There Will Be Fire

Also by Rory Carroll

Comandante: Hugo Chávez's Venezuela

There Will Be Fire

Margaret Thatcher, the IRA,
and Two Minutes That Changed History

Rory Carroll

G. P. PUTNAM'S SONS | NEW YORK

PUTNAM
— EST. 1838 —

G. P. PUTNAM'S SONS
Publishers Since 1838
An imprint of Penguin Random House LLC
penguinrandomhouse.com

Library of Congress Cataloging-in-Publication Data

Names: Carroll, Rory, author.
Title: There will be fire: Margaret Thatcher, the IRA, and two minutes that changed history / Rory Carroll.
Description: New York: G. P. Putnam's Sons, 2023. |
Includes bibliographical references.
Identifiers: LCCN 2022052213 (print) | LCCN 2022052214 (ebook) |
ISBN 9780593419496 (hardcover) | ISBN 9780593419502 (ebook)
Subjects: LCSH: Thatcher, Margaret—Assassination attempts—
England—Brighton. | Irish Republican Army. | Magee, Patrick, 1951– |
Terrorism—England—Brighton—History—20th century. | Attempted assassination—Investigation—England—Brighton—History—20th century. |
Great Britain—Politics and government—1979–1997. | Ireland—Politics and government—1949– | Northern Ireland—Politics and government—1968–1998.
Classification: LCC HV6433.G713 C377 2023 (print) |
LCC HV6433.G713 (ebook) | DDC 363.32509422/5—dc23/eng/20230111
LC record available at https://lccn.loc.gov/2022052213
LC ebook record available at https://lccn.loc.gov/2022052214

Printed in the United States of America
1st Printing

Book design by Elke Sigal

To Alma and Ligi

Contents

PART III | Manhunt

A Note to Readers

I was twelve years old, a kid in Dublin, when the Irish Republican Army came astonishingly close to assassinating Margaret Thatcher. My family listened to the radio report in silence over breakfast.

It was common enough, in 1984, to start the day with news of the latest violence in Northern Ireland, but this was different. The bomb was in Brighton, England, and had targeted the British prime minister. It had almost killed her. It was the fifteenth year of the Troubles, that odd euphemism for sporadic killing, and we were grimly accustomed to reports of attacks on soldiers, police, and civilians. But Thatcher? The world wobbled on its axis. She was a global figure, the Iron Lady, protected by rings of security. How did the IRA get so close? How had they planned it? How did she escape? What if she had died?

So many questions, but they were never really answered. For the British, it was as if dwelling on the enormity of it—publicly, at least—would play into the hands of the IRA. Thatcher led by example, insisting everything must go on as usual. The shock wore off, and the world recovered its equilibrium. An attack that had almost wiped out the British government gradually slipped down the news bulletins and receded into history.

My first job as a newspaper reporter was in Belfast in the mid-1990s, when the Troubles were winding down. In those days, you might occasionally hear whispers about Brighton, about how the IRA did it, but nothing definite. The operation, in the organization's parlance, was still kept "tight." I moved on, joined *The Guardian* in London, and ended up covering other conflicts—the Balkans, Afghanistan, Iraq, Mexico—each with their own dark secrets. In 2018, I returned to Dublin to cover Ireland, north and south, for *The Guardian*. Belfast was transformed, British troops long gone, boutique hotels popping up like toast. But the so-called peace walls dividing Catholic and Protestant areas were still there, and so, too, the hush over certain IRA operations. For those involved, fear of prosecution, or just the old reflex to say nothing, kept the lid screwed tight.

Then I learned that Patrick Magee, an IRA member who had been convicted of planting the Brighton bomb, was writing a memoir. A good topic for an article, I thought. The memoir shed light on his childhood and motives for joining the IRA, and his life since release from prison, but disclosed next to nothing about the Brighton operation. When I interviewed Magee, he was courteous and thoughtful, but implacable in deflecting questions about the plot to kill Thatcher. The story seemed to remain locked in that black box.

But by reviewing newspaper accounts of his 1986 trial, and monitoring the slow release of information in subsequent books, oral histories, court cases, and official documents, I was able to discern an outline of the conspiracy, its zigzag path from conception to execution, and the police hunt for the bombers. After I located a handful of former IRA men willing to talk, the sequence of events became clearer, and I realized that no article could do justice to the story.

From 2020 to 2022, research assistants and I delved into archives in Dublin, Belfast, London, and Brighton, and I conducted more than a hundred interviews with former IRA members, police detectives, bomb disposal experts, politicians, officials, and friends and relatives of key players. Some were proud to go on the record, others requested anonymity and elaborate security precautions. Some were garrulous, others were cagey and keen to find out what I had learned. Gerry Adams, who plays a prominent role in these pages, did not respond to my request to interview him. He has consistently denied being a member of the IRA and repeatedly rejected allegations of his participation in any of its operations. There were dead ends, false leads, breakthroughs. In Dublin, I found the IRA commander who sent Magee to England. In Belfast, I found the veteran IRA bomber whose name Magee borrowed as a pseudonym. Interviews took place in dingy flats, dive bars, plush offices, and the occasional fancy restaurant, not least that at the Grand Hotel, my base in Brighton. Bit by bit, the story emerged.

This is a work of nonfiction. At the back of the book, a note on sources details how I used the information. Every scene and descriptive detail is based on interviews, conducted by me or others, or rooted in the historical record. Where someone is quoted, or their feelings described, there is a source. When accounts of particular events conflicted, I chose one version, the one that seemed to me the most credible, and cited the competing interpretations in endnotes. In time, more secrets, in the form of unsealed official documents and perhaps deathbed confessions, will emerge. But for now, this is the story as I was able to unearth it.

Crucial years of the Troubles play out in these pages, but this is not a history of the conflict. The focus is on one operation, and consequently much is excluded. There is little mention, for instance, of IRA attacks on Protestants in border areas, or loyalist targeting of random Catholics, or controversial security force killings. The story is told through the perspective of a handful of individuals, each representing, in his or her own way, a distinct worldview, and how those collided into each other in this fateful moment.

In a chronicle of murder, I don't claim moral neutrality, but I strived for fairness in narrating why people did what they did. My use of language reflects this. In Northern Ireland, terminology is treacherous, denoting bias, real or perceived. Even the term "Northern Ireland" is contentious. I have stomped through this linguistic minefield by using terminology appropriate to each character.

In researching this book, I've thought a lot about the battle for memory. In the tangled, tortuous history of Britain and Ireland, the past is not a settled matter. There is no grand, shared narrative. Atrocities and justified actions are in the eye of the beholder. Who started the Troubles is as contested as who won and who lost. The most loaded question of all is what the killing achieved. But in Northern Ireland there are no answers, just as there is no settled peace.

With Margaret Thatcher as polarizing in death as in life, and Sinn Féin—once the IRA's political wing—reborn as a respectable party of government, the IRA plot to kill its greatest foe is in danger of becoming myth. It is vital to remember what actually happened.

There Will Be Fire

Invisible Beings

A light breeze salted the Brighton seafront when the taxi carrying Patrick Magee pulled up outside the Grand Hotel.

The driver opened the trunk and gave a cheerful warning to the porter, who reached for the case. "You'd better hold on to your nuts for this one, you'll need 'em."

It was just after noon on September 15, 1984, and it felt like the last day of summer. Sunshine burned through a residue of clouds, warming the pebbles on the beach. The English Channel glistened, serene. The Grand soared over King's Road like an overstuffed wedding cake, eight stories of eaves, cornices, and Victorian elaboration coated cream and white. A Union Jack fluttered from the roof. Built for aristocrats, it had hosted kings and presidents and film stars. Soon it would host Margaret Thatcher—and Magee had come to kill her.

The squawk of gulls competed with the tinkle of fairground music. It was a Saturday and Brighton, perched on the southern coast of England, was a town at play. Tourists strolled along the promenade, a favorite spot to devour ice cream, fudge, and Brighton rock, a cylindrical stick of boiled sugar that resembled dynamite. Others sat in deck chairs facing France, invisible over the horizon. The tide was coming in, covering the sand. Brighton was a town for discreet, raffish fun, so it was anyone's guess which of the couples strolling arm in arm were illicit. The playwright Noël Coward is said to have adored the place: "Ah, dear Brighton—piers, queers and racketeers."

Soccer fans streamed to the Goldstone Ground stadium to watch Brighton & Hove Albion take on their archrivals, Crystal Palace. Teenagers walked to the rhythm of their Walkmans; Stevie Wonder's "I Just Called to Say I Love You" topped the charts. There was a festive mood in the air because that morning Princess Diana and Prince Charles had been driven to St. Mary's Hospital for the birth of their second child. Even Charles did not know if the nation would be celebrating a baby prince or princess.

Magee, age thirty-two, blended in. Clean-shaven, neatly dressed, he could have been a tourist or a traveling salesman. He said and did nothing that would stand out. Anyone paying close attention might have noticed a missing fingertip on his right hand, and perhaps they would have sensed a wariness, a coiled tension in his manner—but no one was watching him.

For more than a decade he had been on the radar of security forces: the Royal Ulster Constabulary in Northern Ireland, the British army, Ireland's An Garda Síochána, London's Metropolitan police, the British domestic intelligence agency MI5, the overseas intelligence agency MI6. Each had files on Patrick Joseph Magee, one of the best operatives in the Irish Republican Army.

· · ·

FOR FIFTEEN YEARS, the IRA had been waging an insurgency to end British rule in Northern Ireland and to unite the region with the Republic of Ireland. It was the latest iteration of a centuries-old conflict between Irish rebels and their dominant neighbor.

In 1921, an earlier version of the IRA had expelled the British from twenty-six of Ireland's thirty-two counties, paving the way for a republic ruled from Dublin. For Irish nationalists, it was as if a malignant cancer—an invasive force that had colonized Ireland's land and people, ravaged its language and culture, poisoned the very idea of Irishness, all in the name of making Ireland British—had finally been excised. But, crucially, it was not gone altogether. The Union Jack still flew over those six northern counties. These were home to 800,000 Protestants—descendants of British settlers who had no desire to join a new independent state dominated by Catholics. So the British government carved out a statelet, Northern Ireland, that became a self-governing region within the United Kingdom.

The problem was that 450,000 Catholics in Northern Ireland felt stuck on the wrong side of the new border. Northern Ireland was run by Protestants for Protestants. The Catholic minority got the worst jobs and housing, and the government in London shrugged. When Catholics marched for civil rights in the late 1960s, police beat them. Riots escalated into an insurgency led by a revived IRA.

The IRA considered its campaign of bombings and shootings a war of liberation to end British imperialism and to unite Ireland. The British and Irish governments called it terrorism by republican ideologues who ignored the wish of most people in Northern Ireland to remain in the UK. By 1984, the conflict had claimed more than 2,500 lives and gained a euphemism: the Troubles.

The IRA had become one of the world's most effective guerrilla forces, capable of sustaining a bloody challenge to the combined might of British military, economic, and political power. But the organization was under pressure. Britain's security forces had gotten smarter, adapted, recruited spies. Instead of retreating from Northern Ireland, the British were entrenching—fortifying police and army bases, wooing investors, building housing estates. Numbed to the violence, Britons found the Troubles dreary, even boring, and mercifully over there, across the Irish Sea.

Magee had come to Brighton to break the stalemate.

This was the one operation that could change the strategic calculus, even reorder history. To give birth, as the Irish writer William Butler Yeats put it, to a terrible beauty. Magee was tasked with wiping out Thatcher and her cabinet. He was to turn the Grand Hotel into a tomb.

It was the most audacious conspiracy against the British Crown since the Gunpowder Plot of 1605, when English Catholics planted barrels of gunpowder beneath the House of Lords. In that instance, they were discovered and their heads ended up on spikes. Centuries later, the English still burned the plotters' effigies on November 5, Bonfire Night, and kids still chanted the same rhyme:

> Remember, remember the fifth of November,
> Gunpowder, treason and plot.
> I see no reason why gunpowder treason
> Should ever be forgot.

Such long memories for a bomb that didn't even go off.

If Magee did his job right, the English would have a new date to remember. The most important fact, as Magee climbed the four steps leading to the Grand's main entrance, was that he had evaded surveillance. Since the early 1970s, British security forces had linked him to dozens of bombings in Northern Ireland and England. For the risks he took they gave him a nickname: the Chancer. A poor choice because in truth he was meticulous. It was the reason he was still alive.

When the IRA made mistakes or was unlucky—a jammed gun, a premature bomb, the wrong victim—British security forces called it the "Paddy Factor," reflecting an old prejudice that the Irish were stupid or feckless, just not up to the job even when the job was killing people. But despite all their files and technology and manpower, their border checks and extradition treaties and anti-terrorism legislation, this Paddy had eluded them. No one knew he had slipped into England and was now stepping through the Grand's revolving glass door.

For Magee, this was a moment to savor. Years of planning had led to this. He felt like a submarine captain rising from the depths and peering through a periscope at an enemy ship. Sunlight flooded the lobby, and its marble floors, leather armchairs, and cream-colored velvet drapes seemed a hymn to old-world opulence. Autumnal bouquets and French polish scented the air. To the left was the Victoria bar, royal portraits forming a gallery along the walls, Queen Victoria stern, Queen Elizabeth smiling. To the right, beyond a concierge's mahogany desk, waited a restaurant's white linen tablecloths, duck-egg-blue walls, and chandeliers. After midday it transitioned from cream teas, served on silver platters, to lunch. Saturday tended to be busy, diners ebbing and flowing while guests hovered in the lobby.

There was a timelessness to the Grand, as if the calendar still said 1862, when British imperial power was at its zenith and the hotel's skeleton first rose over the promenade. Completing the pride of Brighton had required more than three million bricks, 12,560 cubic feet of York and Portland stone, 450 tons of wrought and cast iron, thirty miles of flooring, six miles of gas piping, three acres of tiles and glass, fifteen miles of wallpaper, and 230 marble chimneypieces. Five lifts known as "ascending staircases" inspired wonder. Guest books read like a political who's who—Emperor Louis Napoleon III, former Soviet premiers Georgy Malenkov and Nikolai Bulganin, President John F. Kennedy, every recent British prime minister—and Hollywood celebrities, including Ronald Reagan when he was an actor, added glamour.

Magee was entirely out of his element. He had grown up poor in Belfast, and the often gritty accommodations of life in the IRA—ditches, outhouses, jail cells—in no way prepared him for this kind of splendor. But he could not betray any unease, any hint of interloping into an alien world. To operate in England was a performative act. Magee was behind enemy lines, cut off from the movement's network of sympathizers. He had to cloak himself in a different identity and conceal the West Belfast accent that so alarmed English ears. "A few active, intrepid and intelligent men can do much to annoy and hurt

England," Jeremiah O'Donovan Rossa, an Irish rebel leader, wrote in 1876. "It requires a little band of heroes . . . men who will fly over land and sea like invisible beings."

Striding past the restaurant, passing under a sunlit atrium, Magee was visible to all. But what was there to see? Just another visitor approaching the reception desk. A young receptionist, Trudy Groves, smiled in welcome. Magee requested an upper-floor room with a sea view. Three nights. He was polite and soft-spoken, the accent English, perhaps a hint of the Midlands. The hotel was enjoying a good September but had rooms available. Groves presented a registration card.

Magee would not have been human if he did not hesitate at this moment, a crucial test of fieldcraft he would have rehearsed. The trick was to fill in the card without his hands touching it, to leave no prints, and do so without looking awkward or drawing attention, leaving the receptionist with no memory of this encounter. He was to be forgettable, a blur. The pen hovered, then etched its fictions. Nationality: English. Address: 27 Braxfield Road, London, SE4. Magee printed and signed a name: Roy Walsh. The bill for three nights' bed and half board (two meals included) was £180. Magee paid up front, in cash. Groves filed the registration card and handed over the key to room 629.

.   .   .

As MAGEE ASCENDED to his room, his target was ninety miles north in the Buckinghamshire countryside. Margaret Thatcher, Britain's first female prime minister, was in her fifth year of power. She had won two general elections and a war and was now busy wrenching the UK's economy toward freewheeling capitalism. On this sunny Saturday, Thatcher was at her country residence catching up with friends while keeping tabs on a diplomatic crisis in South Africa, talks with China over Hong Kong, and a coal miners' strike.

There was also the vexing matter of her speech at the upcoming Conservative Party Conference. It would be the climax of her party's annual get-together, a chance for cabinet ministers, members of Parliament, and party activists to give a standing ovation and chant, "Maggie!" They did so every year. But Thatcher agonized over the text. Behind her trademark armor-plated confidence, she fretted the speech would fall flat and disappoint her audience. She was already tormenting her speechwriters with notes and revisions.

Everything had to go right at Brighton.

. . .

STEPPING INTO ROOM 629, Magee discovered the Grand's little secret: its grandeur was slipping. The carpet and wallpaper were worn; the decor and furniture were aged. There was, however, a sweeping vista of the seafront, framed by two piers. Several hundred yards to the left stood the Palace Pier, packed with pavilions and kiosks, jutting over the blue-gray sea. If the sash windows were open, the fairground music poured in. To the right stood the West Pier, empty and derelict. People strolled on the promenade, savoring possibly the last weekend of good weather before autumn bit.

If Magee turned on the TV that afternoon, he would have caught the news: at 4:20 p.m., Princess Diana gave birth to a boy, a yet-to-be-named brother to Prince William. Crowds outside the hospital whooped and cheered. The new prince weighed six pounds, fourteen ounces. With the evening sun casting a glow on the hotel's facade, Magee set to work birthing his own creation: a long-delay time bomb.

It was Margaret Thatcher's policy to treat republican prisoners as common criminals—in theory, no different than burglars, rapists, murderers—and thereby delegitimize the republican cause. Republican prisoners had resisted to the point of starving themselves to death in hunger strikes, and still Thatcher held firm. It earned her the bitter enmity of the IRA, a level of hate not seen for an English leader in centuries. The IRA's Army Council, its governing body, decided to kill her. The assassination could be cloaked in strategy, but the impetus was revenge. Many doubted it could be done. The IRA had never attempted to take out a sitting prime minister. It was too hard, too risky.

But a plot had taken shape, scouts gathered intelligence, bomb makers built and tested prototypes, quartermasters managed supply routes and logistics. Bank raids, kidnap ransoms, and Irish American donations helped pay the bills.

Now it was down to Magee, the last link in the chain. Once he had dreamed of being an artist, but Ireland's history swept away his canvas and conjured a new devotion. His job was to assemble and plant the device. Room 629 was his workshop. Slowly, painstakingly, he would lay out a tangle of wires, batteries, and timers, as well as a mound of gelignite, and step-by-step build a precision weapon.

As the sun slid into the channel on that first night, life unfolded around Magee. Down the corridor, in room 645, a guest hired a photographer to take erotic portraits of his female companion. In the Victoria bar, a red-haired chanteuse named Georgie played piano. A gathering of mystics filled Hove town hall with the aroma of incense. Cinemas dimmed their lights to screen *Indiana Jones and the Temple of Doom*. On the beach, fishermen cast their lines long, for the tide was retreating. As the dusk deepened, lanterns strung along the promenade began to glow.

The Chancer had three days and nights to complete and conceal the bomb. It was to hold its breath for twenty-four days, six hours, and thirty-two minutes. Then, if all went according to plan, from room 629 there would be a blaze of light, a sound like thunder, and the heart of the Grand Hotel would crack, unleashing vengeance on those below.

PART I

——

Genesis of a Plot

PART 1

Genesis of a Plot

CHAPTER ONE

Mountbatten

Louis Mountbatten rose at his usual time, just before 8:00 a.m., to a heartening vista outside his bedroom window. An azure sky unfurled over the Atlantic. After weeks of rain and foaming seas, the old man was finally getting sailing weather for the end of his Irish holiday. Mountbatten performed his calisthenics, a Canadian air force drill, and joined his family for breakfast in the dining room of Classiebawn Castle. He sent the poached egg back to the kitchen—the yolk was watery—but that didn't sour his mood. It was going to be a splendid morning for lobster potting.

It was Monday, August 27, 1979, and Louis Francis Albert Victor Nicholas Mountbatten was enjoying retirement. He was on the periphery of Europe, far from great events, no longer facing monumental decisions, and perfectly content.

Born in 1900, he had led a singular life that threaded the history of the twentieth century. His great-grandmother and godmother was Queen Victoria and his godfather Russia's Tsar Nicholas II. A naval officer and a favorite of Winston Churchill, he served as Supreme

Commander of Allied Powers in Southeast Asia during the war and later became Lord Mountbatten of Burma and the last viceroy of India.

Dickie, as he was known to friends, was cousin to Queen Elizabeth and mentor to her husband, Prince Philip, and their son Prince Charles. Handsome, pompous, playful, exceedingly vain, Mountbatten had graced Europe's palaces and chanceries with movie star looks and scandalous gossip.

On this August morning, his glory years long behind him, his once-ramrod posture somewhat saggy, he bossed around the only people he still could: his family. The grandchildren didn't mind because, since they were small, Grandpapa had been a font of stories, rhymes, and games. "Nick'las, Nick'las, don't be so ridic'las," he used to say to one grandson. Then, turning to Nicholas's identical twin, Timothy: "Timothy Titus, please don't bite us," followed by a lunge and gnashing of teeth.

The grandchildren learned that if a wineglass was ringing, they must stop the reverberation because if it was left to fade into silence, somewhere a sailor would perish. Mountbatten also taught them the Bus Driver's Prayer, a parody of the Lord's Prayer that takes the driver around London:

Our Farnham, who art in Hendon,
Harrow be thy name.
Thy Kingston come; thy Wimbledon,
In Erith as it is in Hendon.
Give us this day our daily Brent
And forgive us our Westminster,
As we forgive those who Westminster against us.

Mountbatten had been coming to Classiebawn, which overlooked Mullaghmore, a village in Sligo on Ireland's northwest coast, for thirty summers. It was a turreted Victorian manor house, not a true castle, but had a fairy-tale look. A flat-topped rock formation, Benbulben, brooded over a landscape of fields, woodland, and beaches. Shipwrecks from the doomed Spanish Armada that had tried to invade England in 1588 dotted the seabed. "No place has ever thrilled me more and I can't wait to move in," Mountbatten had exulted after first visiting Classiebawn.

When not riding horses, writing letters, or playing board games, the old admiral would potter about the bay in his beloved *Shadow V*, a twenty-eight-foot fishing boat. For weeks the weather had been spiteful, the worst in living memory, and the boat had languished unused in Mullaghmore's harbor. Now the sun had finally revived. With just a few days left before the family returned to London, Mountbatten planned to take advantage.

By the time the expedition members assembled in the courtyard, it was 11:15 a.m. Mountbatten crunched over the gravel to tell two Irish police bodyguards—Detective Kevin Henry, armed with a

Lord Louis Mountbatten, far left, with family and friends on *Shadow V* off Mullaghmore in August 1966. | Malcolm Aird/Robert Estall

service revolver, and a uniformed colleague, Kevin Mullins, parked in their usual spot—of the outing. The family piled into a white Ford Granada for the short drive to the harbor, tailed by the policemen. Every radio station seemed to be playing the same song: "I Don't Like Mondays" by the Boomtown Rats.

Shadow V—green hull, cranky diesel engine, pungent little cabin—bobbed by the stone jetty. Mountbatten needed some help down the greasy ladder, as did his eighty-three-year-old mother-in-law, Lady Doreen Brabourne. The other crew members were his daughter Patricia; her husband, John Knatchbull; their fourteen-year-old twins, Nicholas and Timothy; and Paul Maxwell, a fifteen-year-old boat boy from Enniskillen in Northern Ireland. Lady Brabourne sat in the stern with Patricia, while the menfolk took posts on the bow and in the cabin. Mountbatten took the helm and guided *Shadow V* through the other moored boats.

"Astern!" Mountbatten called, opening the throttle and boiling the water beneath. The boat wheeled. "Ahead!" he called, and aimed for the open sea.

"You are having fun today, aren't you?" Knatchbull said, grinning, to his father-in-law.

Mountbatten did not reply. *Shadow V* chugged toward lobster pots a few hundred yards offshore, churning foam in a flat green sea.

Maxwell asked the time, and Timothy looked at his watch: "Eleven thirty-nine and forty seconds." Timothy climbed onto the cabin roof to keep watch for fishing lines that could tangle the propeller, as he knew Grandpapa's eyesight wasn't what it used to be. "Buoy twenty yards ahead and slightly to port!" he called.

Mountbatten, silent, seemed lost in reverie. Maybe he was remembering the war—the sinking of his naval destroyer off of Crete, taking the Japanese surrender at Singapore. Maybe he was wondering if Britain's new prime minister would get on with the Queen. Maybe he was visualizing lobster for dinner.

"Isn't this a beautiful day?" said Lady Brabourne.

From a hilltop the police bodyguards kept vigil. They weren't the only ones watching.

. . .

IRELAND'S TORMENTED RELATIONSHIP with the English Crown was written into the Sligo landscape that so thrilled Mountbatten. A story of blood and soil was etched into mossy gravestones and crumbling ruins.

In limestone caves south of Classiebawn, Irish myth claims that the hunter Finn McCool once found a portal to another world. The quarrelsome Gaelic chieftains who ruled Ireland at that time must have wished he'd closed it before Anglo-Norman mercenaries clanked ashore in 1169 on a mission of conquest blessed by King Henry II of England, ushering in centuries of savage subjugation.

It was no accident, after all, that this archipelago off northwestern Europe would become known as the British Isles. Ireland lay on the western edge, the remoter, smaller neighbor of a powerful kingdom comprising England, Wales, and Scotland. Even on maps, Britain appeared to lean into Ireland.

Even so, the mercenaries never fully tamed Ireland's natives, the Gaels. The two sides intermarried and blurred into each other, complicating England's conquest of this troublesome island—the first colony in what would later become a global empire. The stakes rose after the Reformation when, in the sixteenth century, England sloughed off the pope's religious authority. Under Henry VIII, England became Protestant, while the Indigenous Irish remained Catholic. This gave Spain and other Catholic powers a potential back door to England.

Not long after, in an effort to tame the especially rebellious northern province of Ulster, the English Crown confiscated Gael land and gave it to Protestant settlers, known as planters, from Scotland and England. The natives became outcasts, harried at the point of a sword from the land of their ancestors. When they fought back, massacring settlers, the English response was ferocious: Oliver Cromwell led an avenging army that slaughtered Catholics across Ireland and banished survivors to rocky, infertile soil, a campaign of ethnic cleansing that through violence and disease wiped out more than a fifth of the population. Others were banished overseas as indentured laborers. Some historians would later brand the whole enterprise genocide.

An underclass in their own land, scorned for their language and religion, the Irish still periodically rebelled. On occasion, Protestant radicals joined these doomed enterprises, but mostly they were Catholic affairs. All ended with hangings. Anglo-Irish nobles who sided with the Crown, meanwhile, were rewarded with large estates.

When potato crops failed in the 1840s, more than a million peasants died of starvation and disease in what became known as the Great Famine. Another million emigrated in so-called coffin ships. The historian A. J. P. Taylor, writing a century later, evoked a death camp: "All Ireland was a Belsen."

Queen Victoria's government limited food aid, lest charity foster idleness and other vices in what was deemed an inferior race, as if evolution had taken a wrong turn with these backward Celts in contrast to the eminently superior Anglo-Saxons. English publications caricatured the Irish as apelike brawlers, drinkers, and layabouts, a race predisposed to superstition, savagery, and indolence.

"The judgement of God sent the calamity to teach the Irish a lesson," said Charles Trevelyan, a Treasury mandarin in charge of famine relief. "The real evil with which we have to contend is not the physical evil of the famine, but the moral evil of the selfish, perverse and turbulent character of the people."

Some saw opportunity. Agents for Lord Palmerston, a British statesman who owned ten thousand acres around Mullaghmore, hustled two thousand unwanted tenants onto ships. They landed in Canada, malnourished and half-naked, and many froze to death. Palmerston, oblivious, built Classiebawn Castle and erased a village, Mullach Gearr, to enhance the view. He put no markers to indicate a burial ground. According to legend, stepping on such grass condemned you to ravenous, insatiable hunger. It was *feár gortach*—Irish for "hungry grass"—but the language itself withered as survivors left rural areas and adopted English, the victor's tongue.

The catastrophe traumatized and embittered the natives. Small underground groups such as the Fenians and the Irish Republican Brotherhood (IRB) vowed to end British rule and create an independent Irish republic. They staged bombings and assassinations between the 1860s and the 1890s, to little effect. By now, the British empire straddled the globe and was not going to bow, as authorities saw it, to hooligans and terrorists. Peaceful political agitation proved more successful. By the outbreak of the First World War, moderate Irish nationalists who played the parliamentary game had extracted a promise from London for self-governance after the war.

For the revolutionaries, though, that was too little too late. In April 1916 they launched an insurrection in Dublin, Ireland's capital, and proclaimed an Irish republic. The Easter Rising was a military shambles with little popular support. British soldiers squelched it within a week, leaving the center of Dublin a smoking ruin. But then the authorities made a fateful blunder. They introduced martial law and executed rebel leaders, sixteen in all. These were seen as martyrs, and public sentiment radicalized. William Butler Yeats, who grew up near Classiebawn, immortalized the transformation in his poem "Easter, 1916."

> All changed, changed utterly:
> A terrible beauty is born.

Self-governance was no longer enough. The Irish wanted revolution. They rallied to Sinn Féin, a political party whose name meant "We Ourselves." Outside Protestant areas in the north, it swept the December 1918 election. Instead of taking its seats in the British Parliament at Westminster, the party proclaimed an Irish parliament,

Dáil Éireann, in Dublin. Weeks later, a guerrilla force began ambushing police and soldiers around Ireland. Its name was the Irish Republican Army.

IRA units trained and hid arms within sight of Classiebawn Castle, by then owned by Wilfrid Ashley, a British aristocrat and Conservative member of Parliament. Sensing a turning tide, his family, including his daughter Edwina, Mountbatten's future wife, stopped visiting their summer home. By 1920, the ambushes had escalated into a war of independence. Under Michael Collins, a charismatic leader known as the "big fella," the IRA burned police stations. The rebels also destroyed the grand homes of aristocrats. Classiebawn was mined with explosives, but the local IRA decided to keep it intact to billet guerrillas and hold hostages.

Winston Churchill, then the British secretary of state for war, tried to regain control with an auxiliary force dubbed the "Black and Tans" for its dark and khaki uniforms. It acquired a reputation for atrocity. In response, the IRA escalated its own brutality. From 1919 to 1921, more than two thousand people died in the fighting. With neither side able to score a knockout blow, they agreed to a truce. Collins led a delegation to London and signed a treaty that created an Irish Free State, a self-governing dominion of the British empire, a status similar to Canada. British forces withdrew from twenty-six of Ireland's thirty-two counties. The remaining six northeastern counties formed a new entity, Northern Ireland, which could opt out of the Irish Free State.

It was a stunning achievement. Ragtag rebels had taken on the world's mightiest empire and won de facto independence. The Irish tricolor—green, white, and orange—would fly over Dublin. But some rejected the treaty. It would oblige Irish leaders to swear an oath to the Crown and risked partitioning the island. Where was the republic? The IRA split into pro- and anti-treaty factions and waged a bitter civil war. On August 22, 1922, a convoy carrying Collins was ambushed at a rural crossroads known as Béal na Bláth, Mouth of Flowers. The big fella tumbled to the road, shot dead by a republican purist. Weeks later his side executed and dumped the corpses of six anti-treaty IRA men on the slopes of Benbulben. The pro-treaty side eventually prevailed, formed an elected government, and later declared a republic.

Northern Ireland, however, remained part of the United Kingdom. Function followed form: the British drew the boundary so that Protestants, a minority on the island, outnumbered Catholics in the six counties. The Protestants considered themselves British, loyal subjects of the Crown, and refused to be absorbed into an independent Ireland dominated by Catholics. The UK now consisted of Great Britain—the island comprising England, Scotland, and Wales—and Northern Ireland. The descendants of the seventeeth-century planters took comfort in the border posts that mushroomed along the 310-mile border, separating them from the rebels, traitors, and papists to the south. Their provincial capital, Belfast, thrummed with industry, shipbuilding, and linen mills, and over it flew the Union Jack.

But the Catholic minority felt excluded and alienated. Many lived in slums, struggled to find work, and were not allowed to vote. The police were hostile. Sectarian riots fueled the bigotry. Many Catholics emigrated. Impoverished Ireland offered few opportunities, so they sailed to England or America. Most, however, stayed. They lacked the finances or temperament for exile, for the wrenching farewells and cold uncertainties. Northern Ireland, warts and all, was home. So they stayed, and quietly hoped things would get better. But discrimination endured.

The British government in London ignored the injustice. It wanted to forget about Ireland and its complicated disputes. Northern Ireland was a part of the UK, but a distant one. Successive governments in Dublin made pious declarations about unifying Ireland but did nothing about it. They were done with revolution and focused on turning their impoverished backwater into a nation state.

The only people who felt urgency about ending partition were aging republicans—who had been losers in the civil war—and some young apprentices bewitched by rebel ballads. In the 1940s and the 1950s, this motley crew of dreamers and gunmen tried to revive the IRA and staged sporadic attacks. Lacking public support on either side of the border, the campaigns fizzled. History seemed to swallow the IRA whole.

Then came 1969. Inspired by the US civil rights movement, Northern Ireland's Catholics marched to end discrimination. Police clubbed them to a pulp. The marches turned into riots, and Protestant and Catholic mobs clashed. Streets went up in flames, Catholic refugees fled across the border, and the British government deployed the army to restore order. At first Catholics greeted English squaddies as protectors. The welcome evaporated in a haze of tear gas and clumsy soldiering, and the army came to resemble another layer of oppression. Young men begged grizzled old IRA veterans: Give us guns.

The Troubles were born.

. . .

THE REVIVAL OF the ancient quarrel between the Irish and British did not deter Mountbatten from his Atlantic idyll. "Here it is absolutely quiet and friendliness all round and it is difficult to believe that you are having these horrors just across the border," he wrote to Northern Ireland's governor in 1971. Mountbatten arrived each August with his children and grandchildren. The castle was in the Republic of Ireland, while the newly revived IRA—in theory, at least—confined its armed campaign to the "occupied six counties." But Classiebawn was just twenty miles from the border, and the Irish police—An Garda Síochána—did not take chances. The aristocratic visitors were shadowed by bodyguards, a team of twelve to twenty-four uniformed and plainclothes officers who worked in shifts, two or four on duty at any one time.

In 1976, the battle lines shifted. The IRA extended their campaign across the border by detonating a huge land mine under the car of the British ambassador, Christopher Ewart-Biggs, in Dublin. It was a shocking assassination. In a classified military intelligence report called "Future Terrorist Trends," a brigadier named James Glover warned: "The mature terrorists, including, for instance, the leading bomb makers, are sufficiently cunning to avoid arrest. They are continually learning from mistakes and developing their expertise." It was a gloomy assessment—and not only accurate but prescient.

By 1979, Mountbatten's Irish minders appeared relaxed. The body count in Northern Ireland had fallen. And the old admiral was long retired, a glamorous but cobwebby royal far removed from British government policy in Northern Ireland or anywhere else. Still, before each visit Mountbatten asked British and Irish authorities about security. Violent death, after all, had a way of finding his family. A Russian revolutionary had lobbed a bomb into the carriage of one of his Romanov cousins, Grand Duke Sergei Alexandrovich, scattering his limbs across the Moscow snow. The duke's wife was thrown down a mine shaft. The tsar's children—Mountbatten's playmates—were shot. The *Chicago Tribune* would later observe that "No single family in recorded history, including the Borgias and the Cosa Nostra families of Sicily, Chicago and New York, was more susceptible to violent death among its members than the family of Queen Victoria and her descendants."

Still, Dickie had survived the Luftwaffe and the Japanese Imperial Army, and in Sligo he felt safe. He was sympathetic to the idea of Irish unity and had offered to mediate between republicans and the British government. "The Irish are my friends," he once assured a British police officer.

"Not all of them, my lord," came the reply.

A storm was blowing over London on August 3 when the Mountbattens packed into the family car for their annual pilgrimage west, driving across England, boarding the ferry to Dublin, then bouncing over potholed roads to the far side of Ireland.

Unknown to them, an American journalist named Bill Granger had just published his first novel, *The November Man*, about an IRA plot to blow up a fictional lord, a cousin of the queen, on his boat. A British publisher sought to change details because it sounded too much like Mountbatten. The timing was a fluke, but eerie nonetheless.

Weeks of wind and rain abruptly stopped on Sunday, August 26, creating a glorious sunset. Over dinner, Mountbatten spoke of plans for his funeral—a favorite topic. To ensure appropriate magnificence, he had written an eight-page outline with a four-page appendix, detailing the number of honor guards, the royal banners, the VIP guests, and all the other pomp. He regularly updated it. The funeral, said Mountbatten, would be a very happy day. As he spoke of it, he was beaming. The weather forecast for the next day was excellent. Lobster potting awaited.

That night, Mullaghmore Harbor's newly installed lights inexplicably went out, casting pier and boats into darkness.

. . .

By 11:40 A.M. on August 27, *Shadow V* was putt-putting closer to the pots. Mountbatten at the helm, Lady Brabourne seated beside him, stretching out her legs. Everyone soaking up the sun's warmth. The sea like glass. It was a beautiful day.

The explosion lifted the boat out of the water. An ear-piercing roar rent the air and reverberated across the bay.

At Classiebawn, Philip Knatchbull—a Mountbatten grandson who had skipped the outing—put down his book, Charles Dickens's *Little Dorrit*, and sought out the butler: "Did you just slam a door?"

A German tourist on a beach several miles away heard the bang and joked to her six-year-old daughter: "They've blown up Mounty."

Detective Henry, watching from his patrol car, gasped. "The noise was tremendous, terrifying," he recalled. "There was a huge mushroom-shaped cloud of smoke and multicolored flashes. This cloud rose high above me, and then started to disappear. There was debris in the sky and on the sea and I was hit with a huge shower of sea-spray. I could hear screams of panic and pain."

Shadow V splintered and disintegrated and its occupants tumbled into the water.

A uniformed Garda on the shore gazed through binoculars, ashen, unable to talk. Detective Henry tried to alert Garda HQ from his car. "Classiebawn Car calling Seven Five Two, come in, urgent, urgent. Mountbatten's boat has exploded in the water, send help." The radio hissed and crackled. Henry belted down to a phone box by the harbor. A woman inside refused to hang up. He hauled her out, midsentence, and dialed the Sligo Garda station.

Boats from the harbor swarmed toward the wreckage, fragments of wood swirling in concentric circles. Diesel fuel slicked the water. Rescuers pulled Patricia Knatchbull, half-conscious, aboard a dinghy. Then Lady Brabourne, bloodied, hysterical, screaming, "Where am I?" Next, Patricia's husband, John, bones broken, shouting for his wife. People on another boat spotted Timothy floating and pulled him aboard. His face covered in splinters, shaking, he asked: "What happened?" His identical twin, Nicholas, and Paul the boat boy were dead.

Mountbatten floated facedown. His legs were shredded. Tourists dragged him onto their boat. They placed a towel under his head and followed the little fleet back to the harbor. Tourists and staff from the Pier Head Hotel cut sheets into bandages and made stretchers out of doors as the casualties were hauled ashore. "We were in total shock," recalled one resident, Peter Murtagh. "We just reacted. You go on autopilot and keep on going."

Lady Brabourne, in agony, kept repeating: "Don't worry about me. . . . Tell me, how are the boys?"

John Maxwell, who had scrambled to the harbor after hearing the explosion, cradled the body of his son Paul. He screamed: "I'm a fucking Irishman, these bastards."

Richard Wallace, a vacationing surgeon, examined Mountbatten. "He's dead," he pronounced.

The old man had been knocked unconscious and drowned. A small child, at first overlooked in the tumult, played in a pool of Mountbatten's blood.

. . .

THE IRA HAD planned it for months. One team focused on the bomb, another on reconnaissance. Under cover of darkness they had slipped aboard the *Shadow V* and planted an estimated fifty pounds of gelignite belowdecks. The next day a different team watched Mountbatten and his family board the boat and chug out of the harbor. At the chosen moment, a radio-controlled transmitter detonated the bomb.

By fluke Thomas McMahon, a veteran bomb maker, and Francis McGirl, a young apprentice, were caught fleeing the area two hours *before* the bomb exploded. Halted at a routine police checkpoint eighty miles south of Mullaghmore, they were unable to explain why they were driving a red Ford Escort they didn't own. They were still being questioned when news came of the explosion. Both men had sand from Mullaghmore and traces of nitroglycerine on their clothes. McMahon also had flakes of *Shadow V*'s paint on his shoes and socks. He was sentenced to life in prison. McGirl, on the other hand, was acquitted. No one else was caught.

The operation, in IRA terminology, was a "spectacular"—the organization's term for a headline-dominating attack—and it reminded a world transfixed by Iran's Islamic revolution that the Troubles still raged. Mountbatten, in the words of one IRA supporter, was "a beautiful target." Too bad, one was left to think, about the others on the boat.

In Mullaghmore, people wept. But in the nearby town of Bundoran, a man with a bottle jigged in the street, saying, "The old bastard is dead." Two boatmen, Michael Gilbride and Martin Shelbourne, watched him in silence. They had helped recover the body of Nicholas.

"Come on, we're going for a swim," said Gilbride.

"What on earth do I want to swim for?" said Shelbourne.

"To wash the death off you."

They swam out to the surf.

. . .

BUT THERE WAS more death to come, because the IRA was not done with August 27, 1979. They had prepared another surprise 115 miles to the east, on the other side of the island. At 4:40 p.m., a British army convoy—a Land Rover and two four-ton trucks filled with paratroopers—was making a routine run through Narrow Water, a rural spot in Northern Ireland. It was a bank holiday in the UK and tourists lounged on the shore. Not everyone had heard the shocking news from Mullaghmore.

The vehicles skirted Carlingford Lough, which straddled the border, and neared an Elizabethan castle. A trailer piled with bales of barley straw was parked alongside the road. Two young IRA men, Brendan Burns and Joe Brennan, watched from a vantage point next to a disused railway track just inside the Irish border. Cigarette butts lay in the ferns around them. In the line of sight from their position to the hay trailer stood a round tower, used in Victorian times for river navigation. The IRA had chosen it as a marker. When the last truck passed the tower, Burns pushed a button. It used a model aircraft radio-controlled device to send a pulse to a seven-hundred-pound fertilizer bomb packed into the trailer, along with petrol cans.

A ball of flames erupted, instantly incinerating seven paratroopers. "All I can remember is a flash and a rumble," recalled Tom Caughey, a private who was eighteen years old at the time. "Then there was a sensation of flying, of losing vision. I remember lying on the road and then sitting up and looking about. There were bits of bodies around me, some of them on fire, but I couldn't see anybody moving."

A rescue force of army vehicles and helicopters scrambled to the scene and set up a control point by the gatehouse opposite the castle. But the IRA had anticipated that. At 5:12 p.m., a decoder device in a

Tupperware lunch box was activated. It detonated one thousand pounds of explosives concealed in milk churns lined against a wall. A tornado of flame and granite blocks engulfed the soldiers.

"There was another flash and a rumble and it was the same nightmare again," said Caughey. Lumps of flesh landed in trees. A head splashed into the lough.

"I will always remember the chilling silence after that second explosion, and the total lack of noise of any type," said Captain Tom Schwartz. Surrounded by the corpses of comrades—eighteen dead in all—the surviving soldiers shot wildly toward the Irish side of the border, killing William Michael Hudson, an English tourist. Gardaí caught Burns and Brennan riding away on a motorcycle. They were detained and later released for want of evidence. No one was ever charged for the parachute regiment's biggest loss of life since the Second World War.

The slaughter at Mullaghmore and Narrow Water was a ruthless display of the IRA's capacity for violence that created an unprecedented crisis for the British prime minister. Margaret Thatcher had been in the job 115 days.

CHAPTER TWO

The Friendly Skies of South Armagh

Margaret Thatcher was in her favorite place in England, and therefore the world, when the reports came through, shattering her brief idyll. Chequers was the official country residence of British prime ministers, a rural retreat in the Chiltern Hills of Buckinghamshire for weary leaders burdened by office. By rights, Thatcher should have loathed it. She never retreated, was not weary, and felt no burden. She was fifty-three years old and everything about her suggested propulsive motion, a restless, kinetic energy.

You felt it as soon as she entered a room. She didn't walk, she bustled. She didn't sit so much as coil, poised to spring back up. As she reviewed official documents, her pen tracked the text and swooped on errant phrases and feeble arguments, stabbing the page with underlinings, exclamations, excisions. Running the country didn't halt her domestic chores. She still cleaned her own shoes, ironed her outfits, and cooked supper. When a visitor spilled coffee on the carpet, she spent twenty minutes scrubbing out the stain. Such things, after all, needed to be done correctly.

Thatcher had already made history—first female leader of the Conservative Party, first female British prime minister, first female head of a European government—yet fizzed with impatience because there was so much to *do*. In voice and appearance she embodied old-fashioned Englishness, the clipped enunciation and smooth hair seemingly lifted from an old Pathé newsreel. "She has a pretty, English sort of face—silky, unlined skin, naturally cream and roses," an interviewer observed. But Thatcher's drive was decidedly not English. It ruptured the conceit of establishment elites that success should appear effortless, breezy, a fortuitous product of one's talents or connections or fate. Striving was for the vulgar classes. Yet Thatcher would work late into the night, sleep four or five hours, then rise before dawn to attack another day. Instead of draining her, this schedule generated yet more energy. She had led the Conservatives to an election victory over the incumbent Labour Party four months earlier and was now like a racehorse at the starting gate, straining to run.

Chequers might have made her restless. It was forty miles north of London's power hub—Downing Street, the ministries of Whitehall, Parliament—and somewhat detached from the business of ruling. Even so, Thatcher fell for the vista of wooded hills and endless lawns, the beech-lined drive, the red-brick mansion, the magnificent staircase, the Hawtrey Room where Winston Churchill once rallied the nation with wartime broadcasts. She would still plow through government papers, but on the whole Chequers induced a most unexpected impulse: relaxation.

This bank holiday weekend, she had dined with her son, Mark, who was a struggling businessman, and her sister, Muriel, who was visiting Chequers for the first time. She also had a session with her personal dressmaker. Thatcher attached high importance to appearance. Head to foot, she had to be impeccable. With Daphne Scrimgeour she would sketch ideas for outfits and discuss brooches, pearls, handbags, and shoes. The prime minister's hair had its own weekly routine: washed Monday and combed out Tuesday and Thursday, appointments her engagement diary code-named "Carmen Rollers." Male aides were banned from such rituals.

But on this late August day, all frippery was set aside when an aide relayed the reports from across the Irish Sea.

Mountbatten dead, soldiers massacred. Newsroom telexes around the world were already chattering with details. Margaret Thatcher had her first Northern Ireland crisis. She dispatched her Northern Ireland secretary, Humphrey Atkins, to Belfast, and passed the evening in a blur of phone calls, instructions, and funeral arrangements. Mountbatten would get his pomp.

Early the next morning, Thatcher returned to her residence and office at 10 Downing Street and chaired an emergency meeting with Home Secretary Willie Whitelaw, Defence Secretary Francis Pym, and Ian Gilmour, a minister without portfolio who knew his way around the Defence Ministry and Foreign Office. Later, she sat at her desk with pen and paper and began to write. "My dear Mrs. Rogers, no words of mine can match the grief you and your children will feel at the loss you suffered yesterday. . . ." The letter to the widow of Sergeant Ian Rogers ran over two pages and was written in Thatcher's distinctive longhand. She wrote another seventeen letters, each unique, to the families of the other dead soldiers.

That evening she chaired another meeting, this one joined by Edwin Bramall, chief of the army general staff, and announced that in the morning she would fly to Belfast. The crisis had exposed a humbling truth about her policy on Northern Ireland. She didn't have one.

. . .

ONE OF THE many reasons Margaret Thatcher loathed Irish revolution was that it distracted from her plans for a British revolution. She was a Conservative, yes, but believed that for things to remain the same, everything must change. Thatcher feared Britain's greatness was slipping away, that the island nation that had once ruled the waves was drifting into decline. Having seized the wheel, she sought to chart a new course.

The future prime minister delivered a statement of intent in 1935 when she was ten years old and won a poetry-reciting competition. "You were lucky, Margaret," her school's deputy headmistress told her. Young Maggie's retort would echo down the ages. "I was not lucky," Thatcher said. "I deserved it."

Margaret Hilda Roberts was born in Grantham, a market town in the east of England, to Beatrice, a dressmaker, and Alfred, a grocer. From humble origins they had risen to the lower middle class through thrift and industry. Home was a three-story brick house, all spick-and-span, polished, ordered. The ground floor was Alfred's shop, where young Margaret and her sister, Muriel, worked after school, weighing out tea, sugar, and biscuits.

Alfred Roberts so molded his beloved younger daughter that it was later said that he ruled Britain from beyond the grave. He was a Rotary Club president, a town councillor, and a lay preacher, orating during the week from the council chamber and on Sunday from a pulpit. He steered Margaret toward books, political meetings, and public speaking classes. Elocution lessons turned her Midlands accent regal. He instilled in her a belief in self-reliance and a horror of idleness. The Robertses were devout Methodists, a puritanical Protestant denomination that abjured the bells and smells of Catholicism. "We were Methodists and Methodists means method. We were taught what was right and wrong in very considerable detail," Thatcher later said. A diligent, brainy chatterbox, Margaret played piano so well some wondered if she might become a concert pianist. "Oh no," said her proud mother. "We've got—she's got—higher aspirations than that." Grantham's most famous son, Sir Isaac Newton, had developed a theory of gravity. Thatcher would become its most famous daughter by defying the downward force of a male-dominated world.

Churchill's wartime broadcasts convinced Margaret that with the right leader, Britain could always prevail. She won a place at Oxford to study chemistry, thinking to become a scientist, but politics captivated her. In the university's Conservative Association she found a worldview that matched her principles. Yet at the end of the war, voters dumped Churchill from power and ushered in a left-wing Labour government that promised a welfare state. Margaret seethed—it smacked of socialism. Elected head of the Oxford Young Conservatives, she told her family, "I'm going to be an MP."

After graduation, Margaret sought work in the chemical industry. "This woman is headstrong, obstinate and dangerously self-opinionated," said one firm's personnel department, rejecting her application. After finding a job as a research chemist at a plastics company, she embarked on a law degree, deeming it a springboard to politics, and started to zigzag through the Conservative Party's old boy network.

Impeccably dressed, she spoke confidently, remembered everything, and worked, worked, worked, addressing meetings, canvassing, handing out flyers, quelling hecklers. She supported capital punishment, fiscal restraint, and the atomic bombing of Japan. Socialism, she warned, turned the human spirit into a caged bird. "It has food and it has warmth. But what is the good of all that if it has not the freedom to fly out and live its own life?" The Conservatives rewarded her with the chance to contest an unwinnable, impregnable Labour seat. Twice she lost, and wept.

But Margaret Roberts also fell in love. Missing a train one night in 1947 after a party meeting, she accepted a lift from a businessman in the audience. Denis Thatcher was ten years her senior and ran his family's manufacturing firm. He drove a Jaguar, loved cricket, rugby, and golf, and loathed socialists. Interested in politics but not wanting to be in politics, he cloaked his seriousness in an irreverent persona partial to gin and tonics and off-color jokes. He opened up a new world to his girlfriend, flush with shows, parties, and trips. In other words, fun. Once, Denis had been married—to a blond beauty also named

Margaret, who broke his heart. He thought this new Margaret beautiful and steadfast, a reason to try again.

They married in 1951, a merger of like-minded equals, workaholics who respected each other's space. She prepared a cooked breakfast each morning, bacon burned to a crisp the way Denis liked, then they went their separate ways for marathon days. Denis tried to stop his wife overdoing it—sometimes imploring, "Bed, woman!"—and his wealth let the new Mrs. Thatcher quit chemistry and focus on politics.

In 1953 she gave birth to twins, Mark and Carol. "They look like rabbits," said Denis. "Put them back."

Women were beginning to trickle into Parliament, even the cabinet, but tended to be unmarried and childless. Margaret resisted the gravitational pull of two newborns and society's expectations to complete her law degree and continue politics. She outdrove and outdazzled two hundred other hopefuls to become the Conservative candidate for Finchley, a wealthy suburb in northwest London. In the 1959 general election, her Labour opponent found her formidable and cold. She beat him.

Of the 630 MPs who entered the new parliament, twenty-five were women. The Conservatives, having a majority, formed a government under Harold Macmillan. He appointed Thatcher a junior minister for pensions. The first mother of young children to hold government office drew scrutiny. Always well turned out, a masterful command of policy detail—how did she do it? It was a coded, unfair accusation of neglecting her children. There was a nanny, but Thatcher kept weekends free, organized meals, outfits, trips, holidays, riding lessons, and kept vigil on their classwork and friendships. She quietly urged other female MPs to show superiority over the men. "She had a very strong sense that men were agreeable, playful and in the end not very serious creatures," said Shirley Williams, a Labour MP.

The Conservatives lost the next election, but Finchley's voters kept faith in Thatcher, who retained her seat. When Ted Heath led the

Conservatives back to power in 1970, he appointed her education minister. He found her shrill and opinionated, but Thatcher was competent and a media darling. That changed when she cut free milk for schoolchildren, part of painful budget cuts. Critics pounced with a wounding rhyme: "Thatcher, Thatcher, milk snatcher." The antithesis of motherhood, a depriver of milk. "Is this the most hated woman in Britain?" asked *The Sun*. The attacks toughened Thatcher. She did not retreat, for she believed she was right.

By 1974, Heath's government was floundering. He had promised to tame unions, cut taxes and spending, and make Britain competitive. Instead unions called the shots, spending ballooned, and an energy crisis forced Britain to adopt a three-day week. At the same time, Northern Ireland's turmoil was spilling into England: IRA bombs were exploding in London and other cities. Labour returned to power. Conservative MPs seethed at the hapless Heath. Some wanted to replace him, but with whom? The obvious candidates made clumsy mistakes or lost their nerve, allowing an implausible candidate to emerge. MPs exchanged astonished looks. Thatcher? A woman? Not even Labour's socialists or the louche Continentals across the channel had elected a female leader.

The grocer's daughter challenged for the leadership. It was an audacious gamble: if she lost, she was ruined. "She offended against the English canon: you should never be too keen," said one ally, Edward du Cann.

Airey Neave, an MP and former army officer famous for having escaped a Nazi prison, ran her campaign, and lobbied colleagues with a blend of charm, intimidation, and bluff. On February 11, 1975, Conservative MPs elected her.

The honeymoon was brief. Party grandees whispered that the woman was a mistake. Posh young men in the party's research office snickered at her provincial roots and mockingly referred to her by her middle name, Hilda. Others said her free-market beliefs and hectoring style would alienate voters.

Thatcher got an image makeover—teeth capped, puffball hats purged, voice modulated—and promoted allies to party posts. Invariably men, often handsome. Denis did not seem to mind. Whenever asked about politics, he would shrug and smile. "I leave that to the boss." She made a splash overseas. On a visit to California she discovered a soul mate, Governor Ronald Reagan. "I knew that we were of like mind, and manifestly so did he," she said later. A belligerent Cold War speech about the Soviet Union prompted the Red Army newspaper to dub her the Iron Lady. Recognizing it as a marketing gift from the communist gods, Thatcher embraced the nickname.

When the election was called in the spring of 1979, she crisscrossed the country in a battle bus to an upbeat campaign song, "Hello, Maggie!" to the tune of Jerry Herman's "Hello, Dolly!" She pitched her economic agenda in terms of a sensible, budget-conscious housewife and appealed to patriotism. "I'm in the business to try and make Britain great again," she said.

She did not invest much time in Northern Ireland. She left that to Airey Neave, the only senior Conservative truly passionate about the place. A security hawk, Neave believed the terrorists could be defeated and that local government reform could normalize and integrate the region into the UK. Once in government, Thatcher planned to appoint him secretary of state for Northern Ireland.

Neave was perhaps her closest friend in politics. She found him dashing and original. The war hero considered her brilliant and beautiful. His wiliness had secured her the leadership and would, she hoped, make him a good steward of Northern Ireland. In any case, Neave was the only senior Conservative who wanted the job. Nobody realized that his policy goals, and his closeness to the Tory leader, made him a target.

On the cold afternoon of March 30, 1979, Neave was driving his Vauxhall Cavalier up a ramp in the Palace of Westminster car park when a tilt switch detonated a bomb under the car. The blast blew off his legs. It took half an hour to cut him free and transfer him to the

Westminster hospital. Thatcher received the news while preparing an election broadcast at the BBC. Numbed, she immediately returned to Westminster—where she learned that Neave had died on the operating table. She was devastated. "Thank God one doesn't know when one wakes up in the morning what will happen when one goes to bed at night," she murmured to staff.

Margaret and Denis Thatcher at the funeral of Airey Neave in Oxfordshire in April 1979, a week after he was killed by an INLA bomb.
| PA Images / Alamy Stock Photo

Neave, not yet in government, had lacked protection—but Westminster was the heart of the British state. If the terrorists could reach such a high-value target there, who was next? "Some devils got him," Thatcher told the BBC. "They must never, never, never be allowed to triumph."

It was not the IRA that scored this "spectacular," but a small breakaway group called the Irish National Liberation Army.

Thatcher went on to fight the election. "It sounds callous to say it, but Mrs. Thatcher's campaign benefited from Neave's murder," her biographer Charles Moore later wrote. The assassination diverted media attention from a Conservative electoral gaffe over housing and highlighted Thatcher's principles. "Airey's death diminishes us, but it will enhance our resolve that the God-given freedoms in which he believed, and which are the foundations of our parliamentary democracy, will in the end triumph over the acts of evil men," she said. The murder, according to Moore, subliminally deepened the idea that Thatcher was serious and stood for something important.

The election was held on May 3, 1979. She won.

. . .

WITH THE SUN rising behind her, the prime minister sat in the back of a government Jaguar and headed to RAF Northolt, a Royal Air Force station in West London. It was August 29, two days since the IRA had truncated her Chequers idyll. This trip to Northern Ireland—her first since the election—was intended to show the British state was still in control and to discover precisely what was going on.

London vanished as the RAF jet banked north and flew over the English Midlands, Wales, the choppy waters of the Irish Sea, and then, emerging from a light mist, a rocky shore and green fields: the island that had vexed every English monarch since Henry II. It was the tenth year of the Troubles. Just a few years earlier, Hué, Saigon, and the Mekong Delta had been synonymous with body counts as America's war in Vietnam raged. Now it was Northern Ireland's six counties—Antrim, Armagh, Derry, Down, Fermanagh, Tyrone—making the news bulletins.

Thatcher's briefing papers gave plenty of scope for underlining. The IRA had issued a statement calling the death of Mountbatten a "discriminate operation to bring to the attention of the English people the continuing occupation of our country." There was speculation that the attacks were in part a response to being upstaged by the INLA's murder of Neave. The IRA statement promised more to come. "The

British army acknowledge that after ten years of war it cannot defeat us, but yet the British government continue with the oppression of our people and torture of our comrades in the H-Blocks. Well, for this we will tear out their sentimental, imperialist hearts." Britain's tabloids responded with rage and clamored for revenge. "These Evil Bastards," blared the *Daily Express*'s banner headline. "May the Bastards Rot in Hell," cried *The Sun*.

From the air, Belfast looked normal, even pretty. Straddling the River Lagan, it was an orderly cityscape of gray stone and red brick with three hundred thousand souls, the twelfth-largest city in the UK. It looked provincial, compact, manageable. But the illusion dissolved once Thatcher stepped onto the Aldergrove Airport tarmac. Soldiers and police with rifles stood guard as she transferred to a military helicopter. Blades whumping, it skimmed over the city, giving the prime minister a closer look. Royal Ulster Constabulary police stations were fortresses with walls and steel mesh to repel mortars. Army bases had sandbags, sentries, and watchtowers. Convoys of armored RUC and army Land Rovers hulked through civilian traffic. Checkpoints ringed the city.

The rows of terraced housing looked identical except for the flags and painted curbs delineating affiliation: green, white, and orange for Catholic streets; red, white, and blue for Protestant. Murals depicted armed men in balaclavas striking heroic poses. All sides used graffiti to mark territory. Protestant examples tended to be pithy: "No surrender!" "Fuck the Pope." The British army did its share of spray-painting, especially the parachute regiment. "Though I walk through the valley of the shadow of death I fear no evil because I am one mean bastard (1st Para)." Pro-IRA areas showed flair for rhyme. "Every night is gelignite." And a new one, referencing civil rights demonstrators killed in Bloody Sunday in 1972, soon to be unveiled: "13 dead but not forgotten—we got 18 and Mountbatten."

Walls topped with razor wire—called peace walls, an Orwellian touch—separated Catholic and Protestant areas to impede sectarian death squads. Not that it was hard to find other routes. As reprisal for Mountbatten and Narrow Water, the Ulster Volunteer Force—a Protestant paramilitary group—killed two innocent Catholics. John Hardy was shot in his home and Gerry Lennon was shot while placing fruit in his shop's window display. The killers later said in court: "We were told not to come back without a result."

Residents barely would have cast a glance at Thatcher's helicopter. Military and police helicopters and spotter planes droned overhead night and day. People had adapted. They could distinguish the crack of gelignite from the duller, rolling thud of homemade explosives. Adhesive tape crisscrossed windows to reduce flying glass. Shops and offices posted searchers at entrances to inspect bags. A new breed of entrepreneur—the "hardboard millionaire"—boarded up damaged buildings, notably the Europa, purportedly the continent's most bombed hotel. Thatcher's free-market spirit would have been less impressed with the practice of people lying down on the street after explosions in order to be ferried to a hospital where, lacking visible injury, they would be recorded as suffering shock and be eligible for £300 government compensation.

The prime minister landed at Musgrave Park Hospital. She could not see survivors from Narrow Water, who were too gravely wounded, but toured wards filled with the human debris of other attacks. Noel McConkey, an RUC sergeant missing both legs and an arm, told her: "I hope to get out of here soon and remain in the police, carrying out my duties, perhaps as a clerk." Thatcher was visibly moved. Next stop was city hall, a neo-baroque edifice from the city's industrial heyday. Workmen from the Harland & Wolff shipyard had replicated its carvings on the *Titanic*. Stained glass windows depicted kings and queens and the sacrifice of Ulster's sons in the war to end all wars. During its sequel, Luftwaffe bombers destroyed the roof. A Union Jack fluttered from the rebuilt dome.

For Thatcher, the politicians she met here were a curious breed. The Protestants belonged to unionist parties, so-called because they prized Northern Ireland's union with Great Britain. Some preferred the term "loyalist," emphasizing their loyalty to the Crown. From 1921 to 1972, London had let them rule this outpost—and lord it over Catholics—with their own parliament and executive. The Troubles had prompted London to dissolve local rule and impose direct control in 1972.

Ted Heath had tried to restore local rule with a power-sharing executive in Belfast between Catholics and Protestants, as well as an advisory role for the Irish government, an experiment known as the Sunningdale Agreement. In an irony lost on no one, the Queen's most fervent subjects revolted. Branding the agreement a betrayal of their Britishness, Protestants rioted and staged a general strike. The agreement collapsed and London restored direct rule. So for Thatcher, Northern Ireland's Protestants were a prickly tribe. She, too, cherished the union, and she admired their thrift and patriotism. "They had been jolly loyal to us," she once remarked. This was praise for their contribution in both world wars and a tacit admission that their sense of Britishness differed from her own, that they were not quite "us." She was on their side, but not one of them.

Catholics presented a different puzzle. The IRA were terrorists and criminals, plain and simple. Thatcher had no desire to talk to the group's political wing, Sinn Féin. The original Sinn Féin party had mobilized Irish nationalism until splintering and disappearing after the 1922 civil war. Its successor was little more than a mouthpiece for the IRA, a fringe political force that did not contest elections and had no representatives in city hall. Police and troops had raided its Belfast office the day before. Catholics who favored a united Ireland but rejected IRA methods were termed "moderate nationalists." They supported the Social Democratic and Labour Party (SDLP), which disavowed violence. Though British citizens, they were culturally Irish and, for Thatcher, definitely not "us." She once wondered aloud if Irish nationalists were traitors. "No, no, I shouldn't say that. That is not the right word." She never did find the right one.

The purpose of her visit to city hall was to project assurance that despite the slaughter, the government had a plan to defeat the IRA. "If we do not defeat the terrorists, then democracy is dead," Thatcher told the councillors. She strode out into the early afternoon sunshine to tell the public the same. Trailed by TV crews, she plunged up Donegall Place, a retail district. Police escorts prayed the unannounced walkabout had left the IRA no time to prepare anything.

Shoppers gawked and jostled. Belfast was used to a lot, but not celebrity prime ministers. It was as if Farrah Fawcett had dropped in. "Her dress was £33.95, I have one exactly the same," marveled one woman. Another, sobbing, grasped Thatcher's hand: "Please help us, for God's sake help us." Thatcher held the woman's gaze. "We are doing our best—of course we shall help you. We must all stand absolutely together to defeat terrorism."

A loud, insistent voice pierced the hubbub. "Mrs. Thatcher, Mrs. Thatcher, will you clear H-Block?"

The person raising the question was a small elderly woman in a white cardigan forcing her way forward. Her name was Harriet Kelly, and H-Block was the republican name for a prison outside Belfast where IRA inmates were protesting harsh conditions.

Thatcher reached out, offering her hand, but the woman didn't want it.

"We want H-Block wiped out. We want our boys back out of H-Block." Kelly was jabbing her finger, trembling with fury. "We want the freedom of our country and your soldiers out."

Thatcher was swept on before she could respond.

· · ·

WHAT TO MAKE of Northern Ireland, its divisions, grievances, hatreds? Even language was a casualty. Catholics refused to call it Ulster because the historic province had nine counties and the creators of Northern Ireland had lopped off Monaghan, Donegal, and Cavan to ensure a Protestant majority. Many called this entity "the north," recognizing geography if not the state's legitimacy. Each side inflated vocabulary. Riots were "pogroms," working-class estates were "ghettos," sporadic assassinations were "genocide."

For Thatcher, this was emphatically part of the UK, but also a place apart, and a diversion from her ambition to reshape Britain. Its conundrums aggravated her, but she did not go as far as Denis, who vented callous impatience—"If the Irish want to kill each other that does seem to me to be their business." Thatcher struggled with it earnestly.

She was not the first.

Winston Churchill had confessed his own frustration in 1921. "Whence does this mysterious power of Ireland come? It is a small, poor, sparsely populated island, lapped about by British sea power, accessible on every side, without iron or coal. How is it that she sways our councils, shakes our parties, and infects us with great bitterness, convulses our passions, and deranges our action? How is it she has forced generation after generation to stop the whole traffic of the British Empire in order to debate her domestic affairs?"

After visiting Northern Ireland in 1970, Reginald Maudling, a senior minister, hoped never to return. "For God's sake bring me a large Scotch. What a bloody awful country!" The best to hope for, he had concluded, was an "acceptable level of violence."

Thatcher's Northern Ireland policy had died with Airey Neave. She had appointed Atkins to the job, but he had little interest in the region, and in the government's first months policy drifted. Then came the dual attacks on August 27. Thatcher realized she had to take charge. This visit, then, was not just to boost morale; it was research. She had decisions to make. She had already ruled out significant political initiatives. Northern Ireland would remain part of the UK, immutable. The IRA, the Irish government, and misty-eyed Irish Americans who dreamed of unification would have to accept that. So the problem—and the solution—was security. A few hundred terrorists were waging a homicidal campaign, and they had to be defeated.

But how?

. . .

THE ARMY BELIEVED it had the answer. The task was to persuade Thatcher.

Military escorts whisked her to Girdwood Barracks, strapped her into a helicopter, and flew her thirty miles south to Portadown, headquarters of the 3rd Infantry Brigade. A buffet lunch was laid out in a briefing room. Uniformed senior officers—all army; police were excluded—bobbed around maps and charts, lending an operational atmosphere. The prime minister sat down, plate in her lap, and said, "Come along! Let's get on with this."

Brigadier David Thorne started the briefing. He cut a dashing figure. Everything about Thorne, it was said, was spring-loaded: his salute, his physical vigor, his intellect. His ability to inspire was renowned. Thorne told the visitor the existing security policy of "police primacy," with the army in a supporting role, was not working.

He questioned the RUC's capacity, especially in border areas like South Armagh, to lead the fight. The army—he argued—had the equipment, expertise, and will. Thorne told Thatcher he had walked among the smoldering corpses at Narrow Water. He pulled a lieutenant colonel's epaulet from his pocket and gently placed it on the table. "Madame Prime Minister, this is all I have left of a very brave officer, David Blair."

Other officers pressed the case for army primacy. They wanted direct radio communication with the Irish army, the right to pursue suspects across the border, the right to detain people without charge, a new security overlord to coordinate strategy. A radical change, in other words, to give the military complete control. Thatcher asked to visit the army base in Crossmaglen. It was in South Armagh, an IRA border stronghold known as Bandit Country, and the most dangerous place in Northern Ireland. Her officials blanched. Snipers and land mines made roads too dangerous, so the army supplied the besieged outpost by air.

Donning a camouflage jacket and an Ulster Defence Regiment beret, and clutching her handbag, Thatcher buckled into a Wessex helicopter and found herself skimming over a landscape of fields and hedgerows. The pilot, Brin Sharp, was a jaunty character who lauded the "friendly skies of South Armagh" and said in-flight alcohol was for crew only. He awarded VIP visitors—there weren't many—a scroll certifying their induction into the "lemming club."

The Wessex touched down and Thatcher scrambled inside the tiny fort. She listened to radio chatter and viewed surveillance cameras. An officer indicated spots where some twenty soldiers had been killed. The base was also the home of Rats, a corgi/Jack Russell mix who accompanied patrols. Creative army press officers fed newspapers stories of Rats leaping into helicopters, growling to warn of danger, and fending off vicious republican dogs.

By the time Thatcher took to the skies once again, the top brass were confident they had won her over.

She made one final stop: an RUC station in Gough Barracks. The prime minister had done her homework. She knew of the rivalry between the army and the police, long-running disputes over turf, strategy, and intelligence that had boiled since the carnage at Narrow Water. She wanted to hear the other side. Chief Constable Kenneth Newman was not physically imposing. A pipe-smoking, cerebral policeman, he was nicknamed "the wee man," and his hard-drinking colleagues noted his preference for tonic over gin. He had a law degree and explained the sociology of policing with histograms and flowcharts. Newman had been a rising star in English police forces several years earlier when the RUC advertised for a deputy chief constable.

"What kind of a nut would put in for that?" his wife asked.

"I might," he replied sheepishly.

Thatcher removed her army jacket, sat down, and listened to him for forty minutes. Newman knew what type of briefing the army would have given and calmly dismantled their arguments. Recent slaughter aside, statistics showed violence had peaked in 1972, with 476 deaths. In 1977 the number was 111, in 1978 it was 80. Mullaghmore and Narrow Water were aberrations in a downward trend. IRA intimidation within the nationalist community, a good metric for terrorist activity, was at its lowest in a decade. The army's abandonment of roads in South Armagh gave the IRA too much space to operate, he argued. The police knew what worked and were better placed to contain and defeat the enemy. The Irish army, for instance, would never deal directly with the British army, but the Gardaí would talk to the RUC. His force was getting smarter—a new undercover surveillance unit was tracking IRA supply lines—and gaining public support even in nationalist areas. What was needed, said Newman, was patience.

It was a defense of the "criminalization" strategy initiated by the previous Labour government: tackle terrorists through the police, courts, and prisons, treat them as criminals, not combatants. Strip away their claim to legitimacy. Normalize daily life. Keep the army in the background and prioritize assets such as the Ulster Defence Regiment, with local accents and knowledge, over units from England, Wales, and Scotland. Newman had a final request: more RUC officers.

Thatcher had not interrupted once. She gazed at Newman. The army, she said, had given a bleaker briefing. "Did you say, Chief Constable, that you wanted an extra one thousand men?"

"Yes, prime minister, I did."

"Did you say that if you had them, we could make further reductions in the army?"

"Yes, prime minister, I did."

"Right. You can have them." Thatcher stood up and left.

Back on Downing Street, memos and reports streamed into Whitehall departments. Thatcher had her strategy. She would let the police lead the fight. She would show the people of Northern Ireland, show the world, that the IRA were common murderers and criminals. She would ignore the heckler in the white cardigan, shaking with fury, asking her about the H-Blocks.

No, not asking. Warning.

CHAPTER THREE

———

The Chancer

In the late summer of 1979, Patrick Magee was starting to unravel, one stitch at a time, a thread bound too tight for too long. He was twenty-eight years old and in danger of losing the two things that most mattered: his purpose and his family. A small man with tight brown curls and a matching beard, Magee had the stillness and intensity of a Renaissance portrait and spoke so softly you had to lean in to catch the words. Not that he said much. A quiet one, everybody agreed. He preferred to watch, listen, and let others talk, a policy that had served him well during seven years in the IRA. He was not high in the hierarchy but was one of the operational elite.

At the moment, Magee was on a break from the war and living in Shannon in County Clare on the west coast of Ireland, a world away from Belfast, 250 miles to the north. Shannon was a collection of housing estates built on reclaimed marshland next to an airport and factories. It was Ireland's newest town, but poor design gave it no center, no heart, and exposed residents to wind and rain. Magee had moved here several months earlier under instructions to lie low and take it easy, but that plan, too, had design flaws. He was on edge, restless, and gazing north.

Thatcher's whirlwind visit at the end of August must have stung. Magee had been abused and humiliated in Girdwood Barracks, which the prime minister bustled through on her way to a helicopter. He had been battered in enough interrogation rooms to know all about the policing methods of Chief Constable Newman. And there was Thatcher, gazing into the TV cameras, promising to defeat the IRA.

Magee did not know whether he was still up for the fight. This sabbatical from the frantic pace of operations, supposedly temporary, had given him time to think, too much time, and unleashed a churn of emotions. For seven years his commitment had been absolute. But now, while the new prime minister appraised the battlefield, Magee felt himself sinking into the Shannon swamp. He was no longer just an IRA operative, he was a husband and father. He felt confused, tugged different ways. He did not know if he could still contribute to the movement, still be effective. Memories of operations, of things seen and done, seemed to play in a loop. His nerves jangled. He was having nightmares. Maybe he was done with the IRA.

. . .

SOME PEOPLE SAILED into the IRA as if born to it, bidden by fate. Patrick Joseph Magee edged in like a crab who so easily could have washed onto a different shore.

He was born in May 1951 to Philomena Donegan and John Magee, working-class Catholics who rented a room in a cramped house in Belfast's Market district, a five-minute walk from city hall. Like many Catholics they endured overcrowded, unsanitary housing—rats were a problem—and chafed at discrimination. Protestant mobs had burned Philomena's parents out of their home in 1920. But the Market hummed with extended family—grandparents, nephews, cousins, in-laws—and the bakeries, cobblers, and livestock markets completed a full, vibrant world. It was home.

In pursuit of a paycheck, Magee's father, a steel plate fitter, moved the family to England. For the four-year-old Pat—the family seldom used Patrick—it was a wrenching dislocation. He never forgot the stench of vomit on the ferry crossing and unlike his younger siblings never truly settled in the alienness of Norwich, a provincial city in the east of England. Money was tight, requiring pawnshop visits, and his parents bickered. Pat became a nervous nail-biter. Everyone missed Belfast.

They tried to fit in. His mother instructed the children to stop calling her Mammy, the Belfast practice, and use Mum, like English kids. "To me it was daft. Mammy was mammy," Magee recalled in his memoir, *Where Grieving Begins*, published in 2021. She once had a row with a neighbor, a bowler-hatted man, who responded by calling her an Irish bastard. "I never for a day forgot I was Irish. Nor was I allowed to forget," Magee wrote. At home he was Pat, but outside it he was always Paddy, a version of Patrick, yes, but also a generic name, often said with a sneer, for Irish people.

Small for his age, appearing malnourished, the runty outsider clung to his Irishness. He was hyperactive and easily distracted, but teachers sometimes detected a blazing intelligence. Magee served as an altar boy and sang in the church choir, only to turn into an outspoken atheist by the age of twelve. There was no God, certainly not in England. In 1964, the Magees returned to Belfast for a few weeks. For Pat, it was like he had never left. The aromas of the Market, the jokes, songs, and slang, the old friendships and rituals, all were rekindled. He felt reforged.

Dragged back to Norwich, he became a moody teenage rebel, grew his hair long, rowed with his parents, skipped school, fell in with older teens with a taste for shoplifting, vandalism, and petty theft. Seeking cash, they broke into a butcher's shop. Magee, age fifteen, was arrested and fingerprinted. His prints matched those on a broken glass window. A juvenile court sent him to a young offenders' hostel in London.

By day, Magee found casual jobs as a teaboy and factory worker, working alongside Irish, Caribbean, and other immigrants. He loved London, but with "low esteem" and "pathetically eager to belong"— Magee's words—he again joined older boys in petty crime, including joyriding. "Just the sort of stunt that might convince you that you could get away with anything if you only kept your nerve," he recalled. Narrow escapes from police yielded a life lesson: "Never panic; hold your nerve and examine the options. What I had failed to figure out was how not to get myself into such scrapes."

Back home in Norwich, Magee was caught stealing a motorbike and sentenced to another spell of juvenile detention. There he obtained five O levels—basic high school qualifications—and discovered a talent for drawing. He returned to the family home in August 1969. He was eighteen, and a seductive tide beckoned. The sixties were still swinging, and dreamers and misfits were transforming music and fashion. Rebellion was modish—Black Panthers and Vietnam War protesters in the US, student rioters in Paris. Magee, fancying himself a pacifist and a communist, or at least a socialist, embraced the zeitgeist. He saw Jimi Hendrix, Bob Dylan, and Fleetwood Mac perform live. He read George Orwell's *1984*—a fateful year—and Robert Tressell's *The Ragged-Trousered Philanthropists*.

He signed up for art school, a state-funded alternative to university for those allergic to conventional education that had incubated the likes of John Lennon, Eric Clapton, and David Bowie. Perhaps not the sort of alums to impress Margaret Thatcher, soon to become education minister, but potential role models for Magee. Easily bored, he crashed out after one term, his studies derailed by booze, a smattering of drugs (uppers, downers, LSD once), and wanderlust. He hitched around England, slept rough, worked in bottling plants, factories, warehouses, bars, fruit stalls, and on fishing trawlers. He told himself he was tasting life, harvesting bohemian experience for some future artistic endeavor.

In truth, he was lost.

. . .

THEN IRELAND EXPLODED.

Instead of Vietnam, news bulletins led with Belfast and Derry. Magee had to see for himself. He returned for Christmas 1970 and spent six weeks with relatives observing street clashes. The defiance of those hurling petrol bombs at army vehicles awed him. He drifted back to England for a few months, bobbing from job to job, and returned to Belfast in August 1971.

With no plan beyond a vague desire to bear witness, he stayed with relatives and hung out in bars and illicit drinking dens known as "shebeens." One night some drinkers mistook him for a Brit spy and roughed him up until confirming his identity. Magee resolved to lose his English accent.

In November, his parents—now with four young children—followed their eldest son back to Belfast. It was a war zone, but they worried about Pat and perhaps like him they, too, needed to see things for themselves. They moved into a maze of three-story concrete blocks called Unity Walk. A misnomer. It was a Catholic enclave in a Protestant heartland and to avoid rocks it was best to run. There were also abductions and drive-by shootings. Women and children evacuated during the summer marching season when loyalists celebrated the seventeenth-century victories of King William of Orange with huge bonfires and drumming to waken the dead.

Compounding the sense of siege, soldiers patrolled day and night and barged into homes for destructive searches—furniture smashed, floorboards ripped out, ceilings gouged. The troops surveilled the Unity flats from a small fortified position known as a sangar. Another outpost kept watch from atop a library, which doubled as a helipad. The RUC had their own barracks, completing the encirclement. The security forces were considered in cahoots with loyalist paramilitaries.

Somehow the local IRA eluded this stifling matrix to stage gun and bomb attacks. Magee marveled at their courage. "I had come to realize that the IRA *were* the community—of the people and for the people," he recalled. He wondered if he had what it took to join this secret army and confront the might of the British state. "I couldn't decide whether I was up to the task. What the hell can I do here? Would I be physically up to the task of killing people? That's what we're talking about. And I couldn't answer that question." He felt a poor specimen, not athletic or sporty, prone to chest infections. Even after Bloody Sunday in January 1972, he hesitated. "Was I capable of killing? Of withstanding torture?" Stories abounded of beatings and electric shocks.

Weeks later, Magee was in a shebeen when soldiers stormed in. A random raid. They "lifted"—slang for arrested—Magee and about a dozen inebriated men. Black boots pinned Magee to the floor of an armored personnel carrier and stomped on his hands. The frightened drinkers were hustled into Girdwood Barracks, the main interrogation center for North Belfast, split up into cubicles, and punched, slapped, and taunted for thirty-six hours. "We simply had no rights. The veil was lifted," wrote Magee.

A girlfriend assumed from his bruised, scabbed knuckles he had put up a fight. Well, now he would.

· · ·

THE IRA DID not seek out Magee. The organization offered no salary. In fact, it warned prospective volunteers—the preferred term for members—that what awaited was a jail cell or a hole in the ground. Yet supply of would-be volunteers far outstripped manpower needs. The vast majority were young working-class males. Some were thugs, some were romantics, most were unremarkable. A psychiatric study of convicted "political" killers in Northern Ireland judged them normal in intelligence and mental stability. An informal IRA survey found up to 90 percent of volunteers joined not through ideological conviction but to hit back after security force violence or harassment. They viewed violence as a legitimate response because if the state broke the law, then there was no law. There was also a youthful fascination with guns and bombs. Others joined for respect and approbation and to stand out from the ranks of the unemployed and powerless. There were, in other words, many Pat Magees.

The IRA had split into two factions in 1969 at the outset of the Troubles. The Officials wanted to contest elections and ally with left-wing radicals. The Provisionals—known familiarly as the Provos—rejected electoral politics and claimed the mantle of the Easter 1916 rebels who had proclaimed a provisional government. By 1972, the Provos were ascendant. Magee chose the Provos.

From whispers in the Avenue Bar about "the boys" and "the 'Ra," laudatory slang for the IRA, the local unit's identity was an open secret—though exactly who did what was unclear. Magee, age twenty, discreetly signaled his interest. His English accent still aroused suspicion, but in the spring of 1972 a senior IRA man accepted him on probation, a precaution applied to some newbies. Training was brief. In a tiny bedroom, he and other newbies learned to strip, reassemble, load, and maintain an M1 carbine, an old Webley revolver, and other guns. The IRA also ran training camps in rural areas with firing ranges and explosives workshops. Some city boys didn't see the point of crawling through muddy fields, infantry-style, and they mistook foxes and wild goats for undercover police.

Magee was assigned to G Company of the IRA's Third Battalion, Belfast Brigade. Grandiose terms mimicked conventional military structures while masking a ragtag reality. Volunteers formed companies in their own areas, with several companies forming a battalion and several battalions forming a brigade. Belfast was a brigade area with three battalions. Derry, South Armagh, and East Tyrone had smaller brigades. A seven-member Army Council set IRA policy and appointed a chief of staff to direct operations. Over the years, the total number of volunteers at any one time yo-yoed, from several hundred to perhaps two thousand. The total number, over thirty years, is estimated at ten thousand.

Magee, the former pacifist, found himself in a maelstrom. His first year with the IRA became the bloodiest year of the entire Troubles—497 dead, including 108 soldiers—and the most lethal area was his patch of North Belfast. Unity Walk's proximity to the city center gave G Company an edge in bombing commercial targets, part of a strategy to drain the British Treasury and sap political will. Proximity to loyalist areas induced another dynamic: sectarianism. The IRA professed to target the "British war machine," not ordinary Protestants. But loyalist paramilitaries were especially active in Third Batt's area, prompting some companies to gun down random Protestants in reprisal and claim they were paramilitaries. This inability to stay focused on the larger goal was said to be one reason Third Batt commanders seldom made it to brigade level. This bothered Magee's first mentor, Gerry Bradley, not at all. He didn't give a damn about promotion, he cared only about pushing the Brits into the sea. He was eighteen years old with shoulder-length hair, and he was a veteran of riots, shootings, and bombings. He also had a side job in bank robbery and car theft for funding and transport. Bradley was fearless, daring, ruthless, and reckless. And by August 1972, he was G Company's Officer Commanding (OC). The company had about thirty frontline "operators" supported by forty Fianna (boys) and Cailíní (girls), age fourteen to sixteen, and fifty auxiliaries, older men and women, who acted as lookouts, couriers, and scouts.

The teen commander sustained a ferocious tempo of three to four ops per day. Then again, "operation" was too grand a word, he later recalled in the 2008 memoir *Insider: Gerry Bradley's Life in the IRA*, cowritten with Brian Feeney. "You got a weapon, fired five to ten shots, gave it to a girl: she bolted. No question of washing off residues or anything like that. Forensics didn't come into it then. Just shoot and walk away. We didn't know about forensics. Neither did the Brits. It was just blatter, blatter, blatter, and walk away."

Some guns were kept accessible as "floats," others were in "hides" under the control of a quartermaster, who would lend them for approved operations. Armalites—light, powerful rifles smuggled from the US—were especially prized. Bradley endlessly lobbied for "gear"— the IRA term for weapons. Bombers carried their loads into the city center in biscuit tins, cardboard boxes, and shopping bags. Female teams went well-dressed, like office workers, and planted incendiary devices away from sprinklers and close to flammable material for maximum destruction.

In this heady period, the IRA envisaged military victory. Bradley believed every action brought a British withdrawal, and a united Ireland, within reach. "We couldn't be bate [beat]," he recalled. "We were winning gun battles against the Brits. They had everything: armoured cars, the law, firepower, manpower, CS gas, and still they couldn't win. I genuinely believed that one day the IRA would be chasing the British army down to the docks, firing at them, and the last British officer would be backing up the gangway onto the boat with his pistol in his hand."

. . .

RIGHT FROM THE beginning, Magee was a frontline operator. The journey from apprentice to veteran was short because newbies had to fill gaps left by comrades who had been "scooped"—a popular way to say arrested. Within weeks, Magee was appointed to a position that would define the rest of his life: engineering officer (EO), the IRA term for bomb maker. There wasn't much competition. In the OC's estimation, the other candidates "couldn't be trusted with a box of matches." And in any case, few wanted the job, as EOs had a habit of blowing themselves up. Many bombs used an unstable mix of fertilizer and old-fashioned fuses known as "smokey joes." One fuse-delay technique relied on sulfuric acid dissolving two layers of condoms, after which the acid ignited. Making nail bombs, known as "nailers," entailed inserting a stick of gelignite in a beer can with six-inch nails.

"People who volunteered to work with explosives were regarded either as nutty professors or stark, raving mad," recalled Shane Paul

O'Doherty, a bomb maker. He almost lost an eye in a premature letter bomb explosion. "I had just put it into an envelope and sealed it, when I patted it. As I looked at it, a rainbow seemed to rise from it and speed past my head, quickly followed by a blue light, then an almighty *bang*! I was blown over the chair."

Of 106 IRA volunteers killed between 1969 and 1973, forty-four died in premature explosions. The security forces gleefully referred to these as "own goals"—a soccer term for when a player accidentally puts the ball in his team's net instead of the opponent's. Magee, with some misgivings, received a crash course in nail bombs, incendiaries, and other devices. The job, he discovered, was more about attitude than skill. He needed to be disciplined and methodical, qualities that had eluded him until then.

At some point—the cause is unclear—Magee lost the tip of the little finger on his right hand.

With commercial explosives like gelignite in short supply, the IRA cooked up its own lethal brew, turning a readily available agricultural fertilizer marketed as Net Nitrate into ammonium nitrate, which was then mixed with diesel oil. This was arduous labor that induced headaches and skin rashes, leaving EOs easily identifiable. A hospital consultant who was a sympathizer advised the IRA to use well-ventilated spaces. Magee worked from derelict premises in the Market district, which was undergoing slum clearance, Bradley recalled. "He was based in the Markets making the 'blowy stuff' for the whole [third] battalion for weeks on end."

IRA bomb makers and planters—two different jobs—spoke of exhilaration when a big bomb went off. "There was this incredible boom, and there was a vast pool of gray dust and plaster in the air, and an eerie silence," O'Doherty recalled. "And I looked at it and thought, you know, this is the most incredible power I had ever seen unleashed. And all from striking a box of matches."

On Friday, July 21, 1972, the IRA detonated twenty bombs across Belfast in just over an hour, a logistical feat intended to shock and awe.

Warnings were given, but the security forces and emergency services didn't have time to clear areas, resulting in nine dead and 130 injured, including seventy-seven women and children. Body parts were blown onto rooftops. TV news showed firemen shoveling torsos into bags. Bloody Friday, as it became known, was a disaster for the IRA. Even sympathizers recoiled. Third Batt had planted eleven of the twenty bombs.

British troops bulldozed into previously no-go areas, crimping the IRA's room for maneuver. Patrols scooped more and more operators. Early one afternoon in June 1973, Magee walked up a deserted street—he was on his way to inspect a weapons cache—and straight into a squad of paratroopers. The fake ID didn't fool them, and he was arrested.

. . .

Long Kesh was a former RAF airdrome ten miles west of Belfast that had been converted into a detention camp. Fences with razor wire, checkpoints, and army watchtowers marked the perimeter. Hundreds of republican prisoners were housed in dozens of huts made of corrugated iron, with four or five huts forming a compound called a cage. Most inmates, like Magee, were not charged or convicted of any crime. They were "interned" on the basis of a detention order. This was to be Magee's home for two and a half years.

Inmates at the Spartan prisoner-of-war-style regime at Long Kesh, or the Lazy K as some called it, baked in summer, shivered in winter. Guards with helmets, shields, batons, and sniffer dogs would barge into huts screaming a barracks-style reveille: "Hands off cocks, on with socks." But within the wire, prisoners had the freedom to wear their own clothes and organize. They replicated IRA discipline and structures—drilling, training, planning escapes—and each cage was run by an OC.

Younger inmates used the time to catch up on lost boyhoods, pranking each other, staging water fights. Older men pined for wives and children. There was a cottage industry of brewing and distilling hooch. Magee kept to himself. He exercised, his boots pounding the stony soil. Like many prisoners, he studied Irish to help revive a culture the "sassenach"—a disparaging term for the English used by Irish and Scots—had all but extinguished. Another reason was privacy: the guards did not understand it. He sketched portraits of dead comrades on handkerchiefs as decorative gifts for relatives and supporters outside. Such artwork was so popular that Long Kesh was nicknamed "the hankie factory." He played chess with a seventeen-year-old from Derry called Patsy O'Hara. He read novels and was dismayed to find *The Savage Day*, a Jack Higgins thriller, depicted republicans as sectarian thugs. Other novels gave IRA characters ferrety features and rotting teeth to externalize their moral failings. Magee was indignant. "The republicans I knew were politically intelligent, committed and honorable people."

None more so than the tall, rangy inmate with shoulder-length hair, straggly beard, and thick glasses who arrived a few months after Magee. He wore a T-shirt and bell-bottoms and looked like a hippie. He was still bruised from a beating by soldiers before his transfer to the camp. His name was Gerry Adams. Just twenty-four years old, he was already a quasi-mythical figure, a Belfast commander credited with out-*thinking* the Brits. Known as Gerry A—which was pronounced *Ah*—he helped turn the Kesh into a guerrilla university with discussions and debates about the conflict. Magee attended one lecture in which Adams posed a question. "Does anybody here think this war will be over in two years?"

There were no takers.

"Does anybody think this war'll be over in ten years?"

An uneasy silence.

"Does anybody think this war's going to be over in twenty years?"

The question hung in the air, ominous, dreadful. The audience exchanged glances. It was a glimpse into unfathomable darkness. An endless vista of struggle, sacrifice, death. Adams, however, was not despairing. Republicans could beat the Brits, he said, but they needed to build a political movement and retool the IRA for a "long war."

Magee was electrified. The prognosis was grim—years, *decades* of attrition—but with a route to victory. Gerry A mapped it all out, he later recalled. "We were all too close to the forest floor to perceive the view afforded from the canopy. Adams had foreseen the future course of the struggle more keenly than any of us in that hut."

The aloof EO from G Company began turning himself into a vision of Adams's ideal Provo. He joined Sinn Féin, studied military texts, political tracts, history. He not only learned to speak Irish, he became a *múinteoir*—a teacher. "For the first time in my life, I learned I had the capacity to focus."

In November 1975, Magee was released. By then, a new prison complex with high walls was rising beside Long Kesh. There were eight blocks, each in the shape of an H. Magee, trundling away in a transit van, didn't look back.

. . .

SOME VOLUNTEERS NEVER recovered from incarceration and quit the movement after release. Others rejoined but took low-risk jobs in "punishment" units that targeted young criminals—alleged burglars, joyriders, drug dealers—in Catholic areas. This they accomplished with baseball bats, bricks, spikes, and gunshots to the legs known as kneecappings. Within an hour of his return to Belfast, Magee reported to the IRA for duty and made clear he wanted "active service."

He had resolved, when the time was right, to discreetly lobby for the most prestigious area of operations: England. Many operators had never been abroad, never even left Belfast, whereas he knew the enemy's terrain. "Nothing was clearer to me than where the IRA could maximize its impact, pound for pound. England was where I could most effectively contribute to the struggle."

First, however, the IRA needed Magee in the six counties. Its campaign was faltering, and much had changed during his time behind the wire. Dublin-based IRA chiefs had agreed to a truce with the British, hoping to leverage concessions, even withdrawal, but neither came. The Provos atrophied and engaged in a bloody feud with the Official IRA. Loyalist gangs were butchering Catholics, in some cases literally, with hatchets and carving knives. Security forces were eavesdropping on republicans with listening towers and seemed to have thick files on every operator, sowing paranoia. Sympathizers were afraid to store weapons or shelter gunmen.

Pressure intensified in 1976 when the Labour government's new Northern Ireland secretary, Roy Mason, arrived. A tough, diminutive former miner, he wore a safari suit and boasted of squeezing the IRA like toothpaste. Under Chief Constable Newman, police interrogators extracted confessions with slaps, punches, sleep deprivation, waterboarding, and other methods. They didn't call it torture, it was "slap and tickle." And it seemed to work: conviction rates rose and terror attacks dwindled.

Mason felt confident enough to host the Queen in August 1977. The Royal Yacht *Britannia* sailed into Belfast Lough, guarded by a navy destroyer and thirty-two thousand soldiers and police. The IRA pinpricked the shield around the monarch by exploding two small bombs during her visit to a university. It was the debut of a new Provo technology—long-delay timers—but few noted the significance because the bombs caused no damage.

Magee, by now a mid-ranking operator, was well known to security forces—a "red light," in Provo terminology—and was often arrested and interrogated, sometimes brutally. He never cracked or confessed or was charged. He kept to the Provo code of silence. Released, he would resume a nomadic existence, darting from safe house to safe house. A typical day began with lighting a fire in the hearth and making a to-do list; once the list was clear in his head, he burned it. Likewise with bombs. He always drew a diagram of each device. "The timing mechanisms and the safety routines might be simple, but in the stress of an operation and of the unexpected, it was best to have mentally rehearsed."

The IRA innovated by packing a highly flammable mix of household chemicals with a detonator, battery, and timing mechanism into tape cassettes. It also developed a blast incendiary: strap a small explosive charge to a can of petrol and, *whoosh*, a fireball with the explosive force of a three-hundred-pound bomb. During 1977 and early 1978, some six hundred attacks incinerated shops, offices, cinemas, hotels, and other commercial targets. On February 17, 1978, a blast incendiary engulfed staff and guests at the La Mon Hotel east of Belfast. The device behaved like napalm, coating and scorching skin. Twelve people, all Protestants, were burned alive—one of the worst atrocities of the Troubles. The IRA apologized, saying a broken public phone box and an army checkpoint had delayed the unit phoning a warning.

Somehow during all this, Magee had found time to marry his girlfriend, Eileen McGreevy. A slender woman with brown hair and strong features, she was twenty-one and had been active in the movement. She respected Magee's commitment. The groom wore a disguise for the brief ceremony at St. Patrick's Church on Donegall Street. A son, Padraig, was born in January 1978. Magee's parents and siblings, meanwhile, had returned to England and settled in Kent. They had minimal contact with Magee.

Becoming a father initially did not dim his desire for operations. In fact, it ratcheted up his urgency. "I didn't want my son to grow up to have to face the same set of questions that I had to answer in 1972. To ensure that didn't happen, that we didn't bequeath that choice to this next generation, the struggle had to end with us."

Magee got the nod to join the England campaign. Like a cogwheel in one of his devices, slowly rotating in a mesh of other cogs, Pat Magee's life had come full circle. He was back across the water, a Paddy once more, in the land that had never become home, except this time as a member of a secret army. Operating in England was the holy of holies, a strike at the enemy's heart. Such operators were veiled from ordinary IRA volunteers. Magee could not tell his Belfast comrades where he was going, as British intelligence would pick up any leaks. "You had to keep it tight," Magee recalled. One day, he simply disappeared. Some assumed he had abandoned them and moved south. Quitter Magee.

For nine months he brought the war to England. There were different rules for this underground existence. He could not rely on a web of sympathizers or risk contact with Eileen: no phone calls, no letters, no visits. To protect his false identity, he did not even carry a picture of their newborn son. For much of the time, he was alone. The only people who knew exactly what Magee was up to belonged to the IRA's most secret unit, the England Department.

. . .

IN THE SUMMER of 1979, Magee returned to Ireland one step ahead of the British police, who had been tracking him. They had coined a nickname for the risks he took: the Chancer. His IRA handlers were pleased, and they ordered him to lie low in the republic. He would be tapped again for active service when the time was right. Magee felt like he had been shunted aside. But he was overdue a break and needed to reconnect with Eileen, who had barely seen him in two years of marriage. On the promise he would no longer disappear for long stretches, she quit her job in Belfast and joined him with their child in Shannon. For the first time they could be a proper family.

It went well at first. They got social housing, a three-bedroom home. Magee got a job in a factory. They did a weekly shop at the supermarket. Instead of the drone of army helicopters, they were close to the rhythmic thud of Atlantic waves. But Magee could not settle. People in the south didn't really care about the north. A mob had burned the British embassy in Dublin after Bloody Sunday, but that was a one-off. Southerners tended to disapprove of the IRA and to tune out the Troubles. Magee felt he was in a cloud looking down at this strange other self—exile, husband, father, breadwinner. The conflict raged in his head, possibly a symptom of what would today be recognized as post-traumatic stress. He agonized over reports of jailed comrades enduring horrendous conditions in the H-Blocks. Ghosts of dead volunteers visited his thoughts and dreams. "My new existence," he said, "seemed a betrayal."

The war appeared to be spinning in a new direction. Mountbatten and the paratroopers had been wiped out; now this new prime minister was vowing to crush the movement. When the IRA asked Magee to do an op—the nature of which remains secret—he seized the chance. His absence cost him the factory job and Eileen's trust. In the cold, dark winter of early 1980 she returned with their son to Belfast. While the rest of the world bade farewell to the 1970s and welcomed a new decade, Magee was alone in Shannon, poking at the ashes of his marriage.

He began drinking heavily, and he felt a wild impulse for action. He asked a comrade what kept him going. Hatred, came the reply. Magee felt his old certainties drain away. A realization dawned: "I was of no use as a volunteer. I was burned out."

After eight years of collective struggle, of being part of a greater whole, Magee felt small, insignificant. Slowly, he rebuilt his sense of self. He stopped drinking. He resumed working, saved some money, felt energy and focus returning. But this time it would not serve the movement, it would be for himself, Eileen, and Padraig. He notified the Provos: count me out. It was a myth that once you were in the IRA you were in for life. You *could* quit. Magee felt lighter. An intoxicating thought took hold. *Leave Ireland. Walk away from the past.*

. . .

IT WAS JUST before dawn. The sky was paling, casting a glow over the fields and oak trees of this corner of the southern Netherlands. The air smelled of hay. Pat Magee emerged into the yard and mounted his bicycle. It was September 19, 1980, a Friday. He rode out of the farm onto a small road and headed south. Meadows with poppies gave way to woodland, then a few small factories. The sun was higher by the time he passed the village of Overloon. Magee kept riding. He had a job to go to.

The former Belfast Brigade bomber felt reborn. Initially Magee had planned to move to the United States, but scotched that when the US consulate in Dublin notified him of a British warrant for his arrest. Upon arrival in New York, he would probably be detained and face extradition. So in early summer of 1980 he took a ferry to France and hitchhiked to the Netherlands, drawn by its reputation for protecting political exiles. He was not undercover—he was traveling under his own name. In Amsterdam he spotted an ad for seasonal work and took a train south to Overloon, a sleepy village near the border with West Germany. There he earned a paycheck loading ovens in a brick factory.

He found accommodation with two other young laborers at the farm of Jan Vloet. Home was a renovated stables with a bed, a toilet, and a kitchenette—luxurious compared to life at Long Kesh.

The Vloets were hospitable. On weekends, their lodgers dined in the farmhouse with the family. Magee hit it off with the whole family. They found him polite, genial, a bit shy. He volunteered for chores and taught English to Jan's daughters, Iris, fifteen, and Daphne, eleven. He sketched a portrait of Iris, which she adored. His dimpled chin reminded her of John Travolta's. Magee spoke of injustice and violence in Northern Ireland, but gave no clue about his background. Asked about his fingertip, he said it was a carpentry accident. Mostly Magee spoke of Eileen and baby Padraig. He wanted to bring them to Holland.

Pushing past Overloon on a bike loaned by Jan, Magee had special reason for contentment on this autumnal morning. He no longer heaved bricks into ovens. He had found a better job in a metal factory in Venray, a few miles farther south. He was learning Dutch and had opened a bank account. The Vloets were helping him find an apartment.

Magee pedaled over a small canal and a creek and took a side road that skirted Venray. The factory was on the other side of town.

Leave Ireland. Walk away from the past. It was happening.

A white van appeared behind him.

Soon Eileen and Padraig could join him.

The van accelerated.

In a few months Eileen could be learning Dutch.

By the time Magee was in sight of the factory gates, the van was right behind him. Now he heard it. It roared past, swerved into his path, and screeched to a stop. With no time to brake, he crashed into it. Dazed, sprawled on the ground, Magee heard voices shouting. He looked up. A submachine gun muzzle pointed at his face. Six men in black balaclavas and black overalls surrounded him.

"Stay down!" they yelled.

CHAPTER FOUR

Hunger

Magee stared at the gun and thought, *This is it. I'm about to die.*

A moment later, he processed a second possibility: he was being kidnapped by British agents. After being handcuffed and bundled into the van and discovering the men were Dutch police acting on a British extradition warrant, he had a third thought: there was no escaping his past.

By using his own name and passport, Magee had left tracks. The British authorities had notified Interpol that they wanted to try him in London for bombings in England, and word had gone out to European police forces. All the time Magee thought he was starting a new life at the Vloets' farm, the Dutch domestic intelligence service, Binnenlandse Veiligheidsdienst (BVD), had been tapping the phone and surveilling his movements from a neighbor's attic.

Magee was held on the top floor of an eight-story prison in Maastricht. The only other prisoner on his floor was a Czech spy whom he never saw or heard. The weeks while he was isolated in his cell passed in a sort of fugue. Incidents from the conflict clawed at him and triggered outbursts where he shouted out involuntarily. In calmer moments, he reflected on a painful truth. The IRA had killed innocent civilians. He thought of La Mon, the Birmingham pub bombings, and other horrifying slaughters. These were mistakes, unintended outcomes, Magee told himself. The solution was not to halt the armed struggle but to standardize timing mechanisms and improve warning procedures. The IRA was morally justified. They were forced into war, whereas the Brits chose violence. It was the nature of the imperial beast.

Magee wrote to the Vloets, thanking them for their kindness and apologizing for embarrassing them. He told Jan he would pay any outstanding rent and expressed concern that the bicycle might have been damaged during the arrest. He hoped to see them again. "I pray for a happy ending," he told them. "I hope still that I can live in the Netherlands with my family."

The Vloets retained affection for their former lodger despite the shock of police raiding their home and Dutch and British journalists camping on their doorstep. "The Girl Who Befriended a Murderer," one tabloid headline blared over a photo of Daphne. The family offered to send Magee food and clothes. The Venray factory bosses lauded their former employee's diligence and said his job awaited should he return. "Such a boy should be given a chance," said a director.

The IRA had targeted British soldiers and diplomats in continental Europe, but there is no evidence Magee was involved in any operations during his time at Overloon. But perhaps it was only a matter of time.

Ireland's gravitational pull began to strain his tether to the Netherlands when, on October 27, five weeks after his arrest, seven prisoners in the H-Blocks began a hunger strike. Self-starving was an ancient tactic in Ireland, used to shame power. By whittling away flesh, it turned the body into a bony instrument of protest. Those who went all the way, who died, became martyrs. The most famous example in the twentieth century was Terence MacSwiney, a Lord Mayor of

Cork who died in a British jail in 1920 after refusing food for seventy-four days.

The H-Blocks, officially known as Her Majesty's Prison, the Maze, was a new front in the conflict. The British had bitterly regretted granting de facto prisoner-of-war status to republicans in Long Kesh. After the last detainees were released in 1976, the government closed the camp and opened the adjacent H-Blocks, a modern maximum-security prison that took its official name from a nearby townland called Maze. There would be no more "special category" status for republican prisoners. They would be treated as ordinary criminals and murderers.

For Margaret Thatcher, this was part of the criminalization strategy. But for republicans, it was an existential challenge. The whole struggle rested on the premise that they were combatants resisting colonial occupation. It was this claim that generated public support and funding. Lose legitimacy, you lose the war. In fact, you were even at risk of losing history, because this same coarse brush could be used retrospectively to undermine the struggle's definitive moments, such as the war of independence and the 1916 Rising. So in 1976, H-Block prisoners refused to wear the prison uniform, cloaked themselves in blankets, and demanded political status. Confrontations with warders escalated, triggering harsh punishment. Outside the prison, the IRA retaliated by shooting warders. In 1978, about three hundred prisoners, still in blankets, began the "no-wash" or "dirty protest": they refused to slop out and covered cell walls with their own feces. Warders called them the "shitters" and meted out more beatings.

Thatcher had inherited this conflict-within-a-conflict when she took office. The woman who harangued her during the Belfast walkabout had demanded the H-Blocks be wiped out. Instead, Thatcher had accelerated the prisoner conveyor belt. By October 1980, the prisoners, their resolve chiseled to a fine point by five years of hellish protest, played their most powerful card. If Thatcher did not grant them political status, seven men would starve themselves, unleashing who knew what sort of reaction.

Following this on the radio in his cell seven hundred miles away, Magee felt a tug of comradeship. He knew some of the hunger strikers personally; he, too, was an Irish POW. He told his Dutch jailers he would forgo food over Christmas in solidarity. But on December 18, the hunger strike abruptly ended after fifty-three days. In a confused denouement, the prisoners thought the government had agreed to abolish prison uniforms and was considering other compromises. To save a comrade on the verge of death, they called off the strike. But the concessions turned out to be minor. Thatcher had not backed down. The prisoners reeled, defeated and distraught. The Iron Lady had prevailed.

A few weeks later, in January 1981, three Dutch judges rejected the British extradition request, deeming the evidence against Magee insufficient. British detectives who attended the hearing watched the Chancer walk out of court a free man. A newspaper reported tears in his eyes. Outside the courthouse, banner-waving demonstrators from the Ierland Komitee Nederland, a solidarity group of leftists and anarchists, celebrated a blow against British colonialism. Its members hosted Magee while he decided his next move.

Two journalists from the *Daily Mail* tracked Magee to 40 Frederik Hendrikplantsoen, a five-story tenement building in a run-down part of West Amsterdam occupied by squatters. For a newspaper hostile to terrorists, lefties, foreigners, layabouts, and any other offenses to English decency, the scoop ticked all the boxes. All the story needed was a picture of the Provo in his squalid continental lair. After trying and failing to talk their way in, the reporter and photographer waited in their car, eyes peeled on the door. With no other exit, Magee was stuck. One of his Dutch comrades rustled up a posse of *kraakers*, members of the squatter movement. Led by a towering Amazonian with blue spiky hair and roller skates, they laid siege to the car, bounced on the hood, and hammered on the roof. "Why don't you leave him alone? If you don't there will be big trouble for you. Patrick has nothing to say," cried one. "British pigs, go back home," shouted another.

The distracted journalists did not see Magee slipping out, leaving them without a picture. The *Daily Mail* subsequently ran an indignant article about the fugitive from British justice. "He remained hidden, protected by the gang of punk rockers and out-of-work Leftists," it said. Magee and his friends celebrated their victory by attending a punk concert. But Magee was twitchy. He feared the British would again try to extradite or perhaps even kidnap or assassinate him. Abandoning his Dutch dream, at the end of February he slipped into France and boarded a ferry at Le Havre. Plowing through the English Channel's winter swell, he rounded the southern coast of England and approached Ireland in wind and drizzle. He had no idea what he was going to do.

. . .

THAT SAME WEEK, Margaret Thatcher, fresh from victory over the hunger strikers, was in Washington, DC, enjoying crisp sunshine and a hero's welcome from Ronald Reagan, the new US president. A limousine festooned with US and British flags delivered the Thatchers to the White House. Bugles and trumpets sounded when Margaret emerged, resplendent with pillbox hat and white gloves, onto the red carpet. Reagan and his wife, Nancy, escorted the visitors to the South Lawn while a military band played "God Save the Queen" and "The Star-Spangled Banner." Denis, on his best behavior, looked solemn as he put his hand on his heart for the US anthem.

The president and prime minister pledged fealty and kinship. "The responsibility for freedom is ours to share," said Reagan, squinting in the sunlight. "Britain and America will stand side by side." Thatcher, pale save for red lipstick, said they shared a resolve to unshackle enterprise and proclaim the truth that makes men free. "We must have the courage to reassert our traditional values and the resolve to prevail against those who deny our ideals and threaten our way of life." They waved to the cameras and disappeared inside the Oval Office.

It was impeccable pageantry, but in reality Thatcher was in trouble. Northern Ireland, however, was not the reason. Eighteen months had passed since her visit following the murder of Mountbatten, and her plan of giving the police primacy over the army seemed to be working. Death rates had fallen. There had been no more "spectaculars." Thatcher did not fret about reports of a new hunger strike brewing. The Troubles felt contained.

Thatcher's problems were closer to home. Senior figures in her own Conservative Party muttered she was not up to the job, too radical, too shrill. Some were her own ministers, but she hesitated to fire such "wets"—her term for the half-hearted—as that could trigger a leadership challenge. The other quandary was the economy. It refused to prosper. Her attempts to tame the unions had stalled, unemployment was rising, and her poll ratings had slumped. Reagan's affection for her was genuine and he basked in her Cold War warrior glow, but White House officials pointedly told Congress and the press they would not repeat her domestic mistakes.

The FBI kept an unusually close watch on the prime minister. Two weeks earlier, a reliable source had reported overhearing two men with English or Irish accents in the cocktail lounge of the Boar's Head restaurant in Falls Church, Virginia, discussing an apparent "hit" during her visit. "This will even the score for H," one man allegedly said. The FBI took this as a reference to the H-Blocks. "The Iron Maiden is no better than any other bloody PM," the man went on. He also referred to Bloody Sunday and "blanket men." The bureau's agents took it seriously enough to interview people from the bar and to alert field offices in New York, Boston, Newark, New Haven, and Philadelphia, where the IRA had support. The bureau's relations with the source soured when they asked him to do a polygraph test. Their next request didn't fare well, either. "Source emphatically refused to submit to hypnosis to authenticate his previously furnished information." Thatcher's visit passed without incident.

A would-be assassin, however, was watching from the shadows.

John Hinckley, a disturbed young Texan, wanted to impress the actress Jodie Foster with a historic deed. Thatcher didn't interest him. He was stalking Reagan.

. . .

IT WAS SUPPOSEDLY the start of spring, but Gerry Adams greeted March 1, 1981, with foreboding. A new hunger strike had begun that morning when a prisoner named Bobby Sands refused breakfast in the H-Blocks. Adams was by then deputy president of Sinn Féin and a member of the IRA's Army Council, which directed strategy. Years later, he would consistently deny ever having been a member of the IRA.

Adams opposed the strike. He was sure it would fail, just like the previous one, and almost all other hunger strikes before that. But Bobby and the other prisoners had made up their minds. They would gain political status or die trying. Adams believed Thatcher would let them die. He had been reared on tales of heroic failure—thwarted rebellions, betrayed plots, martyred leaders—and wanted to break the cycle. It was time to be practical, time to win.

It was an irony of the republican movement that a man with poor eyesight was credited with supreme vision. Adams viewed the world through thick glasses and seemed to see everything, the field of battle, the mood in a room, the next move. Maybe it was the lenses, but it was difficult to read those dark brown eyes, even more so when he puffed on his pipe, shrouding his expression in smoke. Adams was thirty-three years old, still lean, bearded, but no longer mistakable for a hippie. His hair was shorter and he combined sports jackets with jeans. He was a powerful man, but not powerful enough to stop the prisoners from launching a doomed battle.

Adams was born into the movement. His mother, Annie Hannaway, and father, Gerry Adams Sr., had republican lineage. Big Gerry, as he was known, had been jailed for wounding a policeman in 1942. He was a founder of the Felons Club, a bar where only those who served prison sentences could be full members. Ten children—three others died in infancy—crammed into the family home in Bally-murphy, a slab of housing estates wedged between the Black Mountain and the Falls Road, a Catholic heartland in West Belfast.

The family had a secret. Their revered father sexually abused some of his children, a shame so well hidden that Gerry Jr. said he discovered it only decades later. Young Gerry learned, perhaps too well, the art of emotional detachment. "A meditative fellow," a schoolteacher mused of his former pupil. "Never showed his hand, you always wondered what was going on in that little mind. Taking everything in." Adams was bookish, but dropped out of school at age sixteen to earn a living. Wrapping his lanky frame around a Honda 50 motorbike, he rode into town to pull pints at the Duke of York pub. The owner didn't like his solemn barman, saying Adams never smiled.

It was the era of mods, rockers, and free love, but Adams was not that sort of rebel. He was a practicing Catholic and a traditional republican. By 1968, he was organizing civil rights protests and showing a flair for public relations, writing letters to the *Irish News* under multiple names, some disputing his other letters, to stir debate. When the Troubles erupted, he led the IRA's small unit in Ballymurphy. When soldiers stormed the neighborhood, Adams ordered the IRA to put away its guns and stand down. Instead of a brief gunfight that would scatter everyone and let the troops return to their barracks, youths responded with rocks, bottles, and barricades. This resulted in wild, freewheeling clashes that lasted days, filling the air with tear gas and engaging the whole community in the art of rioting. One resident got hold of an army megaphone and taunted the soldiers in plummy officer tones: "Disperse or we will throw stones!"

It cemented support for the IRA and became a template for other neighborhoods. Adams acquired a reputation as a street Napoleon. After he busted a British army spying ring, some called Adams the "big lad"—a nod to Michael Collins, the "big fella." Soldiers patrolled Ballymurphy, shouting: "We're looking for Gerry A. Come out, Gerry Adams, you bastard!"

Amid the chaos, he married Colette McArdle, a young woman with green eyes whom he had met at a political meeting. Ever the traditionalist, he asked her father's permission. They had a son, Gearoid. Adams was captured in 1972—an informer had tipped off the Brits—only to be released months later to join IRA leaders for secret talks in London with Ted Heath's government. The former barman wore a ragged sweater as a sartorial rebuttal to dapper Tory ministers. His outfit would have been quite a contrast with Thatcher's pearls and dresses, but as education minister she was not part of the talks.

The negotiations failed and a year later Adams was recaptured, beaten black and blue, and interned in Long Kesh. Young Belfast volunteers like Pat Magee might have revered the new arrival, but others thought him gawky. He lacked the bona fides of a hands-on operator; there is no evidence that Adams ever fired a shot at an enemy. When he attended a lecture on AK-47s "to keep his hand in," he was laughed at.

In the claustrophobic world of IRA leadership, the Army Council's most influential members—Billy McKee, Dáithí Ó Conaill, and Ruairí Ó Brádaigh—had reservations about their cerebral young comrade. Like Shakespeare's Cassius, he had a lean and hungry look. After the British enticed them into the ill-fated truce from 1974 to 1976—it weakened the IRA and mired the organization in feuds and sectarianism—Adams found an opening. He blamed the debacle on out-of-touch armchair generals in Dublin who had fallen into a Brit trap. Too shrewd to explicitly articulate insubordination, he hinted his critique in columns smuggled out to the *Republican News*, published under a pen name, Brownie. He got proxies to float heretical notions about a long war. Then he produced a rescue plan for the IRA: a training manual, which became known as the Green Book, a new cell structure to tighten security, and a new Belfast-based Northern Command to focus on fighting the war while a Dublin-based Southern Command looked after weapons caches.

With republicans still suspicious of politics, which they considered a distraction from military action, Adams used euphemisms to advocate political activity. Some volunteers would be redirected from operations to "civil administration" units that acted as local government, including punishing criminals and miscreants with baseball bats and kneecappings. Adams also suggested a "permanent leadership" to reduce the disruption of arrests. This would mean commanders stepping back from operations to avoid arrest, paving their emergence as public figures. The IRA rescue plan, in other words, doubled up as a blueprint for an Adams takeover. And it worked.

By 1977, the IRA was retooling, and Adams, released from Long Kesh, was on the Army Council. He worked steadily to marginalize his old guard rivals, a master class in Machiavellian maneuvering. The IRA's devastating strikes in Mullaghmore and Narrow Water in 1979 were testament to the lethal efficiency of South Armagh's roving operators, who still carried on largely under their own rules, but Adams's supporters credited his restructuring. They had a powerful mouthpiece: the movement's two newspapers, *An Phoblacht* (The Republic) and *Republican News*, had amalgamated under an Adams protégé, Danny Morrison, and burnished the legend of Gerry A, the man who saved the IRA.

By early 1981, the war had reached a stalemate—and Adams had graduated to vice president of Sinn Féin. The Provos were resilient, switching tactics and targets, but the British were funneling arrested volunteers through interrogation centers, special courts, and the H-Blocks. Adams focused on completing his takeover and edging the movement toward contesting elections. The emphasis would be on housing and jobs, not abstract republican ideology. Adams was determined this generation of republicans would not slide to defeat and irrelevance like their fathers and grandfathers who sang ballads in the Felons Club about thwarted rebellions and dashed dreams, about what might have been. A colleague recalled: "He hammered it home to all of us that something had to come out of all this during our lifetimes, that no matter about previous campaigns this struggle was not going to be for nothing."

And then along came Bobby Sands with a hunger strike that could ruin everything. It would drain resources, divert focus, and hand another victory to Thatcher. "Bobby, we are tactically, strategically, physically and morally opposed to a hunger strike," Adams implored in a smuggled letter.

His appeal did no good.

· · ·

"I AM STANDING on the threshold of another trembling world," Sands wrote on a scrap of toilet paper in his cell. "May God have mercy on my soul."

It was March 1, day one of the fast. Sands was twenty-six, with long, fair hair. He had spent nearly a third of his life in jail—first the Kesh, where he got to know Adams, then H-Block, serving a fourteen-year sentence for possessing a gun. A poet and musician with a slender build and granite stubbornness, Sands was the prisoners' leader. During evening storytellings, shouted from behind locked doors down the corridor, they would listen, rapt, as he recited Leon Uris's *Trinity*, a blockbuster American novel set in Ireland that he had memorized.

After a week, Sands lost six and a half pounds. Other prisoners were to join the fast at regular intervals to reach the point of death in rotation to maximize pressure on the government. As Adams had feared, the public shrugged. The prisoners were out of sight, and many of them had done terrible things. And anyway, the first strike had been anticlimactic. Now the government repeated its mantra: no concessions.

Then history pivoted. On March 16, Frank Maguire, an MP for Fermanagh and South Tyrone, died of a heart attack. Adams suggested running Sands in the by-election as a candidate for Sinn Féin. It was risky. The party had no electoral experience. Catholics might balk at voting for an IRA man. Sands could be humiliated. But Adams convinced the party, and Sands, that the publicity could animate public support for the hunger strike.

With the candidate growing weaker in the H-Blocks, republicans from across the island flocked to Fermanagh and Tyrone for a lesson in democracy. They crisscrossed fields and villages, shook hands, erected posters, blared republican songs. Sinn Féin published poems and essays by Sands. He compared the H-Blocks to an underworld and wrote of a caged lark that starves to death rather than sing in captivity. His family told crowds at rallies that a vote for Bobby could save his life. Even the murder of Joanne Mathers, a young Protestant mother shot by the IRA for collecting a census, did not stop the momentum.

Adams was driving to Dublin when the radio announced the result on April 9: 29,046 votes for the unionist candidate, Harry West, and 30,492 votes for Sands. The Ford Escort wove between the hedgerows as Adams pounded the steering wheel, shouting: "Fuck it, we've done it, we've done it, we've done it." In the H-Blocks, the prisoners brought the warders running with a roar of triumph: "*Bhi an bua againn.*" Victory is ours.

The result—Bobby Sands, MP—made world headlines, which until then had been dominated by the aftermath of the shooting and wounding of Ronald Reagan on March 30. Sands's victory subverted the foundations of British policy in Northern Ireland, which blamed the Troubles on a small gang of thugs who lacked popular support. The *Irish Times*—no friend to the IRA—noted, "The Provos can henceforth claim a mandate for their actions."

Thatcher, on the other hand, was implacable. The result changed nothing. "There can be no possible concession on political status," she said. "A crime is a crime is a crime."

Death by starvation is agonizing. Hunger spasms last weeks, then there is fatigue and a freezing coldness as surface body fat is used up. Talking becomes difficult. After losing protein and fat reserves, the body consumes nonessential muscle. Vitamin deficiencies lead to blindness. There is vertigo and nausea. In the final stage, the body devours the heart and diaphragm. Skin is so dry bones can puncture it. There are tormenting headaches and mouth ulcers, punctuated by hallucinations and flashes of clarity, even transcendence.

Sands turned marble white and gaunt. The Irish government and the Vatican expressed alarm. Three Irish parliamentarians, who were also members of the European parliament, visited Sands in the prison's hospital ward and asked to meet Thatcher. She responded with disdain: "It is not my habit or custom to meet MPs from a foreign country about a citizen of the UK, resident in the UK."

Vigils and marches were held across the island. During disturbances in Derry, an army Land Rover fatally crushed two teenagers. In Sligo, protesters broke into Classiebawn, choosing Mountbatten's castle as a symbol of British imperialism, and unfurled a banner from the roof. With Sands nearing death, and three other prisoners on hunger strike, *An Phoblacht/Republican News* carried a dramatic picture of flames engulfing soldiers in riot gear. The banner headline made a prophecy of worse to come if Sands died. "There Will Be Fire and There Will Be Fury."

In London, police discreetly padlocked one end of Downing Street as part of tighter security measures. Sands, blind and in agony, slipped into a coma. He died, after sixty-six days without food, at 1:17 a.m. on May 5. An army chef in the H-Blocks won £500 in a sweepstake for correctly predicting the time.

.   .   .

REPUBLICANS USED TO bang dustbin lids to warn the community of approaching troops, but now they did so in grief and anger, a deafening clatter of metal on concrete that echoed across Belfast. The funeral was vast, a hundred thousand mourners accompanying the coffin to Milltown Cemetery. Camera crews jostled to record the scene.

Reaction vibrated around the world. The US government expressed deep regret. There were marches in New York, Boston, Chicago, and

Gerry Adams and other mourners watch as IRA members fire
a volley over the coffin of Bobby Sands en route to Belfast's
Milltown Cemetery in May 1981. | PA Images

San Francisco. The Longshoremen's union blocked all British ships for twenty-four hours. "He was a rare one, a young man who thought enough of the place where he lived to want to die for it," said the *New York Daily News*. "The British have persistently misjudged the depth of Irish nationalism," said the *New York Times*. There were protests across Europe and Australia. Students in Milan burned the British flag. The Indian parliament observed a minute's silence. Streets in Tehran, Tripoli, and Le Mans were named after Sands.

Northern Ireland loyalists, in contrast, daubed gleeful graffiti. "Don't be vague, starve a taig"—meaning a Catholic. Some joked about a forthcoming concert by Bobby and the Skeletons. In nationalist areas, murals and posters of Sands and the other hunger strikers channeled Catholic iconography: emaciated, bearded, suffering, the prisoners looked like popular depictions of Christ.

Adams, he of the supreme vision, hadn't seen it coming. He had critiqued republican ideology for its obsession with blood sacrifice and martyrdom. He wanted to make the movement relevant to people's daily concerns like pensions, housing, schools. Yet now the agony of Sands—as well as the other hunger strikers following him—was alchemizing death into rebirth, a mysterious conjuring that Thatcher never understood. She betrayed no doubts in a statement to the House of Commons: "Mr. Sands was a convicted criminal. He chose to take his own life."

Even so, she was not blind to the growing danger. As five more strikers—Francis Hughes, Raymond McCreesh, Patsy O'Hara, Joe McDonnell, and Martin Hurson—succumbed during a long, scorching summer, the government feared a disaster was unfolding. Behind a facade of obduracy, Thatcher let envoys negotiate and offer compromises on the prisoners' five demands. In private, she admired their courage. "You have to hand it to some of these IRA boys. What a waste! What a terrible waste of human life!"

The strike inflicted deep anguish on republicans, while generating political dividends. In a general election in the south, two prisoners were elected to the Dublin parliament. The political path that Adams had yearned for was materializing. The longer the strike lasted, the more republicans would see the benefit of electoral politics. And all the while, authority seeped from Sinn Féin's Dublin headquarters to the Belfast-based hunger strike committee on which Adams sat. Bernadette McAliskey, a committee member, said Adams and his allies coldly weighed dead comrades against political gain. "There was no visible emotion, that total control of whatever emotion they felt was subordinate to the politics. . . . They could do a balance sheet."

Michael Oatley, a British official code-named the Mountain Climber, secretly floated a deal conceding some of the prisoners' demands: they could wear their own clothes, have more visits and letters, but not associate freely outside their cells. The Iron Lady, it turned out, could bend. In late July, with six men dead, Adams and three others visited the surviving strikers in the H-Blocks to discuss ending the protest. There is dispute as to whether Adams fully relayed the British offer, and whether it was him or the prisoners who took the decision, but the offer was rejected. What is beyond doubt is the trust Adams inspired. "We had absolute faith in Adams," one prisoner later said. "Adams to us was a God, an intellectual giant walking among midgets."

In his memoir, Adams recalled the visit as a heartbreaking farewell. The starving men looked ancient, skin stretched across skull-like faces, limbs pencil thin. Some were nearly blind. They smoked cigarettes while Adams puffed on his pipe.

"You could all be dead," he told them. "Everyone left in this room when we leave will be dead."

"*Sin é*," said somebody. That's it.

"We're right," said another. "The British government is wrong and if they think they can break us they're wrong twice. *Lean ar aghaidh*." Keep going.

Adams paused. "Before we leave, have any of you any questions?" he asked. "You might never see us again."

"Have we got any heavy gear yet?" one asked, referring to arms shipments.

"Get us our five demands," said another.

There was a silence. Another prisoner spoke up: "*Beidh an bua againn. Brisfimid Maggie Thatcher.*" We'll win. We'll break Maggie Thatcher.

. . .

FOUR MORE PRISONERS—Kevin Lynch, Kieran Doherty, Thomas McElwee, and Michael Devine—went on to die, making a total of ten men dead, seven from the IRA, three from the INLA, the breakaway rival republican group, before the strike concluded in early October 1981. In the end, Thatcher did not break. In fact, Northern Ireland didn't even hold her attention. Race riots had flared in English cities. Unemployment was spiraling. The prime minister plowed ahead, impervious. She cut government spending and purged her cabinet of wets. She promoted kindred spirits such as Norman Tebbit, a combative MP who yearned to shake Britain free of socialism, lethargy, and mediocrity. Like Thatcher, Tebbit was from humble origins, but never took elocution lessons and was fond of street vernacular. As employment minister, he looked forward to giving trade unions a good wallop.

At a private party in Downing Street, Thatcher kicked off her shoes, stood on a chair, and declared: "I am the rebel head of an establishment government."

Three days after the hunger strike ended, the government granted de facto special status to the H-Block prisoners. It was too late. A great, boiling rage convulsed the republican movement. Marches turned into riots. Security forces fired 29,695 plastic bullets during hunger-strike-related disturbances, killing seven civilians, including Carol Ann Kelly, age twelve, and Julie Livingstone, fourteen.

It all congealed into hatred for Thatcher, a visceral, personal hatred no British leader had evoked since Oliver Cromwell centuries earlier. She was Maggie, the Enemy of Ireland, cold, callous, contemptuous, imperious. Her name dripped in blood-red letters from banners calling her a murderer.

IRA volunteers and supporters clamored for revenge. *An Phoblacht/Republican News*, after all, had promised it: "There Will Be Fire." But few envisaged assassinating the prime minister. That was a fantasy on par with the neon cinema signs advertising *Indiana Jones and the Raiders of the Lost Ark*. For one thing, she was ringed by security, beyond reach. And yet the movement's morale and credibility required major attacks to make the Brits howl, so the Provos were in a quandary. Channeling rage into strategic gain would take time—and meanwhile, the hunger strike had sidetracked operations in the six counties. Instead of planning attacks, commanders had been on H-Block marches. There were riots and barricades and sporadic ambushes on police and army patrols, and a booby-trapped bomb injured a soldier who tried to take down an anti-Thatcher poster in

Crossmaglen—a sly little trick by the South Armagh boys—but overall it was a low-key, incoherent response. It was as if the rain that bucketed down that autumn, the wettest in living memory, had doused the promised conflagration. The IRA counseled patience, pledging vengeance at a time and place of its choosing. Only a handful of people knew that the England Department was preparing an offensive, and that a valued former member would be returning to help.

CHAPTER FIVE

The England Department

The end of the hunger strike on October 3, 1981, coincided with the first hint of winter in Dublin. Wind gusted through the city and rain pounded the streets. But Patrick Magee, now thirty years old, saw things clearly. His sabbatical from the armed campaign, his strange limbo, was over. He was going back to war. Seven months earlier, his Dutch dream in ruins, he had disembarked from a ferry, unsure what Ireland held in store. Irish courts did not extradite IRA suspects to the UK, deeming their crimes political. So, despite the British arrest warrant, Magee could live openly—albeit with snooping by the Irish police, who kept a file on him. His priority had been to try yet again to build a life with Eileen and their son, now age three.

He needed a place to live and a job; the movement provided both. Two IRA comrades on the run from the north, Frankie Rafferty and Frank Mulholland, hosted Magee in their flat in Ballymun, a high-rise concrete ghetto on the north edge of Dublin. One of Gerry Adams's closest confidants, a Sinn Féin official called Ted Howell, offered Magee a job with *An Phoblacht/Republican News*.

The weekly paper's office was at 44 Parnell Square, a dilapidated four-story Georgian townhouse that doubled as the national headquarters of Sinn Féin. The job gave Magee a visceral connection to the hunger strike. It was his responsibility to sort through H-Block "comms"—messages minutely written on toilet paper, wrapped in plastic wrap, hidden in body orifices, and slipped to visitors. They read like telegrams from hell. Magee knew many of the authors. The prisoners chronicled their suffering and defiance in hope of galvanizing solidarity around the world. One comm was addressed to Brigitte Bardot. Magee didn't know whether to laugh or weep at the image of his comrade shivering in a drafty cell, appealing to the French film star.

Eileen and Padraig joined Magee in Ballymun, where the council provided them with their own flat. Eileen also got a job at *AP/RN*, working as a typesetter, while Magee moved to the art department, using his drawing skills for posters, leaflets, and special editions. "Each of Bobby's sixty-six days on hunger strike seemed to mark our every waking moment," Magee recalled. Ten dead in all, including Patsy O'Hara, his chess partner from Long Kesh. It felt like a prolonged nightmare.

By the time the strike ended, Magee's commitment to the struggle blazed anew. He volunteered for active service in England.

. . .

MAGEE KNEW FROM his stint across the water in 1978 and 1979 that England required a set of skills—a degree of tradecraft—distinct from operating in the six counties. Mao Zedong, who knew something about insurgencies, had famously said the guerrilla must move among the people as a fish swims in the sea. That was not an option for the IRA in England because the population was hostile. Some Irish expatriates were sympathetic to republican goals, but police spies and informers had infiltrated the community, forcing IRA operators to steer clear of Irish pubs and neighborhoods. In some areas, an Irish accent was enough to invite suspicion. Hiring a car, renting an apartment, buying batteries—a simple act could prompt a call to the police and compromise an operation. Communicating with other volunteers was risky. The Brits had elevated eavesdropping to a fine art, so phoning Ireland, even from a phone box, was fraught. Operating in England required care and vigilance verging on paranoia. It could be a lonely, atomized existence.

Magee's first foray had succeeded—he hit targets, eluded capture—because the England Department was able to draw on a century-long learning curve of republican fiascoes and disasters.

The Irish Republican Brotherhood set the pattern in 1867 by detonating a wheelbarrow of explosives outside London's Clerkenwell prison. The idea was to blow a hole in the wall and free IRB prisoners. Instead, the blast killed fifteen people in nearby tenements, including children, and maimed dozens. No prisoners escaped.

A decade later, Jeremiah O'Donovan Rossa, an émigré in New York, mustered Irish Americans behind what became known as "the dynamite campaign." "A few active, intrepid and intelligent men can do much to annoy and hurt England," he wrote, envisaging a little band of heroes flying over land and sea like "invisible beings." His Celtic Valkyries planted a bomb by an infantry barracks in Salford that ended up killing a child and wounding a woman. The idea of the "Paddy Factor" was born.

Other blunders followed. William Lomasney, a member of a rival republican group, denounced Rossa's men as "fools and ignoramuses"—only to blow himself up in 1884 while planting a bomb under the London Bridge. Rossa's dynamiters refined their methods and caused minor damage before being caught.

If not chemistry, one dynamiter at least mastered alchemy. Thomas Clarke, possessor of a walrus mustache and fanatical dedication, transformed the England campaign's failure into political sulfur. When Rossa died in 1915, Clarke choreographed the funeral into an emotional rallying cry for Irish freedom that set the stage for the 1916 Rising. "I believe we have struck the first successful blow for freedom," he wrote as he and other leaders of the Rising awaited execution. "In this belief, we die happy."

After Ireland's partition, the IRA mounted sporadic attacks in Britain that accomplished nothing, though the writer Brendan Behan did turn his hapless bombing mission to Liverpool in 1939 into an autobiographical masterpiece, *Borstal Boy*. The ineptitude became almost comic in "The Old Alarm Clock," a 1960s ballad by the folk group the Dubliners about a jailed would-be bomber.

> Sure I'd long ago have left the place if I had only got
> Ah, me couple of sticks of gelignite and me old alarm clock.

The Troubles abruptly ended such jokey, romantic revisionism. The first strike in England was by the Official IRA: a bomb at an army base in 1972 that killed five female kitchen staff, a gardener, and a Catholic priest, a murderous debacle that suggested republicans had learned nothing since O'Donovan Rossa's era. Gerry Adams, that assiduous student of history and military tactics, felt sure the Provos could do better. In early 1973, he assembled a team to cross the water.

. . .

MAYBE ROY WALSH should have listened to his mother.

Annie Walsh was a formidable republican who sheltered IRA men in her little home at 39 Theodore Street off the Falls Road. Yet for some reason she never trusted Adams, did not want him in the house, and called him a "waster." That did not deter Roy, a twenty-four-year-old roof tiler and veteran bomber, from joining the ten-strong team assembled by Adams. The target was London. Roy adopted Thomas Clarke as a pseudonym, an homage to the Fenian dynamiter, he of the walrus mustache who ended up executed in 1916. Early on March 8,

1973, they parked four huge car bombs outside an army recruitment center, the British Forces Broadcasting Service, New Scotland Yard, and the Central Criminal Court, known as the Old Bailey. Warnings would be given; the goal was a symbolic strike at the imperial heart, not a bloodbath. The bombs were in place by 7:30 a.m. Walsh and his crew headed to Heathrow to catch flights to Dublin before the bombs detonated at 3:00 p.m.

Five years earlier, justice had caught up with James Earl Ray, the fugitive assassin of Martin Luther King Jr., at a departure desk at Heathrow. A police detective tapped him on the shoulder and said, "I say, old fellow, would you mind stepping over here for a moment?"

Walsh, queuing with other passengers at Gate 4, Terminal 1, felt safe. The bombs were quietly ticking away, hours from detonation. He had promised his heavily pregnant wife, Mary, he would be home in time for the birth of their daughter. They had chosen a name, Roisin. Minutes passed. Boarding was delayed. Something was wrong. There was a commotion at the gate, police striding through passengers, asking questions, examining tickets. Walsh felt his heart pound. He tried to stay calm, to appear relaxed. There was a tap on his shoulder. A polite voice. "Excuse me . . ."

A Provo informant had tipped off the police about the plot. While hundreds of officers scoured London for suspicious cars, others monitored ports and airports. The order was to "close England"—which meant, in effect, quizzing Irish passengers. They caught all but one of the bombers. Two devices were defused, but the other two exploded. Central London shuddered amid massive blasts reminiscent of the Blitz. They injured 250 people and killed one man, who had a heart attack. The Provos had brought the war to England.

For the IRA, it was a successful operation, except for the capture of the bombers. Trying to extract them so quickly was a costly blunder. Provo planners took note. Future operators would be sleepers who could strike and meld back into the population.

It was too late for Roy Walsh, though. Perhaps proving his mother right, he was sentenced to life imprisonment and vanished inside the English penal system.

. . .

LATER IN 1973, Adams also wound up behind bars, in Long Kesh, and IRA commanders sent a new team to England. This became known as the *Looney Tunes* era, after the name bestowed by Scotland Yard detectives on the wild terrorists who careered around London and other cities in the mid-1970s as if in a Warner Bros. cartoon. There were gun battles, drive-by shootings, car chases, explosions, brawls, drunkenness, a hyperactive blur of mayhem not quite captured by the term "sleeper."

The Balcombe Street Gang, as it became known, was a core of six men, most from the south of Ireland. They rented flats in working-class London neighborhoods. They planted time bombs, lobbed grenade-type devices, hit pubs, trains, barracks, department stores, a bank, a water pumping station, a telephone exchange. They shot up posh restaurants and clubs and sent letter bombs. A faulty one injured the thumb of Reginald Maudling, the former cabinet minister who had declared Northern Ireland "a bloody awful country," and fatally poisoned his dog, which ate the explosives scattered on the carpet. The gang tossed a small bomb at the home of Ted Heath, the former prime minister. He wasn't home. The blast chipped a balcony, broke a window, and slightly damaged a painting by Winston Churchill.

A separate unit in Birmingham planted bombs in two pubs, bungled the warnings, and massacred twenty-one people. Ross Mc-Whirter, a television broadcaster and old friend of Margaret Thatcher who coedited the *Guinness Book of Records*, advocated restrictions on Irish immigrants and launched a bounty to catch the terrorists. The Balcombe Street Gang responded by visiting McWhirter's London home and fatally shooting him in the head and chest with a Magnum revolver. The police assigned detectives to guard public figures, including Thatcher, who was then leader of the opposition.

Other fatalities, unplanned, included a train driver, a homeless man, a cancer researcher—random victims of a campaign that scythed civilians who got in the way. There was, however, method in the madness. Varying targets and modus operandi wrong-footed the police. No one knew where the gang would strike next because the gang itself probably wasn't sure, either. Even so, their success couldn't last. Like the moment Wile E. Coyote runs off a cliff and tumbles into the void, the unit was cornered on Balcombe Street. Its members surrendered after a six-day siege and were jailed for life.

. . .

WHEN MAGEE CROSSED the Irish Sea to bring the war to England in 1978, the IRA had assembled a new team under a new leader: Gerard Tuite. Soft-spoken, with a mop of black hair, he understood that "sleeper" meant "low-key." Though he was the younger of the two, Tuite tutored Magee in the art of operating behind enemy lines: communicate via prearranged calls to phone boxes, speak in codes and euphemisms, stash gear properly, change your appearance, change your name, disarm suspicion with charm.

Tuite used the nom de guerre Gerry Fossett, possibly a nod to Fossett's Circus, which moved between Britain and Ireland. He convinced a nurse he was a German Irishman named David Coyne and moved in with her. He supervised a small network of vehicles, safe houses, and caches with gelignite, timers, detonators, shotguns, and Armalites. Tuite also managed communications with GHQ, operators, couriers, and fixers, a continuous ebb and flow of messages, any of which, if intercepted, could lead to disaster. "In all such struggles the greatest obstacle to effective operations is often secrecy, seen by the conventional as an underground asset but in fact an enormously costly necessity," wrote J. Bowyer Bell, a historian of the IRA. "Secrecy assures confusion, limits the lessons of experience and more than all else clogs communications." Magee, an attentive pupil, learned the craft.

The unit's focus was commercial targets. Magee is believed to have been part of the teams that blew up a gas depot and an oil refinery in January 1979. Seven million cubic feet of natural gas ignited at the gasworks in Greenwich, east of London. "The fire can be seen from one end of London to another. The sky is red with flames," said a fireman. A bomb at the Texaco oil depot at Canvey Island in the Thames estuary gashed open a tank, leaking thousands of gallons of aviation fuel. There were no casualties. An anonymous caller had phoned a warning to the Press Association. He sounded almost civic minded: "For goodness sake do something about it. We want the area cleared because people are living there." *An Phoblacht/Republican News* celebrated the "spectacular" sabotage on its front page. The campaign caused £6 million in damage.

At this point, mentor and protégé parted ways. While Magee was in Shannon having a nervous breakdown, Tuite was captured in London. Ever resourceful, he tunneled through the walls of his cell, scaled a perimeter wall, and escaped to Ireland, earning a place in republican lore.

After volunteering to return to England, Magee might have appreciated teaming up with his old comrade, but Tuite was too well known to security forces. For the coming offensive, Magee was to join a new team. Other operators were in place and the supply line was ready.

· · ·

IN EARLY OCTOBER 1981, a group of men gathered in a room over Brassil's pub in Tralee, County Kerry, on the southwestern tip of Ireland. They hailed from different corners of the republican universe. This was unusual. The IRA tended to extreme insularity; volunteers liked to work alongside people from their own neighborhood. In perilous undertakings, there was comfort if those next to you were kith or kin. The England Department did not have that luxury. The nature of its mission drew people with very different accents and backgrounds.

This gathering in Brassil's was the republican equivalent of the cantina scene from *Star Wars: A New Hope*. Owen Coogan was the head of the England Department. Known as Ownie—and also Jug Head, for his prominent ears—he was a Belfast Brigade veteran and a friend of Adams. They had served time together in Long Kesh until Coogan escaped in a garbage truck. He was a suspect in the La Mon horror but was never arrested or charged.

The second-in-command and quartermaster was Michael "Mick" Hayes, a working-class Dubliner who had been part of the discredited team that bombed Birmingham. Hayes was a romantic who considered the movement his family. When arrested by the police, he would respond to questions with ballads. Some considered Hayes an idiot, but he was dedicated and ruthless. He had a sidekick, Albert Flynn, careful, quiet, who acted as the intelligence officer. And there was Mick Brassil, owner of the pub, a hulking former rugby player with a musical Kerry lilt.

These were the backroom men who would direct and supply operators in England. They were collectively known as the "flat caps." Brassil owned a haulage company that delivered mussels from Cromane, a village facing the Dingle Peninsula, to the Billingsgate fish market in London. It offered cover for smuggling guns and explosives. All was carefully packed and weighed so the crates matched the weight reported in freight documents. A truck took a ferry from Rosslare to Fishguard in Wales, trundled down the M4, and delivered its lethal cargo to London.

The IRA had selected a variety of targets to keep the Brits off-balance. The idea was to show that the IRA could strike anywhere, anytime, and disappear. Coogan and his team were under pressure to deliver results. Republicans wanted to turn on the BBC news at 9:00 p.m. and see reporters with plummy accents standing in front of police tape, describing the latest scene of devastation in London. The Army Council wanted operations sustained week after week, month after month, to pressure Thatcher's government. Operators wanted reliable gear and accessible targets. All these demands had to be managed under the noses of the British security forces. And what was the England Department, really? A handful of men mostly with basic education and average intelligence who juggled jobs, wives, and children with the logistical grind of running a secret army, a treadmill of meetings, briefings, lists, decisions, problems to solve, cock-ups to excuse, and rumors to chase. Even in Ireland, arrests, checkpoints, searches, or just bad luck could scramble best-laid plans. There was little time for grand strategy. Sometimes reaching the end of the week without disaster was achievement enough.

Yet this rickety instrument of terror incubated the Provos' most dangerous, audacious idea, one that could alter the entire conflict and transform it into two phases: before and after. The idea was to kill Margaret Thatcher.

Sending the Iron Lady to hell was not an original notion, not since Bobby Sands was lowered into the ground. But to invest time and effort to really go after her, to methodically probe her security, seek chinks in the armor, identify opportunity, devise a plan—all that was unprecedented. The only time a sitting British prime minister had been murdered was in 1812, when John Bellingham, a businessman with a grudge against the government, shot Spencer Perceval through the heart at point-blank range. Since then, attempts to assassinate a prime minister had belonged in the realm of fiction, and even then the plots usually failed.

In *The Eagle Has Landed*, Jack Higgins conjured an IRA character, Liam Devlin, who leads German soldiers on a mission to kidnap or kill Winston Churchill. In the Troubles-set novel *Vote to Kill*, Douglas Hurd, a minister in Thatcher's cabinet who moonlighted as a writer, imagined an assassin who stalks a prime minister with a crossbow. Gerald Seymour lowered the bar for the Provos in *Harry's Game* by having the assassin target a mere cabinet minister. In reality, the IRA had shied away from high-level assassinations in Britain. They were too difficult, too risky. During the 1919–21 war of independence, one senior IRA figure, Cathal Brugha, tried to send assassins to London to shoot ministers, possibly shooting them from the public gallery at Westminster, but comrades vetoed the plan as harebrained.

The Provos did kill a British ambassador in Dublin in 1976 and another in The Hague in 1979, but they, like Mountbatten, were soft targets not on British soil. The INLA got Thatcher's ally, Airey Neave, with a bomb, but that was before he was in government, without protection. When it came to prestigious English targets, Provo methods spilled more headline ink than blood. Days after Bobby Sands's death, a bomb exploded in the power station of a Scottish oil terminal during a visit by the Queen, but the bomb was so puny that nobody noticed at first. *An Phoblacht/Republican News* was so desperate to project IRA menace it ran a story about a security alert following the mislaying of Thatcher's engagement diary.

Yet by the autumn of 1981, the England Department was beginning to take its wild, intoxicating idea seriously. Motive and means were aligning. The Engineering Department was perfecting long-delay timers. The England operators could gather intelligence. Pat Magee could do reconnaissance. He had done so before, surveilling a Labour Party Conference at Brighton. The realization, like a raindrop swelling at the tip of a leaf, dropped slowly: they could get Thatcher.

PART II

——

Countdown

CHAPTER SIX

The Bomb Burglar and Mr. T

Peter Gurney arrived early, as always, for his shift at the Canon Row police station in Central London. It was Monday, October 26, 1981, a cool, sunlit afternoon in the capital. The Thames flowed sluggishly under Westminster Bridge. Gurney, fifty years old, tall, athletic, balding, in a nondescript suit and tie, might have passed for a bank manager were it not for the military bearing and arch grin that would occasionally slide across his face, heralding a risqué wisecrack. He followed an exhortation to "laugh and live" because he had seen the alternative up close.

Gurney was an "expo" attached to the Explosives Section of the Metropolitan Police Anti-Terrorist Branch. Armed with a knife, screwdrivers, wire cutters, and a small X-ray machine, he was charged with the job of defusing and destroying bombs. Gurney appreciated the binary simplicity. You beat the bomb or the bomb beat you. A bomb situation could be frightening, yes, but it was also *interesting*.

Police called their expo colleagues, all ex-army men, "bomb

doctors." It was a terrifying, exhilarating way to make a living. You arrive at a police cordon, put on body armor, shut the helmet visor—muffling all sound except your own breathing, like a diver underwater—and begin the long walk. Every step toward the device brings new possibilities, imaginary boundary lines demarcating zones of moderate injury, mutilation, annihilation. To awake in a hospital, grievously maimed, condemned to permanent darkness from sightless eyes, was Gurney's great fear. Better an instantaneous death.

Reaching the device, you focus. Each one is unique, the alignment of circuits and timers a signature reflecting the creator's personality. You wonder: Was he a professional or an amateur? What was his purpose? What was going through his mind when he made it? Is there a trap?

Gurney had been handling explosives since he was a boy at his father's army base, turning abandoned cartridges into rockets, then as a soldier himself, a munitions expert tasked with defusing bombs in postwar Germany and Libya, then Northern Ireland. Now he was part of an expo team at the Bungalow, an annex to the police station with its own offices, workshops, bunks, showers, and library of texts on explosives. When there was an alert, the phone had a distinctive ring and flashed a red light. The Canon Row station was close to Parliament, Downing Street, and Whitehall, prestige targets, and Westminster Bridge gave quick access to South London. Gurney chased so many callouts that colleagues nicknamed him the "bomb burglar."

This afternoon, however, he missed one. The police had received an anonymous warning of three bombs on Oxford Street, two in department stores, one in a Wimpy fast-food restaurant, where a suspicious package, a padded envelope and a box taped together, had been found. Gurney arrived at the Bungalow to discover that the duty expo and his best friend, Ken Howorth, was en route to Oxford Street.

The IRA had announced a bloody return to London two weeks earlier with a bomb at a barracks that killed two civilians—Nora Field, fifty-nine, and John Breslin, eighteen—and wounded fifty people, including twenty soldiers, followed by a car bomb on October 17 that sheared a leg off Steuart Pringle, head of the Royal Marines. Now a third attack seemed imminent. Gurney was briefed at the Bungalow while Howorth and a driver sped to the Wimpy in one of the unit's white Land Rovers. An expo had two tempos: high speed on the way to the scene and low speed once he'd arrived.

Police with megaphones were herding people away. "Will you please move away from Oxford Street. . . . Please go in any direction, but away from Oxford Street, please." There was no panic; Londoners were accustomed to bomb alerts. Shoppers and parents with strollers waited behind police tape for the all-clear. A stillness fell over one of the world's most famous thoroughfares. Only the chatter of police radios pierced the silence. Howorth put on a flak jacket and disappeared inside the deserted restaurant. Back at the office, Gurney wondered about the warning. It said the device was in the basement toilets, behind the sink. The IRA were never that helpful, never that specific. Why now?

. . .

GURNEY HAD BEEN battling the Provos since he was an army bomb disposal officer based at Girdwood Barracks in 1972, the Troubles' bloodiest year. In those days, he would devour mounds of eggs, bacon, steak, and chicken and still lose weight because of the frenetic pace on Belfast's streets. Nail bombs, car bombs, blast bombs, incendiaries— the IRA were plastering the city with improvised explosive devices (IEDs). Gurney's initial sympathy for Catholics evaporated as mobs rained insults, rocks, and bottles on him while he tried to defuse devices. One bottle came with a surprise—filled with battery acid, it burned through his combat jacket and peeled paint from his helmet.

So many bomb disposal men died in Northern Ireland—twenty in total—that the officer in charge of postings was nicknamed the Grim

Reaper. "How narrow a tightrope we were walking on," noted George Styles, the unit's commander. "You can train a man to the nth degree, you can give him courage and skill and caution, but you can't give him good luck." There were enough survivors for the unit to be nicknamed Felix, the cat with nine lives.

When the Provos came up with a new device or tactic, the bomb disposal officers, closely watched by IRA spotters, would seek a way to counter it. The use of radio-controlled bombs like the type that killed Mountbatten prompted a chase along the electromagnetic spectrum, with IRA engineers switching frequencies to try to avoid detection and jamming by their opponents. After encountering especially tricky devices, the army sometimes made smug-sounding claims about beating the IRA just to provoke their foes into changing designs. Provo bomb makers tried to short-circuit this technological and psychological battle of wits by targeting their counterparts with customized booby traps and diversionary devices known as "come-ons." Some scrawled taunts on particularly fiendish devices. "IRA—Tee-hee, Hee-hee, Ho-ho, Ha-ha," read one. One army unit roped a captured bomber and forced him to defuse his own device, a tactic that commanders did not let them repeat.

For Gurney, the aftermath of bombings became a blur of sirens, smoke, and screams. In his 1993 memoir, *Braver Men Walk Away*, he recalled one casualty in Belfast, a young office worker: "She can't see me because she can't see anything. She has no face. I cradle her to me and keep the words coming from somewhere. Just once she moves her head as though listening. Through the holes where her cheeks used to be her few remaining teeth clench together, then part." Gurney loathed his IRA opponents, but the battle felt impersonal. He found refuge in gallows humor, sometimes macabre. When IRA members blew themselves up, he celebrated "own goals"; other times, he made plays on words: "If they ever get him to court, he won't have a leg to stand on," or "That's one bomber who's totally armless."

This was the same year Patrick Magee was doing his "blowy stuff" apprenticeship and being hauled into Girdwood for brutal interrogation. The two men did not meet, but over the next decade their careers would intertwine like two tangled wires.

Gurney joined the Met as a civilian expo in 1973, just in time to defuse two of the four massive IRA car bombs in Central London that March. A harrowing afternoon's work, it not only averted devastation but saved the neutralized devices as evidence troves that helped convict Roy Walsh and the rest of the IRA team. Expos, 1; IRA, 0. Gurney spent the rest of the decade defending London from the IRA. He preferred to disarm devices, leaving forensic evidence intact, but on occasion had to follow the bomb doctor injunction "If you don't know it, blow it," which meant using a disrupter, also known as a pigstick. Resembling a telescope with a cable, it fired a water-projectile-shaped charge that destroyed the bomb and sometimes evidence, too. Whatever was recovered was taken under police escort to the Royal Armament Research and Development Establishment (RARDE) for examination.

Gurney tracked evolving Provo technology and methods. Some bombs lacked basic components, pure Paddy Factor. Others were devilish. The terrorists started producing prepacked, easy-to-operate timing power units (TPUs), roughly the size of a videocassette. They converted Memo-Park timers, little gadgets motorists used to remind them when a parking meter was about to expire, into detonation timers. "If you take ten people and try to teach them bomb making, half of them will mess it up, whereas Memo-Park timers made all that easy," Gurney recalled. "All a guy had to do was connect up the detonator, anybody can do that. It meant incompetent bombers could become quite proficient."

They cannibalized video recorders to make long-delay timers, which were first discovered during the Queen's visit to Northern Ireland in 1977. A secret but prophetic Ministry of Defence report in

1979 grasped the significance: "The availability of long-delay timers makes it feasible for bombs to be placed at a target before suspicion arises. Such a system is very accurate and can produce a delay of weeks or even years. We would expect to see more use of these long-delay timers, particularly with a view to causing explosions at sensitive moments, such as the time of a VIP visit." However, the warning was buried in paragraph 57, and few paid heed. After all, the MoD produced so many reports it was difficult to keep up.

Gurney's team kept encountering long-delay timers, including a dozen found in January 1979, under floorboards of an East London flat linked to Gerry Tuite's unit. Later that year, expos defused six letter bombs with an electronic arming circuit similar to long-delay timers. Forensic evaluation led to the arrest warrant for Patrick Magee, which led to the extradition request that a Dutch court later rejected. Gurney tackled other bombs attributed to Magee, including squelching through aviation fuel after the explosion at Canvey Island, but he had little time to dwell on the individual names on Scotland Yard's Warrant Register, which listed suspects for whom warrants were issued. He was too busy chasing the next alert, an obsession that frayed his marriage.

For Londoners, bomb disposal men were heroes. Gurney was moved to tears when some pensioners offered to take a crash course in bomb disposal, deeming their lives more disposable than those of expos. He also politely declined a suggestion from a member of the public for World War II–era barrage balloons to lift suspect cars to the English Channel, where RAF jets could shoot them down.

There were other light moments. Gurney once found himself investigating the cramped, hollow interior of a statue opposite Buckingham Palace and cracked his head against a protrusion. He radioed the driver: "Guess what, you're talking to the only living Englishman to have banged his head on Queen Victoria's clitoris."

Back came the reply: "I've got news for you. I'm looking at her face and she most definitely is not amused."

The expos were a tight-knit brotherhood, with friendships going back decades. On quiet days, Gurney would fish a bottle of Teacher's whiskey from a filing cabinet and discuss cricket with Ken Howorth, a blunt, solidly built Yorkshireman and father of two. He shared Gurney's joy in pranks. No matter the weather or job, Ken always wore the same tattered woolen cardigan, to the mortification of his wife, Ann.

. . . .

As DUSK EDGED across London, the Bungalow's phone flashed red: police had found a second suspect device, this one at the Debenhams department store on Oxford Street. Gurney was being briefed, and still mulling the unusually precise warning for the Wimpy device—in the basement toilets, behind the sink—when news came through of an explosion inside the restaurant. He grabbed his kit and ran to a Land Rover.

People were running away from Oxford Street, some of them screaming. Smoke spewed from the Wimpy's wrecked frontage. Gurney entered the smoldering ruin. Crunching over glass, he wound down a spiral ornamental staircase into a dark basement he would forever remember as "the pit." Steam hissed from broken pipes. Powder from shattered plasterwork hung suspended in the air. There was a stench of burned explosive, excrement from demolished toilets, hamburger mince, and the distinctive odor of shattered body tissue. Ken lay at his feet, half covered in debris. The injuries were massive, and the wounds suggested his face had been close to the bomb. In the gloom, Gurney ran his hands down the body to confirm what he suspected: both arms had been blown off. Ken had been handling the device when it detonated. It was a booby trap tailor-made for a bomb doctor, the first time such a device was used outside Northern Ireland.

Expos, 1; IRA, 1.

Gurney had a mental switch that filtered emotions at moments of extreme stress. It was the only way to retain concentration and do the job, the only way to stay alive. Whatever type of device killed Ken might also await in Debenhams. Gurney sifted through the debris, seeking clues, component fragments, anything that revealed the nature of the device. His fingers touched something soft. A singed, shredded piece of cardigan. It was too much.

Gurney returned to the street and regained control of his emotions, save for a cold, raw anger. He wanted the Debenhams bomb. He wanted to take it apart piece by piece, bit by bit, to extract every last microscopic fragment of forensic evidence. A single thought pulsed in his brain: *Nail the bastards.*

Passing side streets sealed off to traffic, Gurney entered the deserted department store. The package was on a cistern in the first-floor toilets. A box and padded envelope taped together, just as in the Wimpy restaurant. Wires linked an explosive charge to a timing power unit. Leaning in, Gurney heard the tick of a Memo-Park timer. He wanted to see inside the device, but the confined space prevented the X-ray getting a good angle. Gurney stared at the bomb as if the sheer intensity of his gaze could disclose its secrets. There was no safe way to defuse it. Reluctantly he unpacked the disrupter. Targeting the explosive charge, he ran the firing cable out the toilet to the store's showroom, took cover behind a settee, and fired. There was a muffled *thump!* Returning to the toilet, Gurney discovered the disrupter had been too strong. It shattered the explosive charge *and* the timing power unit, potentially destroying precious evidence.

Covered in blood and shit and dirt, he got on his knees and gathered the debris. Maybe it could yet help catch the bastards.

· · ·

WHILE GURNEY TOILED inside the department store, dozens of his colleagues from the Anti-Terrorist Branch fanned across Oxford Street, radios squawking, siren lights flashing in the dusk. Some had hard hats and heavy boots, like laborers, and formed a line outside the Wimpy. Others had cameras. They parted to make way for a small man carrying an aluminum box about the size of a doctor's medical bag.

David Tadd descended into the Wimpy's basement and surveyed

the carnage with a cool eye, visualizing what had happened. He viewed crime scenes almost as Old Master paintings, each one posing the same question: What is the artist trying to tell us? Tadd had analyzed Rembrandt's compositions and he brought the same intellectual interrogation to scenes of robbery, kidnapping, and murder. The grisly tableau before him now, however, was closer to a nightmarish landscape by Hieronymus Bosch. Tadd opened his box, which contained brushes, powders, and chemicals, and set to work.

Tadd was the head of fingerprinting at Scotland Yard's Anti-Terrorist Branch. He was five feet, seven inches, which could seem diminutive beside towering constables, and he had a soccer player's lean physique. At thirty-five, he was an unusually young "guv'nor," or department head, and his staff playfully called him Mr. T. Tadd's team searched for and recovered prints at scenes of terrorist incidents and processed prints from a conveyor belt of evidence sent by bomb doctors, intelligence analysts, surveillance operators, and other departments. It was their job to match a smudge of thumb to a name in Scotland Yard's vast archive of terrorist suspect files. And as if by magic, blaze a spotlight on the IRA's darkest recesses.

Tadd was a working-class South London boy. When he was growing up, the family home had no electricity and the bath was a tin tub in front of a coal fire. He left school at sixteen with an advanced qualification in art and worked as a commercial artist doing advertising layouts. Tadd never took to London's advertising scene and in 1967, age twenty, he joined the Met as a trainee fingerprint expert.

The Fingerprint Bureau was founded in 1901 by a police commissioner, Edward Henry, who saw value in dactylography, the study of fingerprints to establish identity. The ridge arrangement on every finger and palm of every human is unique and does not alter with growth or age. When a hand touches a surface, the papillary ridges on the epidermis leave an impression that can be recovered. It was a revolutionary advance on the most accurate method previously used— measuring skulls with calipers. Eight decades after the Fingerprint

Bureau's formation, there was still no DNA profiling and finger-printing remained the most valued forensic technique.

Tadd, in regulation suit and tie, learned his trade crisscrossing London with his silver box, dusting burgled homes, stolen cars, and forged checks. He examined the cash allegedly used by Lord Lucan, an aristocrat who famously disappeared after being suspected of murder. When not at crime scenes, Tadd was in the office studying prints or in the lab experimenting with chemicals.

Prints were classified by a three-part process: shape and contour; finger positions of the pattern types; coincidental sequence of ridge characteristics. In this precomputer era, identification was a pains-taking process done with the naked eye, aided by a magnifying glass. A working day could last fifteen hours, demanding intense concen-tration from beginning to end. Identifying a print was subjective, a matter of opinion, but required finding sixteen points of similarity, deemed sufficient to confirm a match. The work was highly specialized and largely intuitive. Advanced education and a scientific background didn't seem to help, whereas those with an artistic background often excelled.

Tadd completed the five-year apprenticeship and gained expert status in 1972—then was snapped up by the Bomb Squad, a newly formed specialist unit within the Met that evolved into the Anti-Terrorist Branch. Fingerprints helped to convict Brian Keenan, a senior Provo from the *Looney Tunes* era, and identified members of Gerry Tuite's unit. An IRA safe house had prints on a notebook, a map of London, a milk bottle, and a porcelain cup that matched those taken from a juvenile Patrick Magee in Norwich, though that proved insufficient evidence for the Dutch to extradite him.

Tadd had seen his share of corpses, but the one in the Wimpy's basement was no stranger. Bomb doctors were part of the Anti-Terrorist Branch, and Tadd would bump into Howorth, Gurney, and the others at crime scenes and occasionally in the Tank, a bar on the ground floor of Scotland Yard. Now he surveyed the scene. Fading daylight filtered from a hole above through a shroud of smoke, steam, and dust. Water from the wrecked plumbing flooded the floor. The stench was dreadful. Tadd gazed at the ruined cubicles, the shattered sinks, the blasted walls, the debris of glass, plaster, and tiles, the position and angle of the body. Rembrandt never painted anything like this.

While interpreting the scene, he dictated observations to a colleague, a "scribe," who noted everything in a notebook. Slowly and methodically, Tadd dusted selected areas, working around the shredded remains of Howorth, hoping the bomber had been sloppy and left prints.

"It was very unpleasant," he later recalled with understatement. "A mess." No matter how grim a task, Tadd, like Gurney, was able to compartmentalize his feelings and focus on the job. "I can park it somewhere. I can just park it. I don't let it affect me." Still, they all needed release—and while some colleagues found it in booze, Tadd did so on a soccer field. He played several times a week for his club, the Nomads, and racked up medals in amateur leagues. He could be aggressive, shouldering opponents off the ball. It was his medicine.

There was little time for soccer, or his young family, this October. This was the third IRA bombing in a month. The England Department had gotten smarter. Three people dead, a senior army officer maimed, security forces stretched, millions of Londoners frightened, West End stores facing pre-Christmas losses. The number passing through Santa's grotto on Oxford Street would drop from five thousand a day to sixty-four. A decent result for the bombers, who remained hidden, unknown. Still, each attack left a mound of evidence, or potential evidence. It was a massive, urgent task. A smudge smaller than a postage stamp could unmask a bomber and lead police to the IRA's Active Service Unit.

After a century of Irish bombs in London, Scotland Yard had also gotten smarter. Right from its foundation in 1829, the force had needed to adapt. The public did not welcome the appearance of men in blue tunics, fearing a martial presence on the streets, so the uniforms sprouted swallowtails to conceal truncheons. A public entrance named Great Scotland Yard, built on the site of a former medieval palace for visiting Scottish nobles, gave the force its metonym. The advent of undercover police in civilian clothes was controversial. "There was and always will be something repugnant to the English mind in the bare idea of espionage. It smacks too strongly of France and Austria," said a *Times* editorial in 1845. Satirists mocked the first detective branch as the "defective branch."

Attitudes changed when Fenian bombs started exploding in the 1880s. The home secretary, William Vernon Harcourt, urged the force to gather intelligence by whatever means necessary. "All other objects should be postponed in our efforts to get some light into these dark places. If anything occurs there will be an outcry." So from political pressure was born the Special Irish Branch, tasked with infiltrating and disrupting terror plots. Early successes prompted Harcourt to assure Queen Victoria in 1883 that "we have the enemy by the throat." A premature boast because more bombs followed, an early lesson that against this enemy there would be no permanent victory, just endless vigilance.

The force basked in the glow of Sir Arthur Conan Doyle's Sherlock Holmes, even though the character was not actually a policeman but a "consulting detective." And in any case, real detectives did not need deductive brilliance while the IRA's England operators bungled through much of the twentieth century, leaving elementary evidence trails. By the early 1970s, the Met enjoyed global prestige and occupied a big modern office block on Broadway overlooking St. James's Park. Tourists posed for pictures in front of the revolving New Scotland Yard sign. Every so often there were phone calls from abroad asking to speak to Sherlock Holmes.

The perception of starchy integrity and professionalism concealed rot. When IRA bombs turned pubs into slaughterhouses, the force cracked under the pressure to produce results. Lacking proper intelligence, detectives rounded up innocent Irish people and brutalized them into confessions. Flawed forensic evidence supposedly showed that some had handled explosives. The Birmingham Six, Guildford Four, and Maguire Seven, as they became known, would all serve more than fifteen years in jail until exoneration.

The Anti-Terrorist Branch, known as C13, stuttered in the early years. Lacking specialist skills and knowledge, detectives would trample over evidence. But they learned from experience. By autumn 1981, when IRA bombs returned to London, the C13 men had new protocols. In the trunk of their cars, each had a black canvas bag with a hard hat, steel-toed boots, protective gloves, face masks, and coveralls. Bomb doctors ensured sites were safe and salvaged components, then teams tackled crime scenes in waves. Exhibit officers harvested immediate evidence; artists and photographers recorded scenes; forensic officers took fingerprints; sweepers split sites into zones and gathered every remaining scrap of debris. Scientists processed the data to reconstruct the attack.

. . .

GURNEY AND TADD were very different men with very different skills joined by a shared mission. Each formed a strand of the C13 net that was tasked with capturing the IRA's England Department. Each in his own way would tangle with Patrick Magee.

As darkness swallowed London on that autumn night, each man made his way back to base. Gurney was exhausted. The IRA's claim about a third bomb in another department store had been a hoax that obliged Gurney and officers with sniffer dogs to make a painstaking, nerve-racking, fruitless search. The expos' Bungalow was packed. The bomb burglar had a stiff drink and slept on the operations room floor, too tired to remove his flak jacket.

Tadd went to Scotland Yard headquarters on the other side of Westminster Abbey, half a mile from the Bungalow. From the outside, the two interconnected towers resembled an anonymous office block, not a crime-fighting hub. Inside the reception hall, a perpetually burning flame flickered on a marble stand, beside it a book of remembrance listing staff killed on duty, a melancholy roll of honor that now awaited Howorth's name. Tadd took the elevator to the fifth floor, home to C13. A secure area with two locked doors gave way to private offices and an open-plan operations room with desks, filing cabinets, telephones, radios, a blackboard, and maps. The windows offered sweeping panoramas of the city, but the slat blinds stayed closed for confidentiality and bomb protection. This room was the operational heart of Scotland Yard's fight against the IRA.

Other parts of the security services—MI5, MI6, and the Special Branch—were tasked with spying and gathering intelligence. It was the job of C13, the executive arm, to catch the terrorists. While the spooks were university-educated and posh, many Anti-Terrorist Branch guys were blue-collar and could sound like Cockney fruit sellers. Before joining C13, the detectives had cut their teeth chasing fraudsters, bank robbers, and gangsters through London's underworld. They knew how to catch villains and, just as important, knew how to gather evidence that would stand up in court and secure convictions. C13 was a self-contained universe of several hundred people. Many were technically not police officers but civilian specialists like the bomb doctors and forensic analysts. Tadd had handpicked his fingerprint team, about a dozen men, from the Yard's pool of 250 fingerprint analysts. "I picked them for their expertise and willingness to work stupidly long hours," he said later.

The IRA's bombing offensive turned October into a grueling marathon for the whole section. Witness statements, ports and airports data, bomb component sources, rumors of vehicles used by the bombers—there were a thousand leads to follow, each generating more leads, almost all leading nowhere. On a tip that the IRA was using a lock-up garage, officers searched more than 250,000 premises in Greater London and found nothing. Tea, coffee, and takeaway Cornish pasties from a bakery called Stiles fueled late nights and early mornings on the fifth floor, but what really sustained the IRA hunters was the grim certainty that their foes were planning bigger, bloodier attacks.

CHAPTER SEVEN

———

Friends

A hush settled across the audience when Danny Morrison rose to speak.

Danny was a good talker, a man made for microphones. Not much use with a gun—his nervousness with firearms earned him the nickname Bangers—but Sinn Féin's publicity director could decant the republican cause into a sinuous word flow that charmed and sometimes convinced the journalists who visited the party's West Belfast office. Now Danny was down in Dublin, with the rest of the northerners, for the party's annual Ard Fheis, or conference.

It was October 31, 1981, five days after Ken Howorth's death. A vicious wind whipped through the Irish capital. Under the baleful eye of Irish Special Branch detectives, delegates in jeans, sweaters, and worn suits trooped into the Mansion House. A venue steeped in history, the building was the official residence of the city's Lord Mayor and had hosted the first meeting of Ireland's rebel parliament in 1919. British soldiers had raided it seeking Michael Collins, but he posed as a janitor, sweeping the floor, and escaped.

Now it was the turn of Danny Morrison to address a sea of faces in the Round Room. It might have been a briefer speech had the Ulster Volunteer Force been better terrorists. The terror group had hoped to wipe out Sinn Féin's leaders by placing a concealed bomb in the ceiling above the platform, but the plan came to nothing. In addition to being publicity director, Morrison, age twenty-seven, was the editor of *An Phoblacht/Republican News*, and a protégé of Gerry Adams. As party vice president, Adams sat on the platform with other leaders, sucking his pipe and surveying the audience while Morrison took the podium.

The mood was febrile. The shattering yet energizing hunger strike had ended just weeks earlier. Ten men dead, but Sinn Féin had retained Sands's Westminster seat in a by-election after his death and won two others in the Irish parliament. For Adams, this was a pivotal moment. The party traditionally saw itself as a support group for the IRA and reluctantly contested just the occasional election. It viewed electoral politics as a road to perdition because competing for votes could lead to compromise and dilution of republican principles, an incremental process of moderation that defanged revolution. Sinn Féin made electoral forays only if deemed tactically beneficial. Like a dentist taking an X-ray, the party's instinct was to step away quickly to avoid radiation. But Adams wanted a permanent move to electoral politics, and for candidates to take seats in local government.

Morrison's voice filled the stuffy auditorium. A hard Belfast voice from the war zone, unlike the accents from Cork or Kerry or Dublin, distant from the action. Electoral politics, he said, brandishing his notes, would not diminish republican commitment to the armed struggle. On the contrary, it would complement and fortify armed struggle. It would pave victory. "Who here really believes we can win the war through the ballot box?" Morrison paused. The audience, silent. "But will anyone here object if with a ballot paper in this hand and an Armalite in this hand we take power in Ireland?" The hall erupted.

It was rhetorical lightning. Martin McGuinness, a member of the IRA's Army Council, looked startled. He whispered to a comrade:

"Where the fuck did that come from?" Adams, sphinxlike, said nothing. He didn't have to. His proxy had deftly articulated his strategy. The "Armalite and the ballot box," as it became known, would come to define Provo policy. Delegates overwhelmingly endorsed it. They also voted down a policy of federalism, called Éire Nua, long advocated by Ruairi Ó Brádaigh and other aging leaders based in Dublin. It would be another two years before Adams took formal control of Sinn Féin, but he had routed his rivals.

The IRA's ideological purists and military hawks went along with it all, but they were uneasy. Previous eras showed that at some point killing undermined vote-getting and you had to choose one or the other, splitting the movement between those who wanted to overthrow the state and those who wanted to work inside it. Could they trust Gerry A, up there on the podium in his tweed jacket and turtleneck? And had anyone, for that matter, ever actually seen him fire a gun?

A hairline crack appeared in the movement. On one side, "army" people; on the other, "Shinners," or party people. A similar split had put a bullet in the head of Michael Collins.

The surest way to maintain cohesion and assuage doubt about the political path was high-impact operations, preferably in England. Hits across the water cheered activists and had the bonus of not alienating potential voters in the six counties. Under Morrison's editorship, *An Phoblacht/Republican News* had given readers vivid, blanket coverage of the recent attacks in London. It depicted daring commandos operating behind enemy lines, the tone breathless, almost gleeful.

"IRA Blasts Brits Where It Hurts," blared a banner headline. "By rocket, rifle and remote-control bomb attacks the IRA has proved itself to be an effective and successful guerrilla army," said the article. Briefly acknowledging two "regrettable" civilian deaths in Chelsea, it trumpeted the wounding of twenty-two soldiers with the "devastating shrapnel-type" bomb. "The attack was acclaimed by the republican people throughout the beleaguered nationalist ghettoes and countryside in the occupied six counties as part of the very necessary extension of the war outside of the North, particularly into the very heart of the imperialist monster, London." It illustrated the "carefully planned and coldly executed" operation with photographs of charred vehicles and a map. The art department outdid itself with a detailed graphic showing the barracks, the detonating cable, and the exact position of the blast, all precisely scaled.

The report on the bomb that claimed Sir Steuart Pringle's leg mocked the Anti-Terrorist Branch's response. "An hour after the explosion, police forensic experts covered the car with tarpaulin and removed it on a police lorry for detailed examination which doubtless proved fruitless but at least looked efficient." The following week's splash celebrated the Oxford Street bomb. "Prestige Target: IRA Bomb London Again."

The British government was unable to protect the imperialist capital, said the article, detailing disruption to commuters and commerce. Careful warnings prevented civilian casualties, leaving the Wimpy bomb to claim just one life, it said. "The bomb expert, whose expertise failed to defeat those super experts, the IRA, joined the police in March 1974. . . ."

An Phoblacht/Republican News said that the British media's coverage of the Wimpy bomb—it documented ample newspaper and TV coverage—proved the wisdom of bombing "precise" targets in England. It was a distillation of a concept Adams would come to term "armed propaganda." Some hawks rolled their eyes but didn't protest. Fancy terminology was fine, as long as they could still kill Brits.

. . .

THE ENGLAND DEPARTMENT was forced to pause the campaign. A bomb damaged the home of Sir Michael Havers, the attorney general, and that was the end of the autumn offensive. The security forces were agitated fire ants, crawling everywhere, making it dangerous to surveil targets and move gear. Supplies needed replenishing. And it was time to change operators. The campaign would resume at Christmas, when bombs had extra economic and psychological impact, and be led by Patrick Magee.

The Chancer had not been involved in the October bombings, which were planned well before he volunteered to return to active service. During October and November, he had personal matters to sort out in Dublin, not least Eileen, who was seeing the promise of a semi-normal life once again disintegrate. He needed to be briefed and prepped. It was two years since he had been on a mission. A comrade told Magee it would be quite a comeback. "We'll give these bastards a Christmas they'll never forget."

Shortly after 6:00 p.m. on November 25, Magee and his boss, Danny Devenny, who ran the art department of *An Phoblacht/ Republican News*, were in the foyer of Sinn Féin's Dublin headquarters. Devenny noticed a man acting suspiciously and shouted a warning. The man pulled out a gun and started shooting. Two bullets hit Magee's lower right leg, but he did not feel anything—the heat cauterized nerve endings. One bullet chipped a bone before exiting, the other lodged behind a knee. The gunman fled.

The Ulster Defence Association, a paramilitary group, claimed responsibility. The intended target was thought to be Joe Cahill, a legendary republican. It had been a bungled assassination attempt, a Prot job, except it did hurt the Provos. Magee hobbled out of the hospital—a police guard had kept close tabs on his republican visitors—in mid-December, on crutches, facing a long convalescence, and unfit for active service.

Magee asked a comrade about the planned campaign across the water.

"You were it," came the reply.

London enjoyed a peaceful Christmas.

. . .

THATCHER REMAINED UNWAVERING. She told Parliament that Belfast was in effect as British as the Finchley district of London. "I take the view," she said, "that Northern Ireland is part of the United Kingdom—as much as my constituency is." And what did she have to fear from Irish republicans? She had faced down two hunger strikes. It burnished her reputation as a lady, in her own words, "not for turning." Few in her cabinet recognized the hunger strike's slow-burn impact on Northern Ireland. After all, there were other things to worry about in January 1982. A cold wave plunged Britain into an Arctic freeze. The economy continued to wheeze, seemingly impervious to free-market medicine. Thatcher's ratings slumped to 23 percent, the lowest ever recorded for a prime minister. Her bodyguard wore a raincoat to shield his suit from protesters hurling eggs. Thatcher's nicknames multiplied: Attila the Hen, the Great She-Elephant, That Bloody Woman.

When it seemed nothing else could go wrong, her son, Mark, went missing in the Sahara. Still groping for a career, the twenty-eight-year-old had entered the Paris-Dakar motor rally and disappeared in southern Algeria. While Thatcher was distraught, Denis considered it all ridiculous and said the boy would turn up. He was taking a bath when his wife shouted through the door to say a tycoon had offered a loan of his jet. Would he go and find Mark? "I can't," he shouted back. "I have a dentist's appointment." The boss, of course, prevailed. Denis went. A few days later, after a huge search by Algerian authorities, Mark turned up—a wonky back axle had veered him off course. A tearful mother greeted him at Heathrow.

With such dramas filling the news, Britain quickly forgot the hunger strike. But its sulfurous aftermath was shaping ideas in the minds of dangerous men.

. . .

FOR THE IRA Army Council, it was a simple equation.

To wage war, you need money and gear. To get money and gear, you need friends, especially foreign friends. To get those friends, you put Joe Cahill on a plane. When Joe went out, money and gear came back. In the winter of 1981–82, that meant sending Cahill to Canada to rendezvous with a busload of hockey fans and to slip across the US border. He had an appointment with some gangsters in Boston.

Cahill was sixty-one and looked older, a short, bald Belfast native with thick glasses, invariably dressed in an overcoat and a cloth cap. He was a living fossil, an embodiment of IRA history. He had narrowly escaped hanging for the killing of a policeman in 1942 and partici-pated in sporadic IRA campaigns in the 1950s and early '60s. When loyalist mobs burned Catholic homes in 1969, Cahill helped to birth the Provisional IRA. Elected to its first Army Council, he commanded the Belfast Brigade with ruthlessness.

When the British army had swept through Catholic areas making mass arrests in 1971, a young apprentice named Gerry Adams had orchestrated an audacious press conference for the fugitive commander. Before a phalanx of cameras, Cahill taunted the Brits and showed that he was still free and that the Provos were still in business. It was in-spired theater, the flat-capped pimpernel, and it caught the eye of a young Arab leader 1,800 miles to the south. Muammar Gaddafi, after all, was a connoisseur of showmanship.

An emissary for Libya's revolutionary leader told an IRA intermediary—a French sculptor and sympathizer who lived near Dublin—that Gaddafi wanted to meet Cahill. If he came, "everything would be possible." Cahill got a fake passport and hopscotched through Paris and Rome to Tripoli, where he and several IRA companions were welcomed as dignitaries and installed in a villa with a chef and housekeeping staff. Gaddafi was prickly and mercurial, prone to changing his mind, but he took a shine to old Joe. "He had an awful hatred of England—we never really got down to discussing why," Cahill recalled later. Gaddafi saw the unification of Ireland as part of the international anti-imperialist struggle. Give me your shopping list, he told Cahill.

And so Cahill's guerrilla career swerved in a new direction: donor relations, financial management, and gunrunning. It had a bumpy start. Cahill sailed from Tripoli in a merchant ship, the *Claudia*, laden with five tons of Soviet-made guns and explosives. It was spotted. The Irish navy seized the vessel in the Celtic Sea and Cahill spent three years in jail. Upon release, he resumed responsibility for sourcing money and weapons. By then, Colonel Gaddafi had cooled on the Provos, his eye caught by other, more exciting anti-imperialists, so the IRA needed new patronage.

Working from a drafty hallway in Sinn Féin's Dublin office, Cahill was a tightfisted treasurer, itemizing every expenditure, no matter how trivial, in ledgers. He frowned on tea and sandwiches at party meetings as lavishness, as his own habits were ascetic. Vacation meant squeezing his wife and seven children into an old trailer by a beach. As an incarnation of the struggle's continuity and legitimacy, Cahill was an effective ambassador. Plain talk, a whiff of cordite, a fanatic's integrity. You looked at his scuffed shoes and you knew every penny went to the cause. Irish Americans in particular fell for Uncle Joe. Traveling under the name Joe Brown with wigs and other disguises, he was the main draw at fundraisers organized by the New York–based Northern Aid Committee, or NORAID. A blunt speech, some schmoozing, count the dollars into a plastic shopping bag, and Cahill would be on his way.

The FBI had a habit of intercepting shipments of Armalites—especially since Thatcher had badgered Reagan about the Provos' US pipeline—but Cahill would return for more. South Boston was an especially reliable contributor. Southie's working-class communities traced their lineage to immigrants who had fled the famine. The area's unofficial mascot was a leprechaun, fists balled up, ready to brawl. No celebration was complete without a rebel song like "A Nation Once Again." A liquor store owner painted a mural proclaiming "Ireland Unfree Will Never Be at Peace." Jars and hats passed around bars filled with dollars for the cause.

Cahill had done the Canadian hockey trick before. He would fly in when the Boston Bruins were playing Quebec teams. IRA sympathizers would charter a bus for fans from Southie, induce a few to stay extra days, and have Joe and his companions take their seats on the bus, which was invariably waved through the border on its way home. It was an icy time of year to travel, but Cahill had special reason to visit Boston that winter: there was a potential new benefactor.

James "Whitey" Bulger.

The meeting took place in a private room on the second floor of Triple O, an underworld favorite on West Broadway dubbed a "bucket of blood" for the brawls and lethal plots it incubated. This was Whitey's redoubt. Several other gangsters attended the gathering. An Irish tricolor hung from a brick wall, and a TV and video recorder sat on the bar. Nobody drank; this was business. Cahill had come to ask Whitey to escalate South Boston's contribution to the war effort. Or at least to give his blessing for others to do so.

Not much happened in Southie without Whitey's approval. He was fifty-three, arms and chest pumped from the gym, with the city at his feet. From a teenage thief with a gang called the Shamrocks, he had graduated to forgery, assault, armed robbery, racketeering, and emerged triumphant from 1970s mob wars as Southie's top gangster, master of loan-sharking, bookmaking, and extortion, rumored to have personally killed more than a dozen people, including two women, who were strangled.

Whitey's coldness chilled even his friends. He'd walk into a bar and it was said even the beer would go flat. Yet he could also be paternal and traditional. "A strange, complex amalgam of the depraved and the blandly conventional," a biography would observe.

And yet Whitey had a soft spot for the old country. He had contributed to NORAID and was flattered Cahill had asked to meet him. Southie's underworld respected the Provos. So did much of the political establishment. As president of the Massachusetts senate, Whitey's brother, William Bulger, had welcomed a former H-Block prisoner, Fra McCann, to the state capitol. But asking Whitey to ship weapons was a big ask—all risk, no profit. Where was the angle? Whitey never did anything without an angle.

Cahill then did something that entered gangster lore. He bewitched Whitey Bulger. In his blunt way, he filled the room with tales of battling the Brits, of sacrifice, suffering, and revolution, of an ancient cause, of history calling. He fished a videocassette from a shopping bag. It was a documentary that showed the British army and RUC firing plastic bullets into crowds. "The movie had pictures of little girls, dead," recalled Kevin Weeks, Whitey's mob lieutenant. "They had been shot in the head by plastic bullets."

Cahill turned off the television and, in the silence, turned to face the assembled gangsters. "Lads," he said, folding his hands as if in prayer, "we need your help." It was an appeal to sentiment, and Whitey was possibly the least sentimental Irish American who ever lived. It worked. He agreed to supply the IRA.

Ego was part of it. In Southie's underworld, a connection to the Provos conferred prestige, and Bulger considered himself a refined mobster, a reader of military biographies and tomes on Northern Ireland. He imagined himself a guerrilla strategist. Whether that was reality or fancy, Bulger's associates, who sat beside him in the Triple O, said yes to Cahill. Patrick Nee, a former marine turned mob enforcer, wanted to give Margaret Thatcher payback for the hunger strikers, whom he considered noble warriors. Joe Murray, a cocaine and marijuana trafficker, buzzed at the chance to do something big and patriotic. Rather than watch from the sidelines, Bulger figured it was better to take charge of the enterprise. Not that he would be, out of pocket; he could always persuade others to pay.

Soon Bulger's gang was shipping Armalites, pistols, ammunition, and blocks of C-4 plastic explosives under the false floor of a Dodge van that crossed the Atlantic in a cargo vessel. It disembarked in Le Havre, France, and took a ferry to Ireland. The Provos were delighted. They asked for more, a lot more. It would mean sourcing tons of weapons and a dedicated vessel and crew. It would be risky, complicated, and expensive. Whitey said yes.

This was an alliance rich in irony. As a street commander, Cahill, a practicing Catholic, had refused to outsource car theft to professionals, not wanting to be associated with thieves. The IRA policed Northern Ireland's Catholic neighborhoods by beating and shooting criminals. The hunger strikers had died rather than be labeled criminals. Provo strategy hinged on defeating the British policy of criminalization. Yet here was Cahill courting some of America's most ruthless criminals.

Indeed, when it came to patronage, the Provos were not choosy. Eastern European communist regimes, the Palestine Liberation Organization, conservative Irish Americans—all were cultivated. IRA emissaries could quote Marx, Nasser, or catechism, depending on the audience. The Provos would not have appreciated the comparison, but this was the year Woody Allen filmed *Zelig*, a comedy about a human chameleon who takes on the characteristics of those around him. Bobby Sands and his doomed comrades were propaganda gold, and the narrative framing could be tweaked here and there, emphasizing republicanism, or anti-imperialism, or human rights. But at the end of the day, only one thing remained constant: the villain. Thatcher, Thatcher, life snatcher.

. . .

IT WAS AROUND this time that the most enigmatic personality in the IRA's supply chain started to reemerge. Brother Leader, Universal Theorist, Falcon of Africa, King of Kings, and Supreme Guide of the Great Socialist People's Libyan Arab Jamahiriya—Muammar Gaddafi had racked up additional titles since hosting Joe Cahill in Tripoli a decade earlier.

The colonel's ardor for Irish liberation had faded after Cahill left. He became pickier about his rebels and no longer wrote blank checks. But then, by 1982, Gaddafi was again eyeing the Provos. He was impressed by the hunger strike and had his own reason to loathe the British prime minister. Few leaders were as caricatured as Libya's dictator, a figure of whimsy and menace floating on oil wealth. Intelligent, capricious, with a cosmic ego, he perched on the edge of the Mediterranean looking for entrées into global dramas.

Born in 1942, the goat herder's son had been plucked from school by the army and fast-tracked through the military. He never completed formal education, but could intuit others' motives and weaknesses. A stint in England for military training in 1966 aggravated his disdain for Britain and other colonial powers. With other Arab nationalist officers, he overthrew Libya's pro-Western king in 1969 and declared a revolution. His blend of Islam, socialism, and hippie sentiments turned Libya into a laboratory for half-baked political and economic experiments. The resulting chaos suited Brother Leader. His authority remained inviolate and he was spared the tedium of building a functional state, leaving him to play the philosopher king while amassing an arsenal of warplanes, tanks, guns, and explosives.

Now Gaddafi was agitated and swatting at enemies from his underground bunker. He dispatched assassins to Britain to liquidate political exiles he called "stray dogs." He was tangling with Ronald Reagan. US fighters had downed two Libyan warplanes and Reagan was preparing an oil embargo. Gaddafi took note of the US president's European sidekick. He didn't need a universal theory to conclude Margaret Thatcher was an imperialist accomplice. He sent a message to Ireland: the Falcon of Africa wanted to hear from his old Provo friends.

· · ·

THE LINCHPIN OF the IRA's global supply network, the thread connecting Libya, continental Europe, and Boston, was a former Catholic priest named Patrick Ryan. He laundered the money and smuggled the weapons that kept the Provos in business. The British security services knew all about him. They had thick files that thudded onto ministers' desks and still they couldn't stop him. It was the Paddy Factor in reverse. The Padre, as he was known, had swept-back hair and easy charm. Once, he had heard God calling, but now his faith was republicanism.

Born into a farming family in County Tipperary in southern Ireland, Ryan was ordained in 1954. He served as a missionary in Tanzania and the US before becoming an assistant curate of a small church in East London. When the Troubles flared, something stirred in the young priest. He began funneling money for the African missions to the republican movement. Ryan also wooed and dazzled a shy young Englishwoman named Catherine, who worked with disabled children. On a trip to Rome in 1973, Ryan told Italian priests he hoped the IRA would bomb London. "And they should hit some of the reservoirs as well," he added.

Suspended by his superiors, he volunteered his services to the Provos. They could not believe their luck. A clean record, a respectable front, good at languages—the perfect fixer. Ryan relocated to the continent and began a nomadic existence. Shuttling in a camper van between Luxembourg, Switzerland, France, and Holland, he set up bank accounts in different names and funneled over £1 million. He met Gaddafi in Tripoli—"a fine fella, best I ever met"—and liaised with couriers, truck drivers, and ferry stewards. He set up a base in Le Havre and supervised illicit cargoes of weapons on ferries to Ireland.

Spinning tales of woe about French bureaucracy and a fantasy about their future life together, Ryan persuaded Catherine, his besotted admirer, to smuggle him cash and a fake English driver's license.

In Zurich, he bought a novelty store's entire stock of four hundred Memo-Park timers, the first of several bulk purchases. It earned the gratitude of a generation of IRA bombers. The ticking was probably the last sound Ken Howorth heard.

By 1976, the British security services were onto Ryan. They persuaded Swiss police to arrest him. But he had not committed any offense in Switzerland, and any evidence of IRA activity was deemed political and outside the scope of Switzerland's extradition treaty with the UK. So Ryan walked.

This set a pattern. The British would surveil him, persuade authorities in Spain, France, Italy, and Luxembourg to arrest him, and days or weeks later the errant priest would be released, free to keep the IRA's supply lines humming. "I regret I wasn't even more effective," he recalled later. "But we didn't do too badly."

It was a strange fellowship. A Belfast gunman turned accidental ambassador; an American mobster yearning for glory; an Arab autocrat in the market for terror; a renegade priest with a lethal vocation. They were part of a distribution chain that clanked along, unseen, sometimes slowing, occasionally breaking down altogether, only to revive and clank anew. Without that chain, there was no England Department, no bombs in the imperialist capital for *An Phoblacht/Republican News* to report, no hope of reaching the Iron Lady.

CHAPTER EIGHT

Rejoice

The American Secret Service agents filed into 10 Downing Street, polished shoes clacking on tiles, and politely turned the prime minister's residence upside down. They opened drawers, inspected closets, probed nooks, investigated crannies. They took measurements and notes, looked behind doors and under sofas, scrutinized chandeliers, lamps, fireplaces, vases. They had a problem with clocks; maybe it was the ticking. The cabinet room's ancient grandfather clock aroused particular suspicion, perhaps because it did not chime at the same time as the clock on the mantelpiece. The agents poked around the pendulum and its mysterious machinery. "They broke it, so we could never thereafter get it started again," recalled Charles Powell, Thatcher's private secretary.

It could have been worse. The platoon of interlopers in suits and crew cuts might have been a full troop. "The Secret Service said could they send in an advance team to look at the premises," said Powell. "I said, 'Oh, all right, how many?' And they said a hundred. And I said we only have about twenty people working here. They said we can't do less than a hundred and I said you'll have to, I'll accept forty."

It was the American way: blanket security for any event with the president. The agents had reason for extreme thoroughness. It was June 1982, just a year since their radios had crackled with the dread words "Rawhide down." Rawhide was Ronald Reagan's code name, a tribute to his passion for ranching. On March 30, 1981, agents had vetted the Washington Hilton Hotel for a presidential visit, but failed to secure Reagan's short walk back to his car. From behind a rope line, John Hinckley, that twisted admirer of Jodie Foster's, fired six shots from a .22-caliber revolver. One bullet ricocheted off the president's limousine and pierced his chest, coming to rest an inch from his heart. "Doctors believe bleeding to death," the White House deputy press secretary, Larry Speakes, scribbled in the hospital. "Can't find a wound. 'Think we're going to lose him.' Rapid loss of blood pressure. Touch and go."

Reagan survived, but the shooting was a brutal reminder to the Secret Service that complacency kills. The First Lady, terrified about another assassination attempt, used an astrologer to tweak her husband's schedule. The agents who scoured Downing Street were not about to rely on celestial cycles—or their British hosts—to protect the president during his forty-one-hour visit to England.

Two US marine helicopters preceded Reagan's arrival at Heathrow on June 7. Air Force One, with its own medical suite and electromagnetic-pulse-shielded electronics, beetled into a remote and secure part of the airport. Every stop on Reagan's itinerary had been sanitized—streets sealed off, buildings checked, staff vetted, ordinary people kept at bay. "Anyone rushing forward to hand Mr. Reagan an unscheduled posy would have been brought down within six steps by a security man," noted *The Guardian*.

Thatcher's security was much smaller and lower-key. Scotland Yard's Special Branch had an "A" Squad to provide personal protection to the prime minister and other VIPs. Its 120 officers received training in firearms, unarmed combat, and tactical positioning. A small team was assigned to Thatcher. On a threat scale graded from one to six, she was classified level two, the second highest: "Information and events indicate a high threat to the subject." Specific information that she was the target of an attack would move her to level one.

Before official engagements, Thatcher's protective officers would do reconnaissance, checking exits and sight lines and designating a "safe room" with a phone. Sniffer dogs would check for explosives. During an engagement, such as a speech, the officers would form a pattern, typically a triangular formation, one on each side of Thatcher, another farther back with a wider view. "We're watching different aspects," one protection officer, Barry Stevens, recalled. "The one at the back is our link with the people outside. They may be uniformed officers or the local plainclothes people." Were a gunman to appear, there were two options, said Stevens. "I'd either have to take him out or I'd take her out of the way. My job would be to come between her and the bullet."

· · ·

WHEN THATCHER WELCOMED Reagan to Downing Street, her mind was on security, but not her own. A British military task force was in the South Atlantic, eight thousand miles away, attempting to retake the Falkland Islands from Argentine forces. After weeks of fighting, the British were nearing victory. Thatcher was on tenterhooks awaiting updates.

The British overseas territory was a windswept, rocky archipelago, a footnote of empire, home to ruddy-faced sheep farmers and a million penguins. Most British people could not have located it on a map until the right-wing military junta in Buenos Aires invaded on April 2. Argentina had long claimed sovereignty over what it called Las Malvinas. The generals decided to boost their regime's sagging popularity by seizing the islands. It was a bloodless conquest—the small British garrison surrendered—and yet it seemed the gravest crisis so far of Thatcher's premiership.

Her government had misread Argentine intentions and failed to prepare any defense. Retaking the islands by force seemed outlandish. They were too far, too remote, and the Royal Navy was not what it had been. Thatcher was already weakened by economic recession, the rise of the new Social Democratic Party, and conspiring "wets" in her own party. Now the Falklands humiliation threatened to topple her. In a meeting that came to acquire mythical status, an admiral, Henry Leach, explained the awesome challenges of dispatching a task force.

"Can we do it?" Thatcher asked with piercing urgency.

"We can, Prime Minister," he said.

Others disagreed, but that singular answer was enough for Thatcher. A fleet was assembled and sailed to the other side of the world, shadowed by the specter of disaster and defeat. The distances were vast, the weather horrendous. The Argentines had submarines and warplanes armed with ship-killing Exocet missiles. Thatcher's days filled with military briefings, parliamentary debates, and intense diplomacy. At night, she would fix herself a whiskey, kick off her shoes, and sit on the floor by an electric heater, listening to the BBC World Service, sometimes till dawn. By early June, the Argentine navy had retreated—cowed by the sinking of the cruiser *General Belgrano* and the loss of 321 lives—and British troops were battling across the two main islands.

Thatcher was the first female war leader with executive power in the British Isles since Elizabeth I, and the conflict brought out her best qualities. Courage and resolution, but also caution and focus. Knowing nothing about war, she was humble enough to defer to her generals and admirals and not meddle in operations. Nimble diplomacy built international support. She cared passionately about the islanders and the men she sent into battle. They in turn trusted and adored her. The public also rallied to her banner. Her ratings soared. Privately, the Russians marveled at this demonstration of Western will and capacity. For Thatcher, seizing triumph from disaster became a talisman of what she could do. "In her mind, it helped to create the dangerous idea that she acted best when she acted alone," noted her biographer Charles Moore.

Perhaps not completely alone. Reagan's visit to England in June 1982 cemented their partnership. Early in the Falklands crisis, he had wobbled, not wanting to alienate US allies in Latin America, before giving full support to Thatcher, whom he considered "the only European leader I know with balls." In a speech to MPs and lords, Reagan linked the British troops fighting in the Falklands to a wider "crusade for freedom" to send Marxism-Leninism into the "ash heap of history."

It was a landmark speech that articulated the Reagan doctrine. Many Britons were stunned, thinking it simplistic and dangerous. Thatcher was thrilled. Western values were finally on the offensive. She had done her part by letting the US station nuclear-tipped missiles on British soil despite huge protests by peace campaigners, who warned of Armageddon. She hosted the Reagans for lunch at Downing Street. "As you can see, this is a very simple house, one which has witnessed the shaping of our shared history since it first became the abode of prime ministers in 1732," she told them. She raised her glass: "I ask you all to rise and drink a toast to the enduring alliance between the United States and the United Kingdom."

. . .

WITH A VAULTED ceiling, oak-paneled walls, and crystal chandeliers, Downing Street was no simple house. Thatcher had invested time and some of her own money redecorating. More than a residence, it was her sanctuary. Originally it had been the home of Sir Thomas Knyvet, a parliamentarian who helped foil the Gunpowder Plot of 1605. Rebuilt for prime ministers, it was deceptively large, like Doctor Who's *Tardis* spacecraft: connected to adjacent properties and much roomier than it appeared from the modest front door. Thatcher gave it a makeover, selecting drapes and artwork. She was especially proud of a sitting room overlooking Horse Guards Parade. A patriotic floral pattern of red and blue on a cream background covered settees. You could hear the Queen's Household Cavalry clip-clopping past.

Number 10, said Thatcher, "became my refuge from the rest of the world." Rising at dawn, she would listen to BBC Radio news while working on papers or having her hair done. Meetings started in the first-floor study at 9:00 a.m. She liked to prepare her own lunch, often a salad or poached egg on Bovril toast. After a day at the Commons, she might retire to the sitting room with aides, then prepare supper for Denis and any visitors who lingered. "One MP was so horrified to find his chain of thought constantly interrupted by the prime minister bobbing up and down to check on the simmering frozen peas that he read the riot act to her," her daughter, Carol, recalled. After everyone left, Thatcher worked on that day's boxes of briefs and memos and went to bed around 1:00 a.m.

To the outside world, even admirers, there was something almost inhuman about the Iron Lady. The work rate, the unshakable convictions, the unbending will. All the more so after triumph in the Falklands. "Our country has won a great victory and we are entitled to be proud," she told a party rally in early July. "We rejoice that Britain has re-kindled that spirit which has fired her for generations past and which today has begun to burn as brightly as before. Britain found herself again in the South Atlantic and will not look back from the victory she has won."

This was the public Thatcher, clamorous with certainty. When she was required to change gears and convey compassion, her voice would drop an octave and she would speak slowly. It came across as false. The press dubbed her the "sincerity machine." Her aides despaired. Inside Downing Street they saw another side, a mother who worried about her children, a boss considerate to her staff, a leader who wept at news of soldiers' deaths. "Behind the iron carapace, she was sometimes a woman of damp eyes and vulnerabilities," said one observer, Michael

Dobbs. When feeling insecure, Thatcher would settle her nerves by rereading a poem she had cut out and underlined. It was "No Enemies," by the nineteenth-century Scottish poet Charles Mackay.

> You have no enemies, you say?
> Alas! my friend, the boast is poor;
> He who has mingled in the fray
> Of duty, that the brave endure,
> Must have made foes! If you have none,
> Small is the work that you have done.
> You've hit no traitor on the hip,
> You've dashed no cup from perjured lip,
> You've never turned the wrong to right,
> You've been a coward in the fight.

. . .

THE SUN HUNG in a cloudless sky over London on the morning of July 20, 1982. After the drama of the Falklands and Reagan's visit, the capital was in holiday mode. Jimmy Connors had defeated John McEnroe in a thrilling Wimbledon final. Italy had thrashed Germany in the World Cup final. Londoners wondered when they would get to see *E.T.*, which was packing American multiplexes. "Fame" topped the charts. There was a new royal baby, Prince William, twenty-nine days old. Even by her standards, Thatcher had a busy schedule: a doctor's appointment, prep for Prime Minister's Questions, a weekly parliamentary duel with Labour leaders, then a meeting with ministers to discuss a policy paper on renewing society's values.

Two miles away, sixteen troopers from the Blues and Royals, a regiment of the Queen's Household Cavalry, started their regular trot through Hyde Park to Horse Guards Parade for the changing of the guard near Downing Street. Some of the riders had returned from the Falklands the previous week. Tourists stopped to watch and take pictures. As the soldiers and horses passed a parked blue Morris

Marina, a twenty-five-pound bomb in the trunk was detonated by radio control.

The blast cracked over the city. Thatcher heard it. Black smoke rose into the sky; windows in offices and stores a hundred yards away shattered. Horses and men were lifted into the air and slammed to the ground. A blizzard of four- and six-inch nails tore into them. "I heard screaming around me," recalled Corporal Oliver Pitt, who was blown off his horse. "I saw and felt blood dripping from my head into the road. . . . I looked around me and saw what I can only describe as carnage." Some of the guardsmen had their skulls crushed by the ceremonial helmets. Horses writhed in agony.

The aftermath of an IRA bomb in London's Hyde Park that killed four soldiers and seven horses of the Queen's Household Cavalry in July 1982. | PA Images / Alamy Stock Photo

Two hours later, another shocking attack: a time bomb exploded underneath a bandstand in Regent's Park, where an army band was performing music from *Oliver!* to spectators. Some of the musicians were ripped in half. The two attacks killed eleven soldiers and injured dozens of bystanders. Seven horses were killed or so grievously injured they had to be destroyed.

Rejoice, Thatcher had said of victory in the Falklands, and here was the IRA's response. They rained blood on her triumph. The statement claiming responsibility taunted her by echoing her own words when she had dispatched the task force. "Now it is our turn to properly invoke article 51 of the UN statute and properly quote all Thatcher's fine phrases on the right to self-determination of a people. The Irish people have sovereign and national rights which no task or occupational force can put down."

Thatcher responded in her typical vigorous way, condemning the attacks, visiting the wounded, meeting security chiefs, vowing the perpetrators would be brought to justice, and then trying to draw a line under the atrocities and move on. But the IRA had violated her refuge. How could she now perch on her settee with its floral pattern, listening to the cavalry's clip-clop outside the window, and not remember the men and horses who never made it?

. . .

THE PARK BOMBINGS revolted people around the world. But for the IRA, it was still a success. The dead were all military and the long-war strategy meant wearying and sickening British public opinion. The Army Council wanted to sustain the pressure with more high-impact operations to show that the Brits could not contain the Troubles to an "acceptable level" of violence in Northern Ireland.

It was around this time the England Department floated its proposal to assassinate Margaret Thatcher. Owen Coogan, the Long Kesh escaper with jug ears, and Michael Hayes, who liked to sing ballads to police interrogators, conceived it in Dublin, sometimes meeting in dingy apartments in Ballymun, other times in the open air away from potential eavesdroppers. They came to it via a process of elimination.

A sniper attack—à la Frederick Forsyth's classic novel *The Day of the Jackal*—was impractical. Gaps appeared in Thatcher's protective bubble during her occasional walkabouts and other public events, but such an attack would require advance intel and the IRA didn't have a mole on Downing Street. In any case, marksmanship had never been the IRA's forte. Shootings tended toward assault-rifle *blatter blatter blatter*, as Gerry Bradley put it, or handguns fired at point-blank range. A skilled sniper putting Thatcher's corona in the crosshairs of a telescopic sight and wrapping a finger around the trigger was a stirring thought, but fantasy.

It would have to be a bomb. Like Captain Ahab chasing his white whale in Melville's *Moby Dick*, Coogan and Hayes studied calendars and charts to see where their quarry might surface. Downing Street, Chequers, and Westminster were heavily guarded, and Thatcher's schedule when outside those fortified zones was a tightly guarded secret. But there were two occasions when she was sure to appear. The first was election night, when she would be at the count center in her Finchley constituency. However, there was no date for the election and it was unclear exactly what time or how long she would stay there.

The other opportunity was the annual Conservative Party Conference. It was held over four days every October and alternated between two seaside resorts: Blackpool, in northwest England, and Brighton, on the south coast. Police everywhere, of course, but maybe there was a way. The idea was not new. Patrick Magee had surveilled a Labour Party Conference in Brighton in 1979 when the IRA dreamed of paying back Roy Mason, the safari-suit-wearing former Northern Ireland secretary of state, for the RUC's "slap and tickle" interrogation methods.

Coogan and Hayes concluded the best chance was at the party conference. They pitched the proposal to the Army Council. According to Hayes, the IRA's seven-member ruling body said no. "They said it would be suicide, like kamikazes, and they rejected it. The probability of us getting her seemed impossible to them." The Army Council's deliberations remain secret, but several other IRA sources agree there was hesitation. The operation would be risky and expensive, and it would distract from easier targets. Another reason was that some members were still "spooked" by the furor over Mountbatten's assassination. They did not relish the prospect of British agents hunting them for the rest of their days.

Coogan and Hayes argued the IRA had a duty to go after the most reviled British leader in centuries. "We persisted with it," said Hayes. "I said, 'At least let me do a feasibility study.'" The IRA chiefs assented. In early October 1982, two scouts made a preliminary reconnaissance during the Conservative Party Conference in Brighton. They mingled with delegates, noted schedules, studied police deployments. The feedback emboldened the England Department. With proper planning, the right gear, and serious operators, the plan could work. The Army Council would need to give final authorization, but Coogan and Hayes were confident enough to give the plot a code name: Lochinvar.

Thatcher, it turned out, was not the only one fond of nineteenth-century Scottish verse. "Lochinvar" was the title of a poem by Sir Walter Scott. It depicts a valiant knight who travels east, across a stretch of water, to gate-crash a bridal feast.

> O young Lochinvar is come out of the west,
> Through all the wide Border his steed was the best;
> And save his good broadsword he weapons had none,
> He rode all unarm'd, and he rode all alone.
> So faithful in love, and so dauntless in war,
> There never was knight like the young Lochinvar.

CHAPTER NINE

Blackpool

The call came over the police radio as Steve Atkinson, a rookie constable, walked his usual beat through central Blackpool. A store security guard had caught a shoplifter. Could someone please bring him in? Not the most glamorous assignment, but it promised a bit more excitement than rousting vagrants and directing lost tourists. It was a supermarket called Fine Fare near the train station that sold groceries and souvenirs plugging "Britain's favorite seaside resort."

A favorite spot for inept thieves, too, judging by the number nabbed walking out with stuff they hadn't paid for. The offender this time was a middle-aged Irishman with boozy breath. Atkinson packed him into the back of a police van and sat up front for the ride to the police station. After the suspect was booked, Atkinson and the driver searched the back of the van, a routine practice that sometimes turned up drugs and blades stuffed under seats. They found a handwritten note. It was either gibberish or some sort of code. "It didn't make any sense to us," Atkinson recalled. "But being an Irish guy, we passed it

to Special Branch. That was the last I heard of it." So ended PC Atkinson's cameo in the countdown to kill Margaret Thatcher.

It was autumn 1982, and a chain of events began to unfold. A
Special Branch detective studied the note and was intrigued enough to
quiz the shoplifter. He was a forty-eight-year-old petty criminal called
Raymond O'Connor. Originally from Galway, when not boozing and
thieving he worked in a local café. It didn't take much questioning for
his story to spill out. Earlier that year, O'Connor's stepson, a young
Dublin schoolteacher with republican sympathies named Thomas Maguire, had visited his mother and O'Connor in Blackpool. Out walking
one day, O'Connor and Maguire stopped for a drink in a pub called the
Eagle and Child Inn. O'Connor mentioned the nearby Weeton army
base, home of the 2nd Battalion of the Light Infantry, hosted training
camps for the RUC and the Special Air Service, an elite army unit
better known as the SAS. O'Connor's information was incorrect, but
back in Dublin, Maguire relayed the information to Sinn Féin contacts. Their interest was piqued.

Maguire—who was later acquitted in court of conspiring to cause
explosions—wrote letters to his stepfather about the republican movement's desire to learn more about the base, which he referred to as
"Judy." It was one of these letters that O'Connor tried to hide in the
van. The detective who questioned O'Connor must have bolted upright.
The IRA appeared to be plotting a new attack in England. And Blackpool's very own Special Branch had discovered it. There was not often
opportunity to practice the rarefied arts of counterterrorism in the
northwest corner of England. Blackpool's decaying charms—a promenade, arcades, an Eiffel-esque tower—drew tourists and drunks and
pickpockets, not subversives. The local Special Branch, with responsibility for Lancashire County, had negligible experience of terrorism.
They were distant cousins to the professional IRA hunters of Scotland
Yard, 250 miles to the south. And yet now they had a chance to take
the organization on.

They persuaded Raymond O'Connor, a man "given to the drink," to become a double agent. Under police direction, he played along with his stepson and republican friends in Dublin, who in coded letters requested more details about the camp. In February 1983, O'Connor relayed exciting news to his handlers: the IRA was planning an operation. The England Department had fallen for the trap.

. . .

THE TARGET WAS not Weeton Camp, but the adjacent pub, the Eagle and Child, which was often packed with soldiers. There was also a secondary objective, a task of pure reconnaissance, requiring finesse. It was finally time for Patrick Magee to return to England. The wait must have been frustrating. Instead of blowing up London in early 1982, he had been hobbling around Dublin on crutches, convalescing from the shooting. He became anxious after Irish police caught up with Gerry Tuite, his mentor and comrade.

Tuite was convicted in an Irish court for the 1978–79 London bombing campaign—the first use of a new law allowing suspects to be tried in Ireland for offenses in the UK. Magee reckoned he was next, so he went underground, a return to his former edgy existence. It was the final straw for Eileen. She took Padraig, now age four, back to Belfast. They agreed to divorce. "We both recognized it was for the best. My life was too chaotic," Magee recalled.

His memoir is otherwise silent about 1982. There is no evidence he was involved in the Hyde and Regent's Park bombings. It was another bloody year in Northern Ireland, giving opportunity for Magee's skills, but there were no sightings, no forensic traces. Like footprints in the snow, wherever it is he went that year, his tracks melted.

For Blackpool, the England Department partnered Magee with a volunteer called Patrick "the Pope" Murray. He was forty years old, tall, muscular, with reddish hair. Originally from the west of Ireland, he had grown up in Scotland and served in the British army. His commitment was not in question. He had a "God save the Pope" tattoo on his chest, three shamrocks tattooed on an arm, and a long, violent record on behalf of the IRA. Sean O'Callaghan, an IRA informer, found them an odd couple, deeming Murray a "classic sociopath" with primitive politics, in contrast to Magee. "Highly intelligent and cool, but a strange, moody individual, he and Murray made an unlikely but effective team."

The two Patricks slipped into England and rendezvoused with Raymond O'Connor at Blackpool on April 12, 1983. The city had memories for Magee. During his teenage wanderings, he had worked here as a waiter. Blackpool's promenade had once hosted hordes of vacationers shelling out for donkey rides, puppet shows, and fortune-tellers. The crystal balls didn't foresee (or foretell) cheap flights to Spain siphoning the life out of the place, leaving the Irish Sea to spray a half-deserted pier. The Luftwaffe didn't bomb Blackpool during World War II because Hitler wanted an intact leisure town after invading Britain, and then the Nazis never made it—so double luck for Blackpool. Magee was thinking to end that streak.

Thatcher's Britain left him cold. The government boasted about taming inflation and retooling the economy, but Magee could see for himself the homelessness and ranks of unemployed, their number swollen by laid-off coal miners. It seemed to him that Thatcher's callousness extended to her own people. "The Tories had much to answer for," he wrote in his memoir.

O'Connor was the IRA team's fixer. He rented Magee and Murray a flat and a car, guided them around Weeton's perimeter, showed them the Eagle and Child. All three men were fond of drink, and Magee's staple was vodka, but this was business. Pub bombings had been some of the deadliest attacks on soldiers during the Troubles, invariably with civilian casualties.

While Magee and Murray circled their target, police circled them. Briefed by O'Connor, detectives shadowed the visitors and photographed them with telephoto-lens cameras. In the pictures, Magee is clean-shaven and smartly dressed. The police learned that the IRA men planned to reconnoiter the target, collect explosives, assemble a bomb, and plant it in a van outside the pub. But the police did not know the identities of the IRA duo. O'Connor was never told their names, so he invented nicknames: the big redhead was "the minder," the small dark one was "the mechanic." The minder had a big mouth. "You have the best people over at the moment," he told O'Connor. "Do you remember the bombing of Airey Neave? He"—he was speaking of Magee—"was responsible for that. That's how good he is." In fact, the INLA had killed Thatcher's ally.

On April 16, the detectives sent their grainy black-and-white pictures to Scotland Yard for identification. The two suspects had yet to commit any crime, so there was no point arresting them; they would simply walk free after questioning. But if the minder or mechanic were wanted for previous offenses, the watchers could pounce and deliver them, wrapped in a bow, to Scotland Yard.

Once the photos arrived at Scotland Yard, a clock started ticking. In a filing cabinet on the fifth floor, the Anti-Terrorist Branch had a manila folder on Magee. On the eleventh floor, the Met's Special Branch unit had its own file on him. Each contained mug shots, fingerprints, RUC records of his activities in Northern Ireland, plus the Met's records of his role in the 1978–79 London campaign.

The Chancer had eluded the Met in 1979, slipped free again when the Dutch court released him in 1981, only to stumble into a trap in Blackpool. Once Scotland Yard identified the photographs sent from Lancashire, his running days were over.

Days passed, the world turned. A suicide bomber blew up the US embassy in Beirut. Britain introduced a £1 coin. Soviet astronauts failed to dock with a space station. David Bowie's "Let's Dance" topped the charts. The Lancashire detectives heard nothing from Scotland Yard. They could only guess at the holdup. Were the photos in the wrong pile? Were the IRA hunters overworked, not interested, prioritizing other cases? The Lancashire detectives continued the surveillance in hopes that the suspects would lead them to an arms cache.

On April 22, Magee and Murray sensed they were being followed.

No proof, just a feeling. Then a nagging suspicion about their fixer crystallized into a chilling conviction that Raymond O'Connor was an agent provocateur. Informers, or touts, were the bogeymen of republican nightmares, the Judases within the ranks. They had betrayed and doomed countless rebellions—and apparently this mission, too.

Magee and Murray faced a dilemma. They were under pressure to deliver a result. The IRA had not hit England since the park bombings the previous summer. A spectacular was overdue. And there was the secondary objective: advance reconnaissance of the Conservative Party Conference due in Blackpool in October. This would be the most spectacular operation of all. It was Thatcher's custom to stay in a promenade hotel near the Winter Gardens conference center. Magee visited the Metropole, a potential venue, and probably other hotels. IRA volunteers stuck on punishment squads or fundraising duties would have given their eyeteeth to be on such a mission. This was taking the war to England. This was *it*.

To abort was agonizing. But to proceed while under surveillance would be crazy. On April 26, a gray, drizzly Tuesday, Magee and Murray drove their Ford Cortina out of Blackpool and merged into traffic heading east on the M55. Three of the four police surveillance cars hung back, not wanting to get too close. It was standard practice for one car to keep eyes on the target, then drop back to be replaced by another vehicle. The detectives hoped the suspects might be en route to a clandestine arms dump. Rain pattered on windshields as the flat Lancashire countryside flashed past.

Around this time, a Met detective in Scotland Yard was poring over the photographs sent from Blackpool. One of the men, the shorter one, must have looked familiar because the detective fished out a file and compared its mug shot with the surveillance photos. Bingo. Patrick Joseph Magee. The Chancer himself, back in England, taking one chance too many.

On the other side of England, the IRA duo's Ford Cortina left the

M55 and headed south, toward Preston, three miles away. It began to accelerate.

Scotland Yard had rules for sharing intelligence with other forces. A senior officer would have had to sign off on a call to Lancashire. Minutes slid by.

On the outskirts of Preston, it was as if Nelson Piquet, the Formula 1 champion, had beamed into the Cortina. It revved through traffic and swerved through side streets. Magee and Murray were making a run for it. The surveillance detectives, guessing their cover was blown, raced in pursuit, a frantic slalom through traffic. It was no use. The lead surveillance car lost sight of the target. "We knew we were being followed and just drew them away," Magee recalled. "We'd already a spot in mind where we could get out of the motor and disappear."

It would not have been the first time in law enforcement history that furious swears were yelled over a police radio. Magee and Murray wove south through the center of Preston and abandoned their car outside the railway station, a busy freight and passenger hub.

When the detectives found the Cortina a short while later, the doors were open, the engine running, and the windshield wipers going. About fifteen minutes after the Lancashire detectives realized they had lost the suspects, a phone rang in their headquarters. It was Scotland Yard calling with some important information about "the mechanic." Lancashire made a desperate search around Preston and surrounding areas for the man they now knew to be Patrick Magee. But the Chancer and his companion were gone.

The fugitives had prepared their flight using local knowledge. Murray, years earlier, had sold republican newspapers in Preston. The train station was a ruse. The pair, possibly on foot, met up with Murray's younger brother, James, a laborer who lived near the station. James connected them with an Irish friend, Joseph Calvey, who shared the Murray brothers' County Mayo roots. That same night, April 26, Calvey and James drove the IRA men two hundred miles south to

Newport, in Wales. Magee and Murray caught a ferry back to Dublin—and a jury later cleared Calvey and James Murray of any wrongdoing.

Magee and Murray had been sent on a poisoned mission into the maw of the Special Branch and successfully escaped, but the IRA did not see it that way. The inquest—the Provos routinely held post-mortems to analyze blunders—gave credence to another narrative peddled by the ever-inventive Raymond O'Connor. He said there had been no surveillance, that Magee and Murray had imagined it and panicked. It was impressive chutzpah, though O'Connor had the sense to stay in Blackpool and not risk execution by the IRA's internal security unit, the Nutting Squad. It suited the England Department to doubt Magee and Murray's version, because this absolved those who sent them of culpability, a case of classic bureaucratic ass-covering.

Magee, for the second time in his IRA career, faced an enforced sabbatical from operations. Having waited so long to get back into the field, the demotion must have stung. "It appeared my operational days were over," his memoir said flatly. "It looked as if my contribution would be confined to logistical support."

The attack on the army pub was abandoned. But the other target in Blackpool remained in play.

. . .

SIX WEEKS LATER, on June 9, 1983, Margaret Thatcher led the Conservatives to a landslide reelection. Framing the vote as a choice between greater liberty and smaller government or a return to state socialism, she dominated the campaign. The Labour Party helped by producing a rambling left-wing manifesto dubbed the "longest suicide note in history." In a three-way race, the Tories won 42.4 percent of the vote, marginally less than 1979, but under the first-past-the-post system they took 397 seats, versus 209 for Labour and 23 for the Social Democratic–Liberal Alliance. Thatcher's parliamentary majority was the largest for any government since 1945, and the greatest increase in a ruling majority in parliamentary history.

Before the Falklands, most people, including her own ministers, had expected Thatcher to lose. "Now her enemies—outside her party and within it—lay prostrate before her," wrote her biographer Charles Moore. Celebrations at the Conservative Party's HQ left Peter Cropper, head of the research department, uneasy: "She really did start walking on water. It was wonderful in a way. But the triumphalism horrified me."

In a government shake-up, Thatcher removed Lady Janet Young, the sole woman in the cabinet apart from herself. For the rest of her reign, Thatcher sparkled as the only female in a cabinet of dark suits. And with prosperity finally sprouting, she moved to privatize state industries and cut taxes and spending.

But victory masked vulnerabilities. Having ousted her predecessor, Ted Heath, Thatcher sensed colleagues would eventually turn against her. "I have not long to go," she told an aide. "My party won't want me to lead them into the next election—and I don't blame them." Not every initiative went her way. The new Parliament voted against a restoration of capital punishment, even for terrorist murders.

Then, too, there was another source of agitation. Gerry Adams had become an MP. It beggared belief. The hirsute apologist for the IRA, for an organization Thatcher decried as foul and murderous, was now the Right Honorable member for West Belfast. Sinn Féin's abstentionist policy meant Adams would not take his seat at Westminster, so Thatcher would be spared seeing him in the flesh, but she must have recoiled at the footage of jubilant crowds carrying him on their shoulders up the Falls Road.

"I didn't win the election," Adams had shouted over the cheers, "you people won the election, every one of the sixteen-odd thousand who voted Sinn Féin, all the people who worked for the past three weeks, all the prisoners' families who have suffered over the years, all the widows of the republican volunteers, and of all the people who have died—they won the election today."

The spectacle deepened an urge in Thatcher "to do something about Ireland." So far, she had been reactive—Mountbatten, Narrow Water, the hunger strikes, one crisis after another, limiting her focus to smothering the IRA. Now she wondered if there could be an actual settlement in Northern Ireland, some way for its two communities to come to terms with one another.

Ireland's prime minister, Garret FitzGerald, was nurturing a similar thought. And he was preparing to pitch Thatcher a radical idea.

. . .

ON JULY 30, the *Andersonstown News*, a West Belfast newspaper, published an article about a republican prisoner. For most readers, the name Roy Walsh would have been, at most, a blurry memory. He had been sentenced to life in prison in 1973 with nine others for the Provos' first bomb attacks in London. Some had been repatriated to Northern Ireland, but Walsh remained in England. Serving your time across the water meant isolation and harsher treatment, and few had it as bad as Walsh. His wife, Mary, told the paper about a disastrous visit to Gartree, a maximum-security prison in Leicestershire. Five guards had crowded around her, Roy, and their children in a cramped visitors' room. Roy ended up in a scuffle with a guard and was hauled away, screaming, while the children wept.

Walsh was an unquenchable rebel. During his ten years in English prisons, he had repeatedly attempted to escape, clashed with guards, gone on a hunger strike, and used his skills as a tiler to punch holes in ceilings and stage rooftop protests, earning the nickname the "catman of Brixton." He was routinely banished to solitary confinement and shunted around different prisons, a process known as "ghosting."

For republicans, the *Andersonstown News* article was a heartbreaking chronicle of resistance and English vindictiveness. Six weeks later, on September 17, 1983, a guest checked into the Imperial Hotel in Blackpool under the name Mr. R. Walshe. It might have been Magee. If so, it was a remarkable act of bravado or recklessness, since just five months earlier he had been under surveillance in Blackpool. Whoever it was, the purpose was to test Margaret Thatcher's security in advance of her stay at the hotel in October for the Conservative Party's one-hundredth conference.

The guest calling himself R. Walshe checked out after one night, his research apparently complete. No bomb was planted. The England Department had the timers and technology to attempt an assassination in Blackpool, but it decided to wait. This was, after all, a long war. Success hinged on the bomb being the right size, in the right place, detonating at the right time. A lot could go wrong. And for this operation there could be no margin for error, no Paddy Factor. A chink had been found in Thatcher's security. There would be one, and only one, chance to pierce it. So the organization used Blackpool as a rehearsal.

The IRA would strike the following year, at Brighton.

CHAPTER TEN

Salcey Forest

Wednesday, October 26, 1983, two weeks after the Tory conference at Blackpool, was a crisp, clear day in the woodland around Pangbourne, a village west of London. It was raking season. Leaves carpeted the grounds of country estates, a great brown and yellow quilt that crunched underfoot. A forestry worker's rake snagged on something that turned out to be a dustbin lid, coated in soil. The worker lifted the lid, revealing a concealed bin buried up to its neck, crammed with bags. Just like that, autumnal sunlight streamed into one of the England Department's most precious secrets.

To avert police seizures, Owen Coogan and Michael Hayes had ordered their operators to bury weapons in the countryside, resulting in this cache in the heart of Berkshire, thirty miles south of Chequers. The trove included a submachine gun, two rifles, four handguns, thirty-nine timing devices, sixty-three detonators, and 118 pounds of explosives. A search revealed another bin nearby containing more bomb-making equipment as well as birth certificates and driver's licenses. It was the most comprehensive collection of terrorist equipment and materials ever found in Britain.

The timing was fateful. It was the second anniversary of Ken Howorth's death in the Wimpy basement. His colleagues at the Anti-Terrorist Branch had labored for two years to catch the IRA's England team, with meager results. Peter Gurney compared battling the Provos to an aerial dogfight, the pilots anonymous to each other, and that was the problem. The police needed names and faces. They needed a break. Now they had one.

. . .

THERE HAD BEEN some progress in the previous two years.

After the 1982 park bombings, the Anti-Terrorist Branch had chased every clue—actual or potential—checking shrapnel from dead horses, dredging a lake, searching thousands of premises. All dead ends, save for one long shot: detectives discovered that the car containing the Hyde Park bomb had been in a Knightsbridge car park. They recovered the ticket.

Which meant that David Tadd—Mr. T—had to forget about clattering into opponents on the soccer field for a while. His team worked on the ticket, examining the shapes and contours of fingerprints, counting the ridges in loops, tracing the ridges in whorls. Eventually they found it: sixteen points of similarity with the prints of a suspect on file. His name was John Anthony Downey and he was an IRA operator from County Clare. It was the kind of moment Tadd lived for. "It was all about the chase," he recalled. "There was no better feeling than turning up at the guvnor's door to say 'would you like to know who killed so and so?' or 'who did that incident?' You had that little bit of power for a short while."

Tadd's boss was Commander William Hucklesby. Handsome and debonair, with cropped gray hair and pin-striped suits, Posh Bill, as he was known, filled his office with Regency furniture, oil paintings, and a crystal decanter. But he was a working-class boy who had risen up the ranks the old-fashioned way, catching criminals. Catching terrorists was more complicated. In addition to detective work, it required media appearances and navigating security force rivalries.

The Anti-Terrorist Branch had tetchy relations with its cousins on the eleventh floor—the Special Branch, Scotland Yard's own spy agency. A secretive fiefdom, it used informants and surveillance to spy on terror suspects on the British mainland. In theory, the Special Branch liaised with MI5, which gathered intelligence in Northern Ireland, worked with MI6, which gathered intelligence in the south of Ireland, and funneled the information to Posh Bill's unit, which was tasked with capturing terrorists. In practice, each agency hoarded information to keep an edge in Whitehall's endless bureaucratic jousting for budgets and dominion. "I don't know what they've got; they don't know what I've got; and it's only when you put all the fragments together and start to interpret them and try and understand them that you learn anything," one frustrated spook told the journalist Nick Davies.

Another problem was institutional myopia. The RUC, which fed intelligence from Northern Ireland, grumbled that the Metropolitan Police had "NKIL syndrome"—meaning, not known in London. "If it hasn't happened in London, well, it just hasn't happened," said one RUC officer. The RUC's chief constable, Jack Hermon, was even blunter: "You can always tell a Met man—but not much." The result was that Hucklesby, himself a Met man, was never sure when intelligence nuggets would rattle down from the eleventh floor.

The other complication was jurisdiction. When Tadd bounded into Hucklesby's office to share news of John Downey's identification, it did not result in an arrest. Downey was in the Republic of Ireland, outside the Met's jurisdiction, so Hucklesby passed the fingerprint evidence up the security chain. The Home Office, MI5, the Special Branch, the Ministry of Defence, and the Northern Ireland Office came to the same conclusion: Downey was untouchable. Irish courts seldom extradited IRA suspects, because their offenses were politically motivated. For Ken Howorth's colleagues this was the frustrating reality behind Thatcher's promise to hunt down IRA bombers. They could harvest every scrap of evidence, sieve, dust, fingerprint the whole lot, reenact bombings, interview hundreds of witnesses, chase a thousand leads, identify a suspect, and then come away with nothing.

Ken Howorth, left, and Peter Gurney a short time before an IRA booby trap bomb killed Howorth in the basement of a Wimpy restaurant in London in October 1981. | Peter Gurney

Not that Ken Howorth was forgotten. In August 1983, Peter Gurney had received a medal from the Queen for his bravery at Oxford Street. She had read up on Howorth.

"Did you know him at all?" she asked.

"He was my closest friend for twenty-five years, ma'am," Gurney had replied.

The Queen paused. "But you went in and examined the body . . ." And she froze midsentence, seeming to grasp what he'd experienced.

Two months later came the discovery at Pangbourne.

For five days, Tadd and his team rose at 5:00 a.m., drove to the woodland, and extracted, tagged, and bagged items for examination in the lab and office. "There was so much stuff in those bins. It was a forensic Aladdin's cave," Tadd recalled. It would take months to analyze it all. The Anti-Terrorist Branch had only four scientists and four support staff. Each piece of evidence required painstaking handling, with forensic processes done in the right sequence. It was not just about identifying suspects, it was about obtaining evidence that would stand up in court. Defense lawyers would pounce on any oversight, any divergence from protocol. Might a chemical process have contaminated a fingerprint? When did exhibit B start to rust? Who was in charge of exhibit F during transport from the lab? Tadd and his colleagues operated "cradle to grave" protocols to shepherd evidence from scene to trial, journeys that could take years. "It wasn't about racing to identify suspects," he recalled. "It was about following the process. You didn't want to cock it up."

Even so, within weeks the Pangbourne trove yielded tantalizing results. Material matched microscopic comparisons with debris collected in the aftermath of the 1981 and 1982 bombings: a spool of electrical cord used to detonate the Chelsea Barracks bomb; timers and magnets from the attack on Steuart Pringle; microswitches and detonators similar to those in the bomb that killed Ken Howorth; specialist radio equipment used in the park bombings. And there were fingerprints, lots of them. Tadd's team found matches, giving names and faces to the silhouettes of the IRA's England Department: Patrick "Flash" McVeigh, Paul Kavanagh, Thomas Quigley. A suspected female accomplice was Evelyn Glenholmes. The suspected bomb designer was Dessie Ellis, a Dublin television repairman turned Provo.

"Get some light into these dark places," the home secretary, William Vernon Harcourt, had implored Scotland Yard when the Fenians were bombing London in the 1880s. A century later, dogged detective work and forensics were illuminating one of the IRA's most inner sanctums. Even without extradition, the information gleamed with possibilities. There were other ways for the police and security services to reach out and grasp the bombers.

. . .

THE OPERATORS UNMASKED by Tadd's team were on the England Department's roster of potential candidates to assassinate Margaret Thatcher. Each had proven his or her worth in the field.

Kavanagh and Quigley were an especially effective partnership, perhaps because they had plenty in common: both twenty-six, from Belfast, each with a brother killed by security forces. They had graduated from the mayhem of 1970s Belfast to the 1981 England campaign.

Glenholmes, also twenty-six and from Belfast, was republican royalty: the daughter of Richard "Dickie" Glenholmes, a veteran operator who was in prison. Petite, with long wavy brown hair, she confounded stereotypes of what a terrorist should look like.

John Downey, age thirty-one, had grown up in County Clare steeped in family lore about fighting the Black and Tans. He was soft-spoken, with an easy charm that allayed suspicion.

There were a handful of other trusted operators with experience in England. All had crossed the water and returned undetected. All had skills required for the IRA's most audacious operation. None had bolted home in panic after imagining police surveillance.

But one by one, the England Department began losing candidates for Lochinvar. The first to be crossed out was Downey. Scotland Yard detectives "blew" him in the press, giving his name, age, description, and alleged crime. It was a tacit admission that he was unreachable—but also an unsubtle message to the IRA that Downey had been identified and was now a "red light," too high profile to use in further attacks.

On December 2, 1983, Tommy Quigley, apparently homesick, crossed the border to visit Belfast. He knew the RUC kept tabs on him, but did not know the Pangbourne cache had been discovered and mined for evidence, and thought he was safe. Alighting from a taxi, he was swarmed by police officers, bundled on a plane across the Irish Sea, and delivered to Paddington Green, a police fortress in West London.

Quigley's comrade Kavanagh, on the other hand, was also back in the imperialist capital, but roaming free, undetected, and planning a new campaign. While counting down to the next Tory conference, the England Department needed other operations to sustain morale and show the Brits it was business as usual. Kavanagh was paired with another Belfast volunteer, John Connolly, twenty-nine. They smuggled weapons in a trawler, found a safe house, bought two cars, and counted the days to the festive season. If all went well, they might be tapped for Lochinvar.

. . .

ON THE AFTERNOON of December 17, the last Saturday before Christmas, shoppers with parcels and bags jammed West London's department stores. Christmas trees glowed with fairy lights. Electronic Santa Clauses nodded from window displays. "White Christmas" and an a cappella cover version of "Only You" seeped from department store speakers.

Margaret Thatcher had spent the morning at Chequers discussing outfits with Daphne Scrimgeour and was on her way back to London. David Tadd was playing for his beloved Nomads FC, his mind cleared of whorls, focused only on parting opposition players from the ball. Peter Gurney was driving home with reason to smile. *Nail the bastards*, he had seethed after Ken's death—and with the capture of Thomas Quigley, it had partially come to pass.

Gurney caught the alert on the car radio: an explosion outside Harrods. Tadd learned something was up when his wife appeared by the soccer field, gesticulating. Officials notified Thatcher during a carol concert at the Royal Festival Hall. All headed to the scene to perform very different functions.

Glass shards coated the streets around Harrods like ice, tinkling underfoot. Shopping bags lay in the gutters, spilling wrapped gifts. The dusk was drenched in sweetness, as the blast had obliterated the perfume counters. And, for the police, other, more familiar aromas: burned oil, explosives, burned flesh. The bomb had been in a blue Austin parked on the street. The IRA warning had been confusing and gave little time. Police were evacuating crowds when the fireball erupted, sending a black cloud of smoke boiling into the sky high above the Edwardian facade. Six people died—three police officers, a reporter, a US tourist, a young mother. More than ninety were injured. It was the bloodiest attack on London since the park bombings.

Gurney at first mistook the young mother for a mannequin. She had been blown through a plate-glass window and lay broken upon gaily colored wreckage. Her skirt had been blown off and she had underpants adorned with a heart that embraced the message: *I love you.* Gurney's detachment, for the second time in his career, faltered. Instead of seeing her as a clue to the bomb, as the job demanded, he saw her as a person. *Who had she been, this girl? Who had she loved, and who had loved her?* That night, at home, he wept.

While his team combed debris for prints, Tadd stood back and surveyed the scene, re-creating in his mind the sequence of events and planning his strategy for what would be a huge investigation. "It was pretty grim. A mess. My lasting memory is a car on top of a police sergeant," he recalled. The arm, with three stripes, pointed straight up into the air, as if reaching out for help.

Thatcher, too, crunched over the debris and saw the charred bodies. Later that night, she visited the wounded in the hospital. The attack, she said, was a crime against humanity. "It's difficult to understand the minds of people who can do that. There are very evil people in our society, and we have to do everything we can to catch them."

It partially inspired the composer Andrew Lloyd Webber, a friend of one of the victims, to write his most austere work, *Requiem*. When Harrods reopened two days later, shoppers flocked in solidarity, among them Denis Thatcher. He emerged with two bulging packages and blunt defiance. "No damned Irishman is going to stop me going there."

. . .

ON DECEMBER 23, the prime minister made a surprise visit to Northern Ireland. The initiative was code-named Operation Abercorn, and she traveled by armored car and helicopter, with a medical team on standby. She visited a military barracks and a border post, met police widows, and did a walkabout in Newtownards, a unionist town east of Belfast, eliciting cheers. One well-wisher, Mary Miller, told Thatcher not to worry about security: "I told her she's as safe as a row of houses down here and couldn't have come to a better spot."

Thatcher echoed her husband's defiance, albeit in more prime ministerial language. "I want the people of Northern Ireland to know that they will remain part of the United Kingdom as long as the population here wishes. . . . We're never, never going to be defeated by bombs and bullets. Not here or anywhere else in the world. We believe in certain things very strongly. We believe in our way of life. We're determined to keep it."

A week later, the year ebbed to a close and it became 1984, a year George Orwell had made synonymous with surveillance, propaganda, and fear. For the Anti-Terrorist Branch, Christmas had been effectively canceled. The prime minister's words from Harrods hung over the unit. *Do everything we can to catch them.* The investigation racked up 895 telexes, 3,060 phone messages, 2,600 witness statements, and 5,577 police actions. All done without a computer. The paper filing system collapsed under the strain of trying to collate and cross-reference the avalanche of information. Scientists and technicians worked full speed to process seven dumpsters and 282 garbage cans of debris taken from the scene. When they asked for more resources, all they got was encouragement.

Tadd, already busy preparing a formal evidential package for Quigley's impending committal trial hearing, was yet again glad to have a team "willing to work stupidly long hours." "Years later, police briefed journalists that John Connolly and Paul Kavanagh were prime suspects in the Harrods bombing, but nobody was ever charged or convicted of the attack."

Halfway through January came one of those lucky breaks that policemen dream about. It was not the result of chasing down leads and forensic examination, of the mundane, grinding routines that comprise 99 percent of police work. The IRA simply made a mistake.

A second mistake, that is. Harrods was the first. It was supposed to be a commercial hit—blast the hell out of the store, disrupt retail, frighten Londoners, a splash for *An Phoblacht/Republican News*, no need for corpses. The bungled warning made the Provos look like butchers and violated an unwritten rule: don't kill Americans. Thatcher seized the opportunity to assail NORAID's US fundraising.

The IRA's statement claiming responsibility for the attack was unusually contrite and attempted to absolve the Army Council leadership by tacitly blaming rogue England Department operators: "The Harrods operation was not authorized by the Irish Republican Army. We have taken immediate steps to ensure that there will be no repetition of this type of operation again." Some suspected the remorse was feigned and that the Provos' private calculus weighed any temporary reduction in the flow of dollars from US sympathizers against the value of hitting a prestige target.

Still, Owen Coogan and Michael Hayes had to answer for their operators in the field. Someone needed to cross the water to debrief the England Department on what had happened and to check on arms dumps. Coogan and Hayes were under regular Garda surveillance, so they dispatched a lower profile comrade, Natalino Vella, who handled Provo logistics in Dublin.

That was the second mistake. The Gardaí were also watching Vella. They told Scotland Yard's Special Branch to expect him on a flight into Heathrow on Sunday, January 15. A tall man of Italian heritage traveling with his wife, Vella, age thirty, was not hard to spot among the disembarking passengers. The couple collected their luggage and took the Tube into Central London. Eyes followed them, every step.

Special Branch surveillance specialists were not invisible, simply not memorable. They were selected according to a Goldilocks test: not too tall or small, not too attractive or plain, preferably medium height, medium build, utterly ordinary looking. They had to be able to think on their feet, know when to get close or keep distance, when to stroll, trot, dawdle, stop, browse in a window, enter a phone box, light a cigarette, change appearance. Above all, like Hollywood extras, they had to blend in to match the setting.

Vella was an easy mark, a backroom supplies guy, not a frontline operator. Oblivious to his shadows, Vella and his wife did some shopping and spent the night at a hotel in Earls Court. Vella emerged the next day around midday. He wore purple, police learned later, so that his contact, who did not know him, could identify him. Vella traveled five miles across town to Swiss Cottage. At 2:15 p.m. he entered the public library and there met a short, stocky man with fair hair. They strolled around the block, talking. They parted and Vella spent another night at his hotel. At 7:00 a.m. the next day, Vella took a train to Northampton, a market town seventy miles north of London. Surveillance men boarded the train, while others sped up the motorway to Northampton, racing to arrive first.

In the station buffet, Vella met the stocky man from the day before plus another man. It was 9:20 a.m. The watchers' long-lens cameras clicked. In the car park, the IRA suspects joined a fourth man at the wheel of a white Rover and drove off.

Following them were seventeen plainclothes officers in at least six unmarked cars, plus on motorcycles. The Special Branch was pulling out all the stops. Scotland Yard's most secret unit, originally established to combat Fenian terrorism, was on the cusp of glory. The stocky man was Paul Kavanagh, co-architect of the IRA's 1981 campaign. Also in the Rover was John Connolly, Kavanagh's partner in the recent Harrods attack. The UK's most wanted terrorists, plus Vella and another suspect, dangled within reach, ripe for the plucking.

The watchers, however, did not recognize Kavanagh or Connolly. Like their counterparts in Lancashire the previous year, they planned to observe, not arrest. The Anti-Terrorist Branch would almost certainly have identified Kavanagh, and perhaps Connolly, but none of Posh Bill's men were in Northampton. They were at headquarters, piecing together clues from Harrods, unaware their eleventh-floor colleagues were out on a surveillance operation. Special Branch was flying solo.

The Rover left the motorway and began classic countersurveillance measures, zigzagging across the countryside, speeding up, slowing down, stopping, doubling back. Alternating lead vehicles, the watchers hung back and kept eyes on the target. Windows misted up; it was freezing, the roads icy, the landscape coated in frost. Eight miles south of Northampton, and east of a village called Hartwell, the Rover halted at a rest stop. Two of the four occupants—Kavanagh and Vella—got out and trekked into woodland.

They had reached Salcey Forest, the remnant of a royal hunting forest. Some of the oaks dated back to Henry VI and his unsuccessful attempts to tame Ulster. The men returned to the Rover, which then zigzagged north to another stop in Annesley Forest, where again Kavanagh and Vella disappeared into woodland. The Rover returned to the M1 motorway and veered back onto country roads. Outside the village of Belper, a milk tanker pulled out between the IRA men and the lead surveillance car. Unable to overtake the truck, it lost sight of the target. The Rover vanished.

The IRA's blunder in dispatching Vella to England turned into a debacle for police. After Kavanagh was belatedly identified from photographs, Posh Bill's team tore strips off the Special Branch. "They hadn't got the faintest idea what they were doing," one source briefed a journalist. "They were trying to score points off the Anti-Terrorist Squad by going it alone. It was bloody amazing."

Returning to the woodlands to retrace the IRA men's steps, however, yielded compensation. Detectives discovered bins buried in the frozen earth of Salcey and Annesley Forests. David Tadd was in the middle of building a new kitchen in his house when he got the order to go. It looked like a building site, with wires dangling from the ceiling and cupboards. He exchanged looks with his wife. "Don't rip them out," he said. "And don't touch them." Rembrandt could have painted her expression as he drove away, not to return for a week. "She still talks about it," he said decades later.

Fresh snow covered the forests. Peter Gurney, wearing boots and fire-resistant overalls, went first, probing the soil at each site. Having established there were no booby traps, he watched with grim satisfaction as the contents were extracted and laid on a white sheet: grenades, handguns, submachine guns, Armalite ammunition, mercury tilt switches, radio transmitter receivers. Stuffed inside a pipe, looking deceptively innocuous, were six long-delay timers. Gurney noted they had been set to twenty-four days, six hours, and thirty-six minutes. The timers had markings with small numbers and letters. Two timers were bound together with tape, obscuring the markings. The others, Gurney noted, were 5L, 53E, 35E, 63E. "I assumed they had been tested and the 5L was 'five minutes late' and the 63E was 'sixty-three minutes early,' and so on," he recalled. The IRA had gone to a lot of trouble to produce long-delay timers with exact precision.

Seven weeks later, in the middle of March, Paul Kavanagh repeated Quigley's mistake. Unaware that his prints had been found at the Pangbourne dump, he crossed the border into Northern Ireland to visit his native Belfast. He wanted to see friends and family, and there might have been another lure: he was in love with a fellow volunteer, a former beauty contestant from Derry named Martina Anderson. The

RUC spotted and arrested him. The England Department thus lost another potential knight for Lochinvar. Kavanagh was flown to London and joined Quigley in the dock for murdering Ken Howorth and two civilians in 1981.

Peter Gurney had reason to celebrate. But a detail from the Salcey Forest trove nagged the bomb burglar. The six long-delay timers were numbered 1 to 7. Number 4 was missing.

CHAPTER ELEVEN

Tightrope

On the bright, cold afternoon of March 14, 1984, shortly before the clocks struck one, the only person on earth with both the authority and the motive to halt the assassination attempt against Margaret Thatcher sat on an uncomfortable wooden bench in Belfast's magistrate court. Gerry Adams was a member of the Army Council and the Army Council knew of the plot. Adams had a compelling reason to oppose the plot—it potentially imperiled his political strategy—but saving the prime minister did not preoccupy him at that moment. He was worrying about his own possible appointment with the Grim Reaper. Years later he recalled the prickle of anxiety. "I was unsettled, a familiar feeling, an old friend coming back to warn me of impending danger," he recalled.

Fifteen years into the Troubles, the only reason the Sinn Féin leader still breathed while so many others lay cold in their graves was because he possessed a mix of guile and luck. Loyalist paramilitaries wanted him dead, and he believed the police and army also yearned to see him lowered into the black void at Milltown Cemetery, another martyr to rot beneath a headstone. He had lived in the crosshairs almost his entire adult life. "Gerry Adams will be next," the Ulster Volunteer Force said in 1981 after shooting James "Skipper" Burns, an Adams lieutenant. Visions of his demise included immolation in the bomb— never planted—at the 1981 Sinn Féin Ard Fheis. The Ulster Defence Association magazine ran a "wanted" picture of Adams, Wild West– style. He received bullets in the mail and multiple threats. In 1983, Adams publicly showed a letter purportedly from a policeman's father promising vengeance if his son died. "Do not depend on Monaghan's hoods to save you, they will be useless against the violence I will bring upon you—no matter where you are."

Weeks before this court hearing, the recently elected MP had told reporters he believed there was a 90 percent chance he would be killed. "I have been involved in republican politics a long time and if it happens, it happens. I am fearful I may be assassinated at any time." Adams was unarmed—authorities had rejected his gun permit application—but took precautions. He varied his routes and lodgings, always carrying a toothbrush, since he couldn't be sure where he would be sleeping. He mostly kept to his West Belfast enclave and had not set foot in the city center, just two miles away, in years. He preferred that journalists came to him for interviews held in fortified offices.

And yet here he was in the magistrate's court on Chichester Street, a neoclassical edifice of Corinthian columns a few blocks from city hall, and everyone knew it. He and two Sinn Féin colleagues, Sean Keenan and Bob Murray, had been summoned on a minor charge linked to flying an Irish tricolor during an election cavalcade the previous June. Now Adams sat in court under the gaze of Magistrate Tom Travers. Mutual contempt probably simmered between Travers, a middle-class Catholic from South Belfast who upheld state laws, and Adams, who regarded such people as Crown collaborators.

Soon after midday, Travers adjourned the case for lunch. Security mandated that everyone had to leave the building—which presented a dilemma. The case had been widely reported. Adams's enemies, for once, knew his location and his schedule. The IRA was refining a plan to kill Britain's prime minister based entirely on such foreknowledge. Adams scanned the smattering of people in the public gallery. They gazed back blankly. Any one of them might be a loyalist snoop.

"In the enemy territory of the court building, surrounded and hemmed in, I was bound to be nervous," he recalled. "But this was more than that. My antenna had never let me down before. It was practically screaming 'Danger! Danger!' at me. And yet there was no obvious sign of danger in sight."

Adams asked for permission to remain in court during the break, but Travers said no. The three defendants plus Joe Keenan, a colleague, left the courtroom and lingered in the big hall. Adams eyed the dwindling throngs of people who swept past them on their way out. By 1:00 p.m., it was just the four republicans plus a handful of court officials and RUC men. At 1:20 p.m. they beetled out. Gray skies coated Belfast. Adams, as always, stood out, tall and relatively formal in a woolly sweater, slacks, tweed jacket, and tie, compared to his companions' jeans and windbreakers. They looked left and right. A trundle of traffic, a few parked cars, nothing suspicious.

They strode to a waiting gold-colored Cortina driven by a friend, Kevin Rooney. Adams took the front passenger seat. The Cortina merged into traffic on Chichester Street, named after a suppressor of rebellious Gaels in the seventeenth century, and took a right on Oxford Street. Skirting the River Lagan, Rooney took a right on May Street, bordering the Market area where Patrick Magee had grown up. It was now a straight shot west through the city center. The occupants began to relax. Adams reassured himself they were invisible in the lanes of slow-moving cars, and lunch promised to be tasty: fish and chips at Long's, a fast-food joint.

A few hundred yards behind them, a brown Rover 2000 began to edge through the traffic. It was 1:25 p.m.

"Who's paying for the grub?" Sean Keenan asked.

"I'll pay," said Rooney.

. . .

PASSING THE GREEN dome of city hall, Adams could reflect on how far he had come. Five years earlier, after Mountbatten's execution, Thatcher had stood under that dome and condemned him and other Provos as a handful of evildoers. "If we do not defeat the terrorists then democracy is dead," she had said. But then the Iron Lady had ignored the heckler's warning about the H-Blocks, and everything changed. Sinn Féin rode the hunger strike to electoral breakthrough. Adams and Martin McGuinness won seats in a 1982 Northern Ireland assembly election, and Adams was now also a Westminster MP and president of Sinn Féin, having finally dethroned Ruairi Ó Brádaigh. He was thirty-six.

Britain's tabloids depicted him as a blood-spattered gangster, but in writings and media interviews he was cultivating a softer public image. A 1982 memoir, *Falls Memories*, appeared to have been written not by a guerrilla commander but a community elder. "This persona was presented as wise and well-grounded, civilized and gentle, the feminist man who loves children, the natural democrat," noted a biographer, Malachi O'Doherty. "Though in his mid-thirties, he aspired to being a model of the experience of his community, to be known more for wisdom than anger, a man with organic links to West Belfast who presented basic republican principles as self-evident, at least in his own wise old young head." Confronted with hostile interviewers, Adams projected unflappable reasonableness even when justifying IRA killings. "He pits himself against the broadcaster as a confident and intellectual equal, or superior. . . . This is the sort of combat that suits him," noted O'Doherty.

This had been the Adams on display when left-wing radicals in Britain's opposition Labour Party invited the new MP to London in summer 1983. Enjoying Tory apoplexy, the radicals had invited him back in October for the party's conference. It was in Brighton. Labour's leadership abhorred Adams, so he addressed not the main conference but a nearby gathering of socialists, republican sympathizers, and members of the Troops Out Movement, a coalition of mostly left-wing British activists that favored a British military withdrawal from Northern Ireland. Stooped over a low microphone, Adams framed IRA violence as a working-class-led campaign for self-determination. "The struggle for socialism in Britain will never succeed while the British government denies Irish people their basic rights," he said. The audience nodded and applauded.

A question from the floor threatened to ruin the mood of solidarity. "Do you personally," asked an audience member, "ever have specific knowledge of military acts by the IRA?"

The words hung in the air, accusing, like those of an Old Bailey prosecutor. The Grand Hotel was half a mile away. The IRA had scouted it the previous year, during the 1982 Conservative conference. An IRA scout had recently checked into the Tories' hotel in Blackpool. The Provos were planning to murder Margaret Thatcher.

Adams did not flinch. He leaned into the microphone. "No," he said.

A ripple rolled across the audience. Relief? Disbelief? Both. Sinn Féin's leader leaned back, eyes flicking across the hall. "Never showed his hand, you always wondered what was going on in that little mind," his old school principal had said.

Adams left Brighton with new British friends. But any hope of a Sinn Féin alliance with the British left was shattered two months later in the horror of the Harrods bombing, notwithstanding Adams expressing regret for the civilian casualties. The atrocity exposed the contradiction in the "Armalite and ballot box" strategy. At some point, political and military imperatives diverged. What then?

The answer was unclear. The British were entrenched—a fact stenciled into the streetscape Adams and his companions passed on their way to lunch. Bedford Street, Queen Street, Brunswick Street—names rooted in Englishness and royalty. After independence, Dublin had renamed its own Brunswick Street after Patrick Pearse, a martyred leader of the 1916 Rising. "Ireland unfree shall never be at peace,"

Pearse wrote. Adams had signed up to a war that would be long, but had he signed up for an eternal struggle?

The brown Rover 2000 edged through traffic, closer to the Cortina.

Of the many strategic questions facing Adams in spring 1984, the most urgent, were he in the loop about Operation Lochinvar, was this: Would killing Margaret Thatcher bring victory closer? It would be popular. Christ, the cheers from West Belfast would echo down the ages. And then what? Probably a Brit backlash off the scales. A merciless pursuit of the IRA and the banning of Sinn Féin. Once the whirlwind slackened, might the Brits, disgusted with the whole place, simply withdraw? Adams must have known that was a fantasy. And even if they did withdraw, Northern Ireland was not like Kenya or other abandoned outposts of empire. A million Protestants would fight to keep Brunswick Street and everything else British, paving full-scale sectarian civil war. The Provos might inherit, in the words of the poet, a terrible beauty. Killing Thatcher would transform the conflict, yes, but not necessarily to republican advantage.

The brown Rover 2000 accelerated through a red light, drawing even closer. It was 1:27 p.m.

Heading back to his fiefdom, Adams had reason to ponder threats closer to home. He had served on the Army Council and the Belfast Brigade for over a decade. At one point, he had been chief of staff. Upon becoming MP, he had stood down from direct military roles. It was Provo protocol—being a public figure was incompatible with planning operations. Adams did, however, remain on the seven-member Army Council, which directed overall strategy and appointed a chief of staff, who ran GHQ, which supervised different departments, including the England Department.

So the big lad, as some still called him, walked the tightrope. On one side were the "Shinners," who ran elections and advice centers; on the other, the "army." From a peak of about one thousand in the 1970s, the number of active operators had shrunk to about 250. Since volunteers received a pittance wage, if any, the IRA was cheap to run, just

£2,500 a week to finance the Belfast Brigade. But Sinn Féin's political ambitions swallowed ever more funding, £1 million alone for the 1983 election.

More elections loomed, including a council by-election in Dungannon, a market town in County Tyrone where the local IRA had a particularly fearsome reputation. Adams had recently visited to support the almost surreal candidacy of Peter Sherry. A Provo commander known as the Armalite Kid, Sherry courted votes on the promise of delivering bus shelters and fixing safety hazards.

The militarists were restless. Belfast, once the cockpit of the struggle, accounted for just eleven of the IRA's ninety-five kills in 1983 and 1984. Adams appeared to be curbing operations in his constituency. Dissent stirred. On the eve of the June 1983 general election, an IRA unit had detonated a huge bomb by a police station in the heart of West Belfast, damaging homes and angering potential Adams voters. Adams was said to have shaken his fist when he saw the unit driving back.

Adams liked comparisons with Michael Collins except for the part where erstwhile comrades shot him dead. Though a remote prospect in spring 1984, Adams had acquired a dangerous, powerful rival. Ivor Bell, a former ally from Long Kesh days, suspected that Adams was running down the war effort. Bell was in charge of sourcing weapons— he was liaising with the Libyans and overseeing a shipment from Boston—and also sat on the Army Council, where on occasion he could muster a 4–3 majority against Adams. A series of bungled kidnappings— the targets were business tycoons and a racehorse called Shergar—had undermined Bell's authority, but he remained a threat.

And Adams knew it.

. . .

AT 1:29 P.M., the Cortina paused in traffic at the junction at Fisherwick Place. The Rover drew level. Windows rolled down, inside it three men, eyes locked on Adams and his companions. Once the vehicle was parallel, the Rover's passengers aimed pistols, a .45 Colt and a Walther P38, and opened fire. The Cortina's windows exploded. Adams at first did not realize what was happening, and everything seemed to unfold slowly. "I felt the thumps and thuds as the bullets struck home. The crack of gunfire came after."

"Hit the deck!" yelled Murray. Joe Keenan was screaming. Glass and upholstery exploded and splintered.

Adams mouthed a childhood prayer. *Jesus, Mary, and Joseph, I give you my heart and my soul. Jesus, Mary, and Joseph, assist me in my last agony. Jesus, Mary, and Joseph, may I raise forth my soul in peace with you. Amen.*

Four bullets pierced his body, one in the back of the neck, one in the left shoulder, two in the upper left arm. Gunfire raked the other occupants, save for Murray, who was subsequently nicknamed "Hit-the-deck."

The shooting stopped as abruptly as it had started. The hit squad raced away. The Cortina slowed to a crawl. "Keep driving!" Adams screamed at Rooney. Though wounded, he did so.

"Are you okay?" Adams asked.

"Yes," Rooney said.

"Go straight to the Royal."

Rooney wove through traffic, jumping red lights. Murray asked Adams if he was hit. "Yes, a couple of times, but I'm okay," he replied. Adams crouched down and recited an Act of Contrition to Sean Keenan, who stared back silently, blood pouring from his face. Catholics are advised to do this for those who are near death and cannot repent unaided.

Rooney, also bleeding, made it to the Royal Victoria Hospital, a mile away. Murray ran into the emergency department shouting that four men outside had been shot. Medical teams scrambled to the car.

Adams, fighting to retain consciousness, was put on a trolley and given a chest drain. One bullet had come within millimeters of his spine. Another just missed his heart. His spirit remained intact: when his wife, Colette, and a journalist named Eamonn Mallie arrived, he argued with police to let them into his room. Before police had confirmed the shooting, even before surgeons removed three bullets, he was giving an interview.

All four casualties survived. The UDA—using its cover name, the Ulster Freedom Fighters—claimed responsibility, saying Adams was an IRA leader and a legitimate target. British soldiers in civilian clothes intercepted the would-be assassins a few blocks from the shooting, prompting rival theories. Adams said the British knew of the pending attack and hovered for posthumous law enforcement. "They let it take place as it happened and then arrested those involved. I think it was a miraculous escape for all of us." Loyalists said the soldiers were shadowing the Sinn Féin leader to protect him. Authorities said the soldiers were there by chance and simply reacted to what they witnessed.

Beyond republican circles, few wept for Adams's wounds. "It's the natural order that you reap what you sow," said Ian Paisley, leader of the Democratic Unionist Party.

. . .

THREE WEEKS LATER, Magistrate Tom Travers, who had presided over Adams's court case, attended Sunday mass at St. Brigid's church near his home in South Belfast. An owlish man with wavy gray hair and thick glasses, he was accompanied by his wife, Joan, and their daughter, Mary, a twenty-two-year-old teacher.

When the Travers family emerged from the church, two IRA gunmen approached. They shot the magistrate six times and his daughter once. They attempted to shoot his wife, but the gun jammed. Tom Travers survived. His daughter died. "Mary lay dying on her mum's breast," he later recalled, "her gentle heart pouring its pure blood onto a dusty street in Belfast."

. . .

ADAMS WAS CONVALESCING near Buncrana, a seaside town in County Donegal, a few miles from the border, and apparently had no advance knowledge of the attack on the Traverses. Nor did he know that he was being slowly poisoned. The surgeons had missed a fourth bullet lodged in his upper arm. When it swelled and caused agonizing pain, he was told it was shrapnel and tweed from his jacket making their way to the surface of the skin. In fact, it was a .45-millimeter bullet slowly traveling around his arm, occasionally hitting bone. Its copper jacket had fractured, and lead was seeping into Adams's bloodstream. When a surgeon belatedly detected and removed the bullet, the infection emitted an odious stench.

Donegal, with its beaches, cliffs, pubs, and remote villages, was a mecca for republicans needing a time-out from the six counties. It was also a favorite location for the Army Council. It met irregularly and in different locations throughout Ireland, but Donegal's convenience was hard to beat. The venue and date of the meeting that conducted a final review of Operation Lochinvar remains secret. Nor is there a known record of what was said. This much can be guessed: it took place in spring or early summer and presented Adams—if informed—with a complicated calculus.

The chief of staff, Kevin McKenna, a gruff, monosyllabic character from a County Tyrone farming family, would have been tasked with reiterating the England Department's plan. Scouts, he probably reminded his listeners, had surveilled the Tories in Brighton in 1982 and at Blackpool in 1983. They had observed the police protocols, the conference schedule, the hotel room assignments, and Thatcher's habits. "We knew she would be doing her speech, she had a habit of writing at nighttime, and we knew that she would have a window open looking out onto the beach," recalled Michael Hayes.

There was something else. The England Department had dispatched a construction engineer to study the Grand Hotel. He had noted the mix of Sussex bricks and wrought iron, the use of Yorkstone (a sandstone), Portland stone (a limestone), and load-bearing walls embedded with granite rocks. "We established that it was granite. We understood that with a certain amount of explosives gone up under a room, it would bring down the roof," said Hayes.

The England Department had done its homework. This was a one-off opportunity. After Brighton, the Brits would doubtless tighten security for future conferences. The IRA would never again have such a chance. The Army Council would surely have had questions, and a discussion, but not necessarily a vote. It preferred to reach decisions by consensus. Some members worried killing Thatcher would leave them forever hunted—prey for the British agents and Special Air Service squads tasked with finding and possibly executing them. "Shot while resisting arrest," as the official report would put it.

Of course, there were even worse fates. Leaders of the 1605 Gunpowder Plot were hanged, cut down while still conscious, castrated, disemboweled, and quartered, with their heads put on spikes outside the House of Lords. And their bomb didn't even go off.

But if the IRA's bomb exploded, if the operation succeeded, the reward would be incalculable: Maggie Thatcher, dead beneath a thousand tons of rubble. The British state punished for its crimes. The hunger strikers avenged. The world's gaze fixed on the six counties. Ballads and poems about the men who dared.

Strategic reflection was not a Provo forte. For over a decade—since Roy Walsh's 1973 mission to London—they had taken the war to England, slaughtering soldiers, police, public figures, and civilians, in hope the Brits would eventually say, "Enough, take your six counties and sod off." But it wasn't working. The British had little love for Northern Ireland or its Union Jack–waving Protestants, but showed no sign of bowing to the IRA. Even so, the Provo instinct was to keep bombing.

Adams, however, was quietly eyeing another path. He had sold electoral politics to the IRA on the promise it would complement the armed struggle. In June 1984 came a setback: his ally Danny Morrison, who had articulated the ballot box and Armalite dualism, lost a European Parliament election to John Hume, leader of the SDLP, the moderate nationalist party that rejected IRA violence. Shepherding republicans to pure politics would be a rocky, treacherous trail. Still, as 1984 progressed, Adams was contemplating using electoral politics to replace the armed struggle—which was republican heresy. In the privacy of a monastery off the Falls Road, Adams was discussing alternatives to violence with a Belfast priest, Alec Reid, who had contacts in the Irish and British governments. The conversations were exploratory, speculative, and secret. Adams did not even tell the Army Council.

All of which—were he included in the meeting about Lochinvar—begged the question: To murder, or not to murder, Margaret Thatcher? A bomb in Brighton might bury not just the prime minister but any chance of negotiations. Alternatively, in the Rubik's Cube of possibilities, might her successor, after requisite acts of vengeance, prove more flexible? The Americans, after all, had pulled their marines from peacekeeping duties in Lebanon after bombers killed 241 US service personnel in October 1983.

Adams alone would have had both a rationale and the authority to veto the plot. He could cite any number of compelling-sounding strategic reasons to the Army Council, playing on their individual fears, and probably prevail. But the whisper would escape, a genie from the bottle, that it was Gerry Adams who lacked the guts to go after Thatcher. A poison would enter the republican bloodstream, infecting his credibility and authority. Adams would become vulnerable to Ivor Bell and the others who wanted him out.

Lochinvar was a roll of the dice. The bomber might be caught planting the device. The bomb might be discovered. It might explode at the wrong time, or not at all. Thatcher could live, die, be maimed. In the calculus of possibilities, there were two certainties. First: the attack would placate the militarists. Second: while the IRA remained in the killing business, better to do it in England, where Sinn Féin was not seeking votes.

Word filtered back to the England Department: proceed.

——————

CHAPTER TWELVE

Room 629

Shortly before midday on September 15, 1984, a British Rail train emerged from the Sussex countryside and chugged to a halt at Brighton station. The doors hissed open. Patrick Magee, smartly dressed, stepped onto the platform and inhaled a familiar tang of sea air. Gripping a suitcase, he joined the throng heading for the exit gate. Gulls liked to perch on carriages to monitor disembarking passengers in hope of a stray sandwich, but there were no human sentinels scrutinizing the arrivals, no Special Branch surveillance cameras clicking. The Chancer was in the clear.

Magee walked to the taxi stand behind the station café, the layout unchanged since his visit in 1979 to surveil the Labour Party Conference. He asked to be dropped at the Grand Hotel. The driver, an exuberant man named Dennis Palmer, did not get much chat from his fare as they cruised down the hill to Queen's Road past stores filled with Cornish fudge, plastic sunglasses, and I LOVE BRIGHTON T-shirts. Newspaper posters blared the big news: Princess Diana was in labor. Bookies were slashing odds on the baby, if a boy, being named George.

It was a Saturday and day-trippers had colonized Brighton. Sunshine pierced the clouds in valediction of summer. People peeled off their jackets and lounged outside pubs, clutching pints of lager. It was derby day: Brighton's soccer team, Albion, was hosting its fellow second division rivals, Crystal Palace, from London. A grudge match—and there was a history of ructions between the fans.

Halfway down the hill, around the clock tower where Queen's Road became West Street, Magee could glimpse the blue-gray water of the English Channel.

The cab turned right on King's Road, a busy thoroughfare with four lanes of traffic. The promenade ran alongside it, wide, paved, sticky with gum, an esplanade for joggers, dog walkers, couples, families. Steps led to a lower promenade at shore level: a grittier affair of pubs and public toilets. The Palace Pier, a 1,700-foot-long landmark with iron pillars, jutted over the water, a jumble of carnival rides and arcades. Farther down the promenade, the West Pier lay silent and derelict. Deck chairs faced France, which lay invisible over the horizon. The tide was coming in, the swash clacking pebbles on the beach. It was virtually all shingle, not sand, and the current had a habit of sweeping away unwary swimmers. The taxi passed a gray concrete hulk resembling a lunar fortress: a conference center in the 1970s brutalist style. It won no beauty contests, but its size and convenience enticed gatherings to the seafront year-round.

Towering over the center, separated by just a few feet and a century of aesthetic values, all creamy and white and stately, was the Grand. After 120 years, the name remained apt. An eight-story monument to Victorian engineering and adornment, the hotel was an immensity of brick, stone, and wrought iron topped by chimney stacks. A Union Jack fluttered from the roof.

The hotel looked out to the sea, oblivious to its squat neighbor. But the grand old lady, as some called it, relied on the center for trade. Soon the center would host the Conservative Party and most of the Grand's 178 rooms would fill with Tories. Its cheaper rooms faced north, toward town. VIPs got sea views.

Palmer pulled Magee's suitcase from the trunk. It was heavy, and he grinned as he passed it to a slightly built uniformed doorman. "You'd better hold on to your nuts for this one, you'll need 'em." Magee paid his fare in cash, climbed the four steps to the entrance, and pushed through the revolving door. And then the Chancer glided into the Grand's foyer with a wallet full of cash, an English accent, and a request for a sea-facing room.

.   .   .

IT WAS QUITE the comeback. A year earlier, the IRA had sidelined him in Dublin on suspicion of panicking in Blackpool. The suspicion was that he had lost his nerve, got rusty, bottled. Magee had feared his operating days were over, his contribution confined to logistical support and errands for the England Department in Ireland. He must have wondered if the commitment and sacrifice, the years of running and hiding, of crazy risks and broken promises to Elaine, had been worth it. Some comrades seemed not to fully trust him, and what was the cause without comradeship?

For the Brighton operation, Magee had seemed set to be, at most, a link in the supply chain, one of perhaps thirty people tasked with assembling, checking, transporting, and sorting the gear, the money, the logistics, a thousand little details. Most did not know the target. The few who did spoke of the operation in hushed tones, wondering if they were kidding themselves, if this were some fantastical quest on par with dragon hunting.

And then, one by one, the candidates to plant the bomb were vacuumed up by the RUC and Scotland Yard, a malign rapture. "A series of setbacks resulting in the arrest of several key operators," as Magee's memoir dryly put it. Few volunteered to replace them, he added. "There was no endless queue for recruits for the England campaign." The fate of Thomas Quigley and Paul Kavanagh, swallowed inside the English penal system along with Roy Walsh, may have dimmed enthusiasm.

And so came the call.

Magee's life seemed to be completing a circle. The drifter who never settled in Norwich and found purpose, as he saw it, in defending his community in Belfast was returning to England to settle accounts with the enemy.

. . .

THE GRAND'S LOBBY was a portal to old-world splendor. Marble floors, leather armchairs, mahogany tables, velvet drapes—this had been a home away from home for Emperor Louis Napoleon III and other European leaders. To Magee's left was the Victoria bar, with a rogues' gallery of royalty on the wall above the cash register, Queen Victoria plump and grumpy, flanked by Queen Elizabeth, Prince Philip, Prince Charles, and Princess Diana. To Magee's right, past a concierge's desk, the restaurant was transitioning from cream teas, a fancy term for eating cake in the morning, to lunch. A grand staircase with brass railings zigzagged to the top floor. Sunlight poured through an atrium.

This was not the moment for Magee to reflect on his previous lodgings, cramped terrace homes, juvenile detention centers, Long Kesh cages, interrogation cells, moldy safe houses. Operating in England was a performative act. He had to appear relaxed, a denizen of opulence. Magee had no reservation, but phone calls the previous day and that morning had confirmed availability. He approached the reception desk. Trudy Groves, a young woman in a dark blazer, smiled in welcome. Magee requested an upper-floor room with a sea view for three nights. The accent may have had a hint of England's Midlands. Groves would have consulted the room planner.

Based on bombing expertise, the Grand's architecture, and Margaret Thatcher's probable location, the IRA had identified a short list of acceptable rooms. Groves offered 629, saying it had a wonderful sea view, and Magee accepted. "The room was actually offered and we could have changed it, but it suited," he recalled.

It was on the sixth floor, close to the center of the hotel, in a vertical line down to the Napoleon Suite on the first floor, which encompassed two rooms, 129 and 130. The Napoleon was being refurbished, the work almost complete.

Groves asked the guest his name. Roy Walsh, he said.

History clanged. Walsh was a common Irish surname thought to have originated as a reference to the Welshmen who joined the 1190 Anglo-Norman invasion of Ireland. Irish immigrants spread the name across North America and Britain. It figured in about a million UK census records. But as far as the IRA, Scotland Yard, and the English penal system were concerned, there was only one Roy Walsh: the London bomber. For his own pseudonym in 1973, Walsh had chosen Thomas Clarke, the name of a Fenian bomber. And so Magee's pseudonym threaded a century of republican history.

Magee would later say he chose the name at random and that it had no hidden significance. Other Provos didn't buy that. They believed it was an homage, one member of the brotherhood saluting another. "For some extraordinary reason he chose the name of one of the London bombers. I could never come to terms with that. I called him an idiot," Michael Hayes, the deputy head of the IRA's England Department, said later.

Groves, oblivious to her role in Irish republicanism's own Rosebud-style enigma, handed Magee a registration card, a white sheet about the size of a postcard.

He would have rehearsed this moment. Quigley and Kavanagh and who knew how many more operators had been caught through fingerprints. The challenge was to complete the form, not touch it with his hands, and not arouse the receptionist's suspicion. The less she remembered about this check-in, the better. By coincidence a convention of psychics and palm readers was meeting nearby, in Hove Town Hall, to divine futures in the lines on people's hands.

The pen hovered; then Magee wrote.

Name: WALSH ROY.
Address: 27 BRAXFIELD RD, LONDON SE4
Nationality: ENGLISH.

He signed as *R.Walsh*, connecting the *R* and *W.* He left the passport number and place of issue blank, a common practice in that era. In the registration card's top right-hand corner, Groves wrote *CHANCE*. It was the hotel's term for walk-in guests without reservations, and the closest anyone came that day to identifying the Chancer.

The bill for three nights' bed and half board was £180. Under normal circumstances, it was the sort of expenditure to give Joe Cahill, itemizing the movement's every cent in his ledger at Sinn Féin's HQ, a heart attack. Just this once, though, he might have approved. Magee paid up front, in cash. Groves filed the registration card and handed over a key with a metal fob stenciled *629*.

·   ·   ·

WHILE MAGEE'S ELEVATOR glided to the sixth floor, an Atlantic hurricane three thousand miles to the west was threatening to sink James "Whitey" Bulger's dreams of glory. Huge waves off the coast of Nova Scotia pounded the steel hull of the *Valhalla*, an eighty-seven-foot fishing trawler laden with seven tons of weapons for the IRA. Two nights earlier, Whitey had monitored the loading and watched the boat chug out of Gloucester Harbor, just north of Boston. "How great is this?" he had murmured.

Since Joe Cahill's heartfelt appeal at the Triple O, Whitey had embraced the role of a gunrunning Irish patriot. He had persuaded the drug smuggler Joe Murray to buy $500,000 worth of weapons. Other gangsters chipped in cash and weapons. It conferred underworld prestige, recalled Patrick Nee, a Whitey accomplice. "It was like a status symbol to have one of your guns on the *Valhalla*."

The crew comprised the skipper, Bob Andersen, a marine mechanic named John McIntyre, an ex-US marine turned IRA volunteer named John Crawley, and assorted Southie criminals. Whitey considered the shipment, the biggest in IRA history, a historic act of charity for the old country. If it survived the hurricane, the *Valhalla* would take about two weeks to reach a rendezvous point off Ireland's coast.

. . .

Magee stepped inside 629 and closed the door. The room had two beds, a desk and chair, a cupboard, a television, an en suite bathroom. It was bright, clean, comfortable, not a bad place to spend three days and nights. Grandeur, however, had been left in the foyer. The room's furniture and pale decor had a dated look; the carpet was worn; the beds had blankets, not duvets; and the white towels appeared to be old. There were no little chocolates left on the pillows, and air freshener could do only so much to purge years of cigarette smoke. The Grand, a former manager later confided, was "tired."

On the other hand, Miss Groves had not lied about the view. Sash windows framed a vista of the English Channel. Cargo ships and tankers occasionally crossed the horizon, and a fishing boat might appear closer to shore, but otherwise it was empty blueness. People paid for a sea view and nothing happened out there, the same manager mused, but guests liked the tranquility.

Magee did not linger in the room. He had a lunch appointment. At 12:55 p.m., he appeared in the restaurant and shared a table with a companion. They ate a light meal washed down with a glass of milk and a cup of tea. Fellow diners barely noticed them. The identity of Magee's accomplices at the Grand remains one of the Provisional IRA's most closely guarded secrets. Magee refers to "we," but declines to elaborate. According to Michael Hayes, two female couriers, elegantly dressed, delivered bomb materials to the room—and another volunteer, a man, visited over several days to help prepare the bomb, but did not stay overnight. This matches accounts from hotel staff who encountered a man seemingly other than Magee in 629. It is unlikely that more than four people were involved. The IRA wanted to keep this operation, above all, "tight."

The explosives were commercial nitroglycerine-based gelignite. "To be certain of killing Thatcher, only the use of a high explosive such as plastic or dynamite could ensure success. I only had gelignite to work with, albeit a sizable amount," Magee noted later. He and the IRA later claimed to have used one hundred pounds of explosives. Investigators estimated it was about twenty-five pounds.

The other two crucial elements of the device were a PP9 nine-volt battery about six inches high and two inches wide, and a timing power unit. This almost certainly contained the long-delay timer—number 4—missing from the Salcey Forest cache. Police later surmised all the materials would have fitted into a briefcase or a small suitcase.

After the restaurant lunch, Magee returned to his room and appeared not to have left it until checkout three days later. Once he had unpacked explosives materials, he could not risk leaving the room, lest a staff member enter and discover his purpose. Plus, he was busy.

The most complex part of the bomb was already done—a bomb maker in Ireland had made the TPU's integrated circuits. Once activated, the timer would count down twenty-four days, six hours, and thirty-six minutes. As Peter Gurney had observed with the other timers, it would have been tested for precision. But much remained to be done. The device had at least two timers, two batteries, and two independent circuits, so if one circuit failed there was a backup. A Memo-Park timer was used, almost certainly as part of an anti-handling device similar to that which killed Ken Howorth. Patrick Ryan's shopping expeditions in Zurich were still paying off. The explosives needed to be molded into the required shape and wrapped in plastic wrap dozens of times—a slow, painstaking process—to mask the marzipan-like odor.

Magee had refined his method with the "blowy stuff" in Belfast a decade earlier: ventilation, a to-do list, *always* draw diagrams of devices before working on them. "In the stress of an operation and of the unexpected, it was best to have mentally rehearsed." There was also the matter of preparing a hiding place where the bomb would remain undetected and cause maximum destruction. The England Department had identified the location: beneath the bath, in a cavity concealed behind a detachable panel.

The stars were aligning. Until now the IRA had assassinated senior government figures only in pulp fiction. In reality, the organization had to spread its meager resources over multiple fronts—land mines in South Armagh, car bombs in Derry, shootings in Tyrone, kneecappings in Belfast—to sustain its claim to be waging a war of national liberation. This required relentless effort amid relentless pressure from security forces. Most plans ended up abandoned or thwarted. It was not easy to focus on an operation years in the planning when every week brought a new crisis.

And yet the Provos had zigzagged to this moment, slowly building experience, expertise, ambition. In 1974, a unit threw a small bomb at the London home of Ted Heath, the former prime minister. In 1977, small long-delay time bombs exploded at Ulster University before the Queen's visit. In 1979, they got Mountbatten, a prestigious but soft target, and Magee had shadowed Roy Mason at the Labour's conference in Brighton. In 1981, a small time-delay bomb popped at a Scottish oil terminal during the Queen's visit. Rehearsals, really, that had led to this: an operator in room 629 of the Grand Hotel with the opportunity to wipe out Margaret Thatcher and her government.

Magee was the last link in the chain. The teenager with the English accent who was almost turned down by G Company, the loner of Long Kesh, he was still proving himself, and felt the weight of responsibility. "The enormity of it. It's down to you, simple as that. It's down to you, so you have to just do it to the best of your ability," Magee recalled. Having got so far, there could be no Paddy Factor, not on his watch. If the plan worked, history would pivot. And Patrick Magee, whether he liked it or not, would enter a pantheon of assassins, his name forever bracketed with John Wilkes Booth, Gavrilo Princip, and Lee Harvey Oswald. Unless, of course, he eluded detection, leaving only a silhouette, the unknown avenger.

. . .

As MAGEE SET to work on that first afternoon, life unspooled around him. For the Brighton police, the only noteworthy violent acts committed on September 15 were scuffles between rival groups of Crystal Palace and Albion supporters, leading to twenty arrests. The rest of Britain raised a toast to the announcement that at 4:20 p.m., Princess Diana gave birth to a boy, a yet-to-be-named brother to Prince William. Less cheery was the collapse of talks between the government and the National Union of Mineworkers, auguring further turbulent strikes. In London, a German submarine commander had a reunion with survivors from a British freighter he sank in 1942. "Instead of recriminations Capt. Karl-Friedrich Merten, commander of U16, met a warm welcome," marveled the press reports.

By dusk, Brighton's pubs began to fill with students, day-trippers, stag parties, hen parties, and clubbers. There were several discreet gay pubs, which on occasion were raided by police wearing rubber gloves as protection from a new scourge called AIDS. The Duke of York's cinema screened *Mephisto*.

In the Grand, a chanteuse named Georgie settled onto her stool at the lounge bar piano to entertain diners with a medley of old pop songs, her voice drifting up the staircase. In room 645, a guest paid a photographer to take erotic portraits of his female companion. By now, room 629, down the hall, would have resembled a workshop: jumbles of wires, cables, batteries, timers, and other electronic parts requiring sorting and testing. If Magee took a break to watch the sunset from his balcony that first night, he would have seen it slide and disappear into the sea. Victorian-style lanterns strung along the promenade glowed. Any bobbing glimmers from the water would have been fishing boats.

Sunday, September 16, dawned with a gulls' chorus and a patch of sky paling over the Palace Pier. The Grand's manager, Paul Boswell, had a daily ritual of raising the Union Jack over the center of the roof, almost directly over Magee's head. That afternoon, a caller from 629 phoned room service and requested turkey sandwiches and tea. The waiter knocked on the door and heard a man's voice inside. The man who opened the door was tall, about six feet, two inches. He turned away from the waiter and said in the direction of the bathroom, "They're here," before taking the platter. The testing and assembling of components continued. The sunset came two minutes earlier than the previous night. Autumn had its own timer.

Monday, September 17: again the dawn chorus and Boswell raising the flag, but the weather now cooler, showers sprinkling the cars and buses whooshing up and down King's Road. To avoid "gelly headache," the window in 629 was probably open. At some point during the day, Magee and his accomplice paused from their work for tea and sandwiches.

Pamela Plappert was keen to get into the room. The veteran chambermaid liked to keep her rooms spick-and-span. She lived in staff quarters and took pride in her job. She waited in vain for 629's DO NOT DISTURB sign to be removed. Sometimes boldness was the only way. Plappert knocked and, without waiting for a reply, opened the door. "There was a voice . . . [it] said you can't come in, so I went out again," she later recalled. "He was in there all the time doing something but I don't know what it was." She shut the door and scuttled down the corridor. The cleaning would have to wait until the gentleman checked out.

Bombs were in the news. Activists from Brighton joined the occupation of a runway at a US air base in Oxfordshire to protest nuclear missiles. In Derry, an IRA unit set explosive charges in the fuel tanks of a fleet of telecom vans, but troops disarmed the devices. The impact of falling masonry on the human body was the lead story in Brighton's local newspaper, the *Evening Argus*. "Buried in Trap of Terror," blared the headline. A wall at a building site half a mile from the Grand had fallen on an Irish laborer named Joseph Barrie, crushing him under five tons of rubble. "He lay face down in the muddy pit as his mates and workmen from a nearby office block construction team clawed through bricks and steel to reach him," said the article. Barrie survived with broken legs.

During his Dutch prison reveries four years earlier, Magee had pondered ways to minimize civilian casualties. Now he was preparing to blow up, without warning, a hotel filled with hundreds of civilians. In Provo terminology, the Conservatives were members of the ruling class that presided over the "war machine" occupying the six counties. This made them legitimate targets. Anyone else caught up in the blast—hotel staff, tourists, journalists—were unfortunates in the wrong place at the wrong time. Mercy was not an option when the target was so important. The same logic had justified blowing up children on Mountbatten's boat. Magee's desire to minimize civilian casualties was doubtless sincere, but the IRA campaign, just like Pinkie, the anti-hero in Graham Greene's novel *Brighton Rock*, could not change. "I've never changed. It's like those sticks of rock: bite it all the way down, you'll still read Brighton."

The Provos had studied the Grand's architecture but could still only guess at the bomb's impact. The explosion itself was just the spark. The real weapon would be the hotel itself, its bricks, stone, marble, and glass loosened from 120 years of compact solidity and turned into a great, sweeping avalanche. The gunshots of Booth, Princip, and Oswald, by contrast, had been surgical. Magee's method was closer to that of the suicide truck bombers who a year earlier had destroyed the US marine barracks and other targets in Beirut. On the other hand, the Chancer had no intention of dying with his bomb.

The one element of IRA precision was time. The TPU was already configured, but needed to be activated. Then it would count down to twenty-four days, six hours, and thirty-six minutes. Thatcher usually spent three to four days and nights at her party conference. The surest time to catch her in the hotel was late at night and early morning, the witching hours. That would also be when fewest hotel staff were in the Grand, Magee said later. "Our conflict was not directed at the ordinary working-class people. We were trying to target those we deemed most culpable."

The IRA chose just before 3:00 a.m. on October 12, the conference's final day, for its surprise. This meant Magee and his accomplice had to finish assembling and arming the device by around 8:20 p.m. on September 17. They probably had to wait another hour for the circuits to engage automatically after completing the manual settings to be sure the bomb was primed.

Centuries of enmity and three years of planning had led to this moment. The hotel went about its business, untroubled. Guests padded down the corridor. Diners clinked glasses in the restaurant. Margaret Thatcher was on Downing Street, attending a farewell party for members of her policy unit before having supper in her flat.

At approximately 9:20 p.m., the bombers would have known the device was primed. The dragon, as the Chinese inventors of gunpowder would have put it, had inhaled. All that was left was to replace the tile beneath the bath and clean up. Magee did not pause to picture the possible scene three weeks hence: the blast, the dust, the screaming. "You're putting a bomb in designed to kill people, but you don't dwell on it," he said later. "Years afterward you can dwell on that, but while you're doing it, no."

After 10:00 p.m., the bar received an order from 629: a bottle of vodka and three bottles of Coca-Cola. A waiter delivered them on a tray. It was an act of extravagance—the bar charged per nip—but Joe Cahill didn't need to know. Magee could have checked out then, but he spent the night in 629 with his bomb armed and primed. "We were still undercover," he recalled. "I mean, you have to go through the motions. You've booked into a hotel and you book out like everybody else does, that's part of the cover."

At approximately 9:00 a.m. on Tuesday, September 18, he checked out, walked out onto King's Road, and disappeared. Pamela Plappert finally got into 629. Only one bed had been slept in. And there were grease marks around the bath, but a good scrub fixed that. Room 629 was soon ready for the next guest.

In the dark cavity beneath the tub, the electronic timer pulsed in silence.

CHAPTER THIRTEEN

Clockwork

Margaret Thatcher emerged from 10 Downing Street and eased into the backseat of her jet-black government Daimler shortly before 9:00 a.m. She wore a green tweed suit and matching shoes, a favorite outfit, and carried a briefcase and a small handbag. The hair, done the previous morning, was immaculate, offset with pearl earrings. Gray clouds menaced drizzle, but autumn's chill had not reached the capital. It was Tuesday, October 9, 1984, the first day of the 101st Conservative Party Conference, and the prime minister was on her way to Brighton.

The Daimler cruised into place between police escorts and snaked through traffic, Big Ben sounding a sonorous bong on the hour over the Gothic towers of Westminster. In a few weeks, Parliament would reconvene with a little ceremony: the Yeomen of the Guard, wearing scarlet and gold Tudor uniforms and carrying lanterns, would make a symbolic search of the cellars where Guy Fawkes was caught with barrels of explosives in 1605. For his trouble, each guard would earn, according to tradition, half a pint of port.

A warning of a possible IRA attack in England a few weeks earlier had prompted the prime minister's security team to check sewers and service tunnels along the route from Downing Street to Westminster. They found nothing. The security threat level for Brighton was deemed low. In fact, there was good news about the IRA: on September 29, the Irish navy had intercepted a boat with seven tons of weapons sent from the US, and arrested all aboard.

Navigating morning rush hour, the prime minister's little convoy crossed the Thames and picked up speed after joining the A23, a fifty-three-mile arrow to Brighton that followed the Romans' direct route to the coast. The Daimler's sleekness concealed drawbacks. West of England cloth, a material favored by the royal family, trimmed the interior, but stained easily. More seriously, the headrests did not support Thatcher's head and neck. When she dozed, her head dropped forward, only to jerk up when the car braked or turned. Her bodyguards fretted about whiplash. Naps were becoming more common. Since her reelection a year earlier, aides had noticed that the Iron Lady's superhuman energy level had dipped—she started having vitamin B_{12} injections in her buttocks to sustain her. Her eyesight was weaker and there was just a hint of shuffle in her walk. She would turn fifty-nine on Saturday, a day after the conference wrapped.

While the prime minister sped down the motorway, her party colleagues already in Brighton bowed their heads inside the cavernous conference center on the promenade. The vicar of Brighton, John Hester, opened proceedings with a prayer for the Queen, Parliament, and the people, followed by the Lord's Prayer and a reading from Paul's letter to the Philippians. Then the assembled Tories sang a hymn, "Lord of All Hopefulness," to the melody of an Irish folk song. It invoked a God of gentleness, calm, and contentment. "Be there at our sleeping, and give us, we pray, Your peace in our hearts, Lord, at the end of the day."

Indeed, the prime minister had reason for contentment. Five years into her premiership, she was reshaping the economy and society, and she dominated her party. The wets, her nickname for colleagues deemed pusillanimous, were long routed. Gone, too, was the nickname "Hilda," an old snickering tilt at her provincial roots. Now many colleagues called her, without irony, "Mother."

Spitting Image, a satirical television puppet show, depicted Thatcher as a cross-dressing dominatrix who chomped cigars and bullied her ministers. A famous skit had them seated in a restaurant, where Thatcher orders raw steak.

"And what about the vegetables?" asks the waitress.

"Oh, they'll have the same as me."

It was funny because there was truth to it. Thatcher had become more hectoring and dismissive. Some ministers did feel bullied. Behind the carapace, however, Thatcher's sense of vulnerability endured. As sure as apples fell from trees, parties tired of their leaders and voters tired of their governments. The trick was to delay gravity. One way was a barnstorming conference speech, a walloping one-two of oratory and conviction to enthrall the faithful and show everybody else the chief was still in charge. Thatcher pulled it off each year, but her relief at doing so lasted just as long as the standing ovation, and once the audience sat down, she began to worry about next year's speech. As the conference neared, her anxiety mounted. The leader's keynote could not really be precooked. It was on the last day of the conference—in this case, Friday, October 12—and had to encapsulate its spirit.

"Throughout the week of party conference Mrs. Thatcher keeps The Speech on the boil, like some terrible peasant stew, feeding it each night with more words tossed in by her writers and aides," Simon Hoggart, a newspaper columnist, observed. "You started at the beginning. You went through to the end, and then you started again at the beginning, and you went through it time and time again," recalled

John Whittingdale, a speechwriter. "Then she would turn around and say, 'No, it's absolutely hopeless, the whole thing is useless.'"

With London behind her and the green hills of Surrey flashing past, Thatcher had extra motivation to make this speech perfect. The coal miners' strike was into its thirty-first week. Miners protesting the closure of pits deemed uneconomic were fighting pitched battles with riot police and clashing with miners who continued to work, the anguish playing out nightly on TV screens, splitting Britain into those who supported or opposed the strikers. It was a defining moment for Thatcher's determination to reshape her country.

Seldom had Britain felt so polarized. Conference-goers would belt out "Hello, Maggie!" to the tune of the Broadway hit "Hello, Dolly!," hailing their leader for winning back the Falklands, reversing the nation's slide to mediocrity, and facing down militant socialism. The London yuppies who gabbed into brick-sized mobile phones seemed reflected in songs like "Gold" by Spandau Ballet, and a new wave of shiny, aspirational pop music.

Others, however, viewed Thatcherism as a cold, callous creed that gutted industries and communities while telling the unemployed—to paraphrase her cabinet minister Norman Tebbit—"on your bike." These critics had their own anthems, such as the Specials' "Ghost Town" and the Jam's "Town Called Malice." "Thatcher was an absolute fairy godmother. Christ, you're an anarchist band trying to complain about the workings of capitalist society and you get someone like Thatcher. What a joy!" Penny Rimbaud, of the punk band Crass, recalled.

It was not just left-wing artists. Anglican bishops, mainstream commentators, and even John Biffen, one of Thatcher's ministers, worried about ideological zealotry. Opinion polls found that voters respected the Iron Lady's toughness, but considered her dictatorial and uncaring about ordinary people. Jack Foster, an *Evening Argus* columnist, urged her to unite the country. "She goes to the gleaming assembly as prime minister of a society that is as divided and violent as we can remember. . . . Sensible Tories will not object if Mrs. Thatcher thinks now is the moment for compassion," he wrote. "Perhaps the Iron Lady is about to show a softer side. She should."

But Thatcher was planning on neither balm nor calm. She was going to attack, attack, attack. The draft speech in her briefcase depicted British politics as a Manichaean struggle between liberty and tyranny, order and chaos, democracy and communism. It said extremists had hijacked the Labour Party and planned to destroy freedom. They were the "enemy within" and would, just like the Argentinian junta, be defeated. Her pen had already lacerated the typed draft with multiple excisions, underlinings, and comments, and would continue to do so all week, but the core message was there. The lady was not for turning.

The only obstacle that could stop Thatcher on this autumn morning were roadworks near Pyecombe, a West Sussex village just north of Brighton, which delayed the convoy for fifteen minutes. As the Daimler purred down the final stretch of the A23, Thatcher may have reflected on what she would *not* say. Her draft barely mentioned Northern Ireland. Likewise, the 160-page conference handbook, which gave it a cameo on page 98. But behind the scenes, Thatcher was inching toward a radical idea, one floated a year earlier by Ireland's prime minister, Garret FitzGerald. In return for the Dublin government formally recognizing Northern Ireland's place in the UK, something it had never done, she was considering giving the Irish a role—an advisory role—in running the province. If agreed, it would be a historic treaty. It would not end the Troubles, but could be a stepping-stone to a final settlement, to peace. Thatcher had perhaps surprised herself by setting aside her unionist sympathies and instinctive distrust of the Irish to reach this point. Even so, it was still just a proposal. Nothing had been signed.

The convoy trundled through the heart of Brighton and turned onto King's Road just before 11:00 a.m. The Palace Pier tinkled and twinkled, but there would have been few takers on a damp Tuesday morning. The Daimler pulled up in front of the Grand. Thatcher stepped out, clutching handbag and briefcase. A handful of protesters on the promenade beyond the security cordon barely had time to react. Some passersby applauded, others just stared. One man, restraining a barking dog on a lead, suddenly realized who had arrived. "Maggie out!" he shouted. The prime minister wove though a handful of uniformed and plainclothes police and beamed at a scrum of photographers and TV crews. "Good morning, good morning. How are you?"

She stepped through the revolving doors into the lobby, click-clacked across the polished floor, and paused at reception. Guests were putting their names to charity raffle tickets. Thatcher bought six. The winning tickets would be drawn from an antique tombola drum, a random lottery.

The prime minister was ushered up one floor to her home for the next four days, the Napoleon Suite. A Frenchman would not have been her first choice of name for the hotel's finest suite. She had a complex relationship with the French, and they with her. President François Mitterrand reportedly said she had "the eyes of Caligula and the mouth of Marilyn Monroe."

Thatcher may have sniffed evidence of the recent refurbishment and painting. The suite, spanning rooms 129 and 130, was well furnished, comfortable, not opulent. Tall windows, a rich sea-green carpet, full-length drapes. An apricot-colored bathroom, a drawing room, an oval dinner table, a bedroom with two double beds—needless, as she and Denis, who would join her the following day, shared a bed. The hotel staff may have plucked up the courage to tell her that ABBA partied there after winning the 1974 Eurovision Song Contest with "Waterloo." Beyond the ornate wrought-iron balcony, Thatcher could see part of the seafront had been cordoned off for security. But traffic still rumbled past and people strolled on the promenade. It was all pleasingly normal.

She went to the neighboring conference center for a day of

speeches, debates, and social events. Souvenir sellers were doing brisk trade in marzipan models of Thatcher, £2.50 each. She would return to her suite later to work on her own speech. Aides delivered red boxes with government papers, and the "Garden Girls"—secretaries whose office overlooked number 10's garden—set up shop in a room across the corridor. For one week, Britain would be governed from Brighton, and the Grand Hotel became 10 Downing Street.

. . .

At 6:01 P.M. on Wednesday, while Thatcher attended a party treasurers' reception in the Grand, the deputy assistant commissioner of the Metropolitan Police sent a secure telegram to the UK's fifty-two chief constables, each in charge of a territorial police force, about the Provisional IRA.

1. You will be aware from press reports that the PIRA have suffered severe blows to their morale in recent weeks through the action of security forces in the Republic of Ireland.

2. The Provisional Sinn Féin Ard Fheis (annual conference) is due to be held in Dublin on November 3–4, and leaders of the movement will be anxious to take military action to restore the spirits of adherents before that date. The most likely area of attack remains Northern Ireland, but a brief campaign on the mainland cannot be discounted. It is our assessment that potential military and political targets should be given special attention over the weeks preceding the Ard Fheis.

The RUC had relayed intelligence to the Met's Special Branch that the IRA might be planning an attack in England somewhere outside of London. There were no other details. The DAC's telegram raised the national BIKINI alert state—a benchmark similar to the US's

DEFCON—to Black Alpha, just below the maximum, a cue for military bases to tighten security.

Roger Birch, the chief constable of Sussex Police, would later say he did not receive the message. Even if he did, it was vague and probably would not have changed his arrangements for the conference. Birch—prim, slender, clean-cut—was in charge of 1,800 police officers in East and West Sussex. He had designed his strategy for the week around the prospect of angry miners pouring off buses, waving placards, and perhaps attempting to storm the conference center. Almost one thousand police officers, far more than usual, had been deployed at barricades, checkpoints, and rooftops. Teams searched the conference center each morning and operated a color code for passes: red for ordinary attendees, gold for platform speakers, yellow for MPs and peers, green for the press. Specially trained Sussex protection officers reinforced Thatcher's usual retinue of bodyguards.

A police dog handler with a German shepherd had searched the first floor of the Grand before Thatcher's arrival. A rushed, incomplete sweep because the hotel was still operating as normal, with hundreds of guests and staff milling around. "They didn't shut it down or anything," recalled the officer who conducted the sweep. "I had to search Maggie's suite. I had just over half an hour to do it. And there were flunkies in there, you know, all making like, flowers. I'm trying to search, trying to work a dog. But you can't, you've got people all round you. . . . I couldn't do it properly." Other rooms on the first floor were searched, but nowhere else. The operation was not far off a Yeomen of the Guard ceremony, minus lanterns. Uniformed officers were posted outside the hotel and plainclothes Sussex officers, plus the Met's close protection unit, were inside the Grand. Some people entering the hotel were searched, others not.

It was a striking contrast with the clock-wrecking thoroughness of the US Secret Service. Before Ronald Reagan had arrived in Dallas for the Republican convention in August, all guests at the Loews Anatole hotel were awoken at 7:00 a.m. and told to be out by 11:00 a.m. Agents, police, and a special army unit scoured the hotel's 1,620 rooms, plus storm drains and air-conditioning ducts, with metal detectors and bomb-sniffing dogs, after which the hotel became a fortress with X-ray machines. No one without a pass could enter. To the British, such meticulousness seemed impractical. Who would reimburse the hotel? Who would pay for the police overtime? How could a conference be a conference without the freewheeling socializing?

Britain's alphabet soup of security services had networks of informers, spies, and electronic surveillance. They had battery-pulse detector units and radios to sweep for bombs, they had files on virtually every IRA suspect, including Patrick Magee, and his immediate superiors Owen Coogan and Michael Hayes, but there were no whispers of any operation in Brighton, and nobody remembered the Ministry of Defence's prophetic 1979 assessment about long-delay timers: "Such a system is very accurate and can produce a delay of weeks or even years. We would expect to see more use of these long-delay timers, particularly with a view to causing explosions at sensitive moments, such as the time of a VIP visit." MI5 would later assert that for several consecutive years it had flagged intelligence that the IRA planned to target a Tory conference, but there is no corroboration of such warnings. The hasty, incomplete search of the Grand was the responsibility of the local Sussex police—but in that still-innocent era, that verged on standard practice. Nobody expected the police to search an entire hotel. The IRA had closed in on its top target using well-known operators and well-worn technology, but the security services did not join the dots. The failure to properly protect Margaret Thatcher was a failure of imagination.

The DAC's telegram sat in the Sussex Police headquarters in Lewes that Wednesday evening, causing not a ripple of concern to the thousand police officers at Brighton, ten miles away. The promenade was quiet. The miners had not turned up. A full moon glowed over the channel.

. . .

As WEDNESDAY NIGHT ebbed into Thursday morning, Harvey Thomas was getting ready for bed and daring to relax, just a little. The set had not collapsed, the teleprompter had behaved, and there was no sign of hecklers or egg throwers. Thomas was the conference's technical coordinator. Age forty-five, built like a polar bear, with thick glasses, he was responsible for making everything run smoothly and look good on television. Not always easy when Tory grandees grumbled at radical innovations, such as adjustable electronic lecterns. Thomas also insisted on rehearsals, which provoked more spluttering, but got his way. Mother, after all, believed in him, and so apparently did God.

A devout Christian, as a young man he had helped organize a visit to England by the American televangelist Billy Graham, and ended up joining Graham's globe-trotting religious road show as a logistics and PR man. After returning to Britain in 1977 he offered his services to the Conservatives. Two elections and six party conferences later, Thomas was the party's Mr. Fix-it, roving the vast Brighton center checking plugs, cables, and camera angles, adjusting the teleprompter, clearing the platform of clutter. He splashed water on the pale blue canvas backdrop to tauten it like a drum skin.

Conferences were not government events but party events organized by the Conservative Central Office on behalf of local associations. It was a chance for constituency branch chairpersons, treasurers, secretaries, and activists to spend a week by the sea rubbing shoulders with MPs and ministers. In contrast to the rowdy slugfests and insurrections of Labour's annual get-togethers, Conservative conferences were usually smooth as brandy, with no contentious votes or rebel motions to trouble the leadership.

Attendees—they were not called delegates but representatives— no longer had blue-rinsed hair or double-breasted serge suits, but still looked pink and portly, said the *Evening Argus*'s waspish political diarist, Adam Trimingham. "The party hierarchy still consists largely

of noble nonentities whose names sound like a roll call of old comedians," he wrote, noting the number of lords, barons, and dames. Au-
diences spent their days applauding speeches before spilling out to
bars, restaurants, and hotels for schmoozing and buttonholing; ministers, journalists, students, and activists all merrily jumbled. The
conference program had a blank page for the starstruck to collect autographs from their political heroes.

Even by Harvey Thomas's standards, Tuesday and Wednesday had
gone like clockwork. Ministers thundered against the old reliables—
socialists, criminals, peaceniks—the audience lustily applauded, and
the BBC gave blanket coverage. On Tuesday night, the party faithful
had watched, enraptured, as Thatcher danced with the Tory mayor of
Brighton. "You look gorgeous," gushed the mayor. On Wednesday
night, the faithful had watched, enraptured, as she danced with the
Tory mayor of Hove.

There had been one glitch: some Young Conservatives had piled
out of a disco onto the beach and vandalized a mock seventy-five-foot-
long nuclear submarine to be used in a protest by the Campaign for
Nuclear Disarmament. This embarrassment was offset by the spectacle
of lashing wind and rain harrying the peaceniks, who truncated their
protest. Some demonstrators from Troops Out and the Irish Freedom
Movement had chanted and distributed leaflets, and somebody threw
a stink bomb, but otherwise all was going splendidly.

As the sun rose on Thursday, October 11, Thomas took a moment
to enjoy the celestial display of dawn light. Conference hotel room al-
location was subject to elaborate etiquette. By tradition, only notables
from constituency associations got prize rooms with sea views, but
Thomas had snaffled one for himself: room 729.

. . .

ONCE GUESTS DEPARTED for the morning, the Grand's chambermaids
worked quickly, room by room, floor by floor, vacuuming, changing
sheets, scrubbing baths. As the Tories walked toward the conference

center, a plane buzzed in a bright blue sky, trailing a banner: IT'S
BETTER IN BLACKPOOL, a marketing stunt by the rival resort. The
day's first session began at 9:30 a.m., debates on food and farming,
homes and land, employment. Ivor Humphrey, a fifty-seven-year-old
sales executive who had lost his job, ruptured the self-congratulatory
mood with a speech that accused the government of lacking compassion for the unemployed. "Fellow Conservatives . . . there has to be
an alternative, otherwise one day you will experience an explosion the
like of which you have never witnessed before." Shouts of "Rubbish"
greeted this intervention. Thatcher sat on the podium, impassive.

The morning's other surprise was news of a shocking act of
violence. The *Evening Argus* reported on its front page that a mugger
had stabbed Michael Keith Smith, president of Portsmouth South
Young Conservatives, necessitating fifteen stitches to his hand. Britain
should restore corporal punishment with birch rods, said the victim.

Thatcher returned to the Grand for meetings and to work on her
speech. It was 11:30 a.m. She was escorted by burly protection officers,
but still slipped unnoticed past about two hundred Sussex Young Socialists, who did not get to chant insults. "I didn't even know she had
left," fumed an organizer.

The afternoon belonged to Norman Tebbit. Thin as a whip, and
just as sharp, the fifty-one-year-old trade and industry minister was in
some ways more Thatcherite than Thatcher: more combative, more
radical, possibly more ambitious. She had originally promoted Tebbit
to the cabinet as employment minister to battle trade unions, which he
did with relish. Now he was leading the charge to privatize nation-
alized industries. Opponents called him a semi-house-trained polecat,
the Prince of Darkness, and worse. His conference speeches always
galvanized the Tories.

At 2:30 p.m., he stood at the lectern, almost five thousand faces
looking at him, and gave a passionate defense of the government's
right-wing agenda. The Conservatives had widened their appeal to
represent all of Britain, rich and poor, he declared. "There is a prize to

Margaret Thatcher and Norman Tebbit, her secretary of state for employment, at a press conference in June 1983. | Bettmann via Getty Images

be won, and win it we will." It earned the conference's longest standing ovation. The newspapermen headed off to the cramped press room to file articles anointing Tebbit the darling of the 101st conference.

Tebbit savored a familiar glow. Twelve months earlier he had emerged from the conference in Blackpool to triumphant headlines and speculation that he was Thatcher's heir. Brighton was proving even more agreeable. The MP for Chingford was on top of his game, and looked ever more like a future leader. And Margaret, *his* Margaret, his wife of twenty-eight years, seemed finally free of the mental darkness that had imprisoned her.

Tebbit owed nothing to privilege. He had grown up in Ponders End, a working-class London neighborhood, during the Great Depression, and watched his father cycle around the city seeking work—the origin of Tebbit's later exhortation to the unemployed to get on their own bikes. Evacuated to Wales during the war, Tebbit stayed in a house packed with books, which he devoured, and glimpsed a world beyond his family's poverty. Leaving school at sixteen, he escaped by flying, piloting fighters for the RAF—he narrowly escaped death in a fiery crash—then transatlantic flights for British Airways. To soar over clouds was bliss—but less so his dealings with airline unions and managers, who in his opinion connived to bloat and featherbed the industry. Economic distortions and social permissiveness, Tebbit concluded, were ruining Britain, convictions that fueled his entry to Parliament. He favored tougher interrogation of IRA suspects and cheered Thatcher's handling of the hunger strikes. In the cabinet he became one of her ablest media performers. *Spitting Image* lampooned him as a leather-clad skinhead who beat up colleagues, and indeed he reveled in political combat, albeit only with a sharp tongue and acid wit.

"Heard a chap on the radio this morning talking with a Cockney accent," Harold Macmillan, an upper-crust former prime minister, said after hearing Tebbit's everyman tones for the first time. "They tell me he is one of Her Majesty's ministers."

At the department of trade and industry, Tebbit powered Thatcherism's engine. And the idea that whenever the boss stepped aside he was the obvious successor was apparently shared by the conference audience as they rose to their feet to applaud. "There's a rather warm glow inside you when you have achieved that," he said. It would, on the other hand, mean yet more aggravation for Thatcher's speechwriters; when a minister made a successful speech, she felt duty bound to better it.

After the day's last speech ended and he joined the throngs filing out into the cool evening air, Tebbit had another reason for contentment. His wife was well. More than well: happy. They had met in 1955, she a nurse, he a pilot, and love "sort of crept on us," as she put it. They had spent summer evenings gardening. But the birth of their third child, William, was difficult. Margaret did not remember giving birth. "Who is he?" she had asked her husband. Postnatal depression consumed her. She feared she might kill her children. "The memory of seeing her personality disintegrate is more painful than any other experience I have undergone," Tebbit recalled. Margaret was hospitalized, and recovered, but the illness returned. Tebbit had juggled parliamentary business with cooking, cleaning, parenting, and visiting his wife.

By 1984, Margaret was back to her cheerful, multitasking self, working as a volunteer at a hospital, and the Tebbits counted their blessings. They had recently become grandparents and acquired a country retreat, a house in Devon, and were itching to transform its garden. They considered leaving Brighton that night to motor to Devon. They could watch Thatcher's speech the next day on television. However, Norman had missed her speech in Blackpool the previous year, to attend a son's awards ceremony, and dared not do so again lest the press depict it as a snub.

So, the Tebbits stayed for the final night.

. . .

INSIDE THE GRAND, chandeliers blazed. Bars and reception rooms were packed. This was the final night to hobnob, flirt, and settle scores before Mother's speech the next day wrapped the week and scattered the tribe. Waiters emerged with platters of oysters and prawns. Younger Tories, some wearing top hat and tails, had supper at Top Rank, a nearby entertainment complex, blissfully unaware the bowls of grated Parmesan-type cheese had earlier hosted cockroaches. Maria Pali, a nineteen-year-old cleaner and punk rocker, did not warn them. Thatcher's policies had reduced many Britons to scavengers, so why not let insects inflict some revenge, she reasoned.

At 10:30 p.m., Thatcher, taking a break from her speech preparations, called into Top Rank, where a ball was in full swing. A band called Zoochi struck the familiar chords and 1,200 revelers belted out the lyrics.

Hello, Maggie, it's so nice to have you back where you belong.
You're looking swell, Maggie . . .

Resplendent in a silver-spangled blouse and a blue ball gown with ruff collar, she acknowledged the cheers. Denis, dressed in a tuxedo and armed with a baton, led the orchestra as his wife danced a quickstep with a local party official before taking her for a spin himself. Thatcher signed autographs and posed with a big blue teddy bear, a raffle prize. Her watch said 11:10 p.m. Security men ushered her out under a starlit sky to the Daimler, which drove her the two hundred yards back to the Grand. It was 11:15 p.m.

The Tebbits were at a reception hosted by the party treasurer, Alistair McAlpine, a bon vivant whose gatherings were famous for flowing champagne. Over the chatter and laughter, few noticed the clocks striking midnight, ushering in Friday, October 12. For Brighton's emergency services, it was a routine night—ambulances summoned for two women in labor, the fire brigade called out to a burning mound of garbage and a motel's smoldering tumble dryer. Police responded to an armed robbery and a minor road accident. Soon after midnight, the Tebbits said their goodbyes and withdrew. Norman paused on the staircase to chat to John Cole, the BBC's political correspondent, then bid adieu, saying his wife would soon be asleep and he did not want to risk waking "higher management." The Tebbits were in room 228, behind the hotel sign that adorned the Grand's facade. The minister changed into his pajamas, climbed into bed beside his wife, and was soon asleep.

In the rooms above them, other couples followed suit. In 328, two Jack Russells, Smudge and Lucky, yapped when Sir Anthony Berry and Lady Sarah Berry, eighteen years married, glamorous in a tuxedo and a red dress, returned to their room. Sir Anthony was an aristocratic MP and junior government figure. He walked the dogs before climbing into bed around 2:30 a.m. Normally Sarah slept to his right, but she had calls to make in the morning, so she slept on the other side, by the phone.

Approximately thirty feet above, in room 428, John and Roberta Wakeham, nineteen years married, were deeply asleep after a hectic few days. As the government's chief whip, tasked with keeping MPs in line, John had to be everywhere, taking the pulse of the party, gathering intelligence for Thatcher. He was diligently supported by Roberta, a vivacious personality who disguised it all as fun.

In 528, Eric and Jennifer Taylor, twenty-four years married, got into bed around 2:00 a.m. A week in Brighton had been Eric's reward for serving as chairman of the North-West Conservative Association, a low-profile cog in the party machine. On Monday, he would return to his data-managing job and Jennifer would resume running a beauty salon.

In 628, Gordon and Jeanne Shattock, thirty-two years married, were in bed by midnight. Gordon had wanted to be an MP, but his veterinary practice left little time and money to run for office, so he settled for being chairman of the party's western area. Jeanne was a magistrate and a school governess, and chaired a cancer charity. The conference was their big week off, an annual adventure. After noisy guests woke the Shattocks around 2:30 a.m., the couple struggled to get back to sleep.

Beside them, in room 629, dozed Donald and Muriel Maclean, twenty-seven years married. Donald was president of the Scottish Conservatives, a grand title for a soft-spoken optician who lived in a bungalow in the coastal town of Ayr. Muriel shared his interest in politics, but looked forward to returning to her embroidery and hill walks.

By 2:35 a.m., the lounge bar had stopped serving, but the portrait of Queen Victoria still had dozens of lingering drinkers to scowl at. As the bomb in room 629 counted down its final minutes, the Grand Hotel's roof enclosed 286 people: 220 residents, 32 visitors, 11 staff, and 23 police officers.

.   .   .

PATRICK MAGEE WAS approximately six hundred miles to the west, in a remote part of Cork, near Ireland's Atlantic coast. He lay in bed in a safe house, tormented with thoughts of all that could go wrong. A dud fuse. A dead battery. A break in the circuit. Discovery of the device. A premature explosion. No explosion. A failed operation. The IRA's best chance of killing Thatcher, wasted. Or maybe, at the appointed moment, a blinding flash.

A week earlier, Magee had briefed an IRA superior in Dublin. On a bar napkin, he had sketched the Grand's facade, marked the bomb's position with an *X*, and with a circle showed the likely scope of destruction. "My view," he recalled, "was that the explosion would directly reach the third floor but that debris and falling masonry just might extend the bomb's effective killing range." The Army Council had considered putting all volunteers on standby to flee or hide if Thatcher was killed and the Brits came roaring. It decided not to. There were too many informers in the ranks, a reality underlined by the Irish navy's seizure of the arms shipment from Boston. The authorities had been waiting for the trawler, which meant somebody had blabbed. So there would be no putting volunteers on standby. The Brits would get wind that something big was up and maybe put two and two together.

In his billet, Magee knew he would not sleep. A transistor radio sat by the bed, and all it could catch was an offshore pirate radio station with crackly reception. A syndicated news bulletin came on the hour, but after midnight it just repeated the previous bulletin. Pop songs filled the gaps. The chart-topper was still Stevie Wonder's "I Just Called to Say I Love You." Magee listened in the darkness.

He stared at the clock. It was 2:40 a.m. He wondered when they would update the news.

. . .

At 2:45 a.m., Margaret Thatcher was wide-awake, still in her ball gown, seated in an armchair in the Napoleon Suite lounge. The promenade outside was deserted save for a few police guards. The prime minister was pleased. She had just approved final amendments to her speech. The writers filed out, exhausted, and handed the text to the secretaries in the room across the hallway for typing.

Denis was in the suite's bedroom, asleep. Robin Butler, Thatcher's most senior civil servant, sat opposite her, eyelids drooping, looking forward to bed. He suggested leaving a few pending minor government matters till morning.

"I'd much rather do it now," said the prime minister.

Butler nodded. Of course she would.

He waited while Thatcher rose and went to the bathroom. Even the Iron Lady needed time-outs. Seconds ticked by, the Napoleon Suite silent. Thatcher reappeared at 2:52 a.m. and sat in the armchair.

Butler handed her a document about funding for the Liverpool Garden Festival. In the cavity beneath the bath in room 629, the timer pulsed into its final minute.

CHAPTER FOURTEEN

—

A White Light

Fifty seconds from detonation, the only sound on the Brighton promenade came from the English Channel. The tide was high, waves thudding ashore, a few fishermen standing in the surf like moonlit sentinels.

Forty seconds. Barely a breeze to ruffle the night. The biting wind and rain that had seemed to presage winter earlier in the week had given way to stillness. It was not even cold. Darkness draped the Grand's eight-story facade, its windows black squares save for a few scattered glows, like a giant crossword.

Thirty seconds. Two pedestrians—a DJ and a manager from the Pink Coconut nightclub making their way home—turned from West Street onto the promenade. A police transit van, a rattling old Bedford, trundled past them toward the Grand. In the car park behind the hotel, weary constables clambered into another van, their shift over.

Twenty seconds. In the Victoria bar, the night's last revelers clinked glasses. A contingent of councillors and party officials from Bradford, in tuxedos and gowns, wheeled another three bottles of champagne from the closed bar for a farewell toast to the 101st conference. A cabinet minister's secretary discussed sharing a taxi back to the hotel of Richard Whitely, host of a TV show called *Countdown*.

Ten seconds. In his safe house, Patrick Magee stared at the clock.

In the Napoleon Suite, the world's most powerful woman worked her way through the day's final dregs of government business.

Five seconds. A surveillance camera positioned on the conference center scanned the prime minister's balcony. Imprinted on the top right-hand corner was the date and time: 12-10-84.

At 02:54:01, the bomb in the bathroom of room 629 detonated. A brilliant, blinding white light pierced the walls and corridors and brick facade. It exploded into the night air, dazzling and blurring the surveillance camera.

A fireball whooshed through the sixth floor, driven by the exponentially expanding force of the explosives' compressed power. Blast waves radiated outward through brick and stone, unleashing a roar like thunder. In 629, Donald and Muriel Maclean flew out of bed and spun through the air. Muriel, age fifty-four, hurtled sideways. Her husband seemed to go upward. The wall separating the bathrooms of 629 and 628 dissolved just as Jeanne Shattock, age fifty-five, was in her bathroom bending over the bath. The bomb's heat seared her flesh. Fragments of metal, ceramic, wood, and a green plastic lipstick holder stabbed her with the force of rifle bullets. The blast propelled her body across the corridor into a cupboard in room 638. She was decapitated. Gordon Shattock glimpsed the flash in the bathroom and felt a burning sensation before being hurled out of bed. The surge of heat appeared to pursue him through the air.

In the room above, 729, Harvey Thomas found himself flying through space. He thought he was dreaming about asteroids.

The blast wave continued upward through the eighth floor and exploded through the roof, shooting tiles into a starlit sky. A flagpole snapped off and arced over the promenade onto the beach.

The eruption engulfed one of the two great chimney stacks with velocity greater than a typhoon's. For generations, these eleven-foot-tall stacks, each with five stone funnels, had belched smoke from hundreds of fireplaces. Central heating had made them redundant, but still they soared with symmetrical precision over the center of the Grand. Now the western stack, a five-ton exemplar of Victorian engineering, encountered the full force of late-twentieth-century terrorist technology. An unequal match. The stack fell.

With a rumble never forgotten by those who heard it, the masonry cracked and smashed through the roof, gathering speed and violence as it plunged downward, room by room, impelled not by explosives but that other unforgiving force: gravity.

Harvey Thomas realized he was not dreaming but flailing through a void filled with bashing objects. Gordon Shattock experienced a slow-motion descent into Hades. "There was no floor and I started to fall into a pit," he recalled. Girders, concrete, and bricks crashed down with him. "I seemed to be falling faster than the debris and I had the feeling if I hit anything solid the debris would catch me up."

The avalanche punched through the ceiling of 528 and collected Eric and Jennifer Taylor and everything else in their room as it hurtled down into 428, where it swept up John and Roberta Wakeham. Then 328 was obliterated, casting Anthony and Sarah Berry and their dogs into the vortex.

In 228, Norman Tebbit, lying in bed, eyes wide open since the blast a few moments earlier, saw the chandelier sway above him. "It's a bomb," he shouted to his wife. Then came a deafening roar, and the maelstrom swallowed them.

When the bomb detonated, Margaret Thatcher heard a muffled crash and felt the room shake. Plaster dropped from the ceiling. A slab of glass from a shattered window splintered into shards on the green carpet. She knew immediately it was a bomb. There were a few seconds of silence, then a rumble of falling masonry. The prime minister stood up and went to the window, suspecting a car bomb on the promenade.

Robin Butler said: "I think you ought to come away from the

window." Thatcher ignored him. Then, oblivious to the homicidal cascade falling above, she darted for the bedroom. "I must see if Denis is all right." She opened the door and vanished into darkness. Butler watched in horror. He could hear the Napoleon Suite's bathroom collapsing. A thought honed by decades in government assailed the prime minister's chief civil servant. "If she's gone to her death, what am I going to tell the commission of inquiry?"

A moment later, to Butler's immense relief, Thatcher reappeared with Denis, who was pulling clothes over his pajamas and digesting the destruction to the bathroom. "I've never seen so much glass in my life."

They went out to the corridor and saw a police bodyguard trying to kick open a door to a suite occupied by Geoffrey Howe, the foreign secretary, and his wife, Elspeth. The Thatchers and Butler scrambled into the secretaries' office opposite the Napoleon Suite. The Garden Girls were unharmed, but shaken. Thatcher consoled one of them. "It's probably a bomb, but don't worry, dear."

With the Grand Hotel still groaning and cracking, the prime minister sat in a chair and murmured to no one in particular: "I think that was an assassination attempt, don't you?"

. . .

THE BOMB MISSED the Iron Lady. It did not even scratch her. But it came very, very close.

Through planning—not least, dispatching a construction engineer to study the Grand—the IRA multiplied the device's destructive force by toppling the chimney stack. Like a monstrous guillotine, it sliced through concrete, steel, and wood, all the way to the ground floor. What saved Thatcher was the path it took. It toppled through the blast hole, then veered sideways and plunged down a vertical stack of rooms with numbers ending in *8*. It merely clipped those rooms, including Thatcher's Napoleon Suite, with numbers ending in *9*.

Had Thatcher still been in her bathroom she would have been cut

The shattered bathroom in Margaret Thatcher's Napoleon Suite, in Brighton's Grand Hotel, after the IRA bomb exploded on October 12, 1984. | PA Images

to ribbons, perhaps fatally. The briefest extension of the speechwriting marathon—a final musing over a certain adjective, or haggling over a particular verb—could have placed her in the bathroom precisely at the moment of detonation, leaving her sprayed by a blizzard of broken glass, ceramic, and concrete. Instead, she emerged with two minutes to spare and was in the lounge, about a dozen feet from the bathroom, when the carnage began. Even there, she might have perished. Had the chimney stack toppled a slightly different way, the tons of debris could have smashed into her suite and flattened the lounge. Revenge for the dead hunger strikers would have been served, and a major

Western democracy would have convulsed. Thatcherism might have died with her. The attorney general would probably have designated Willie Whitelaw, a traditional Tory grandee, as caretaker prime minister while the Conservatives chose a successor. History pirouetted on a twist of geometry.

With alarm bells hammering and a great cloud of thick, choking dust enveloping the hotel, Thatcher had no time to mull over what might have been. Chaos reigned. The attempt to murder her and wipe out her government was a defining moment that stripped personal and political instincts to their essence. Hunkered in the secretaries' office, Thatcher did not know the extent of the damage, or that friends and colleagues were buried in rubble fighting for oxygen, for life. She knew she had to escape the bedlam in the Grand and take charge of the crisis.

The lights stayed on in Thatcher's part of the hotel, permitting an air of deceptive normality. Cabinet ministers and officials emerged from nearby rooms, some in dressing gowns and pajamas, and huddled with the prime minister. Aides packed her documents and clothes, while bodyguards discussed an exit plan. Michael Alison, Thatcher's devout Christian parliamentary private secretary, said to her quietly: "Thank God you're all right, Margaret."

"I do," she replied. "I do thank him."

. . .

SEVERAL BLOCKS AWAY, three fire engines raced through Brighton's deserted streets. Fred Bishop swayed in the lead vehicle, untroubled. The Grand's alarm system had automatically triggered a tape-recorded voice to the fire brigade: "Fire, Grand Hotel, Brighton." The message had been relayed to Preston Circus station, two miles from the hotel, where eleven men from Green Watch were on duty. Bishop was in charge. His team scrambled within twenty-eight seconds, blue lights flashing, with little expectation of action. Hotel calls were usually false alarms, or trivial, like a smoking toaster. "Someone's broken a fire alarm to get Maggie out of bed," said a fireman.

A small, compact man with a thick mustache, Bishop loved his job. Being trained and paid to save people, what was better? His blunt honesty sometimes discommoded the higher-ups, but his men did not complain. Fred never asked anything he would not do himself. He did not really follow politics, but knew about the Tory conference and agreed with his colleague: probably a hoax call.

The trucks turned onto the promenade. "Here, it's suddenly got misty," said someone. Bishop peered ahead. Indeed, a gray miasma coated King's Road. Then he saw sheets and pillowcases and curtains hanging from lampposts and lanterns. He realized the mist was dust, a billowing, smothering plume that obscured the hotel and seafront. "The dust was so thick it looked like Sleeping Beauty, as if the place had been asleep for 100 years," one witness later said. Stumbling through it were ghostly apparitions, policemen and people in ball gowns and tuxedos, dazed and ragged, some bleeding, like other-worldly survivors tottering ashore from an ancient shipwreck.

"There was screaming, you could hear crashes of masonry and metal," said Lesley Brett, a passerby. She never forgot the arrival of the fire trucks. "There was no nee-naw, just blue lights coming out of this huge cloud of dust. They arrived absolutely silently, like angels from heaven."

Bishop ordered Green Watch to park in front of the stricken Grand and asked a policeman what had happened. "Um, it just went bang," came the bewildered reply.

Broken bricks, glass, and fragments of railings littered the ground. Bishop surveyed the hotel facade. A huge V-shaped gash ran from top to center, with more destruction visible on lower floors. Possible causes included a bomb, a gas leak, or a roof collapse. Over the blare of fire alarms, he could hear shouts for help. A hotel employee told him there were about three hundred people inside. Under brigade rules, if

The Grand Hotel's ruined facade hours after Patrick Magee's bomb
detonated on the sixth floor on October 12, 1984. | PA Images

there was a bomb or suspected bomb, the crew was to park two streets
away, maintain radio silence, and wait for the police bomb squad,
unless there was a fire. There appeared to be no fire. Bishop gathered
his men. "Something dreadful's happened here. It may well have been
a bomb . . . so I can't officially order you to go in, because we don't
know. There are going to be dangers inside the building. I'm going in,
to find out what the problem is, as much as I can, and sort out the
rescues." To a man, Green Watch volunteered to go in.

"Everyone said, 'Well if you're going in, governor, we're going in
with you.' And that was the end of it," Bishop recalled. He radioed
headquarters that three hundred people were unaccounted for, requested ten more fire engines and multiple ambulances, then led his
crew into the Grand.

.   .   .

THATCHER'S BODYGUARDS FEARED a secondary device—a lesson from
the Narrow Water ambush—and wanted to move her to another lo-

cation. They also feared the possibility of a sniper waiting outside to finish the job. There was also a transport problem; no one could access the prime minister's car, which was locked up for the night. By chance, one of the first rescue ladders was laid against the Napoleon Suite balcony, but bodyguards vetoed the idea of the prime minister clambering down to the promenade in full glare of streetlights. They checked the rear exit for rogue gunmen—it seemed to be clear—and rustled up another car. At 3:10 a.m., they led the prime minister down the first-floor corridor and encountered Fred Bishop's team.

Thatcher, impeccable in her ball gown, not a hair out of place, greeted the rescuers with a courtesy so formal it bordered on surreal, given the chaos. "Good morning, I'm delighted to see you. Thank you for coming." If the firemen were flummoxed, they did not show it. "You've got to think, 'Well, didn't have a lot of choice really,'" Bishop said. "But you didn't say it back to her, obviously."

After leading the group down a dead end, a fireman led Thatcher, her husband, and a few officials down the main staircase to the lobby, where Patrick Magee had checked in three weeks earlier. Cement dust coated their clothes and hair and filled their mouths, making Thatcher cough. She saw rubble in the entrance and foyer—her first inkling of the carnage.

Outside, beyond her line of sight, scores of guests huddled on the promenade. They had escaped through windows, broken doors, and dust-filled corridors. Those with shoes carried the barefooted over the debris. Off-duty nurses who had been at a dinner tore their evening dresses to bandage the wounded. There was no screaming, no panic, just numb shock. "They were shaking and kept saying, 'We're cold, we're cold,'" recalled Ivor Gaber, a BBC producer who had been staying at the neighboring Metropole hotel when the explosion jolted him out of bed. "It's shock, because it wasn't that cold, it was quite a warm evening."

People wandered in a daze. Keith Joseph, the education minister, in slippers and a paisley dressing gown, perched on his "red boxes"—ministerial briefcases with official papers. Lord Jock Bruce-Gardyne

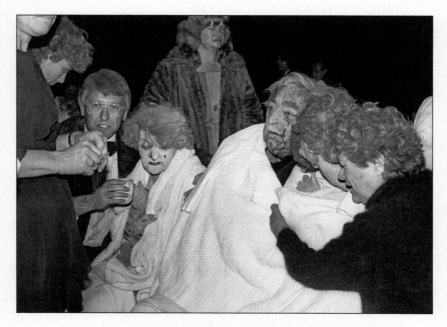

Dazed and injured guests huddle outside the Grand Hotel
after the explosion. | Martin Mayer

wore a three-piece suit and club tie, a vision of elegance sabotaged by a
missing sock, subsequently earning him the nickname One Sock Jock.
Lord Gowrie, a former Northern Ireland minister, fetched dozens of
deck chairs from the beach. Gaber itched to film everything, but to
save money the BBC, and ITV, had lodged cameramen and their kit at
cheaper hotels outside Brighton. As fire engines and ambulances filled
King's Road, the survivors gazed at the ruined hotel, dumbstruck.
Anguish deepened when a rumor spread that Thatcher was dead.

In fact, she was in the lobby, delaying her exit to ask about reception staff. Assured they were all right, she followed the firemen and
bodyguards toward the rear exit, clambering over discarded belongings
and broken furniture. "It still never occurred to me that anyone would
have died," she later said.

Dead, dying, and desperate colleagues were just yards away, invisible, entombed in rubble that stretched from the basement to the

first floor. Norman and Margaret Tebbit were actually suspended above Thatcher, encased in debris about twelve feet over the reception area. Both were grievously injured and contorted, unable to move, locked in a black, muffled hell. They could not hear sirens or alarms, only the groans and chokes of others trapped nearby. Norman called for his wife and she replied from somewhere close. She was just inches away. He moved his left arm slightly, and their fingers touched.

Oblivious to such agonies, Thatcher was shepherded outside. Gulping in night air, she climbed into the backseat of a waiting car with Denis and Cynthia Crawford, her personal aide. A photographer captured the moment. Crawford, gaping; Denis, disheveled; the Iron Lady, jaw firmly set, gaze fixed ahead, like a figurehead on the bow of a ship. Shortly after 3:15 a.m., police escorts led the way to a designated safe haven, the Brighton police station, a mile away. En route, Denis raged. "The IRA, those bastards." His wife remained calm, inscrutable.

The five-story police station on John Street briefly became the power center of Britain. Thatcher sailed in, one officer commented,

Margaret Thatcher, flanked by her husband, Denis, and personal assistant, Cynthia Crawford, is driven from the Grand Hotel after the bomb. | John Downing via Getty Images

"like a battleship." After changing into a navy-blue suit, the prime minister and her inner circle sipped sweet, strong tea in the office of Superintendent Dennis Williams. Other ministers and officials arrived, filling corridors, some in pajamas, like a bizarre VIP sleepover. The US ambassador, Charles Price, was shoeless. Thatcher noticed police struggling to squeeze past the throng. She stepped out. "You people, come in here out of the way," she ordered. The corridor duly unblocked. With a glint in her eye, she told a police officer: "I'm playing the schoolmarm today, aren't I?"

While senior officers and officials discussed her accommodation, and how to get her back to London, Thatcher tapped her fingers on the desk. Then she snapped. "Gentlemen, I have sat here listening to this discussion for some time and a decision needs to be made. I do not mind where you take me but there is one clear instruction. You must have me back at the conference center by 9 a.m. Is that understood?"

A ghastly realization struck her listeners. The woman intended to go on. An unprecedented attack on the British government, casualties unknown, the promenade a war zone, and she wanted to resume the conference.

Just before 4:00 a.m., Thatcher emerged from the police station to a media scrum. Ignoring bodyguards' attempts to shoo her into a car, she gave an impromptu press conference, TV camera lights illuminating the darkness. She described hearing the bomb and her escape from the Grand. "You hear about these atrocities, these bombs, you don't expect them to happen to you. But life must go on, as usual," she said.

"And the conference will go on?" asked the BBC's political correspondent, John Cole.

"The conference will go on," Thatcher said. "The conference will go on, *as usual.*"

The bodyguards exhaled when she climbed into the car, only to see her climb out again to ask Cole if he needed another take. An hour after being almost being murdered, Thatcher wanted to get the sound bite just right. Her survival was not enough. She wanted to deny the IRA even the satisfaction of halting the conference. Her speech was to go ahead, on schedule.

. . .

AMONG THE REFUGEES at the promenade, word swiftly spread. "Maggie's safe!" Such was the relief, strangers shook hands and embraced, though in silence. Inside the Grand other fire crews joined Fred Bishop's team in evacuating rooms. Remarkably, some guests had slept through the explosion and alarms and awoke to hammering on their doors and men in helmets and dark tunics bursting into their rooms. Some protested. "Get out!" one government figure shouted. He was, the interloping fireman later recalled, "in bed with a young lady that wasn't his wife."

As Bishop made his way to upper floors, he grasped the pattern of destruction. The initial blast had destroyed several rooms on the sixth and seventh floors and the chimney stack had cleaved a path down through 528, 428, 328, 228, and 128 like a deadly lift shaft, dumping a two-story-high heap of wreckage. While sea-facing rooms that formed part of the facade had collapsed, rear sections of the hotel were untouched. Most guests were unscathed. Bishop realized that casualties were likely to be in the remnants of the upper floors and in the mound of debris below.

He ordered his men to turn off and, if necessary, smash the clattering alarms, to better hear the plaintive cries of the trapped. On upper floors, rescuers operated in darkness and fog-like dust on the jagged edges of a crumbling chasm. Each step risked fresh collapse. The blast had shredded a fifteen-thousand-gallon water tank on the roof, dousing everything below. Water spurted from broken pipes. Live power cables snaked and sparked. Bishop and his men attached themselves to ropes in case of a tumble into the void. Bishop was risking not only his career but his life. A brigade chief briefly entered the Grand to fulminate about him leading his crew into a bomb zone.

"If I lose anybody, anybody injured of my men," said the chief, "I'm having your guts for garters."

An official building surveyor arrived, took one look at the shaky edifice, and said the Grand was going to fall down. The rescuers ignored him. Their adrenaline was pumping; they were going to find survivors.

Gordon Shattock and Jennifer Taylor were in the basement, miraculously alive and with only minor injuries despite having fallen from the sixth and fifth floors, respectively. They groped toward each other's voices and stumbled out, hand in hand. Gordon did not know his wife, Jeanne, was dead. "Where's Eric?" sobbed Jennifer, clutching a blanket around her bloodstained nightdress. Her husband, the North-West Conservative Association chairman, was deep inside the mound above her, seriously hurt and running out of oxygen.

On a precipice of what was left of Patrick Magee's former room, 629, firemen found Muriel Maclean, her head gashed, her right leg mangled, in excruciating pain. Using an aerial ladder, they lowered her on a stretcher to the pavement. Guided by his cries they found her husband, Donald, president of the Scottish Conservatives, on the fifth floor, battered and buried under wreckage. He, too, was extracted.

"Hilp! Hilp!" Another faint voice on the fifth floor. Harvey Thomas may have been built like a bear, but he was immobile under tons of debris, with water leaking into his nose and mouth, and was not so much calling as gurgling. "Hilp!" he repeated. He prayed—and then Billy Graham's protégé heard the seven sweetest words of his life: "Quiet, quiet. There's somebody alive down there."

One of Bishop's team beamed a torch and asked if he could see the light.

Blinded by mud, Thomas replied, "I saw the light years ago, brother, but I can't see yours."

The firemen found Thomas suspended over a chasm, his head and feet wedged in debris, with a bath full of masonry and roof timbers on his chest. They began a slow, perilous extraction. The conference's technical coordinator tried to ignore electric cables sizzling nearby. He worried about his wife, Marlies, back home, four days overdue for the birth of their first child.

"Harvey, we're going to get you there."

After ninety minutes, he was free. A TV crew recorded seven firemen stretchering his naked bulk, covered with blankets, down the stairs. "If we'd realized what you weighed, we would have gone to rescue somebody else," said one.

Down in the foyer, near floor level, another crew heard a distant noise that sounded like barking.

"Silence!" shouted Chris Reid, a veteran fireman. In the hush they heard it again, a yapping. With picks and bare hands, they tunneled into the debris, then heard a woman's muffled screams. They tunneled closer to the spot from which the voice seemed to emanate.

"What's your name?" Reid shouted into the debris.

A pause, then a voice seeped out. "Lady Berry."

The wife of Sir Anthony Berry was buried alive with a broken pelvis, but Britain's aristocratic titles endured. Reid, accustomed to rapport on first-name terms, hesitated. "I wasn't then sure how to address her," he recalled. As he tunneled closer, she became Sarah, and he learned that her two Jack Russells, Smudge and Lucky, were with her. She was trapped between the hotel's revolving door and twisted flooring. Of her MP husband, there was no sign.

Somewhere beneath her, far deeper in the dense mass of stone and timber, came another voice. "Who is that?" called a fireman.

"My name is Eric."

This was Eric Taylor. The rescuers started burrowing toward him.

Perched on a ladder leaning against twelve feet of debris, over the remains of reception, a fireman made another startling discovery: three hands poking out. Two were moving. Fred Bishop climbed up and grasped one.

"Who's that up there?" asked a voice within.

"No, who's that in there?" said Bishop.

"No, I asked first," said the voice.

Margaret Tebbit, speaking from her tomb. Another voice, one that had boomed from the podium and electrified the Tory faithful a day earlier, croaked from the rubble. This was Norman Tebbit. Both were still alive, if only just. The industry minister was curled into a fetal position, wedged into a mattress, dust and grit filling his mouth. Electric cables fizzed nearby. His left side was a sticky mass of broken ribs and a punctured lung. He could hear his guts sloshing. His skull was squeezed by debris as if it were a vise. Excruciating pain came in waves. Margaret was bent double, a huge weight pressing on her neck, yet felt little pain. As a nurse, she knew what that probably signified. Alone in the blackness, they had spoken about their children, comforted and lied to each other. Norman did not mention that he could not feel his left arm, which he feared was severed, nor that he was touching the cold limb of what he assumed was a corpse. Margaret did not mention the paralysis creeping through her body.

When she had first cried for help, Norman shushed her. "Wait until you can hear them digging, or you'll exhaust yourself. It'll be a long time yet." He visualized a total collapse like bombed barracks in Beirut. He wondered if Thatcher and the rest of the cabinet were dead, and who would run the government. His fingers lost their grasp on Margaret's hand. She did not seem able to grip back.

A searing pain, the strongest yet, racked his body. "So this is death," he thought. "How strange. What a waste."

Then the agony ebbed. It had been an electric shock. Then he heard a voice. An unseen hand gripped his and reunited it with Margaret's.

Bishop's team faced a dilemma. The Tebbits were ensnared in a compressed mass of broken brick, metal, wiring, and wood, and would not last much longer. But burrowing into the wreckage risked fresh collapse. Standing on ladders, unable to use heavy tools, with Bishop taking the lead, the rescuers used their hands, knives, and saws to clear a little passageway downward toward the couple, keeping them talking to be guided by their voices.

They reached Margaret first. "Get Norman out," she said. "Get him out first."

Bishop vetoed that. She was above her husband and he could see the weight pressing on her neck.

"How do you feel?" Bishop asked.

"Very cold," she replied. She did not say more, not wanting to alert Norman to the gravity of her injuries.

Bishop appraised her. "Pass me a collar, Stan."

He knows the truth, thought Margaret.

They pulled her out, shredding her nightdress. She felt nothing. Yet when they wrapped her in a tinfoil-type space blanket, she mustered a smile. "I feel just like a chicken being wrapped up to go into the oven," she said.

This woman, thought Bishop, has been in hell for three hours, knows she's paralyzed, and cracks a joke. Absolutely incredible.

With Margaret stretchered away, Bishop cut and clawed his way toward her husband. The lifeless arm Norman had felt turned out to be his own, still attached, just with no circulation. The firemen took turns keeping him talking, about his pilot days, football, childhood games of conkers, anything to keep him from lapsing unconscious.

"How's Margaret?" Norman asked.

"Margaret's fine," lied Bishop. "We've got her off to hospital, just to get checked over."

As salvation neared, Tebbit's desperation increased. He gripped Bishop's hand and refused to let go. "I've never held a man's hand this long before," he said.

A colleague cut through an electric cable. There was a flash and a loud bang, and the Grand's foyer plunged into darkness. The firemen summoned a BBC crew and used TV lights to illuminate their work. And so a waking nation watched, incredulous, as breakfast TV broadcast the rescue of Margaret Thatcher's right-hand man. It became a defining drama of the Brighton bomb.

To complete the rescue, Bishop removed his helmet and clawed like a mole into a tiny space, with just his feet sticking out. Colleagues thought him mad. If the debris came down, he'd had it. The chiefs, of course, would give him another rocket for breaking more brigade rules. Some water was dabbed on Tebbit's cracked lips. "That was bloody marvelous," he croaked.

To grip Tebbit, who was curled up, Bishop rested his stomach on Tebbit's feet.

The minister shrieked, as if on fire. "Get off my bloody feet, Fred!"

"Norman, if I get off your bloody feet you'll fall into this bloody hole."

They laughed, breaking the tension. Bishop hauled him free, leaving his hands and leggings coated in Tebbit's blood.

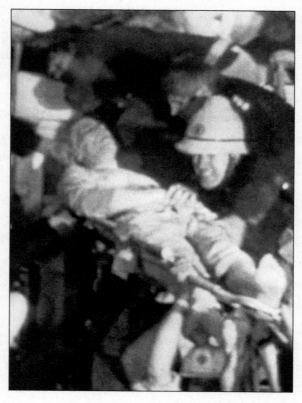

Firemen stretcher Norman Tebbit from the rubble of the Grand—
a still image taken from BBC TV news. | PA Images

Viewers watched transfixed as Tebbit, grimacing, was stretchered down, a broken doll in blue pajamas. It was 6:53 a.m.

In the ambulance, his spirit revived. A paramedic preparing drips and painkillers asked if he was allergic to anything.

"Yes," said the minister. "Bombs."

. . .

PATRICK MAGEE REMAINED awake in his Cork hideaway, glued to the transistor radio, willing the pirate station to update its hourly news bulletin. Finally, it came. A report of a large bomb at the Conservative Party Conference in Brighton. Details were sketchy, but it seemed at least two people had died, and Margaret Thatcher had survived. Relief washed over Magee. His bomb had detonated. No dud fuse. No Paddy Factor. As the last link in the chain, the operator, he had delivered what was asked, a strike at the heart of the British state.

Thatcher lived. Well, she and her government now knew that the Troubles could not be contained. The Provos had brought the war not just to England but to her inner sanctum. It was for the Army Council to decide if that constituted success.

Drained by tension, Magee sank into bed and fell asleep.

. . .

BY 7:00 A.M., the sun rose in a clear blue sky over Brighton. The English Channel appeared serene. It was going to be a balmy autumn day. The promenade vibrated with fire engines and police vehicles. Tape sealed off King's Road. Men in blue overalls—detectives from the Anti-Terrorist Branch, C13—collected debris from asphalt and shingle.

Daylight was not kind to the Grand. A jagged, ugly gash yawned deep and wide across the creamy wedding cake facade. It looked as though a ravenous giant had scooped chunks out of the top, leaving the insides dangling. TV crews and photographers multiplied on the seafront. The proud Grand sign sagged, as if shamed of attention in such a state. From what was left of the roof, a Union Jack hung limply from its broken pole.

Inside the Grand, phones trilled in abandoned bedrooms: automated wake-up calls requested the previous night. A switchboard printer in a back office clunked out its paper record: *No answer, no answer, no answer.* Pauline Banks, the head telephonist, was brought in to field desperate—and macabre—calls. "One man asked: 'Are you selling anything? Are you selling the toilet seat Margaret Thatcher sat on?'" she recalled.

Among the ruins, rescuers were running out of lives to save. The faint, quavering voice of Eric Taylor had fallen silent. No one had heard cries from Sir Anthony Berry and Roberta Wakeham, who were unaccounted for. The coroner later established that all three suffocated. Trapped in dust and darkness, gasping for breath—their terror and suffering can only be imagined. Jeanne Shattock's mutilated body remained on the sixth floor. Muriel Maclean would die of her injuries the following month. Five dead, all told.

One voice still called from the rubble. John Wakeham, the government chief whip, lay under timber and masonry in what was left of the foyer. Firemen borrowed heavy-duty chain saws from a construction rental firm to clear a path.

The injured were treated two miles away at Royal Sussex County Hospital, a hilltop jumble of Victorian-era buildings and a modern fourteen-story tower. Staff had streamed in overnight as ambulances delivered dusty, bleeding patients. Carlos Perez-Avila, a senior doctor, marveled at the stoicism. "In El Salvador, where I come from, there probably would have been hysteria and crying and yelling and 'Ahhh!'" he later said. "Here the so-called stiff upper lip was amazing. . . . There were serious, serious injuries and nobody really moaned or screamed."

Despite his parlous state, Norman Tebbit addressed staff by their titles. Asked about his tolerance for pain, Thatcher's right-wing lieutenant managed another quip: "I'm not known for my tolerance."

Donald Maclean found himself being X-rayed by a radiographer with a broad Irish accent. "Her very first comments were to apologize for being Irish and advising me that if this was upsetting me she would get one of her colleagues to do the work," he said. Maclean was touched and saddened she felt the need to offer.

Instead of hundreds of casualties, as initially feared, the hospital treated thirty-three. These included Pamela Plappert, the chambermaid who lived in the Grand, plus five police officers. Calls from around the world, among them kings and presidents, swamped the hospital's old-fashioned manual switchboard. Journalists filing copy besieged two public pay phones in the accident and emergency department. The hospital's press officer corralled them in an adjacent room, close enough to see what was happening without intruding, with a trolley of bacon sandwiches as added incentive to stay put. To feed their voracious appetite for interviews, the hospital produced an irrepressible Harvey Thomas.

The conference coordinator was cut and bruised but otherwise remarkably undamaged and happy to talk. He initially thought the explosion was an earthquake, he told the journalists. "But then I thought, no, you don't have earthquakes in Brighton, at least not during a Tory party conference." Back at the promenade, the Grand's displaced guests milled in the neighboring Metropole hotel. Numb with shock, some shaking, they picked at eggs and bacon. Word reached Alistair McAlpine, the party treasurer, that Thatcher intended to go on with the conference. A pajama-clad audience would not do. McAlpine made some calls. At 8:00 a.m., a coach and a fleet of taxis ferried the Tories to a Marks & Spencer department store, which opened early. Staff helped them select suits, dresses, and shoes, then the convoy returned to the promenade, with the party covering all expenses. The organization, marveled Ivor Gaber, the BBC producer, was flawless. "You could see how the Conservatives always win elections."

By then, news bulletins were reporting an IRA statement issued via its press bureau in Dublin. It read: "The IRA claims responsibility for the detonation of 100lb of gelignite in Brighton against the British cabinet and Tory warmongers. Thatcher will now realise that Britain cannot occupy our country, torture our prisoners and shoot our people in their own streets and get away with it." There was a chilling addendum: "Today we were unlucky, but remember we have only to be lucky once, you will have to be lucky always. Give Ireland peace and there will be no war."

When news of the attack reached the H-Blocks, republican prisoners erupted in cheers. There were shouts of "Fuck Thatcher" and "Up the 'Ra," Anthony McIntyre, a former prisoner, said. "We were cock-a-hoop, punching the air." Not killing Thatcher was a disappointment, but inmates still considered the attack a daring blow and payback for the ten comrades who starved to death.

Governments around the world condemned the bomb in telexes that chattered into the Foreign and Commonwealth Office in London. The Queen, who was in Kentucky inspecting horses, sent a statement expressing shock and sympathy—a reversal from the Mountbatten bombing five years earlier, when Thatcher had written to the Queen. Ronald Reagan denounced the "barbarous" attempt to murder his British ally.

Someone else who was in Washington took a personal interest: David Tadd, the Anti-Terrorist Branch's fingerprint chief, was with C13 colleagues attending the final day of a federal court case on behalf of the Bureau of Alcohol, Tobacco, and Firearms. He studied the images of the bombed Grand on US television. *This,* he thought, *is going to be one bugger of a job.*

. . .

ROGER BIRCH, THE chief constable of the Sussex Police, waited with other senior officers at the rear entrance of the conference center. They could not stop the prime minister from going ahead with the conference, but had asked her to use the back door for security. She arrived at 9:25 a.m. and swept in the main entrance. "We all stood about like lemons at the back while she breezed in at the front," Birch recalled.

Thatcher was determined to show no concession, no weakness. She had barely slept. After her predawn press conference outside the police station, she had been driven to Lewes Police College, a training facility just outside of Brighton. In a small bedroom, she had kneeled and prayed in silence before lying down, fully clothed, for a fitful nap. She awoke to the sound of television news broadcasting Norman Tebbit's rescue. Briefed about the other casualties, she did not waver: the conference would go on. Downing coffee and devouring grapefruit—a police motorcyclist had scoured Brighton overnight to obtain her favorite fruit—she returned in a convoy to Brighton and saw the Grand's wrecked facade. Somewhere inside, she knew, John Wakeham was fighting for his life, and his wife was dead. Days earlier, she had hosted them for lunch.

At 9:30 a.m., she entered the hall. Security checks delayed people entering, so many seats were empty, but those who were there hollered and cheered as she made her way to the platform. There was a two-minute silence for the dead, then the conference held its scheduled debate, which happened to be about Northern Ireland. On camera, at least, things were unfolding *as usual*.

Thatcher retired to a side office with ministers and writers to rework her speech. Out went the denunciations of left-wing opponents as the "enemy within." Neil Kinnock, Labour's leader, had expressed solidarity; this was not the time for partisanship. Ironically, an act of violence softened her speech.

A flow of flowers, messages, and visitors interrupted the drafting. There was one light moment. An old friend of Harvey Thomas from his Bible college days in Minneapolis sent a telegram addressed to "Harvey Thomas, care of Margaret Thatcher, Brighton, England." When Thomas himself turned up, Thatcher smiled and offered to read it aloud. "It says: 'Dear Harvey, I saw you on television here in California this morning. Do you know, we've known each other 25 years and I've never seen you naked before? Love, Diane.'"

It was a brief respite. As the hall filled to capacity, the Tories' sense of shock and anxiety seemed to deepen. Something had changed, perhaps forever. Conference security, Britain's whole way of doing politics, was in question. Never again could terrorists be allowed to come so close.

Confirmation that some of the missing were indeed dead reached relatives across Britain. In London, Joanne Berry, the daughter of Anthony Berry, walked in a daze down the street. "Dad's dead, Dad's dead, Dad's dead," she repeated. Passersby asked if she was all right. "No," she said, and kept walking.

At 2:00 p.m., the prime minister strode onto the platform to close the conference. She had typed pages but no teleprompter; Harvey had pulled it to underline this was Margaret Thatcher in the raw, speaking from the gut. Her words rang out over a hushed hall. "The bomb attack . . . was first and foremost an inhuman and indiscriminating attempt to massacre innocent and unsuspecting people," she said, face pale, voice strong. "The attack was not only an attempt to disrupt and terminate our conference. It was an attempt to cripple Her Majesty's democratically elected government. That is the scale of the outrage in which we have all shared. And the fact that we are gathered here now, shocked but composed and determined, is a sign not only that this attack has failed, but that all attempts to destroy democracy by terrorism will fail."

The speech ranged widely—economics, philosophy, foreign affairs— to show that government went on. Life went on. Every phrase radiated defiance. The IRA had tried to murder her? Well, here she was, unbowed. A leader who mingled in the fray, no coward in the fight. Even those in Britain who loathed her were awed. They could see her mettle, and it gleamed. The ovation seemed never to end. It was her finest hour.

. . .

PATRICK MAGEE WATCHED from a pub. After a few hours of sleep that morning, he had left his billet and gone into the city of Cork looking for cable television news. The bar was packed, all eyes on the reports from Brighton. Few people spoke. There was Thatcher, looking grim, determined. The Grand Hotel, wrecked. Policemen crawling over the scene, carting things away, like ants.

Feigning disinterest, Magee waited for his Guinness to settle, the blackness rising up the glass. The operation, he realized, would follow him.

"What struck me forcefully was that this bomb would have profound implications for me directly, deeper than any from my previous involvement," he noted later. "The Brits would pull out all the stops in pursuit of those they held responsible. I knew that my name would be in the frame," he reflected. "I would always be looking over my shoulder. They would never forget."

PART III

—

Manhunt

CHAPTER FIFTEEN

———

Wetting Worms

Detective Chief Superintendent Jack Reece crunched through the rubble of the Grand and again heaved his bulk up six flights of stairs. A cold breeze wafted through the shattered facade. The destroyed roof's jagged beams and masonry framed a starlit sky. It was the evening of October 12, 1984, more than eighteen hours since the bomb.

The reason Reece was making another ascent to the suspected seat of the explosion was that Jeanne Shattock's remains had been discovered nearby. A large, pear-shaped fifty-five-year-old, he was fitter than he looked. A balding head, gold-rimmed glasses, and a consistently stern expression gave the impression of a crumpled owl. White dust powdered his hard hat and suit by the time he reached room 638.

There, a pathologist was leaning into a cupboard to examine Mrs. Shattock. Fred Bishop and his team had wanted to remove her, but detectives said no bloody way. The body was forensic evidence and needed to be left in situ. After a standoff, the firemen withdrew. There was no one left to rescue. The Grand was now a crime scene under police control.

Margaret Thatcher had left. After her conference speech, she had visited the injured in the hospital before being driven at high speed to Chequers, police motorbikes cleaving a path. The Brighton she left behind was no longer just a town but an event, its implications still ricocheting. As head of the Sussex Criminal Investigation Department (CID), Reece was responsible for solving the crime. It had happened on his patch, on his watch. Britain had no FBI-type agency authorized to elbow aside local police and take charge. Scotland Yard covered just metropolitan London, with specialist units dispatched outside the capital only if needed. Policing in Britain was subdivided by region, and Brighton fell under the authority of the Sussex Police, a midsize county force. Each station had a unit of plainclothes CID detectives from Sussex Police headquarters at Lewes, ten miles northeast of Brighton. These units were overseen by Reece. It was his job to gather evidence, identify suspects, and build a case that would stand up in court. To lead, in other words, the UK's biggest-ever manhunt. Known as Big Jack for his heft, and Pinky Reece for his choleric temper, Reece was considered by his officers and even the criminals he put away to be a straight player. He answered the phone with a single blunt syllable: "Reece."

He could be intimidating, and you didn't want to feel a slap from those meaty hands. But he didn't plant evidence or tweak confessions. Reece was an old-school copper. "Always spoke his mind, always. Never, ever held back. A tough guy, old Jack," observed his deputy, Bernie Wells.

Reece's father, a Yorkshire coal miner, had died in a pit accident when Reece was eight. His mother moved to Hastings on the Sussex coast and young Jack grew up fishing and hunting gulls' eggs. He got his start in crime fighting during army service when cigarettes and cash started disappearing from soldiers' lockers. One evening Reece hid in a locker—he was skinny then—and observed a soldier from a neighboring barracks sneaking in to pilfer. "I clocked him a good 'un and sat on him until the rest of the guys began arriving back from dinner," he said. His fellow soldiers nicknamed him Sherlock.

Reece joined the Hastings police in 1951, when he was twenty-two, and married Daphne Hyland, an office worker and an inspired cook. They never had children, heartache for a man who yearned to be a father. Reece found solace in work, starting as a police driver before becoming a detective and rising up the CID ranks. The big body contained a nimble brain. He learned to type and would spend hours hunched over manuals and books. Reece investigated corrupt London detectives, caught the attempted kidnapper of a viscountess, and interrogated Alfredo Astiz, the Argentine junta's "blond angel of death," who was extradited after the Falklands War. "Jack Reece was an amazing man, really," recalled Jon Buss, the *Evening Argus*'s crime correspondent. Previous CID chiefs would hold court in pubs, swaying on

Detective Chief Superintendent Jack Reece briefs the media about the Brighton bomb investigation. | Argus/Sussex News and Pictures

their feet, said Buss. "You had to sort of step back because they were so inebriated they were spilling drink on you as they were telling you things. Jack Reece wasn't like that. He was a very clever man, a self-taught clever man, who had worked his way up from the bottom."

With his dark suits, silver hair, and jowls, Reece could have passed for a bank manager, but he was a hunter—and not only of criminals. He was also champion angler, his arms oak-hard from reeling in sharks and swordfish. Before casting a line, he would toss a coin in the sea as an offering to Neptune. "Here you are, Neppy, send us a big 'un," he would murmur. Reece was said to be the first person to catch a porbeagle—a mackerel shark—off the Hastings coast. Often rising before dawn to catch his own bait, he compared fishing to gathering evidence. You hooked big fish with little fish, and those you hooked with worms, which needed to be kept moist. "Unless you are wetting worms, you don't catch the fish."

The night before the bomb, Reece had kissed Daphne good night and gone to sleep at their home in Hastings, feeling secure about his future. Soon he would retire and collect his pension. He would go shooting for pheasants, which Daphne cooked up, and then perhaps add more fish to the giant aquarium in the spare bedroom, where he bred exotic fish like neon tetra and kissing gourami. And he would trawl the world's oceans. He had heard of "monster" sharks off the Azores.

Then the operations room woke him to report an explosion at the prime minister's hotel. Even under normal circumstances, Reece savored speed—even if it terrified his passengers—and he knew every curve of the forty miles to Brighton. One look at the stricken Grand and its casualties convinced him to postpone retirement. It would be the biggest case of his career, of any British policeman's career.

Scanning the waterfront, Reece had noticed potted shrubs tangled with debris. Move them in, he ordered, before the incoming tide washed evidence away. And with the Grand's alarm bells still ringing he had given another instruction: get the Anti-Terrorist Branch.

After a chaotic day shuttling between the seafront and the Brighton police station, Reece was now hunkered in room 638, observing the pathologist's macabre work, and getting his first glimpse of the C13 detectives in action. Wearing boots, helmets, and blue coveralls, they toiled above, below, and around him on every floor, organizing task zones, prioritizing areas, sifting rubble. Amid carnage, they had method. It was the first time the Anti-Terrorist Branch had deployed to a bomb scene outside of metropolitan London.

Reece was relieved. He would never admit it publicly, but Sussex CID was out of its depth. "I was thinking, 'God, you know, what on earth are we going to do?'" Wells, his deputy, confided later. "Nobody within Sussex, certainly, had ever had to deal with an explosion. . . . My knowledge was . . . to say limited is putting it mildly. Was nil."

When journalists had asked if the bomb was a TPU—a timing power unit—Wells had fobbed them off, having no idea what TPU meant. Reece exuded gruff authority but had never handled a terrorist case. Sussex Police was a provincial force with no experience of bombs or the IRA. Reece knew about burglars, car thieves, and drunken murderers. He knew all about the knocker boys—antique dealers who knocked on old people's doors, scattered sawdust on floors, declared woodworm, and bought heirlooms for a pittance. But he knew nothing about the Provos. Yet now he was to lead a vast, complex investigation into the most audacious terrorist attack in British history. Rather than commute home, he took to sleeping in his office.

A clamor for results dinged his ears. World leaders expressed hope the perpetrators would be swiftly caught. Ronald Reagan offered US help to "thwart this scourge against humanity," adding: "I have directed that my experts be available to work with yours to assist in bringing the perpetrators to justice." Conservative politicians said the bombers—once caught—should be charged with high treason and hanged. Britain's hugely popular tabloids demanded instant, brutal action. "Track down these pitiless Provos like the rats they are," exhorted *The Sun*. "They must be hunted remorselessly and exterminated like rats. . . . There MUST now be all-out war to crush them." The *Sunday Express* foamed with xenophobic rage. "Wouldn't you rather admit to being a pig than to being Irish?"

Reece also had to dodge the poison darts that began flying between rival fiefdoms in the police and security services, each keen to deflect blame for not averting the IRA plot. The Met's Special Branch accused Sussex Police of ignoring its warning of a possible attack in England. MI5 chiefs said the bomb showed why it, rather than the Special Branch, should run counterterrorism in Britain. The RUC accused its English colleagues of ignoring lessons from Northern Ireland, a blind spot it dubbed the Not Known in London (NKIL) syndrome. The Home Office solution was a new coordination committee called Terrorist Intelligence Gathering Evaluation Research, dressing bureaucratic fluff in a menacing acronym.

The press hammered Roger Birch, the Sussex chief constable, as the scapegoat and asked if he would resign. Birch put on a brave face. "Jon, I very much enjoyed reading my obituary in the *Evening Argus* today," he said, smiling, to Jon Buss before a press conference. Despite government support, Birch feared his career was over. "You feel pretty lonely," he said later. Birch invited John Hoddinott, the chief constable of a neighboring county, to evaluate Sussex's conference arrangements. Birch was a suave, svelte, wonky contrast to Reece, who seemed from an earlier era, but they respected each other and worked in tandem. "My job was to protect Jack Reece and his team so they could get on with the job," Birch said. In addition to soaking up hostile press attention, Birch dealt with politicians and officials who insisted on visiting the Grand. "They're a blooming nuisance because you've got to show them round and introduce them to the key players," Birch recalled, "and really you want the key players to get on with the job."

For updates on the investigation, the press swarmed William Hucklesby, the ever-dapper, media-savvy commander of the Anti-Terrorist Branch. If Reece envied the attention, he never showed it.

Shielded from the politics and the press, he was able to focus on a sprawling, intricate job of detection.

. . .

THE COMBINED MIGHT of Britain's security services came up blank— no intelligence, no suspects, no leads. The Provos, so often riven with informers, had kept the operation tight. "I expected our Special Branch to be filling us with names, but nothing," Wells recalled. Reece's team would have to find answers in the Grand itself.

The investigation had two prongs. The first was to mine the rubble for clues. "Somewhere in that lot is the identity of the bomber. We have got to try to find it," one officer told the searchers. They sought forensic evidence that a bomb had indeed caused the explosion and sought fragments of the device to establish provenance, design, and any other details that might help reconstruct events and trace the bomb maker and planter. The goal was not only to identify suspects but to harvest enough evidence for conviction. Defense lawyers would pounce on any gaps to seed doubt in a jury. True coppers did not celebrate when cuffs snapped around a suspect's wrists. They waited for a guilty verdict to drain all hope from his eyes.

Sussex police officers manned checkpoints and barriers around the promenade, which closed to traffic, while Anti-Terrorist Branch detectives controlled an inner cordon around the hotel. The task was monumental and would take weeks. Somewhere in the eight-floor ruin, with thousands of tons of debris sandwiched at the base, lay clues, some potentially microscopic. Having mapped out a plan, the C13 men struck up a routine. Dig, shovel, sift, wheel away. Dig, shovel, sift, wheel away.

Bit by bit, the entire edifice would be scoured and 880 tons of evidence would be sent to the Royal Armament Research and Development Establishment (RARDE) at Fort Halstead, in Kent, where scientists with special sieves performed more detailed forensic analysis.

Police officers nicknamed "flour graders" sift and collect potential evidence
from the ruins of the Grand Hotel in October 1984. | · Alamy

Dennis Williams, a senior Sussex officer, phoned headquarters to
request dustbins, lots of them. "How many do you want, then?" they
asked. "Enough to put the Grand Hotel in," he replied. Hundreds of
large, black plastic bins—all new, to avoid contamination—were delivered and promptly filled. Hundreds more followed. Then a thousand.
It wasn't enough. "How many more bloody dustbins do you want, for
God's sake?" grumbled Mike Godlee, a chief superintendent in charge
of Sussex's budget. The eventual answer: 3,798. It caused a bin shortage
in southeast England. Godlee tried to claw back money by returning
unused lids.

The labor left detectives bashed, bruised, and aching. The weather
turned bitter, wind and rain lashing the exposed edifice. The unstable
ruin threatened to bury everyone in a fresh collapse. One officer had
the job of staring at upper floors and blowing a whistle if masonry
wobbled. Choking dust clouded the air. Blue asbestos, the most fatal
type of the mineral, was discovered, but masks were often unavailable
or unusable—they filled with sweat, impairing vision. One detective,

Jonathan Woods, was to die of mesothelioma, a cancer caused by as-bestos fibers in the lung, in 2015.

Detective Sergeant Michael Colacicco found himself swinging on a rope that stretched from the eighth floor to the sixth to swab walls for explosive residue. "We're not trained to abseil . . . we're detectives. But that's how things operated," he said later. Sussex officers joined the rubble search, raising the total number of operators on-site to 228. For sorting through rubble, dust, plaster, and brickwork, they were nick-named "flour graders." Even the young, tough riot officers faltered, Colacicco said. "We burned them out quite quickly, they didn't seem to stand the pace too well." Colacicco rebuffed a planning official who tried to halt the work as too dangerous. "I threatened to arrest him for obstructing the police if he didn't piss off."

The first few days yielded no bomb parts, but the searchers logged troves of bric-a-brac such as "yellow sponge with green scourer," "Brighton area telephone directory," "box of matches." A pair of contact lenses were identified and reunited with their owner—an MP's mother. Peter Gurney, the bomb burglar, inspected the Grand and returned to London to survey buildings that hosted VIPs. He was dismayed to discover that these structures were designed to cope with downward, not upward, thrusts. "You can put tremendous weights on some floors, but apply a tenth of that force in an upward direction and they will break," he noted. It was too expensive to retrofit buildings, so author-ities sat on Gurney's survey and prayed the IRA would never get a copy.

While his colleagues on the seafront sifted wreckage, Reece set up the investigation's second prong a mile away at the Brighton police station, the five-story office complex that had briefly hosted Thatcher. Armed guards hovered outside, reflecting fear about a follow-up IRA attack. Inside, it was like any other police station with metal desks, plastic chairs, and stale cigarette smoke. This would be the nucleus of the hunt.

Gurney's team of "bomb doctors" told Reece's detectives that a time-delay device had been planted in one of four rooms—528, 529,

628, or 629—days, weeks, or possibly three months in advance, as that was the IRA's longest known time bomb. Reece organized the investigation around this time frame. The terrorist might have posed as a guest, a hotel employee, or a visiting tradesman. There might have been accomplices, such as reconnaissance scouts. The investigation therefore needed to rewind to July 1 and identify and track everybody that had set foot inside the Grand since then. That was more than a thousand people, every one of them a potential suspect. Some on Reece's team wondered if this was feasible. There were, of course, no mobile phones or social media, no such thing as digital footprints. Even the technology of the time was in short supply: the Grand had no interior CCTV cameras and it did not ask guests for identity documents or credit cards. Guests came from all over the world. If one signed in with a false name, there might be no way of tracking them. Neppy had sent Jack Reece a big 'un, all right, a monster, but the ocean was vast and dark.

Reece called counterparts in the RUC and the Metropolitan Anti-Terrorist Branch and Special Branch for a crash course in the IRA. With the prime minister nearly assassinated, four people dead, and dozens injured, the UK's entire security network was at his disposal. But he stuck to CID procedure: set up an incident room, gather evidence, take statements, log, index, and cross-reference everything. The difference was scale. Reece would supervise a team of two hundred detectives, most from Sussex, and liaise with a satellite team based at the Anti-Terrorist Branch's Scotland Yard HQ. It might give Mike Godlee palpitations, but money would be no object. Cars, equipment, overtime, travel, translators, a bigger computer, whatever Jack wanted. The investigation would need to trace hundreds of people scattered across Europe, Africa, Asia, and the Americas. Interpol wouldn't know what hit it.

The CID method was no different from that used by police detectives all over the world. It boiled down to organizing resources and information. Instead of hunches or epiphanies, Reece needed facts and systems to filter them through. The government was in the process of computerizing complex police investigations under the Home Office Large Major Enquiry System, or HOLMES, a bureaucratic homage to Arthur Conan Doyle's fictional detective. It was incomplete, but some of Reece's detectives had trained on it.

An incident room—in reality, a warren of rooms spread over two floors in the Brighton station—became the investigation hub. "It was a bit like an ant colony where you had all these worker ants everywhere, going off, shooting off into little sorts of tributaries," one detective recalled.

Detective Inspector John Byford, a fraud squad veteran comfortable with data, directed the rapidly swelling paper flows. Allocators assigned actions to different teams. Some interviewed Grand guests and employees, others started examining hundreds of thousands of cards that visitors from Ireland had completed upon arrival in Britain. Statement readers digested what came back, which generated more actions. "Every inquiry is an action, and it has an action as its number. So the numbers are absolutely the center of it all," Byford said. "You index the indexes . . . so you've got shortcuts to find things." It sounded more like a library than a manhunt, but Reece's team was fired up. This was how investigations worked, and everyone wanted in on this one. It felt simultaneously historic and urgent, because surely the terrorists intended to strike again. Politics didn't come into it, but police officers tended to admire Thatcher, so that didn't hurt. And they all liked overtime.

On Sunday, October 14, day three of the investigation, Byford's deputy, Detective Sergeant Alan Snelling, headed to the Grand. His rubble-rat colleagues had spotted something tantalizing in the basement: steel filing cabinets containing what looked like registration cards. The hotel manager, Paul Boswell, had been summoned and confirmed it. The hotel's archive of registration cards—its sole record of guests—had survived.

The reception area resembled a ruined, forgotten castle. "It was very eerie," Snelling said. "The whole place was a mass of empty bottles and everything was covered in a thick layer of dust." Twice, Snelling scrambled down through debris and reached the filing cabinets, only to retreat when unstable masonry triggered evacuation orders. It took four attempts to collect all the cards. It was the first major break in the investigation.

Back at the station, it was Hilary Pownall's job to make two copies of each card. Each was in a transparent plastic wallet. After days answering phones, Pownall, a woman police constable, or WPC, had volunteered for the photocopying. It was a welcome break from the calls. The machine hummed and clicked as Pownall, wearing latex gloves, fed one card at a time. She felt a frisson that the bomber's card might be among them. She had once dreamed of becoming a chief constable. Thatcher, after all, had shattered gender stereotypes. But a decade of casual sexism and thwarted promotion had withered her ambition. Pownall found solace in the thought, as the light passed under each card, that this secretarial duty fleetingly put her at the heart of a major investigation.

The next morning, Monday, October 15, Jack Reece returned to the Grand. In suit and tie and hard hat, he made his way to the Napoleon Suite, stepped over a bathroom floor littered with broken glass and tiles, and gazed up at the cracked ceiling. A photographer captured the moment. He looked pensive. Perhaps he was reminding himself how close the bomber got to killing the prime minister. Later that morning, Reece got a second break. The Anti-Terrorist Branch disclosed that—in Salcey Forest, ten months earlier—it had found six timers set for twenty-four days, six hours, and thirty-six minutes, with a seventh timer missing. If the bomber had used this timer—a supposition—it would have been activated on September 17.

Alan Snelling pulled the hotel registration cards for the four priority rooms—528, 529, 628, 629—covering that day. He relayed the names and addresses of each guest to Scotland Yard. Before the sun set

The Grand Hotel registration card completed by Patrick Magee using
the pseudonym Roy Walsh. It is in a police evidence bag that contains a
smaller card detailing when it was last sealed. "Chance" was the hotel's
term for walk-in guests who had not reserved in advance.
| Brighton Old Police Cells Museum

on October 15, the London detectives phoned back to say one of the
names appeared to be false. Nobody at 27 Braxfield Road had heard of
Roy Walsh.

. . .

WHILE JACK REECE digested the possibility that he might have caught
his fish, Margaret Thatcher was in Downing Street. She was hosting
Jacques Delors, the French president-designate of the European Commission, for a working dinner. Elegant in a dark dress offset with a
pearl necklace, she greeted her guest with a warm smile. Three days
after her conference triumph, the prime minister exuded business as
usual. Her morning and afternoon had been spent dealing with the
coal strike, the handover of Hong Kong to China, and a public
spending review. Now she was getting a jump start on Brussels' new

chief before he'd even started the job. She was showing the world, and perhaps herself, that she was undented. In fact, she seemed to gleam even brighter. A Soviet politburo member, Mikhail Gorbachev, had for months ignored an invitation to meet Thatcher. Now, perhaps out of admiration or curiosity, he suddenly accepted, and his wife, Raisa, wanted to come, too.

The prime minister appeared to process Brighton with typical brisk attentiveness. She was briefed on the investigation but did not meddle. "It's the sort of thing that she believed was a field for professionals to deal with. She had a huge respect for the law and following legal process," recalled Charles Powell, a senior aide. She sought specialist medical attention for the injured, wrote letters thanking hotel staff and emergency services, and apologized to her hairdresser for canceling their October 12 appointment. Duty done, Thatcher immersed herself in Downing Street routine. It was as if she considered it cowardly or soft to show too much of a reaction—like the old British army wearing bright scarlet uniforms, signaling indifference to danger, her biographer later noted. This produced a restrained security response. Despite goading by the tabloid press and certain Tories, there were no new repressive laws or mass arrests. "She wasn't a very ordinary person," Powell said. "She was not out there demanding revenge and arrests of suspects, no. For her this was a security problem like many other IRA murders which had to be investigated."

The bomb did, however, sour Thatcher's negotiations with the Irish government over Northern Ireland. "We must go *very* slow on these talks if not stop them. It could look as if we were bombed into making concessions," she wrote in a memo. She moved a summit with the Irish prime minister from Dublin to Chequers, saying: "The IRA will probably get me in the end, but I don't see why I should offer myself on a plate." The summit went badly, leaving Garret FitzGerald humiliated. Thatcher did not, however, pull the plug. The attempt to reach a historic agreement stumbled on.

Behind the bravura, the bomb did affect Thatcher. Tears had come during a religious service a few days after the attack. "The sun was just coming through the stained-glass windows and falling on some flowers right across the church and it just occurred to me that this was the day I was meant not to see," she said.

The suffering of the dead and injured haunted her. She seemed to feel responsible and could not help thinking Margaret Tebbit's paralysis might have been her own fate. Thatcher started to keep a torch beside her bed and kept the bedroom door open to avoid being trapped. "When something like that happens to you, you never forget it. It's marked on her soul," said Cynthia Crawford, her personal assistant.

The assassination later that month of India's prime minister, Indira Gandhi, further rattled Thatcher. Denis bought his wife a watch and enclosed a note: "Every minute is precious." Despite ramped-up security, Thatcher told aides she believed the IRA would try again and succeed in killing her. She "doubted now if she would die in her bed," an official later confided. It wasn't just the bomb, it was the taunting message. *Remember we have only to be lucky once, you will have to be lucky always.* "The quote stuck with her. It was a quote you wouldn't forget," recalled Powell.

. . .

WITH THAT DEFT propaganda, the IRA was following in the footsteps of Danny Morrison, who had captured rhetorical lightning three years earlier with the "Armalite and ballot box" conjunction. Conflating luck with menace cast the Provos as agents of fate, players in a cosmic lottery rigged in their favor. It was so catchy that the IRA recycled it. On October 18, *An Phoblacht/Republican News* published an interview with an anonymous GHQ spokesman, who said attacks in Britain would continue at a time and place of the IRA's choosing. "We feel we are going to be very lucky."

The sentiment was contagious. On October 19, a unit from the Special Air Service, the army's elite undercover unit, ambushed a vanload of IRA gunmen in County Tyrone. They were allegedly on their way to kill an Ulster Defence Regiment major. The SAS, fore-warned, had lain in wait. IRA teams had been wiped out by such ambushes in the past; this one, however, swerved through the gunfire and escaped. The commander was believed to be Peter Sherry, aka the Armalite Kid, who had stood for Sinn Féin—and lost—in a council election seven months earlier on the promise of fixing safety hazards. Days after the ambush, Sherry was brought into Gough Barracks for questioning. Three men with English accents in faux jocular tones congratulated Sherry on escaping their trap. Then one leaned very close to him: "Remember, we have only to be lucky once, you will have to be lucky always."

Not everyone appreciated Danny Morrison's Brighton zinger. Per-haps he thought it invoked gambling, perhaps he thought it frivolous—whatever the reason, Muammar Gaddafi disapproved. The IRA envoy to Tripoli who was told this never learned why.

The attack itself, however, impressed the Libyan leader very much. With his own reasons to loathe Thatcher, Gaddafi pondered a dramatic move. He was considering sending the IRA enough explosives for a thousand Brightons.

. . .

AFTER THE MESSAGE from Scotland Yard about Roy Walsh, Reece dispatched his own detectives, led by Bernie Wells, to the card's ad-dress on Braxfield Road. It was a row of two-story terraced houses in southeast London. Number 27, like its neighbors, had a tiled roof and a small front garden. It was the home of a plumber, George Henry Foster, and he had not heard of Roy Walsh. Wells had an easygoing charm that made people chatty, and he deployed every ounce of it on Braxfield Road, tramping door-to-door, asking if anyone knew a Roy Walsh, or perhaps a Ray Walsh, or anyone called Walsh. There was a D. R. Walsh, who was known to the Special Branch because he was a member of Britain's Communist Party, but he had not visited the Grand. Nor, it seemed, had anyone else on that road.

The detectives returned to Sussex satisfied that whoever had signed in to room 629 under the name Roy Walsh had, if nothing else, lied about his address. Instinct told them he had also lied about his name and was probably the bomber, Wells recalled. "We really felt we'd got the man, Roy Walsh was the man, whoever he was. That's our man, who we've got to find."

Working on the assumption that "Roy Walsh" would not have checked in without some form of identification, Reece's team checked the Passport Office and the Driver and Vehicle Licensing Council for reissues in that name. They trawled registers of births, deaths, and marriages. For birth certificates, they had to wade through 750,000 reissues stored in date order rather than alphabetical. They found multiple Roy Walshes, all of whom were checked and eliminated.

Other detectives worked through hotel staff, who were questioned and fingerprinted. Trudy Groves, the receptionist, remembered the guest had requested a sea-facing room and that she chose 629 because of its view, but could not recall anything about the guest himself, not his appearance, accent, or if he had a companion. Waiters remembered delivering sandwiches and the vodka with Cokes, but struggled to describe the man who opened the door. Pamela Plappert, the housekeeper, remembered trying and failing to gain entry, and seeing grease marks around the bath panel. "We were able to corroborate that yes, this is where the bomb had been placed, behind the bath," said Paul Gibbon, a detective constable who interviewed Plappert. Pieces of the puzzle were beginning to fit together. The detectives drafted a timeline of Walsh's known movements from the moment he checked in.

For three days, Sussex fingerprint experts studied Roy Walsh's registration card. Already it was a talisman, the one tangible connection to the prime suspect. They identified and eliminated prints belonging to hotel staff and, by naked eye and by microscope, pored over every millimeter for other marks. Nothing. They tried again. Still nothing. It seemed either that Roy Walsh had not touched the card or his marks had been erased by other prints. Reece must have ground his teeth. Just when the investigation had been gathering speed, a dead end.

Still, some hope remained for prints. Scotland Yard had high-tech forensic equipment unavailable in Sussex. On Thursday, October 19, a Sussex officer delivered a transparent, tamper-proof sealed exhibit bag to David Tadd at Scotland Yard. Tadd had been expecting it. Since returning from the US the previous week, he had visited Brighton and prepped his team for any evidence that might emerge from the Grand. Reece wanted the cards of several guests checked, starting with that of Roy Walsh. A separate copy of Walsh's card was given to the Met's handwriting expert, David Ellen. Some of the letters, especially the E's, were distinctive.

Tadd placed the exhibit bag in his briefcase, pulled on his jacket, and summoned his driver. A humid haze hung over London as they motored down Victoria Street toward the Thames. They crossed Lambeth Bridge and pulled into a great iceberg of concrete and steel. There were no signs to indicate this anonymous complex was the Metropolitan Police forensic science laboratory, the brain stem of British policing.

The car descended into a secure car park. Tadd took a lift to reception, showed his ID, and walked through a warren of brightly lit hallways to the Serious Crime Unit section. He entered his usual lab, a dimly lit, windowless space. Donning a white coat and gloves, he prepared in a shallow tray a solution of ninhydrin, a chemical that reacts to the amino acids contained in human sweat. The reaction can expose latent prints by producing a deep purple known as Ruhemann's purple, named after the chemist who discovered the method. Unlike fingerprint powders, ninhydrin did not contaminate evidence for other tests. The downside was you had to wait about ten days for the chemical to react. Tadd broke the seal on the exhibit bag and extracted Walsh's card with tweezers. He placed it in the tray, letting the transparent liquid seep across the card. He extracted the card and placed it in a small, warm oven.

After approximately thirty minutes, the card was dry. Tadd packed away the bottles and tray, returned the card to the exhibit bag, placed it in his briefcase, and returned to Scotland Yard. Once the card was ready to extract, he placed the exhibit bag in a steel cabinet in his office and locked it. With luck, the chemical would complete its process and give him something to work with by the end of the month.

. . .

BACK IN BRIGHTON, the investigation found a rhythm. Around eight o'clock each morning, dozens of detectives would gather in the police station's ground-floor gymnasium for a briefing. Usually Reece or Wells, standing on a little podium, would run through the previous day's developments and outline a plan for the day. Morale was high, as this beat chasing burglars and shoplifters. And this level of manpower would surely produce a result. After the briefing, allocators in the incident room assigned tasks to detectives, who tended to work in pairs.

The focus on Roy Walsh did not obviate the need to trace everyone who had set foot in the Grand from July 1 to October 12. Accomplices may have stayed in other rooms before and after Walsh's mid-September visit. Other guests may have encountered the plotters, perhaps even inadvertently photographed them. A huge chart in Byford's office, about twelve feet long and four feet deep, tracked progress. Columns representing 160 rooms intersected columns representing 104 days, producing thousands of boxes, each representing a guest or guests that needed to be tracked down, questioned, and eliminated or arrested.

False leads multiplied: a group of Irishmen in the Metropole who jeered Tories the night of the bomb; a dark-skinned man with an Afro seen running from the scene; another "strange man" with a blue rucksack seen in the foyer shortly before the blast—all required investigation. The most time-consuming red herring was a housekeeper's memory of a bearded man with a silver-colored case entering 629 several days before the conference. Exhaustive inquiries established he was a TV repairman.

Quite a few guests turned out to have registered under false names; they were in the Grand for extramarital affairs. Detectives called them the Mr. and Mrs. Smiths. Some were tracked down through credit cards, others by phone calls to home from their rooms, which the hotel logged. When contacted, some panicked and dissembled. Reece seethed, as this nonsense was slowing the investigation. "We interviewed one woman who said she was the wife of so-and-so but when we called to the man's home his real wife was most surprised," he told journalists. "We are urging people to come forward and avoid potential problems like this." The tabloids, meanwhile, hunted for the mistress of the minister said to have had a tryst at the Grand. Rumors spread, such as the *Washington Post* reportedly sacking a correspondent for sleeping through the bomb.

The guest hunters plowed on, not always tactfully. "Are you of medium height, with brown hair and very bad skin?" one asked journalist David Davin-Power over the phone. Davin-Power, normally an affable soul, prickled—and in response the English policeman got defensive. "That's what's in front of me. No offense, mate, just ticking boxes."

Reece's team lodged 851 inquiry requests with Interpol to trace people in more than fifty countries spanning Belgium to Botswana, Mexico to Malaysia. Some responses generated more inquiries, raising the total to 1,301, the single biggest investigation Interpol had ever handled. Day by day, more boxes on the wall chart were filled in. Sergeant Ted Wilkinson organized the growing paper mountain despite a broken leg and became a hobbling human database, able to recall endless investigation arcana, but even he had a limit. So did the Sussex force's computer, which became overloaded. A commercial database was rented and that, too, proved insufficient for an investigation that produced 8,200 actions, 13,000 officer reports, and other documents—some 58,000 records in all, a crime inquiry record. Another record was the price tag: £1 million. Eventually, the investigation linked to the Police National Computer mainframe.

On October 27, after sixteen days of searching through rubble, Detective Constable Ian Macleod spotted an ice cream cone–shaped object in the U-bend of a muddy toilet in the ruins of room 329. He recognized it as part of a Memo-Park timer. The haystack had at last betrayed the needle. Another searcher found the casing of a nine-volt Eveready battery. After all the digging and hauling, these were the most valuable prizes recovered so far. It was enough for scientists at RARDE to piece together the bomb's probable design. They concluded that it had two independent circuits and two timers, a Memo-Park and one similar or identical to those found in Salcey Forest. It bolstered the evidence pointing to Roy Walsh.

The rubble search concluded on October 30. The last bin was wheeled out, leaving the Grand a gutted shell, its fate uncertain. The flour graders celebrated by forming a line and marching into the sea with their dusty overalls and steel-capped boots. A newspaper photographer captured their grins. "What it's not telling you in the picture is, the boots filling up with water and some of the guys nearly drowning and having to be pulled out," Michael Colacicco recalled. Sussex police hosted a farewell dinner for their Anti-Terrorist Branch colleagues. Reece and his team presented ties and cuff links with a bin motif, inscribed: *Thanks for a Grand job.* The Met detectives handed out mock flour-grading certificates. The mementos were heartfelt. Lifetime friendships had been forged.

A week later, on November 6, Reece appeared on a prime-time BBC TV show called *Crimewatch*, which enlisted viewers' help in solving crimes. Its dramatic theme song emulated the whump of a helicopter's blades. "Sussex Police have asked *Crimewatch* to make a special appeal for one man who booked in using the name Roy Walsh," the presenter intoned. "If the man who gave his name as Roy Walsh rings now, Mr. Reece guarantees that his call will be treated in absolute confidence." The camera panned to a somber-looking Reece, who sat at a desk with a phone, pen poised over a notepad. It was theater. What Reece wanted more than anything was for the man who gave his name as Roy Walsh not to phone. If he did call and turned out to be another guest who had been hiding an illicit romantic liaison, the investigation was buggered.

The hotline lit up. "Lots of calls," said the presenter.

All, it turned out, were from viewers who thought they could identify Roy Walsh. None claimed to *be* Roy Walsh. Off camera, Big Jack surely smiled. He was chasing the right fish.

CHAPTER SIXTEEN

Hypothenar Evidence

On November 13, a doctor emerged from the intensive care unit at Royal Sussex County Hospital and approached Donald Maclean with a somber expression. The Brighton bomb had claimed its fifth life. "From the look on his face, I knew very well what he was there to say," Maclean recalled. His wife, Muriel, was gone.

For thirty-two days, since the moment they were blown out of room 629, she had hovered between life and death. Shrapnel had shredded her legs; then the wounds became infected and she struggled to breathe. She had been under sedation when doctors asked Donald for authorization to amputate her lower right leg. The chairman of Scotland's Conservative Association thought of their twenty-seven years together, of their two children, of Muriel walking her beloved hills around Ayr, where on a clear day you could see Northern Ireland. He said yes. Still the infection spread, to her lungs, causing pneumonia. Then her kidneys failed. She died without regaining consciousness.

Four other families struggled with their own grief. Jennifer Taylor wandered her rambling farmhouse, keeping the radio on to deflect the shattering absence of her husband, Eric. Gordon Shattock convalesced at his daughter's home, dreading the emptiness when he returned to the thatched house he had shared with his wife, Jeanne. John Wakeham, the Tory chief whip, would have to learn to walk again while raising his sons Benedict, nine, and Jonathan, eleven, without his wife, Roberta. Sarah Berry sensed a darkness settling over, despite the efforts of relatives—including her cousin Princess Diana—to console her.

Jack Reece would have felt each bereavement. He made a point of staying in touch with murder victims' families. It was a human impulse, but also a professional one: he often needed their help in investigations. "In almost any murder you try and get close to the people that are left," he once said. His crash course in the IRA, which would have included background on nationalist grievances in Northern Ireland, did not change his opinion of the bomber. "I don't think it takes a lot of courage to walk into a hotel and hide a bomb behind the panel of the bath. That in my view is a cowardly act," he said later.

Like a wheel around an axle, the investigation spun on a central question: Who was Roy Walsh? Evidently, he was not the jailed bomber of that name, so who was he, really? His silence in response to the *Crimewatch* appeal suggested guilt, but Reece was no closer to discovering his real identity. Viewers phoned in reports about multiple Roy Walshes, but none had stayed at the Grand in mid-September. As November crept into winter, the pressure for results—or at least reportable progress—weighed more heavily. Reece had to give updates to Roger Birch and his assistant chief constable, David Scott, who in turn briefed the home secretary, Leon Brittan, who briefed the cabinet. A cartoon in the satirical magazine *Private Eye* advised readers not to expect a breakthrough. When Thatcher said, "I'm going to bring back hanging!! Of course it will only be for terrorist offenses," a minister opposed to capital punishment replied: "Well that's all right then, we never catch any of those."

"Get some light into these dark places," a home secretary had exhorted Scotland Yard when Fenians were bombing London. A century later, the police had better intelligence and forensics but still groped in shadows. Reece's colleagues in the RUC and Scotland Yard, and the spooks of MI5, scavenged for intelligence by quizzing IRA informants and trawling intercepted electronic communications. They learned little of use. A thick cloak seemed to have been draped over the Brighton operation. There was speculation that the IRA had used "clean skins," operators unknown to the authorities. The best the security force's professional IRA hunters could do was whittle down the twenty thousand IRA suspects on file—a vast archive dating from the dawn of the Troubles—into a short list of their best guesses. It had about a dozen names. Patrick Magee was not on it.

Reece had received tantalizing but inconclusive news from David Tadd about the hotel registration card. Since applying the ninhydrin solution on October 19, Tadd had unlocked his cabinet each morning and inspected the card, which was turning a hazy shade of purple. In early November, four deep purple marks emerged. To the untrained eye, they were just dark smudges. But to Tadd, they were previously undetected prints. He labeled them A, B, C, and D.

On November 5, Tadd returned to his lab, where a forensic photographer photographed the marks. This was of utmost importance. The photographs of marks, not the card itself, were used for search and comparison. No longer needing the card, Tadd placed it in the exhibit bag, sealed and signed it, and returned it to a Sussex police exhibit officer.

On November 13, the day Muriel Maclean died, Tadd received copies of the photographs. Now the real work could begin. His team swiftly identified marks A and D as the prints of a receptionist. That left B and C. The most promising was C, a palm print, because it was on the card's lower right-hand corner, close to the signature. Tadd directed the team to focus on C. It tapered upward and leaned to the left, bearing a rough resemblance to the outline of Britain. Despite the generic term "fingerprint," the ridge system can identify someone from the tips of fingers to the flex of wrists. For fingerprint analysts, palms were a realm apart from fingers. A fingerprint had dozens of individual ridge characteristics, all grouped into three pattern types: loops, whorls, and arches. The combinations were almost infinite; each of the world's 4.74 billion people was believed to have a unique set.

A finger's shape and size oriented the process of identification— you could usually tell which bit of the finger you were looking at, which facilitated comparison. A palm, however, had no loops or whorls or arches, only ridge characteristics, and in this case it was not clear which part of the palm had left the mark. The hand could have been at any angle, lying flat or leaning on its side, perhaps sliding. Tadd's analysts spent days filling in blank registration cards to simulate the writing of Walsh's card. They determined that it was from the hypothenar eminence, the name of a muscular protrusion on the medial side of the palm at the base of the little finger. Now they could start comparing it with the prints of IRA suspects.

A palm might have a thousand identifying characteristics, ten times that of a finger. The task was to compare the mark's ridge characteristics, which might have been left by the fake Roy Walsh, with prints of IRA suspects, starting with the dozen-strong short list supplied by the Special Branch. If that yielded no matches, Tadd's team would start comparing the prints of approximately two hundred other IRA bombers on file. It would be a grueling process of elimination: stare at the hotel print, stare at those of a known IRA suspect, stare again at the hotel print, back and forth, back and forth, moving from fragment to fragment, hunting for sixteen points of similarity that indicated a match. Prints could be enlarged and projected side by side on a screen called an epidiascope. The process prioritized accuracy over speed. It could take the team an entire day to eliminate just one suspect.

Reece's team in Brighton, meanwhile, continued eliminating hotel guests one box at a time on the incident room's great chart. With the promise of confidentiality, some but not all suspected Mr. and Mrs.

Smiths came forward. Interpol connected the detectives with overseas counterparts who tracked down and interviewed former Grand guests. A response from Japan came on rice paper. Some US forces sent verbatim transcripts complete with "ums" and "ahs." It took a while, but forces in Africa also relayed information to Brighton. The tardiest responders, for some reason, were the French. The more guests who were eliminated, the more the guest who signed in as Roy Walsh gleamed even brighter as the primary suspect. But Reece got no further establishing his real identity. He did not even have a reliable description. Witnesses' accounts of Walsh were vague and contradictory. His accomplices, if they existed, remained phantasms.

The taxi driver, Dennis Palmer, remembered picking up a passenger from Brighton train station shortly before midday on September 15 and delivering him to the Grand. The rider wore a camel hair coat and had a heavy bag, which Palmer recalled passing to the doorman with a cheery warning about its weight. This matched Walsh's known timeline, but Palmer could not give a precise description of the passenger. Nor could the receptionist who checked him in, nor the housekeeper and room service staff who knocked on his door, nor the waiters and fellow diners who were in the restaurant on the day Walsh lunched there with a companion.

"We plotted up that restaurant, and we found everybody in that restaurant, except those two people at the table," Bernie Wells said. "Everyone seemed to remember everybody except those two. It was incredible . . . but we know they were there because they had a meal, and put it on their bill." Detective Chief Inspector Graham Hill, another senior member of Reece's team, said Walsh was a void. "I don't think there was any information at all. . . . I don't recall anybody that was able to tell us what he looked like, or what he was carrying or what he was wearing when he came in, nor at any stage in the hotel." A suppressed cry of frustration bubbled under the dry prose of a Sussex Police briefing paper marked confidential and "For Police Eyes Only": "No one recalls seeing Walsh's companion. Only one of the beds in

629 was slept in during the 3 days and all the clothing in the room during the period is believed to have been male. Several members of staff recall seeing the man Walsh. Descriptions are hazy and unreliable. Description is as follows: 27–45 years, 5'10"–6'2", slim build, dark medium length hair, softly spoken. Most witnesses recall Walsh as having no accent although one describes his accent as Dutch or German."

In public, Reece continued to exude optimism. His detectives' morale hinged on the belief they were making progress, that slowly but surely a net was closing around the Brighton bomber. Bernie Wells knew the reality. They were stalled. "We weren't sort of, really making progress," he said. "There was bits and pieces, names thrown up . . . but we never really had anything, you know."

Roy Walsh, whoever he was, appeared to have heeded the old Fenian injunction: operate like an invisible being.

Reece tried a long shot. He dispatched Graham Hill and Detective Constable Paul Gibbon to a top-security prison on the Isle of Wight to interview Paul Kavanagh. The stocky England Department veteran was awaiting trial for the murder of Ken Howorth and two others during the 1981 London campaign. He was also suspected of the Harrods bomb. Before his arrest in March 1984, Kavanagh had shown Natalino Vella the arms cache in Salcey Forest, so he possibly knew about the missing timer and preparations for Brighton. Guards reported that Kavanagh had multiple phone calls around the time of the bombing. There was no reason for the Belfast man to break IRA *omertà*, but Reece figured it worth a try.

As the gates clanged behind the visiting policemen, Gibbon churned with tension. One of the police officers killed at Harrods, Stephen Dodd, had been a close friend. Now Gibbon was about to meet his alleged murderer. Kavanagh refused to leave his cell, so guards dragged him to the interview room and sat him down. The IRA man eyed the visitors with disdain. "I'm not talking to the likes of youse." He locked his eyes on a spot on the wall behind Gibbon and Hill and did not utter another word. It was a counter-interrogation tactic enshrined in the Provos' Green Book. "And that was it. That's all he said," Gibbon recalled. "My emotions, I want to get up and fucking kill the guy. . . . Very, very emotional moment, never forget that." The detectives persisted with questions, all met with silence, and returned to Brighton empty-handed.

Roy Walsh remained a blank canvas. No one from the investigation, however, attempted to interview the IRA's real Roy Walsh. He was fifty miles north of Brighton, in Wandsworth Prison. It was probably deemed pointless. After eleven years in English jails, he was a figure from another era, far removed from Provo planning. In any case, his clashes with guards led to him often being in solitary confinement or "ghosted"—moved without warning—from jail to jail. The first Walsh knew about the plot to kill Margaret Thatcher was a TV report showing the ruins of the Grand. "I saw it on the news," he said later. "I thought it was a good operation, to strike at the heart." One early November morning, six guards studied him as he ate his porridge before ghosting him to Wandsworth. This observation was a puzzle to Walsh, as he had not been causing any trouble. A few days later, he learned the reason: a copper on *Crimewatch* had named Roy Walsh as a person of interest in the Brighton investigation. "The screws were all whispering and talking about it," he said.

After previous IRA attacks—Mountbatten, Narrow Water, Hyde Park—Walsh, along with other IRA inmates, had faced harassment and assaults from guards and English prisoners. But the disclosure that he shared the name of the prime suspect for Brighton seemed to confuse and worry his antagonists, he recalled. Was it a coincidence, some sort of message, a warning? Walsh himself had no idea, but saw an opportunity for leverage. "I played on it a wee bit with the screws: 'Fuck about with me, I'll get you done.' And they backed off."

As November drew to a close, Jack Reece was worrying about the fake Roy Walsh. David Tadd's team had found no matching prints on the Special Branch short list and was now slogging through the prints of approximately two hundred other IRA suspects.

Not a single person from the Grand could give a decent description. Which meant that Reece was chasing a ghost.

. . .

ON SATURDAY, NOVEMBER 30, James "Whitey" Bulger waited in the kitchen of 799 East Third Street, near Boston Harbor, with two mob lieutenants, Kevin Weeks and Stephen Flemmi. Someone had blabbed to US authorities about the IRA weapons shipment. Whitey had identified a suspect and now awaited his delivery. He had a duffel bag with interrogation tools: handcuffs, leg chains, rope, guns. The house had a basement with a dirt floor that he used as a secret burial ground. He called it "The Haunty."

Instead of glory, the gunrunning had brought trouble. The *Valhalla* had transferred its cargo off the Irish coast, as planned, to another vessel, the *Marita Ann*. But then the *Marita Ann* chugged into the waiting arms of the Irish navy, as a Kerry-based IRA informer named Sean O'Callaghan had tipped off Irish authorities. US Coast Guard and Customs agents then swooped in on the *Valhalla* after it returned to Boston and arrested the crew members. Soon, federal agents began investigating Whitey. He suspected the crew's mechanic, John McIntyre, had ratted him out.

A henchman duly delivered McIntyre. They shackled him to a chair. Whitey sat opposite, his eyes stones. McIntyre crumbled before a single question. "I'm sorry," he said. "I was weak." For six hours, Whitey grilled the prisoner about what he had told US authorities, then marched him down to the basement. He wrapped a rope around McIntyre's neck and pulled. McIntyre gurgled, but kept breathing. The rope was too thick. "This ain't working," said Whitey. He shot McIntyre in the head and face. Flemmi used pliers to extract the teeth to prevent identification.

As he was shielded from prosecution, Ireland's Troubles were no longer Whitey's troubles. He was done with revolution.

. . .

OVER A LUNCH of beef and Dover sole in the dining room at Chequers, Margaret Thatcher delivered such a violent barrage of accusations that the guest seated beside her considered walking out. Mikhail Gorbachev was getting the full Thatcher blast. Soviet failings in economics, human rights, foreign affairs—the indictment went on and on.

It was Sunday, December 16, and Thatcher had moved on from the bomb. Work was therapy, none more so than this intense, high-stakes encounter. Gorbachev was tipped to be the next Soviet leader, so she had rolled out the red carpet, then blasted facts, statistics, and provocative declarations at him, what her aides called the full "hair dryer treatment." Gorbachev recovered from his shock and proved an able match, rebutting his host with confidence and humor. Over six hours of electric debate, the two leaders, ideological opposites, forged such a personal bond that the Cold War no longer felt quite the same.

"I like Mr. Gorbachev," Thatcher declared to the BBC. "We can do business together."

She flew to Camp David to tell Ronald Reagan that here was a chance for a great East-West opening. The US president listened, rapt. The Iron Lady was perhaps at her zenith. It was a reminder that when the Grand's avalanche of rubble swerved in its path, sparing Thatcher, history spun on a thread.

A few days after the Thatcher-Gorbachev summit, snow blanketed Chequers. Fires burned in the hearths, but the great Gothic mansion was silent. The Russians were gone, the prime minister was abroad. A solitary, stooped figure with a cane limped up the sweeping staircase.

Norman Tebbit was a ravaged specter. Previously gaunt, he now looked emaciated. Thatcher had invited her convalescing trade and industry minister to stay at the estate for Christmas because it was close to Stoke Mandeville Hospital, where his wife was being treated.

Tebbit had gratefully accepted. But there was no elevator, and he winced with every step up to his room. Thatcher had given him Churchill's favorite suite. After the housekeeper removed his supper tray and closed the door behind her, Tebbit realized that for the first time since the bomb he was alone. He wondered if it had been a mistake leaving the hospital; he wondered if he could get undressed without help.

Britain had seen two versions of Tebbit at Brighton. A grimacing casualty dragged out in his pajamas, then, in a blink, a resilient, wise-cracking survivor. The minister had vowed to keep running Thatcherism's economic engine—he had British Telecom to privatize, the biggest state sell-off yet. He gave a breezy hospital bed interview to Chris Moncrieff of the Press Association News Agency, saying he had not bothered to count his broken ribs. "I simply have to sit here and ooze. But overall I am not in too much pain."

Tebbit still seemed Thatcher's natural heir. "He has the party in his pocket whenever Mrs. Thatcher decides to go. . . . His ordeal at the hands of the IRA will only add to his credentials as the most likely to succeed, should he so wish," said the *Sunday Times*. But Tebbit had grievous wounds and would be in pain for years. And his wife, Margaret, it became clear, would never recover. Weeks after the bomb, Tebbit had become withdrawn. Doctors became so concerned they spirited in Fred Bishop and two other firemen for a clandestine visit. They discussed the bomb, the rubble, the rescue. It worked, and Tebbit surfaced from despair. "A couple of days later [staff] phoned us and said, 'Absolutely brilliant, it's done what we needed to get him coming back up again,'" Bishop said later. Letters from well-wishers around the world, especially Ireland, piled up—but not everyone wished the couple well. Britain remained deeply polarized. Tebbit had been seen as Thatcher's hatchet man. "Some people would say to me: 'Why didn't you leave them in there, why did you have to get them out?'" Bishop recalled. There were jokes and taunts. A college designer in Northampton turned the image of Tebbit's famous grimace of agony into jigsaw puzzles that he sold for £4.95. A Teesside student newspaper ran a similar picture as a caption competition, with the prize being a night out with Margaret Tebbit. Comedians in mining communities offered to collect money for the IRA to target the Tories again.

By the time Tebbit moved into Chequers, he had partially recovered. He was firing memos to his department and steering the £4 billion BT flotation. The press predicted a great comeback. But the press did not see his struggle up the staircase, or his winces as he undressed, or his utter desolation about Margaret. She would, at best, be paraplegic. Their future was a frightening vista, and the prospect of Christmas only made it worse.

"I thought of our house, dark, lonely and silent," he said later.

Bitterness welled up, and tension was creeping into his relationship with the other Margaret. She had been supportive, keeping his job open for him, urging him to take whatever time he needed. But her own sense of guilt at having escaped mixed uneasily with the Tebbits' struggle. "That in a way made him unwelcome to her because you don't like to be reminded of your guilt by seeing someone who makes you feel guilty," said her biographer Charles Moore.

Finally in his pajamas, Tebbit climbed into Churchill's old bed, a great oak four-poster with a soft feather mattress. But his crushed vertebrae required a firmer surface. Tebbit dragged blankets off the bed and lay them on the floor. As he fell asleep, he wondered whether Churchill's ghost, if he haunted Chequers, would be more displeased to find him on the floor than in his bed.

. . .

On the night of December 20, around the time Tebbit would have been making his improvised bed, Jack Reece returned to *Crimewatch*. Six weeks since his previous appearance, he had come to make another prime-time appeal about Roy Walsh.

"It's looking increasingly like this is your man, is it?" asked the host, Nick Ross. Reece, in a dark suit and tie, gazed through his glasses, his features arranged into a blank mask. His hands were folded on the desk, the only hint of nerves from his thumbs, twiddling and twirling. "Well, the more time that elapses, the more interesting and significant Mr. Walsh becomes," he said.

The formal wording and neutral expression conveyed authority, and the hive of detectives in the background, working the studio phones beneath a wall-sized map, emitted urgency. But the truth was that Reece was running out of options. Sixty-nine days since a fireball had roared through the Grand, and sixty-six days since the man posing as Roy Walsh had emerged as the main suspect, Reece still had no idea who he was. Tadd's team had found no matches for the palm print. No one in Brighton who might have encountered Walsh during those four September days possessed actionable information. So Reece had returned to the BBC studio to cast another line into his sunless sea— hoping it might hook Walsh himself, or at least fresh information that could lead to him.

He had decided to share Walsh's registration card, the investigation's prime exhibit, to see if anyone recognized the handwriting. It flashed up on the screen. A white rectangle with GRAND HOTEL, BRIGHTON printed in capital letters across the top, and beneath that Roy Walsh's name, address, nationality, and signature, written in black ink by a careful hand.

"If your viewers look at the *e* in 'Braxfield' and the *E* in 'SE4,' you'll notice that there is a peculiarity and we would like any of your viewers who know people with handwriting like that to tell us," said Reece. The distinctive feature was also apparent in the *E* in "English." A diagonal stroke connected the bottom right tip to the vertical line on the left, so the pen did not leave the paper when the upper two horizontal strokes were formed.

"It's almost as though he's drawn either an *l*, or a downward stroke and then a *z* backward," said Ross.

"That's right," said Reece, "backward up through the upright."

Perhaps the fake Roy Walsh had registered at other guesthouses and hotels, signed receipts, invoices, left a note, and somebody would remember the peculiar *E*. And perhaps Detective Chief Superintendent Jack Reece had become desperate. The *Crimewatch* hotlines lit up, but none led anywhere. He was losing his fish.

. . .

STEVE TURNER STARED at the screen of the epidiascope, fighting off fatigue. It was 8:00 p.m. on Thursday, January 17, 1985, and Turner was one of the few analysts left in the Anti-Terrorist Branch's fingerprint room on the fifth floor of Scotland Yard. He was part of the team seeking a match for the Roy Walsh registration card. Almost a month had passed since Jack Reece's televised appeal, a new year had dawned, and the identity of the man who had posed as Walsh remained a mystery.

Eleven hours at a desk studying prints left Turner's eyes pulsing, his back aching, and his brain feeling like broiled mince. Then again, it was a familiar sensation. Turner, age twenty-eight, had been a fingerprint officer for a decade and was accustomed to folding his lean, six-foot-two frame into his chair for protracted shifts. He was not one of those preternatural talents that could intuit a pattern in one glance, but was easygoing, diligent, and uncomplaining. "A willing horse," in David Tadd's words.

Scotland Yard's two office towers were turning dark as colleagues flicked off lights and filed out into a freezing, snowy London night. A handful of analysts were still at their desks, peering at prints. Turner had an hour left before clocking off.

Twelve-hour shifts, enough caffeine to wake the dead, and excursions to Stiles Bakery for pastries—this had been the routine since November 13, when Tadd directed half of his dozen-strong team to focus on mark C from Roy Walsh's registration card. The rest were needed for other cases.

Each analyst on the Brighton team had a copy of mark C, courtesy of the ninhydrin solution, and compared it with the latest print pulled from the bundle of approximately two hundred IRA suspects. Occasionally an analyst slid prints under an epidiascope for enlargement. Epidiascopes were projectors, not computers, and the method of seeking a match was essentially unchanged from a century earlier: eyeball the prints and rely on intuition, training, and experience to establish if the sequence of ridge characteristics matched. A match was a matter of opinion, subjective, more art than science. For certainty, and for evidence to be admissible in court, three analysts needed to independently check and agree that a match had sixteen points of similarity. Analysts used felt-tip pens to dot epidiascope screens and damp cloths to erase and start again. After two months, the Brighton team had eliminated about fifty suspects. To go any faster risked missing a match. The name on the latest file was Patrick Joseph Magee.

The world had moved on since Margaret Thatcher's near assassination. A famine in Ethiopia had galvanized pop stars to make a charity record. The US and Soviet Union were planning arms control talks. The UK had just got its first mobile phone network. Thatcher, on this wintry night, was at the London Coliseum watching *Rigoletto*, a story of vengeance not ending well.

The names on the IRA files meant little to most of the team. This latest file, however, did have a curiosity: the print was not from Northern Ireland but Norwich, and taken in 1967. Fastidious coppers in Norwich. Not every force bothered to print palms as well as fingers, especially in those days.

Turner kept peering at his screen, at an enlarged thumbnail-sized fragment of the Britain-shaped smudge on the Roy Walsh card, then at a fragment of the hypothenar area of the palm on the Norwich print.

It was 8:20 p.m. By now, Tadd and most of the others had left for home.

Turner's pen dotted the screen. He paused, then raised the pen. A few more dots. Turner blinked. His pen hovered and he stared some more. The pen returned to the screen. More dots, more staring.

Then it was 8:30 p.m. and the adrenaline was flowing. But he had to be sure. He counted the dots. Sixteen.

Stephen Turner had discovered who planted the Brighton bomb. The second person in the security services to learn the secret was Matt Egan, Turner's team leader. Early the next morning, Friday, January 18, Egan performed his own analysis to verify what Turner had told him. Egan was a strict disciplinarian who frowned on excitable claims. He studied the samples identified by Turner without viewing Turner's marks, per the rules, to see if he could independently find sixteen points of similarity. To Turner's immense relief, Egan found them.

He took the prints up to the sixth floor, where Tadd had a small, private office. Egan, not about to break a lifetime habit of reserve, kept his voice neutral. "Guv'nor, we think we've got an identification for Brighton."

Tadd jolted in his seat. He had feared the palm print, mark C, would prove a bust. Egan's announcement, if correct, was momentous. The three-tier checking process required Tadd to make his own comparison independent of the first two checks. After Egan left, closing the door, Tadd slotted the prints into the epidiascope on his desk. The only sound in his office was his breathing. Outside, the metropolis endured another Baltic afternoon, drizzle and mist replacing snow. Traffic skidded down Broadway, while pedestrians negotiated icy pavements. Tadd uncapped his pen and set to work. He had been doing this since the original Roy Walsh was nicked in 1973. Ken Howorth, the park bombings, the forensic troves at Pangbourne and Salcey Forest—he was a veteran of IRA cases, yet his scalp prickled now with a new kind of excitement. Tadd had got to know Jack Reece, liked his directness, and knew how much hinged on the registration card. His eyes roved the two prints. Several points of similarity materialized, immediately obvious to him. His pen dabbed the screen. He tracked the ridges. More points appeared. Nine, ten, eleven. Out in the corridor, footsteps and voices came and went. Then Tadd saw the other ridge characteristics. Fourteen, fifteen, sixteen points. They had him.

Patrick Joseph Magee.

Tadd exhaled. This was a moment to savor. Coppers and spooks had been chasing a specter; now he could give it a face and a name. He pulled out an A4 sheet of paper and swiftly wrote a briefing note for Commander William Hucklesby, detailing Turner's discovery, the nature of the match, Egan's corroboration as well as his own. Tadd left the space for the name blank—he guessed Posh Bill would want to keep it secret. Then Tadd strode to the typing pool and handed the report to a typist renowned for speed and accuracy.

"I need this now," he murmured.

By 5:00 p.m., he had the typed report plus a carbon copy. With night enveloping London, he filled in Magee's name by hand and made his way to Hucklesby's office. Tadd noticed his heart was racing. "It was the first time I had got so excited, a lovely feeling," he recalled.

The commander's door was ajar. Tadd knocked anyway.

Hucklesby looked up.

"Guv'nor," said Tadd, "you'll be pleased to know we've got a result on Brighton."

Posh Bill's whiskey decanter was going to end the day a little lighter. But first the Anti-Terrorist Branch chief made a call to Sussex. The voice on the other end answered with a gruff declaration.

"Reece."

CHAPTER SEVENTEEN

Dublin

Eileen Magee shut the door of 299 Hillman Street and walked past the two-story red-brick houses of her neighbors, past the walls daubed with IRA slogans in yard-high white letters and the fortified RUC station, and headed toward central Belfast. She was slender, with shoulder-length brown hair, and had a preference for jeans like just about every other young woman in the city. But the detail that most interested the surveillance officers who had been shadowing her for several days was the gold wedding ring on her left hand. She remained the wife of Patrick Magee.

The RUC Special Branch knew quite a bit about Eileen. Age twenty-nine, maiden name McGreevy, former office clerk, married Patrick on June 24, 1977, shared his republican beliefs, lived with him in the south for several years before moving back to Belfast. Their son, Padraig, had recently turned seven. The marriage was under strain. All this and more was in her husband's Special Branch file, number 9004. But as she made her way to the Great Victoria Street railway station and queued to buy a ticket on this cold January day, what the surveillance officers most wanted to know was her destination. Which turned out to be Dublin.

The watchers would have had just over two hours to alert their counterparts in the Garda Síochána as the train pulled out of Belfast. It trundled southwest, stopping at Lisburn and Portadown before turning directly south, stopping at Newry, then crossing the border into the Republic of Ireland. An unchanging landscape of suburbs, fields, and towns rolled past, but now the RUC found themselves in a different country; here, they had no jurisdiction. Between Dundalk and Drogheda, the train skirted the gray churn of the Irish Sea before slowing to a halt under the cast-iron Victorian canopy of Connolly Station. Named after an executed leader of the 1916 Rising, this was Ireland's busiest rail hub, in the heart of the capital. The waiting Irish surveillance team would have been briefed on Eileen Magee's appearance, seat, and carriage number. "An easy follow," one Special Branch detective recalled.

Her double-decker bus edged north through the inner city's Georgian grime, rounded Croke Park stadium, and continued north. The city petered out into small housing estates and wasteland only to abruptly rise back up in the form of hulking concrete tower blocks. Ballymun. Thirty-six towers in total, the tallest fifteen stories, forming a vast urban warren. Once envisaged as a modernist showcase for those cleared from inner-city slums, Ballymun had become known for crime, drugs, and decay. The bus stopped. Eileen Magee stepped out and started walking. A few gnarled trees lined the pavement, their branches stripped bare by winter. She turned onto Shangan Road and entered an eight-story tower opposite the Virgin Mary national school. On bad days, the towers' communal areas smelled of urine and were strewn with junkies' discarded needles. There was only one person who could draw Eileen Magee here.

The Irish police had found the Brighton bomber. No need for wiretaps or informants or scouring the city. Just one easy follow. And it was easy because Magee was not hiding. Three months earlier, he had hunkered in Cork—but after the bomb detonated, there had been no mass arrests, no public mention of his name. So he returned to Ballymun, his on-off base since 1981. Ireland was too small to hide in forever. Magee was already known to the Irish Special Branch, which kept sporadic watch on IRA suspects in Dublin. Prolonged absences piqued the detectives' curiosity, so Magee returned to routine, to what passed for his normality. Which included monthly visits by Eileen.

. . .

CONFIRMATION THAT MAGEE had been located flashed across the top levels of Britain's security services. Even among the donnish agents of MI5, there may have been hugs and clinks of scotch. They had the suspect's name, knew where he was, and had evidence of his crimes. The elation did not last. It withered as an implication sank in. There was no obvious way to get Magee.

A forthcoming James Bond film, *A View to a Kill*, had Roger Moore pursuing villains up the Eiffel Tower and the Golden Gate Bridge. But off the silver screen, banal reality crimped the securocrats. To begin with, they had no jurisdiction in Ireland. They could ask the Gardaí to arrest Magee and have the satisfaction of clicking handcuffs around his wrists, only to see him freed days or weeks later. Irish courts routinely rejected British extradition requests if the alleged offense was deemed politically motivated. Shoot, bomb, hijack—if you convinced a judge it was for some political goal, you almost always walked.

Thatcher had long accused Ireland of giving safe haven to terrorists. The Irish government denied this, saying the courts were independent and merely followed the law, but in truth Ireland was ambivalent about the Provos. IRA atrocities in the UK horrified the Irish public, and when Provos committed offenses in the republic—bank raids, arms smuggling, occasional shootings—the Gardaí and the courts fell on them like hammers. Support for Sinn Féin was small, but many southerners had a sneaking regard for the "boys" sticking it to the Brits and felt uneasy about handing them over to the old enemy.

British authorities had tried to circumvent this by allowing Irish courts to try suspects for certain offenses in the UK—that's how they nobbled Gerard Tuite in 1982—but the innovation faltered. Irish courts had started signaling more flexibility on extradition—until a fiasco in November 1984, when Britain's *Sunday Times* disclosed an imminent attempt to extradite Evelyn Glenholmes, a suspect in the IRA's 1981–82 London campaign. The Irish authorities felt the British were trying to pressure them and the attempt collapsed in acrimony, leaving all sides trading blame.

Britain's security chiefs feared an extradition request would not only fail but reveal to Magee that he was wanted for Brighton. If he valued his liberty, he would know to remain in the republic. There was another option: sit tight and wait for Magee to return to the UK. He might feel emboldened to do so since the arrest warrant for his role in the 1978–79 bombings was gathering dust, seemingly forgotten. If he remained unaware that he was wanted for Brighton, perhaps he would slip across the border to visit friends and relatives in Belfast, the same homesickness that had collared Thomas Quigley and Paul Kavanagh. Or he might return to England for a new IRA operation. In either case, Britain's security apparatus would be waiting for him. Assuming, of course, it could track him. The British would need the Gardaí to maintain discreet surveillance in Dublin. The Chancer was slippery and had different routes into the UK. It would be a huge gamble.

Competing bureaucratic fiefdoms complicated the dilemma. Gathering intelligence on Irish terrorism was the responsibility of the Special Branch in England: MI5 in Northern Ireland and MI6 in the republic. Each agency jealously guarded its turf. The involvement of the RUC, Sussex Police, the Met's Anti-Terrorist Branch, and the Home Office added ingredients to the stew. A top-level conference, whose details remain secret, imposed a truce on the competing agencies and forged a decision. They would watch and wait.

The identification of Patrick Magee became one of the government's most closely guarded secrets. The home secretary, Leon Brittan, gave nothing away when he updated the House of Commons on January 22. The Brighton investigation was seeking a man who had stayed in room 629 and gave a false address, he told the chamber. "Inquiries to trace him and other inquiries related to electronic devices recovered from the debris are continuing. The House will not expect me to go into further details about them." The handful of secret service and police chiefs who knew the truth were under an edict seemingly culled from the title of a Seamus Heaney poem: "Whatever you say, say nothing."

This did not bother David Tadd. Identification done, he had moved on to other jobs, such as preparing evidence exhibits for the upcoming trial of Paul Kavanagh and Thomas Quigley, accused of killing bomb disposal expert Ken Howorth, among others, in London in 1981. They ended up convicted, with long sentences. Jack Reece, however, entered a strange, uncomfortable limbo. At William Hucklesby's office he had listened, rapt, as Tadd detailed the palm print evidence. Since *Crimewatch*, Reece had become the public face of the hunt for the bomber. Now here was a breakthrough, validation of his team's efforts, but he could not stomp aboard a flight to Dublin and bag the suspect. With few guests left to trace, the investigation's manpower dwindled, but the incident room projected brisk activity, as if the effort to identify Roy Walsh was still at full steam. After a lifetime of brusque straight-talking, Reece had to be evasive with colleagues, journalists, and bomb survivors about the status of an investigation that had racked up a significant cost. Under the glare of press conference lights, he would have to bullshit for his country.

Reece took a calculated risk in sharing Magee's identification with some members of the investigation. They had worked hard and he felt they deserved to know. He trusted them to keep the secret. "In true detective style in those days we would have gone upstairs to the social club or to a local pub and got on the piss. But that didn't happen because nobody was to know. We had to carry on as if we didn't know," Detective Constable Paul Gibbon recalled.

It was astonishing nobody blabbed, said DI Byford. "It was the best-kept secret of my police career. There are lots of secrets in the police and half an hour later they [are] no longer secret. But this one was kept."

Actually, not entirely. Reece's phone rang one day. The soft, silky tones of Peter Burden flowed down the line. The *Daily Mail* crime correspondent understood the investigation had identified a primary suspect, a veteran IRA man named Patrick Magee. Burden's mass-selling tabloid planned to splash on the story. Did the detective chief superintendent care to comment? Several choice comments would have occurred to Reece. Burden was the doyen of Fleet Street crime reporters. He would wine and dine senior Met officers over bottles of chilled Sancerre and smoked salmon, then return to his desk at Northcliffe House and weave their tattle into banner headlines. Whoever had blabbed to Burden was probably not a Sussex man, but that was no comfort to Reece. He could have bluffed and told Burden he had the wrong name, or he could have bullied and threatened him. Instead Reece took a high-risk approach seldom recommended in media management: he appealed to Burden's civic sensibility. "If you break this now, you'll destroy one of the most important criminal investigations that we've ever had to face."

It worked. On the promise of a tip-off when Magee was caught, Burden spiked his scoop. The secret remained safe.

Waiting for Magee to surface was perhaps the most frustrating time in Reece's career. Instead of capturing and interrogating his suspect he had to act out a pantomime, the continuing mystery of Roy Walsh, for public consumption. His great passion, as ever, provided a consoling analogy. Catching a villain, Reece once said, was like fishing. "You don't make a noise, so the fish doesn't know you're there."

· · ·

PATRICK MAGEE WONDERED if he was getting paranoid. An unfamiliar car started to cruise around Shangan Road—then another, and another. Four, in fact, seemingly at random, just driving around the neighborhood. Were they taking turns? Other cars were parking in the school grounds opposite his block, affording a view of comings and goings. When Magee took a bus into town, an unmarked car seemed to follow, or on occasion went in front. He scrutinized fellow bus passengers for telltale signs they might be police or informers, and relayed the license plates, makes, and colors of suspicious vehicles up the IRA chain. The feedback was not reassuring: eleven cars had been spotted surveilling his area. Had the Brits linked him to the bomb?

Since watching the TV footage of police crawling over the Grand's rubble, Magee had become even quieter and broodier than usual. *I would always be looking over my shoulder. They would never forget.* He had assumed he was on a short list of suspects, but had not detected surveillance until now, three months later. Maybe he was surrounded by British intelligence agents and Garda Special Branch. Maybe they were preparing a snatch squad, just like the Dutch police years earlier. Or maybe he was imagining things. Ballymun was home to heroin dealers, criminal gangs, and undercover units from the Garda drug squad. They all watched each other. And if it was the Special Branch, maybe it was routine surveillance. Spying on republicans was their job. Maybe they had nothing on him. Maybe he was in the clear. There was no way to know. One thing Magee was sure of: no matter who might be watching, he could, at a moment of his choosing, vanish. That was the beauty of Ballymun.

The city planners who had unleashed this urban experiment in the 1960s named the seven tallest tower blocks after the leaders of the 1916 Rising, a patriotic gesture, but neglected to add amenities and connections to the rest of Dublin. This left Ballymun to molder on the northern fringe as a concrete labyrinth for the poor and the unemployed. Families served their time here before escaping to better social housing, a transient flux that drew squatters, strays, and a trickle of Provos on sabbatical from the war zone. Most laid low, though an IRA bomb maker called Jack McCabe accidentally blew himself up in his garage while mixing explosives. Some joined a community vigilante group that intimidated and evicted drug dealers; if Whitey Bulger had possessed a sense of irony, he might have smiled.

A Sinn Féin caravan held weekly clinics, but this was a political wilderness, Ray Corcoran, a former Sinn Féin councillor, remembered. "Ballymun was anything but a republican stronghold. It was anything goes. A lot of different tribes, different things going on." Tabloid newspapers would splash stories about criminals with nicknames like "Psycho" and nobody in Ballymun would bat an eye. Gardaí were not welcome, a murder squad detective said. "There were so many gangsters there, they'd smell a cop a mile away. It was a very difficult place for us. So many lookouts, fellows on the watch, scouts." With just a few roads in and out, Gardaí could monitor targets in cars and buses but struggled to keep eyes on those who hoofed through the maze on foot. Magee knew this better than anyone. "There were numerous shortcuts, alleyways, footpaths and playing fields, none of which could be effectively monitored by surveillance teams without drawing attention," he later recalled.

Ballymun was relatively safe for Magee, but if he stayed here, what would he do? He had almost wiped out the British government, but that did not alter the fundamentals of his life. He was thirty-three and barely getting by on a meager IRA stipend—the Army Council didn't pay performance bonuses. His marriage was on the rocks, as Eileen preferred Belfast to his squirrelly existence in the south. His skills were not the sort to put on a CV, were he inclined ever to seek a conventional career. Magee looked at his future and saw just one path: continued IRA operations, whatever danger that brought.

Brighton, he believed, had broken Britain's strategy of containment. No longer could Thatcher or any government in London expect to constrain the Troubles to Northern Ireland. When the Grand's ceilings crashed down, so, too, did the ruling elite's sense of inviolability. "We had upped the ante. But we had to maintain the momentum," he later said. "That meant a continuation of the England campaign. Only sustainable, dogged pressure would move the British."

It was the strategy long favored by Magee and the rest of the England Department, but not all the comrades had been convinced.

Some viewed the unit as detached, arrogant, even an indulgence. Bombs across the water generated splashy headlines, but such operations were expensive and fitful and diverted scarce resources from the home front. Sustaining the war in the six counties was hard enough. Informers known as supergrasses were landing dozens of IRA members in court. The RUC and SAS were ambushing volunteers, racking up body counts. Thatcher and the Irish government seemed to be edging toward a deal to try to marginalize republicans. The IRA needed to hit back on home ground. Some Provos dreamed of amassing enough weapons, especially anti-helicopter missiles, to create and hold a "liberated zone."

It was around this time that Ivor Bell, the hawkish Army Council member, made his move against Gerry Adams. Bell accused his former ally of running down the war effort to further Sinn Féin's electoral ambitions. He tried to rally like-minded volunteers in a de facto coup, but it flopped. He was no match for Adams's in-fighting jujitsu. A court-martial expelled him.

It was amid this intrigue and strategic calculation that the England Department pitched an ambitious new overseas campaign. Having come so close to killing Thatcher, it made a persuasive case for further investment in England operations. Owen Coogan's unit got the green light.

"After Brighton, as a direct consequence, the movement were fully won over to the conviction—which beforehand only a rump had held—that we could best further our objectives by a long term, sustained and sustainable campaign of operations across the water," Magee recalled.

There was no need for Magee to cross the Irish Sea again. If caught and linked to Brighton, he would be jailed for decades. He could stay in Dublin, help with logistics, and tutor his successors in fieldcraft. After all, he had worked for years behind enemy lines; nobody would begrudge him taking a supporting role. A Chancer's luck, after all, could not last forever. Magee did not agonize over the decision. Self-esteem, something he had lacked as a youth, may have been part of it. A frontline operator was part of the IRA's military elite, part of a brotherhood. In his quiet way, he had ego. While other IRA men were tasked with kneecapping teenage joyriders, Magee could again bring the war to England, be a player in Gerry Adams's grand strategy.

He volunteered to go back.

·   ·   ·

WHILE MAGEE PREPARED a new campaign in the spring of 1985, Harvey Thomas took a flight to Boston and fell into conversation with his neighboring passenger, a young American. Upon discovering he worked for the Conservatives, she smiled. "What funny seatmates! I'm with the IRA." She raised funds for the armed struggle, she said.

Thomas gazed at her. "I was caught up in one of your things, it was last year," he said. "I got blown up in the Brighton bomb."

There was a pause, each digesting this unexpected encounter above the clouds. "I've nothing against you personally," she said, "but that was one of the happiest days of my life. We almost brought that government down."

·   ·   ·

THE IDEA HAD marinated since 1979, when the Basque separatist group ETA bombed Mediterranean beach resorts to hurt Spain's tourism industry. It was a sporadic, patchy campaign with limited success, but Owen Coogan and Michael Hayes sensed potential. What if an IRA unit hit one British resort after another, more than a dozen bombs dotted across England primed to explode over consecutive days and weeks? A remorseless chain of detonations at beaches and hotels that would sow panic, devastate tourism, and humiliate the security forces. There would be warnings to avert—or at least minimize—civilian casualties, but in traditional IRA style, the warnings would be vague enough to maximize evacuations and disruption. With the police overstretched and focused on the next bomb, the team would switch to assassination. Not Thatcher, who was now too well guarded, but other high-value targets. It would give the Brits a summer they would not forget.

"The complexity of the campaign required meticulous logistical planning," Magee recalled with great understatement. It required an intricate clockwork of researching and scouting targets and constructing, delivering, and planting bombs in accordance with a strict calendar of dates, all without alerting a security apparatus that had moles inside the IRA and monitored Britain's points of entry. Plus, the Gardaí seemed to be taking a close interest in Magee. That made him a potential liability, a "red light." But the England Department did not have a huge pool of available, willing, competent candidates. And Magee was keen to go.

He was to be part of a tight-knit team of four operators that took shape in early 1985. Even by Provo standards, it was an eclectic group. Gerry "Blute" McDonnell was thirty-two, a bearded, big-boned, bullet-headed republican from the Falls Road. A blunt manner and gorilla physique—he towered over Magee—masked a streetwise canniness. Trained in electronics, he had previously operated in England. In 1983, he had escaped with thirty-seven other IRA prisoners from the Maze, the biggest breakout in UK penal history, and resumed active service.

Martina Anderson, age twenty-one, was a vivacious personality who had competed in a beauty contest in Derry before being charged in 1981 with causing an explosion and possessing weapons. She skipped bail and moved to the republic. Her subsequent movements were veiled, but she formed a romantic relationship with Paul Kavanagh, who was busy planting bombs in London, including the device that killed Ken Howorth.

Ella O'Dwyer, age twenty-four, had no republican lineage. She was from a farming hamlet in County Tipperary, far removed from Northern Ireland's violence. Quiet and cerebral, she studied English, linguistics, and philosophy at University College Dublin and thought to become an academic or journalist. Then came the hunger strikes. She joined Sinn Féin and eventually the IRA. She was a "clean skin," not known to any police force.

The four met and bonded probably in a remote setting, away from prying eyes, in January and February. Personal chemistry mattered. Across the water, they would be completely reliant on each other. "You don't just walk into a bomb team—you have to earn its confidence and trust," noted Shane Paul O'Doherty, a former bomber. They would have studied potential targets, undertaken inductions and refreshers in shooting and bomb making, memorized aliases.

Blute had a birth certificate and finance card in the name of Michael Garvey. Anderson would travel under the name Mary Webster, using a passport that was part of a batch stolen in May 1984 from the Dublin Passport Office. O'Dwyer had a passport from the same batch, doctored by the same expert hand, in the name of Sandra Holland, plus a driver's license in that name. Magee had a British passport in the name of David Henry. Forged organ donor cards and other documents would supply additional identities.

A fifth member was assigned as a fixer. Donal Craig, age twenty-six, was a carpenter from Ardara, a County Donegal village. His family had republican sympathies but no involvement in the struggle. Consequently, Craig could travel freely to Britain, rent flats, source vehicles, and perform other errands without suspicion. Wiry, handsome, exuberant, he was bursting to help the cause. A sixth member, a gunman, would be needed later.

Their campaign would rely on the anonymity of Britain's cities. "England was a big field of haystacks within which to lose a needle," Magee recalled, "and once there we had the element of invisibility and surprise."

. . .

As February turned to March, Magee remained under surveillance. But he does not seem to have been *closely* watched. There is no evidence his apartment was bugged, or that adjacent properties were used for twenty-four-hour monitoring. The IRA's estimate of eleven cars surveilling the area, according to one Garda source, was exaggerated. There was no more than a handful.

British spycraft was sophisticated—the KGB's London bureau chief, Oleg Gordievsky, was a double agent working for MI6. Tracking devices were planted in IRA vehicles and weapons in Northern Ireland. Yet Magee could on occasion elude Irish police surveillance in Ballymun. It was the price of letting him think he had got away with Brighton in hope he would return to the UK. Perhaps fearing it would leak, the British did not tell the Irish government about Magee's identification. Instead they used informal channels between Scotland Yard and the Irish police, who routinely exchanged favors and information, to request the surveillance. There were no Klaxons declaring it a national security priority. Brighton may not even have been mentioned, but some Gardaí made the connection. A retired sergeant told Tim Pat Coogan, the editor of the *Irish Press*, that Magee was wanted for Brighton. Coogan did not know if the tip was accurate and did not use it. So a handful of undercover Gardaí continued to cruise around Shangan Road.

The British gamble succeeded. Magee, despite his suspicion about surveillance, decided to return to Britain, just as his enemies hoped. But like the woodcutter who summoned death in Aesop's fable, they should have been careful what they wished for. Their informants within the IRA were not able to say where or when Magee would cross the Irish Sea.

In March, Magee bade farewell to Eileen and Padraig before they boarded a train back to Belfast. He knew it would be a long time before he saw them again. Days later, he left his tower block and walked down Shangan Road for the last time. Ballymun swallowed him up. The watchers did not see where he emerged. They did not see him make his way to a harbor and board a vessel—the IRA had several sea routes—and sail from Ireland. They had no idea he was gone.

Toward the end of March, a polite young couple stepped across the threshold of 17 James Gray Street, a four-story sandstone tenement in Shawlands, a residential neighborhood of Glasgow, Scotland's biggest city. They sipped tea in the living room with the landlady, Frances Boyle, and introduced themselves as Anne and Tom Smith. Anne did most of the talking, while Tom sat in an armchair, silent. A tenant's toddler badgered him for conversation and delivered a kick on the shin, but Tom remained impassive. Boyle had an attic room to rent. It was small, just a bed and sleeper sofa, with a bathroom down the hall. It cost £16 a week. The Smiths said they would take it. They paid £48 in advance for three weeks. Ella O'Dwyer and Patrick Magee had found a base.

. . . .

Two weeks later, on April 17, at the other end of Britain, Jack Reece faced another public prodding over his investigation. The coroner's inquest into the Brighton bomb asked him about the guest known as Roy Walsh. Reece, stretching his thespian skills, continued the fiction that Walsh's identity was a mystery and that his "description was too imprecise to be released." He still hoped the fish would surface if the investigation did not make a noise. The waiting and not knowing, one colleague recalled, was "awful."

By late April, the reports from Dublin were alarming. Magee had not been seen in weeks. Eileen Magee no longer visited. By early May, alarm turned to dread. There was no longer any doubt.

The Chancer was gone.

CHAPTER EIGHTEEN

——

London

All morning, the crowds had streamed down the Mall to claim a spot before the ceremony. Union Jacks hung from lampposts that lined the procession route. The asphalt stretching toward Buckingham Palace was tinted red, like a giant carpet. Ushers steered generals, admirals, and government ministers to vantage points around Horse Guards Parade. Horses crunched over the gravel of the immaculate parade ground, their riders' sabers gleaming in the pale sunlight. Three regiments of the Household Division in scarlet tunics and bearskin caps formed phalanxes, while drum majors in gold lace tunics directed bands into position. Regimental banners fluttered. A hush fell across the crowd.

"Present arms!" cried an officer. A crack resounded as hundreds of troops shouldered rifles at exactly the same instant. A bugle sounded, then drums, pipes, trumpets, and flutes filled the morning air. Queen Elizabeth was on her way. It was Saturday, June 15, and England was celebrating the annual Trooping of the Colour, a venerable military ritual held on the sovereign's official birthday. Cheers rolled down the

Mall as horse-drawn carriages ferried the royal family from Buckingham Palace to the parade ground, followed by the Queen, riding sidesaddle atop her favorite mare, Burmese.

Troopers on gray horses with kettledrums swelled the martial symphony with thumping cadences to stir even a pacifist's fighting spirit. Standard-bearers held aloft ensigns embroidered with old battles: Arras, Egypt, Namur, Rhineland, Salamanca, Sevastopol, Tunis, Tangier, Waterloo. For two hours, horses and men performed ceremonial drills, conjuring the centuries when this island race sailed distant seas and marched across hostile deserts. After a thunderous rendition of "God Save the Queen," the royals returned to Buckingham Palace and appeared on the balcony to salute the crowds. Princess Diana was a vision in pink, nine-month-old Prince Harry clutched to her like a koala. And then the finale: a roar overhead as nine Royal Air Force jets in arrow formation trailed blue, red, and white streams.

It was a spectacle to stiffen British spines and delight tourists, a demonstration of tradition and fealty to the Crown delivered with such panache it was possible to forget Mountbatten, Hyde Park, Brighton, and all the other atrocities that seeped from the dreary conflict across the Irish Sea, to forget that a corner of the United Kingdom contested its Britishness and viewed these pretty soldiers with their sashes and plumes as a force of occupation.

Later that evening, after the horses were stabled and the regimental banners carefully stored, Patrick Magee wound his way through London, an unobtrusive addition to a sea of seven million people.

A month earlier, on May 10, his face and name had been added to a routine internal circular of wanted fugitives issued to all UK police forces. Having lost track of their prime suspect, Jack Reece and the intelligence services felt compelled to flag Magee to all British law enforcement, though they didn't mention the Brighton bomb. No one had spotted him. The Chancer's hunters had no confirmation he was in Britain. He could have been in Bogotá or Bordeaux.

In fact, he had been in the country at least ten weeks, since he and Ella O'Dwyer had rented the Glasgow apartment in late March. They had made slow, careful preparations, researching targets, acquiring bomb components, testing electronics. Gerry "Blute" McDonnell and Martina Anderson had followed in May. The plan was to plant sixteen time bombs, with the chain of explosions starting in mid-July, still a month away. Magee had come to London to plant the first device.

The West End was throbbing, voices and laughter from pubs and restaurants spilling into the summer evening. Tourists packed theaters, but no show could compete with the Queen's birthday parade that morning. Roger Moore, pointing a gun, gazed down from cinema posters. "Has James Bond finally met his match?" asked the tagline. Magee made his way up Buckingham Palace Road, which coiled around the southern section of the palace grounds.

He halted by the Royal Mews, a rear entrance to the palace that housed the monarch's horses, carriages, and vehicles. Stone pillars topped by a lion and unicorn flanked the black iron gates. The palace was protected by Scotland Yard's Royal Palaces Division, half a company of army troops plus infrared cameras, beams, alarms, and Semtracks, an electronic trip wire. None of this troubled Magee. His target was opposite the Royal Mews, outside the palace grounds, on the other side of the road: the Rubens Hotel. A six-story Edwardian edifice popular with foreign tourists. "Few hotels can claim to be neighbors of the Queen," boasted its brochure. Its lights glowed in the dusk. It was approximately 9:30 p.m.

Magee stepped past a gray-suited doorman into the lobby. In the adjacent bar, a pianist tinkled a soft tune. Magee approached the reception desk. He had phoned half an hour earlier to book a room with a palace view. The receptionist, Lynn Natividad, handed him a registration card. She would remember that he had a female companion, who was probably O'Dwyer. Exactly nine months since he had checked into the Grand, Magee's pen hovered over another registration card. There was no encore for Roy Walsh. Magee signed in as T. Morton, an old English name, and gave his address as 11 Woodford Road, Watford, a town north of London. He paid £70 up front in cash for one night, pocketed the receipt, collected a key from the porter's desk, and took the elevator to the first floor. Room 112 was compact and plain, with a small desk and chair, a double bed, a bedside cabinet. Parting the mauve curtains, he gazed directly at the Royal Mews.

While Magee set to work, others relaxed. Margaret Thatcher was at Chequers, her diary free of engagements. David Tadd was at his home across the Thames, watching TV. Jack Reece liked to spend Saturday evenings at home in Hastings, digesting one of Daphne's big weekend dishes. From his case, Magee extracted a bright yellow *Masters of the Universe* lunch box and undid the clasps. The bomb was a snug fit. It was probably already fully assembled and just needed activation. Three pounds and nine ounces (1.6 kilograms) of gelignite—stolen from Irish Industrial Explosives, a company near Dublin—had been wrapped in plastic wrap more than seventy times. A long-delay timer the size of a cigarette packet, similar to that used in Brighton, was already running. A Memo-Park timer and travel alarm clock acted as an additional timer. A nine-volt battery powered the device. There were two booby traps, a microswitch on the lid and a mercury tilting device. If an unsuspecting hand tried to open or move the box more than 0.4 of an inch, the bomb would detonate.

The bedside cabinet rested on a plinth connected to the wall by four screws. Magee or his accomplice undid the screws and lifted the plinth and the cabinet. They placed the lunch box against the skirting board, put back the cabinet and plinth, which fitted over the lunch box, and reinserted the screws.

The bomb was protected and invisible. By fluke or by design, the hiding spot was beside a disused chimney, which would amplify the impact. Though less powerful than the Brighton bomb, the device could bring down one floor—or possibly two—and explode outward, gouging a great hole in the Rubens. The rumble would resound across

Buckingham Palace and remind Britain of a conflict missing from the royal regimental banners.

As in Brighton, Magee slept beside his bomb. He checked out the next morning, Sunday, June 16. The bomb was timed to explode in six weeks, at 1:00 p.m. on July 29.

. . .

MAGEE HAD ERRANDS that required several more days in the capital before returning to Glasgow. O'Dwyer, meanwhile, reappeared in Glasgow. Magee's first task was to shed the identity of T. Morton of Watford and become Alan Woods of Shipley, West Yorkshire. He headed to Finsbury Park, in North London. As he crossed the metropolis, Magee had reason to be satisfied. Preparations for the IRA's most complex campaign in Britain were well advanced. Glasgow was proving a good choice of base.

Scotland had a unique place in IRA lore and tactics. It was from here that King James I of England encouraged Protestant settlers to sail to the north of Ireland in the 1600s to occupy land seized from rebellious Irish Catholics. So the place was a source of original sin, but the Provos redressed the balance by smuggling personnel and material aboard the ferries and merchant vessels that sailed from Belfast and Larne, turning Scotland into a launching pad to attack England. It was easy for operators to blend in. Scotland had a big Irish immigrant community and some Scottish Catholics had sympathy for IRA goals, if not methods. Though part of the British mainland, it felt far from the prying eyes of London's counterterrorism specialists. Local Special Branch detectives tended to focus not on republican but loyalist paramilitaries who flaunted ties to the land of their ancestors. The IRA kept a low profile by eschewing attacks in Scotland, instead using it for safe houses and supply lines, a sort of Celtic Ho Chi Minh Trail.

An IRA sympathizer in Glasgow named Shaun McShane had connected Magee and O'Dwyer to Frances Boyle, the landlady who rented rooms in her tenement at 17 James Gray Street. The location was good: residential, quiet, a transient population with accents from all over Ireland. It overlooked Queen's Park, a lush sixty acres named not after any English monarch but Mary Stuart, a Catholic who ruled Scotland in the sixteenth century. The property itself was not ideal—Magee and O'Dwyer shared it with other tenants, families with children who tromped up and down the stairs. Tom and Anne Smith, as their neighbors knew them, put extra bolts on their door, paid their rent on time, kept to themselves, and hauled their groceries—and other supplies—up the stairs in a shopping cart.

In early April, about a week after moving in to James Gray Street, Magee had traveled a hundred miles south to Carlisle and brought Donal Craig back with him. Craig, a chain-smoker, was told to puff by the window. They gave him approximately £1,000 in cash and dispatched him to London with instructions to buy a car and rent a flat using his false identity documents. The apartment had filled up with the arrival of Martina Anderson and Gerry "Blute" McDonnell, who introduced themselves to neighbors as Mary and Pat. The team had amassed an arsenal—handguns, automatic rifles, more than 130 pounds of gelignite, batteries, modified alarm clocks, microswitches, mercury tilt switches, toggle switches, circuit testers, disposable gloves, tweezers, crocodile clips—and turned the attic space into a workshop, soldering wires and packing explosives. The landlady's son, John Boyle, noted high electricity usage, but did not seem to suspect anything. Shaun McShane, the team's Glasgow gofer, stumbled in and discovered O'Dwyer and Anderson, wearing gloves, using an ammeter to check timers and power units. "They're making fucking bombs up there," he told his wife. The couple did not alert police.

The IRA team sorted timetables, brochures, cuttings, and other documents into folders and envelopes with names like "Work Information," "Newspaper Information," and "Events" covering late May to late September. Using wigs and hair dye to alter their appearance, the unit had split up for reconnaissance across England, Magee and

O'Dwyer forming A-team, Blute and Anderson B-team. Traveling by train and car they visited hotels, boardinghouses, and beaches. They stockpiled brochures, noted public events, and devised a bombing calendar: July 19, Brighton; July 20, Dover and Ramsgate; July 22, London; July 23, Blackpool; July 24, London; July 25, Eastbourne; July 26, London; July 27, Bournemouth; July 29, London; July 30, Torquay; July 31, Great Yarmouth; August 1, Folkestone; August 2, Margate; August 3, Southend; August 5, Southampton. Sixteen bombs over eighteen days, with lulls on Sundays. It would be a chance to revive the old graffiti: *Every night is gelignite.*

Each target on the calendar had an *H* or a *B* beside it, *H* for "hotel," *B* for "boardinghouse" or "beach." Connected on a map, it was one long thread from Blackpool, in the northwest, stretching to London and sprouting multiple legs, like a dangling spider. In addition to the Rubens device, three of the intended bombs appeared to shadow the Queen, who was due to visit Brighton on July 19, Great Yarmouth on August 1, and Southampton on August 7. Warnings could minimize casualties, while leaving the royal itinerary, along with Britain's tourism industry, in chaos.

The team had also prepared a potential assassination campaign. The team's research archive included a newspaper profile of Major General Peter De La Billière and copies of *Soldier* magazine, with veterans' reunion meetings underlined.

In cramped quarters, unable to safely socialize, arrest an ever-present risk, the team must have experienced claustrophobia on the top floor of 17 James Gray Street. Like it or not, all they had was each other. Electronic surveillance ruled out phone calls to loved ones: Blute's new wife, O'Dwyer's parents and siblings, Anderson's family, all cut off. Anderson had also lost her boyfriend, Paul Kavanagh, who in March had been sentenced to life in prison. He sent her greetings through the columns of *An Phoblacht/Republican News*, signing himself "P." Magee's dying marriage showed the personal cost of long operations across the water.

On May 29, Magee had turned thirty-four. He received two cards. "I hope your birthday meets up to your expectations," said one, signed Mary, from Anderson. The other had a picture of a stick of dynamite on the cover and was signed "Jean," one of O'Dwyer's aliases. "To the successful fulfillment of all your varied faculties in the future," the message said.

Two weeks later, her birthday wish for Magee seemed to be coming true. He had successfully planted the first bomb and was switching identities. At Finsbury Park station, he bought a London travel card under the name Alan Woods, of 11 Taunton Street, Shipley, West Yorkshire. He walked three hundred yards down Seven Sisters Road, turned right onto Queen's Drive, and as Alan Woods booked into the Gloucester Hotel, one of the many small, run-down lodgings in this part of London, a hub for immigrants and travelers. O'Dwyer's message expressed a truth about Magee: he had varied skills, including logistics, electronics, subterfuge, and complete dedication to the cause. This had made him Britain's most wanted man, yet here he was, a few miles from Scotland Yard, mounting a new IRA campaign.

Magee's versatility, however, did not stretch to psychiatry—which would have helped with one of his tasks in London. Donal Craig was unraveling. Fizzing with energy, keen to impress, the Donegal carpenter had seemed a promising fixer but had made one blunder after another. He bought an Alfasud car with just two doors and rented a flat with just one exit, liabilities in any emergency, and did so under his own name, not his false identity. He fell in love with a local woman, Una Lowney, confided in her about what he was doing, and fretted he would be arrested and lose her. He started to drink heavily and his moods swung from elation to despair, exactly the chauffeur you don't want when surveilling bombing targets. Blute and Anderson had got a close view of his disintegration when he ferried them around London. O'Dwyer had seen it in the port town of Whitehaven when he drove the wrong way down a one-way street, prompting police to stop them and O'Dwyer to reach for her shoulder bag, prepared to shoot. The danger passed, but Craig seemed close to complete breakdown. Only later would his manic depression be diagnosed. Magee had to manage the fiasco. To safeguard the operation, the England Department wanted Craig shot or withdrawn. In a meeting with Craig, Magee did neither—and Craig handed Magee a resignation letter. He was quitting the campaign and quitting the IRA. As long as he kept his mouth shut, this could be a solution.

On Thursday, June 20, Magee completed a final task when he rented a flat at 53 Hackney Road in London's East End. Using the name Alan Cooper, he paid an estate agent two months' rent. It was a one-bedroom flat on the top floor of a three-story building in a nondescript row of shops and fast-food outlets. It was to be the unit's London base. He hid a loaded handgun, a soldering iron, pliers, wires, and other bomb-making equipment under the floorboards. Labors over, Magee did a newspaper crossword and may have treated himself to a vodka. Despite all of the obstacles, the plot's final pieces were falling into place. The Rubens bomb was planted and ticking. The bombs stored at James Gray Street in Glasgow were largely ready. While still renting the original apartment, the team itself had recently moved to a new, more private apartment at 236 Langside Road, on the other side of Queen's Park. Nobody took it as a bad omen that Langside was named after the battle that led to Queen Mary's defeat and eventual execution in England. Gazing out his window at the Hackney Road traffic on this warm Thursday afternoon, Magee could congratulate himself on reaching this point in the campaign. He had two days to lie low before rejoining the others in Glasgow, with a brief stop en route: a rendezvous to collect a new member of the team.

.   .   .

WHILE THE CHANCER installed himself at Hackney Road, Chief Inspector Ian Phoenix spent Thursday afternoon pacing his office in Belfast, four hundred miles away, waiting for surveillance photographs to develop in his unit's darkroom. Rain drummed on the roof of the

Ian Phoenix with his hunting dogs in the County
Antrim hills in 1993. | Dr. Susan Phoenix

portacabin, one of many behind the fortress gray walls of the Royal
Ulster Constabulary base in Lisnasharragh. It took all of Phoenix's
willpower not to charge into the darkroom and roar at the chemicals
to hurry up. A six-week operation to uncover a suspected IRA smuggling route across the Irish Sea hinged on the blurry image of a suspect
slowly materializing behind the darkroom door. Phoenix was pretty
sure he knew the man's identity. He just needed confirmation, and fast.

Phoenix was forty-two, with a mop of brown hair and a body
hardened by running, hiking, and climbing. When not working, he
was at his converted farmhouse with his family, tending beehives,
glazing windows, mowing the lawn, making wine, always *doing*. He
was possibly the worst-dressed plainclothes officer in the RUC, a
walking jumble of ill-matched trousers and shirts, and possibly the
bluntest man on the force, lacking any aptitude or appetite for bureaucratic niceties. "Okay, what's happening and what the fuck are you
doing about it?" he asked his team each morning.

Phoenix had grown up playing cowboys and Indians in the fields of County Tyrone and spent years as an army paratrooper jumping from planes and hunting insurgents in Malaysian jungles before returning to Northern Ireland, marrying an English nurse, Susan, and joining the RUC in 1970 as the Troubles were exploding. He was shot at, blown up, and lived in perpetual risk of assassination. Phoenix worked for the British state, but considered himself Irish and viewed the IRA as a twisted perversion of Irish identity. He called them "bastards" and "gougers." He believed solid policing and soldiering could defeat them—it was a matter of identifying and taking out key players. He got the chance to prove it after joining a covert surveillance unit within the RUC's Special Branch called Echo 4 Alpha, or E4A. A clandestine force within a force, its members trained at an SAS-style boot camp and learned espionage arts from MI5.

E4A operatives had to be ordinary looking—not too short or tall, no distinctive features—and able to blend into any setting, using disguises if necessary. They hid in derelict buildings, hedgerows, wherever there was cover, communicating with colleagues via radio clicks and taking photographs with customized cameras. "You had to be happy to pee into a plastic bucket lying sideways," said one former "boot man" who hid in car trunks with peepholes. "Take in water and a sandwich and just lie there. You had your pistol and a shotgun and a boot release switch. The worry always was that if someone rumbled you, they would pour petrol on you and set you alight." The operations room was filled with charts, maps, and pictures of suspects, and the pace of operations was nonstop—multiple jobs every day, he recalled.

Phoenix ran the Belfast office like a ship on fire, with no time for protocol or intra-agency communication channels. His nickname was Captain Chaos. He did not hide his opinion that many RUC superiors and English intelligence chiefs were careerists and chinless wonders, earning him powerful enemies in senior ranks. Phoenix's combative streak extended even to the English language, which he battled when writing reports, cursing his way through spelling and grammar doubts.

Phoenix was intimidating, maddening, inspiring. And, on this rainy Thursday afternoon, probably using more expletives than usual as he paced outside E4A's darkroom.

Two separate surveillance operations appeared to have intersected. Operation Drain had begun six weeks earlier, in early May, after a source who worked on a coal boat told his handler the Provos wished to smuggle someone aboard. The crew member would meet his IRA contact, a mid-ranking republican fixer, in a pub called the White Horse on Garmoyle Street in Belfast's docklands. Phoenix dispatched a four-man team. Two frequented the pub, posing as off-duty painters, while the other two hid in their van, parked outside, and photographed people entering and leaving. The republican discussed arrangements with the crew member, but withheld the passenger's identity.

In early June, a Portadown-based E4A unit that covered towns and rural areas south of Belfast received a separate tip: Peter Sherry, a commander of the IRA's East Tyrone Brigade, was apparently preparing to relocate. Where, when, and for what purpose was unclear, but it was presumed to be for an important operation outside Tyrone. The RUC had a thick file on the enigmatic Sherry. Age twenty-nine, a former law clerk, soft-spoken, with a slight build but a fearsome reputation, Sherry was the so-called Armalite Kid. After hijacking vehicles, he was jailed in the early 1970s, shared a cage with Gerry Adams, and upon release graduated to alleged shootings. He canvassed with the family of Bobby Sands when Sands ran for Parliament during the hunger strike, then was jailed from 1982 to 1983 on the word of a supergrass. When the supergrass lost his nerve, Sherry was released without charge and allegedly resumed attacks on security forces in Tyrone. They masked their fear by calling him "Little Peter." Adams canvassed for Sherry in March 1984 when he stood for Sinn Féin in a council by-election, embodying the Armalite and ballot box strategy. He lost the election but won mystique among Provos seven months later for surviving the SAS ambush.

Sherry's luck seemed to run out in November 1984 when Ken

Maginnis, the unionist MP for Fermanagh and South Tyrone—the seat Bobby Sands had held briefly—made a remarkable statement in the House of Commons. "Is the Secretary of State aware that one Peter Sherry, who stood as a Sinn Féin candidate in a local government by-election, recently used his manifesto to forecast which people would be murdered, and three of those murders have already been carried out?" The manifesto had accused a Tyrone hospital and other employers of anti-Catholic discrimination and subsequent IRA attacks took place at or near some of those locations.

Maginnis's claim, justified or not, painted Sherry in bright neon colors for security forces and loyalist paramilitaries. "It made life more difficult," Sherry said later. "My life was very difficult anyway. I was being arrested on a regular basis."

With Sherry no longer able to operate effectively in Tyrone, the IRA suggested a mission farther afield. "The logic was that things were too hot and I needed to go somewhere else." To swap, in other words, the claustrophobic attentions of the RUC and UDR for anonymity across the water. One of the passports stolen from the Dublin Passport Office was customized for Sherry, giving him the name Peter Burns. He made discreet preparations to depart, unaware the RUC had learned something was up. In June, the E4A unit asked the local Ulster Defence Regiment, which routinely monitored and harassed Sherry, to step back—an "out-of-bounds," or OOB, notice. "We were told to lay off," a UDR officer said. The idea was to give Sherry space to breathe and move.

In mid-June, while Magee was staying at the Gloucester Hotel in Finsbury Park, Sherry left his council estate home in Dungannon and headed for the M1 motorway. The E4A team had placed a crude magnetic tracking device under the car and followed at a distance, the control box beeping as he drove east, curling around Lough Neagh and turning north, to Belfast. On the outskirts of the city, the southern-based E4A unit handed over to one of Ian Phoenix's Belfast teams. "Okay, that's him coming off the motorway." Near the Kennedy Way roundabout, the tracking device fell off. Sherry did not notice. The watchers kept eyes on him for the rest of his journey to a house in West Belfast, where he stayed the night. It was not a known republican safe house. The IRA was using a clean property to try to keep Sherry off the radar.

Phoenix had not spent all of June obsessing over the Armalite Kid's murky travel plans. E4A teams were tracking dozens of Provos, including Gerry Adams, and trying to thwart deadly mortar and land mine attacks across Northern Ireland. Most surveillance ops ended inconclusively. Perhaps Sherry would lead to something interesting, perhaps not. But by the time Sherry arrived in Belfast, the surveillance logs and intelligence reports made Phoenix suspect he was the passenger to be smuggled aboard the coal boat, the *Ballykern*. That would signal something big brewing across the water. The problem was that Sherry lodged on a street where not even boot men could safely keep watch. So Operation Drain's E4A team kept monitoring the docks to see if he turned up.

On the afternoon of June 20, while Patrick Magee moved into Hackney Road, the E4A painters' van parked in the drizzle outside the White Horse bar by the River Lagan, close to where the *Titanic* had been built. The officers who were hidden inside photographed everyone entering and leaving, while their two colleagues strolled in and ordered drinks. After six weeks of such appearances, it was like the bar in the TV show *Cheers*: everyone knew their names, which of course were false. The undercover officers would have shown no flicker when the republican fixer walked in and met the *Ballykern* crewman. The IRA man passed an envelope, later revealed to be a £5,000 payment. The fixer turned and nodded to a man at the back of the pub, his face obscured to the officers. The fixer and the crewman walked out and parted ways, the fixer turning left toward the city center, while the crewman headed for his ship. The detectives followed the fixer, hoping he would lead them to the mystery passenger, but he met no one of interest. A short while later, the crewman contacted his handler to say the passenger had slipped aboard. It was the man the fixer had nodded to. He was slim, with brown hair, a description that applied to perhaps five hundred known Provos. The only way to confirm it was Sherry was from photographs of those who had entered and left the bar.

So, like an expectant father Phoenix paced outside E4A's darkroom while a colleague extracted prints slick from chemical solution and hung them under the red light. Minutes passed. The door opened. The developer may have worn a wide grin. There in black and white, unmistakably, was Peter Sherry. It was a cue to whoop and crack out the whiskey, except there was no time to exult. The *Ballykern* was due to sail the next day to Ayr, a port on the southwest coast of Scotland. The RUC had no jurisdiction across the water, so Phoenix needed Scottish police to continue the surveillance. An urgent request was relayed to Strathclyde Police, the force that covered southwest Scotland. But a faxed, grainy photograph left margin for error—they might miss Sherry. Officers that knew Sherry by sight should be there. Phoenix wanted to be there, too. He no longer jumped out of airplanes but could still hunt. That meant catching that evening's 6:30 p.m. ferry. Mustering a sergeant and four detective constables, his posse left the RUC base in two cars and raced to the Port of Larne. Lacking time to submit a travel expenses request via the RUC system, Captain Chaos paid the fares himself.

It was still drizzling when the ferry blasted its horn and slid into the North Channel for the thirty-mile crossing to Scotland. The Scots had a word for such bleak days—*dreich*—but in the gray mist that cloaked the horizon, Phoenix saw only rich possibility. His team would rendezvous with Scottish police and be in position when Peter Sherry disembarked at Ayr the next day.

CHAPTER NINETEEN

———

Glasgow

Peter Sherry sailed out of Belfast on the morning of Friday, June 21, 1985. The endless drizzle of recent days hardened and peppered wintry snow grain over the city he left behind. The *Ballykern* would have felt damp and smelled of diesel. Sherry hunkered in the cabin while the propellers churned a path through the North Channel. The Tyrone Provo was not a fugitive—the attempted murder case against him the previous year had collapsed—but the Special Branch monitored passenger ferries, so to enter Scotland undetected meant playing merchant sailor. Sherry was joining the team across the water, probably as a triggerman. He had a holdall, more than a thousand pounds in cash, a fake passport, and three medallions. One was hollow and contained a message written in tiny letters on cigarette paper: "WHS 3.30 meet."

The ship moored at Ayr's small commercial harbor in the early afternoon. Sherry stepped ashore and made his way through railway sidings toward the port's exit. Several sets of eyes kept a discreet watch as he turned south, toward the spire overlooking the town center.

The watchers did not know if his holdall carried guns or bombs, but Ayr had already experienced a small, controlled explosion in the form of Chief Inspector Ian Phoenix.

The previous evening, his E4A team had disembarked at the ferry port of Stranraer, fifty miles south, and motored up to Ayr, where they had a late-night strategy meeting with two detective constables from the Strathclyde Police Special Branch, who had driven down from Glasgow. It did not go well. The Scots said they would arrest Sherry on sight and could handle it alone. One brandished a huge revolver, as if auditioning for *Miami Vice*. Phoenix erupted, saying the point was to see where Sherry would lead them. "The two plebs had no foresight and were obviously in a hurry to get their supper or whatever," he would write in his diary, after cooling down.

The next morning, Phoenix's sergeant met other members of the Strathclyde team and forged a détente. The RUC men could join the surveillance. Tension prickled again when the visitors said the undercover officers staked out around the port were too obvious and Sherry would spot them. The Scots were accustomed to surveilling loyalist paramilitaries on boozy arms-purchasing missions, not tracking active-service IRA operators. Harmony restored, both teams followed Sherry through Ayr.

Sherry continued to the railway station and bought a ScotRail ticket to Glasgow, forty miles north. On the hour-long journey, he did not notice the watchers in the neighboring carriage, nor the watchers at Glasgow Central Station, who saw him buy another ticket and board a London-bound train. When the train chugged past the English border, so ended the uneasy partnership between Ian Phoenix and Strathclyde Police, which no longer had jurisdiction.

Captain Chaos now had to partner with the Metropolitan Special Branch, which was responsible for surveilling IRA suspects in England. *You can always tell a Met man, but not much,* Jack Hermon, the RUC's chief constable, had once cracked. The E4A team assumed

Sherry was bound for the capital, but he disembarked at the first stop after Scotland: Carlisle. He booked into a nearby hotel. A Met surveillance team arrived that night, about a dozen strong, with several female officers. Most looked scruffy, even unkempt. It was their standard look, since their targets usually inhabited gritty pubs and council estates. Weary from the drive, they took turns monitoring the hotel, while the others checked into their own lodging and studied photographs of fugitive Provos. It was a long night in Carlisle.

. . .

ON THE MORNING of Saturday, June 22, London shivered under the wet chill blanketing the British Isles. It was a day for dodging puddles and lamenting the absent summer. No one paid any notice to the small, compact man with a mustache and stubble who made his way to Euston train station. He collected a ticket and strode to a platform, bound for the north.

Two decades earlier, the direction of travel had been in reverse, a troubled teen from Norwich sent to a young offenders hostel in the capital. Desperate to belong, he had joined older boys in joyriding. "Just the sort of stunt that might convince you that you could get away with anything if you only kept your nerve," Patrick Magee later reflected. With the IRA, the rebel had found his cause, taking one risk after another, and gotten away with it. Perhaps Magee still believed it was a matter of nerve.

He found his carriage and settled into his seat. At 11:45 a.m. the train jolted into motion. It was an Inter-City 125, so-called because the engine's wedge-shaped nose cone reached 125 miles per hour. It was 260 miles to Carlisle.

Carlisle, a border city, was built by watchers, the Romans at the edge of empire eyeing unruly tribes to the north, the Normans on battlements overlooking hostile Gaels—and now, a more discreet form of vigil. While Magee sped through the English countryside, the Met and E4A teams observed Peter Sherry checking out of his hotel and entering a nearby pub, where he sipped a few drinks. An hour passed, then another, each marked by a clock tower's chimes. Sherry paid for his drinks, picked up his holdall, and walked to the station. It was busy, trains pulling in and out every few minutes, passengers milling on platforms. Diesel and coffee perfumed the damp air. Ding-dong chimes from speakers presaged an echoey metallic voice announcing arrivals and departures. Sherry went to a newsagent store on the concourse, W. H. Smith, and stood. It was approximately 2:30 p.m.

A canoodling couple occupied a nearby bench. The man stroked the woman's hair and murmured into her ear. She smiled and murmured back. They appeared besotted, but really they were Met Special Branch officers.

The woman's hair concealed a microphone linked to the team's radio system. Colleagues staked spots farther away. Others were parked outside. Sherry could detect anomalies in the County Tyrone landscape, an open gate that should be shut, a car parked at an odd angle, but sensed nothing out of place in this English train station. He stayed where he was. Minutes slid by. Shortly before 3:00 p.m., a small man with stubble and a mustache emerged from the throng and greeted Sherry. The speakers boomed as they conversed.

The surveillance officers with a direct view of the scene unfolding outside the W. H. Smith may have felt their mouths go dry with the first tingle of adrenaline. They had an obscured view of the stranger, whom they called the UK, or Unknown. They assumed this was Sherry's contact. Such a moment dissolved the job's tribulations—the weeks cooped in a van, pissing in bottles, missing family events—and made the heart thump. The couple on the bench still appeared to have eyes only for each other, but cast surreptitious glances, trying for a proper look at Sherry's interlocutor. They had studied dozens, possibly hundreds, of images of IRA suspects overnight.

The female officer leaned into the microphone. "I think it's Magee."

The two suspects walked to the station buffet. The watchers needed to be sure. A veteran Met undercover operative, originally from

Northern Ireland, ambled through the concourse and discreetly eyed the smaller, darker man. "I started looking for the finger because I knew he had part of his finger missing," he recalled. "I said yes, I'm 90 percent certain—you never said 100 percent—I said I'm 90 percent certain it's Magee."

They had found the Chancer.

Seven years after his London bombing campaign, eight months after the Brighton bomb, and a week after planting the Rubens bomb, Pat Magee had stumbled into British police crosshairs. He remained oblivious. Feeling camouflaged in the station's bustle, his words drowned by the speakers, he continued talking quietly to Sherry.

Jack Reece had paved the way, methodically whittling the biggest manhunt in British history to the Grand Hotel guest who posed as Roy Walsh. David Tadd had made the link to Magee. Intelligence chiefs had held their nerve, waiting for him to return to the UK. And here he was. Yet the discovery was a fluke, haphazard, a spin-off from an RUC operation in Northern Ireland. The watchers in Carlisle did not know Magee was wanted for Brighton. They knew only that he was on a police circular of wanted fugitives, because secrecy still veiled the Brighton investigation.

As their eyes bored into the targets, the watchers confronted the dread question of surveillance operations: To swoop, or not to swoop? They did not know if Magee and Sherry carried guns or had explosives in the holdall. They did not know what they were planning. The temptation was to storm the concourse, guns drawn, and arrest them. The press, duly briefed by Scotland Yard, would hail a meticulous police sting.

But this option faced a menacing obstacle in the form of Chief Inspector Ian Phoenix. Records of the urgent parley between the RUC and Met teams remain sealed, but the gist was that any attempt to grab the bastards now would first require shackling Captain Chaos in a soundproofed bunker to muffle his thundering denunciations of witless

English policing. Let the targets run, Phoenix implored. Let them run to see where they go, to see what they are planning.

The Met team, which was in charge of the operation, hesitated. Magee was slippery. He had wriggled free from Holland in 1981, eluded Lancashire police in 1983, and slipped back into Britain undetected. The surveillance operation at Salcey Forest in 1984 had ended with the IRA team speeding away. There had been enough fiascos. To let Magee run, and lose him, could end the careers of those deemed culpable. "You had to be prepared for the hindsight experts, who never made a decision in real time in their lives, to descend like a flock of vultures to pick over your bones," an RUC man recalled.

The Met team referred the decision to a duty commander at Scotland Yard. Because it was a Saturday, a commander of lower rank than normal was in position, and his identity remains shielded. He would have known Magee was wanted for the attempted assassination of Margaret Thatcher and her cabinet and that the prime minister would eventually be briefed on the outcome of his decision. His reputation and possibly his pension hung in the balance. In the Met's largely deserted headquarters, overlooking a gray, miserable afternoon in London, the commander may have faced the loneliest moment in his career. It was too late for the old policeman's prayer: "Please, dear Lord, not while I'm on duty." He relayed his verdict to Carlisle. "I have confidence in this team . . . let the guy run, and see where he leads us."

The operation was given a code name to reflect its Northern Ireland, Scotland, and England dimensions: Tricorn.

Magee and Sherry left the restaurant and headed for the platforms. The watchers expected them to take a southbound train to London. Instead, they crossed a bridge to the northbound side and boarded the 3:47 p.m. Inter-City to Glasgow. The move to Scotland meant that Ian Phoenix's E4A team had to step back; jurisdiction rules meant it would now become a joint operation between the Scottish police and the Met. The London-based officers had not worked in Scotland before and could not make arrests there; their role would be to surveil and advise. The Met team split up. About half boarded the train and took seats close to the IRA men. The rest joined their colleagues parked outside. To beat the train, they had to escape Carlisle's street maze, drive a hundred miles on the M74, zigzag into the heart of Glasgow, in lashing rain, in eighty-two minutes.

. . .

WHILE ONE OF the most critical manhunts in British history abruptly revived and roared toward Glasgow, Detective Chief Superintendent Ian Robinson, the head of Strathclyde Police Special Branch, was at home in Dumbarton, a picturesque town fifteen miles northwest of Scotland's largest city, painting his back garden gate a new shade of emerald green. He was enjoying domestic tranquility this Saturday afternoon—the painting was relaxing—thanks to the swift resolution of the Peter Sherry business. At the RUC's request, Robinson had dispatched officers to Ayr to shadow the target, who had the good grace to bugger off to England the previous evening, leaving Robinson and his officers to breathe easy, their role done, and look forward to a quiet weekend, with a skeleton team on duty.

Sometime before 4:00 p.m., Robinson's wife came out to the garden. The office wanted to speak to him. Setting down his brush, Robinson entered the hallway and picked up the phone. It was the duty officer from the Strathclyde Special Branch control room. The Met had reported that Sherry and a second IRA suspect had just boarded a northbound train at Carlisle. It was due into Glasgow at 5:10 p.m. Robinson stared at the phone. *Jesus Christ*, he thought.

Strathclyde was the biggest of Scotland's regional police forces. The main purpose of its eighty-strong Special Branch, based on the second floor at the Pitt Street headquarters in central Glasgow, was to spy on Northern Ireland loyalists. The Ulster Defence Association and Ulster Volunteer Force came to Scotland to carouse, raise funds, source weapons and, very occasionally, bomb local pubs deemed to be Catholic. They were not the sharpest operators and Robinson was good at catching them. The quiet-spoken former soldier had attended posh schools, but rose through the police ranks the hard way—catching criminals—and knew how to get the best out of his streetwise officers. He delegated to trusted lieutenants and motivated without banging the table. But his team had negligible experience of the IRA and had never encountered an Active Service Unit. Now two Provos were en route—to do what, nobody knew.

Robinson digested the duty officer's information. "Call in the surveillance team," he said. Minutes later, paint still on his hands, Robinson was on the A82 aiming for Glasgow. "I've never driven faster in my life," he recalled. A pale mist shrouded the city as he parked at Pitt Street. Robinson bounded up the stairs and punched in the code for the Special Branch entrance. A handful of officers were in the control room, some huddled by radios wearing headsets, others on the phone.

Strathclyde's radios used a different frequency than Met radios, so the Met officers driving up from Carlisle radioed short, staccato bursts of information to their Scotland Yard headquarters in London, which relayed the information via phone to Pitt Street, which relayed it via radio to the Scottish officers starting to deploy around Glasgow Central Station, half a mile away. Sherry's companion was said to be a known IRA man named Patrick Joseph Magee. There was no mention of Brighton.

By 5:05 p.m., about eight Strathclyde surveillance officers were in place around the station. They were as scruffy as the Met undercover team. Met HQ notified Pitt Street that the Met cars had reached the center of the city and were nearing the station.

The Inter-City slowed as it approached Glasgow's southeastern outskirts, passing housing estates, factories, warehouses. Rounding the Eglinton Toll junction, it chuntered directly north for the final stretch, brakes squealing as it eased to a leisurely trundle over the Caledonian Railway Bridge, the Clyde's brown waters bubbling below, and halted under the great canopy of Central Station. It was packed. Thousands of people billowed down a dozen platforms and across the vast concourse. Magee and Sherry stepped onto the platform and were swept into the throng. Met officers from the train followed, straining to keep visual contact without getting too close.

A big surveillance operation worked in relay. A few officers would maintain "eyeball," a direct line of sight, or "control," which meant the target was not visible but in a contained location, and murmur running commentary into concealed mics. Radios were carried in pockets or harnesses concealed under jackets and connected by wire to earpieces and mics. Everyone else kept distance until the closest watchers moved back to avoid suspicion and others took their place. As the IRA men moved through the crowd, the Met officers who had driven joined their colleagues from the train plus the Strathclyde team scattered around the station, about twenty officers in total.

Without warning, the closest watchers lost eyeball. The suspects vanished into the human froth of one of Europe's busiest train stations, a Byzantium of halls, stairwells, cafés, shops, offices. A desperate plea ricocheted into earpieces. Could anyone see them? No one could. Seconds turned to minutes, and hearts hammered. *Please, dear Lord, not while I'm on duty.* And then as if spat out by the multitude or providence, Magee and Sherry reappeared, calmly making their way toward the east exit, unaware they had briefly escaped the net. They emerged onto Union Street, stepping into a city granted respite from the torrents in the form of hazy sunshine, and walked to a bus stop.

Detective Sergeant Hamish Innes was suddenly glad he had stuck with the Strathclyde Special Branch. A surveillance specialist, he was thirty-six and had been with the unit eleven years. Too long, probably, and his career had stalled. He didn't quite get on with the bosses or fit into the cliques. It was time to move. But then this humdrum Saturday had exploded into a heart-stopper of a job. An IRA team on the move, right here on his patch. While some watchers hovered on foot, waiting to board the suspects' bus, Innes and others scrambled in different directions to cars with waiting drivers. As Innes jumped into a vehicle, an unfamiliar young woman rapped on the window.

"You're one of us, aren't you?" she said. She was one of the Met officers from the train.

Innes nodded.

"Get in."

They drove down Union Street, guided by radio messages that the suspects had boarded a southbound double-decker bus, number 57. The targets had gone upstairs, then downstairs. About four other Special Branch cars joined the clandestine convoy. After two miles, Magee and Sherry alighted in Govanhill, a quiet residential neighborhood, and started to stroll. Wherever they were going, they were taking their time. They meandered for a few streets before entering a 150-acre blaze of greenery: Queen's Park.

Innes and his Met colleague left their ride and followed on foot, Innes murmuring into his mic. "Eyeballs on target one and target two." His companion radioed a similar message to the Met watchers. It was a signal to everyone else to hang back or stake out positions ahead.

Joggers and families were out taking advantage of the break in the weather. The IRA men ambled on. "They walked fairly slowly, didn't look behind them," Innes said later. "I put my arm around the girl as if we were a couple."

The targets passed a pond and a playground, then retraced their steps and exited the park by the main entrance on the northern side. Innes and his partner followed them up a street. Halfway up, the IRA men turned and walked back the way they had come, a countersurveillance technique known as dry-cleaning, used to check if you are being tailed. Innes and his partner were on the opposite sidewalk and kept walking. "It was a tense moment because you knew exactly what was happening," he recalled. Sherry and Magee continued chatting and did not appear to spot anything odd about the couple.

While Innes and his companion kept walking away from the IRA men, other officers picked up control, supplying updates to their respective teams. "Heading back to the park. . . . Heading up Victoria Road."

A block from the park, Magee and Sherry entered the Queen's Park Cafe. It was small and narrow with a long counter and seats that gave a good view of traffic and pedestrians on Victoria Road. It appeared to be another dry-cleaning exercise.

Innes knew the café—surveillance work generated encyclopedic knowledge of greasy spoons and pubs. It had no other entrance or exit. He led his partner to a sheltered bus stop on the other side of Victoria Road. "Have control of the target. Taking control of the exit." Five minutes inched by, then ten.

Five minutes more and Magee and Sherry emerged from the café and turned right up Victoria Road. Innes and his partner stayed at the bus stop and passed control to another team. Eyeballed all the way, the IRA men walked three blocks north toward Allison Street, briefly stepped into a grocery shop, then turned the corner and entered a brown sandstone four-story tenement. A wooden and glass door swung shut behind them. Its panes were too narrow to let the watchers see into the dimly lit hallway. The address was 236 Langside Road.

. . .

MAGEE LED SHERRY down the short, narrow passageway to a black door on the left-hand side. Beyond it, a narrow staircase zigzagged to the top floor, but there was no need to climb. The IRA unit occupied the ground-level flat. Compared to the garret-like room at James Gray Street, this new abode was spacious, with its own bathroom, proper kitchen, and two bedrooms. With the bombs and rifles stored in the other flat, it did not resemble a terrorist hub. The furniture was sparse and functional, the decor pink, beige, and cream. The front windows were shielded from the road by curtains and a hedge, and the kitchen at the rear overlooked a courtyard ringed by other tenements. The base was discreet and—until the moment Magee and Sherry had entered the building—one of the IRA's best-kept secrets.

The two men had almost certainly met before and had a lot to discuss. Magee was doubtless hungry for news from back home: the Provos' new mortar technology, rumors of a major weapons shipment. Magee also needed to bring Sherry up to speed on the imminent bombing campaign and possible assassination targets.

Ella O'Dwyer, Martina Anderson, and Gerard "Blute" McDonnell were in the flat to welcome their comrades when they walked through the door: the new boy Sherry, and Magee back safe after his stint in London. It was probably at this point he handed over Donal Craig's resignation letter, plus a diagram of the Rubens bomb, which Blute placed in a money belt around his waist. The belt also contained a list of dates and locations of all the intended bombs. For an organization as parochial as the IRA, this was a varied group: Magee and Blute, Belfast blue collars; Anderson, a Derry factory worker; Sherry, a former clerk from the sticks; O'Dwyer, the farm girl turned university graduate.

Each had taken different routes to this point, using false identities in a foreign city, prepared to kill strangers and possibly sacrifice their own lives in the name of a united Ireland. Soon they would split up and crisscross England to ignite a trail of mayhem. Until then, they would hunker here. There had been a brief alarm the night before when a noise in the courtyard turned out to be some drunks taking a piss. They were expecting a visitor later, the landlord collecting his rent. An envelope with cash rested on the mantelpiece. McDonnell, who had experience shooting his way out of trouble, was not taking chances; he kept an automatic Browning pistol with ten bullets close to hand, safety catch off. A second handgun hid in Anderson's gray handbag. But this was an evening to relax and bond. They opened bottles of juice, cracked a few cans of Foster's lager, and started preparing supper.

. . .

IN A CAR parked across the street, Hamish Innes and his Met colleague kept their eyes fixed on the door of 236. Other undercover officers staked out a spot farther down Langside Road. Others took up positions to the rear of the tenement. It was 6:00 p.m. Nobody had entered or left since Magee and Sherry had vanished inside.

Three miles to the north, Ian Robinson was at the Pitt Street headquarters feeling like his garden idyll belonged to a distant epoch. In the past hour, a Met team had swarmed into his patch and an IRA duo had been followed, briefly lost, found again, and tracked to an apartment block. Nobody knew if they were armed, had accomplices, or were planning an imminent operation. The surveillance around Langside Road was perilous; at any moment, another IRA member could walk by and spot the watchers.

Robinson's counterpart in London sounded increasingly anxious. He had let Magee run, now he wanted him bagged. Strathclyde had jurisdiction, and would be responsible for any bagging, so it was Robinson's call. Maintaining surveillance overnight risked exposure and a messy gun battle in a densely populated area. Robinson decided it was better to strike while holding the initiative.

But there was a problem. The tenement had four floors, each apparently with two flats, eight in total. No one knew which one Magee occupied, or who else besides Sherry might be with him.

Robinson could call in a SWAT team. Helmets, boots, body armor, assault rifles, the works, to smash into every apartment. It was the orthodox option—but Robinson didn't like it. Too volatile, too militaristic for a building full of families. He preferred the Special Branch way.

"I decided to do it the way we were used to," he recalled, "going in quietly."

The plan was for plainclothes officers to knock on every door, identify the hideout, and seize the suspects. Robinson wanted at least two officers per flat, at least one of them armed, plus several more covering the street. So, about two dozen officers, half of them armed. This raised a dilemma American law enforcement might have found quaint: not enough guns.

To allay fears of a martial presence on the streets, police in Britain had been mostly unarmed since the Met's foundation in 1829. Strathclyde's Special Branch and some other Glasgow units did have firearms training and access to guns, but this was Saturday evening. Most officers were at home or in the pub.

Robinson was a methodical man, but had precious little time to prepare his raid. First, he phoned the duty assistant chief constable, who was at home, to obtain verbal permission to issue firearms. The Special Branch did not have enough available officers or guns to do the job solo, so Robinson called other unit commanders across Glasgow. He was direct but vague. "There is a serious situation and I need firearms officers." Coming from the head of Special Branch, they would have guessed it was something to do with terrorism. Robinson made the calls over the phone, not the general police radio, which the press monitored. The last thing he needed was photographers turning up at Langside Road.

While the other commanders rang around their own units, Robinson called the Stewart Street police station, a large facility with interrogation rooms and cells that was the designated base to handle any terrorist incident. If there were to be prisoners—as opposed to corpses—Robinson would need a secure, private place for questioning. Quickly and noisily, drunks, brawlers, and other prisoners were herded out of cells and transferred to another station, leaving Stewart Street empty and expectant.

By 6:45 p.m., the heads of the Serious Crime Squad and Regional Crime Squad called Robinson. They had rustled up about a dozen men. Robinson ordered them and other members of the raiding force to assemble at the Craigie Street police station, three blocks from Langside Road. He bounded down his headquarters' steps to a waiting car and driver.

Anybody standing in the middle of Craigie Street at approximately 7:00 p.m. would have seen a stream of men in suits park unmarked cars and hustle toward the handsome Scots Renaissance-style police station adorned with the city motto, "Let Glasgow Flourish."

They gathered inside a large room with chairs and not much else, a so-called muster room. Few knew exactly why they were there. All thrummed with nervous anticipation. Robinson did not know the other units' officers but appreciated their enthusiasm. His briefing was short and to the point. Some 350 yards away, a tenement contained IRA members who were probably armed. The officers were to knock on eight doors simultaneously, identify the flat with the suspects, and seize them.

"They have to be arrested," he said. "Don't take any chances."

The room was silent. Robinson knew, and the assembled men knew, it could all go violently wrong.

"It was IRA, I wasn't expecting them to come quietly," Robinson recalled later.

He tasked his deputy, Detective Inspector Brian Watson, with leading the raid. Watson was a tough, burly wingman who knew the streets. He had helped track Sherry and Magee from the train station, so he knew what they looked like, and he had observed the external layout at Langside Road. He was in radio contact with the watchers outside the complex, who reported no movement. Watson divided the officers into squads and allocated flats. That was all. No diagrams, no maps, no photographs. Strathclyde did not have photos of Magee on file nor photos from the previous day's surveillance of Sherry. Obtaining photos was a luxury; the priority was speed.

The biggest manhunt in UK history, a prodigious collective effort by hundreds of detectives, spies, and scientists to salve a national wound, had zigzagged to this: a hasty briefing to an improvised, patchily armed posse. Its members did not even know Magee was wanted for the Brighton bombing.

At approximately 7:35 p.m., the raiding party streamed out of

Craigie Street into the waning light of June 22, 1985. Clouds obscured a setting sun. One by one, their cars pulled out for the short drive to Patrick Magee. Margaret Thatcher, the prime minister he had tried to kill, was at a black-tie dinner at Dorneywood, an estate near Chequers, oblivious to the denouement unfolding four hundred miles to the north.

The convoy drove through somnolent streets and reached Langside Road in about three minutes. They parked away from number 236 and half walked, half jogged to the tenement. Hamish Innes left his stakeout vehicle and joined them. The watching Met officers had to stay in their cars. Watson spotted Innes. "You, come with me."

At precisely 7:40 p.m., the vanguard pushed through the front door and rushed down the dingy corridor, the others following, twenty-three policemen in all, eleven of them armed. Seventeen pounded up the staircase and formed little clusters outside the upper-floor flats. On the ground floor, three officers assigned to the flat on the right discovered it was a derelict space. They joined Watson, Innes, and another officer at the flat on the other side of the corridor. Which left six men at this one door. Watson had reserved it for himself. The position at ground level made it the flat he would choose if he were a terrorist. And it afforded him a view of the stairwell.

There was a moment's hush while Watson checked that everyone was in place. Then his voice shattered the silence. "Go!"

Knuckles rapped on seven doors.

.   .   .

PATRICK MAGEE AND the rest of the IRA unit were seated at the kitchen table at the rear of the flat, finishing a dinner of potatoes, sprouts, and steak. They had not seen or heard any commotion out the front or on the stairs, but they heard the knock.

Magee rose. The landlord, he thought. He fetched the envelope from the mantelpiece and walked down the hallway. He opened the door. In the gloom he saw two burly men. Straightaway he guessed they were police, and his brain swam. Maybe they were investigating a burglary or some other local matter. Maybe he could bluff it out, buy time.

"Can I help you?" he asked. The accent was English, the tone amiable, just like at the Grand Hotel reception. A responsible citizen willing to assist these strangers.

Watson and Innes grabbed Magee and hurled him into the passageway. "Take him!" said Watson. More beefy hands emerged from the shadows and slammed Magee to the ground. "Ground-floor flat!" Watson yelled.

The Chancer stared transfixed at the gaping barrel of a gun pointed at his face while a blur of bodies hurtled over and around him, their number multiplying as more stampeded down the stairs and crashed past, all storming into the Provisional IRA's Scottish sanctum.

McDonnell emerged from the kitchen into the hallway with the pistol tucked into his jeans, but he seemed in slow motion compared to the horde barreling toward him. Before he could reach for the gun, they were upon him, pinning his arms and legs. The charge continued through the lounge into the kitchen, where Sherry, O'Dwyer, and Anderson rose from their chairs, faces white, eyes wide as their plates. There was nowhere to run.

More officers swarmed into the kitchen in a bedlam of shouts and lunges. They looked like a small army. The three IRA operators did not resist or protest as they were seized. This brutal violation of their refuge shocked them into muteness. The realization was too hideous: they were caught.

With all the suspects immobilized, the stampede stopped. The officers caught their breath. It seemed impossible that a small flat could contain so many people. The prisoners remained silent, ashen. Some of the officers began to smile. Hamish Innes wondered if his heart would ever slow down.

In the corridor, officers handcuffed Patrick Magee and removed his shoes. They marched him out in his socks. Police vehicles lined the street, voices seeping from radios. Neighbors had come out of their homes and lined the pavement, gaping. Wedged into a backseat between detectives, the Chancer let his imagination take flight. He visualized escape, scrutinized every moment and space for an exploitable weakness, as if sheer willpower could conjure a way out: a gun to grab, a window to hurl through, a porthole out of the chaos.

The car eased down Langside Road and began the long drive away.

CHAPTER TWENTY

—

Reckonings

Detective Chief Superintendent Ian Robinson entered the interview room at the Stewart Street station and studied the man seated in a chair. He looked scruffy, like the other four suspects in other interview rooms, all brought in an hour earlier. And like the others, Patrick Magee was gazing at a spot high on the wall as if it held the secret of the universe. Two other Strathclyde officers were in the room, tasked with the interrogation. Every question elicited the same blankness, Magee staring over their shoulders without a flicker. It was uncanny, like the policemen were phantasms, unseen and unheard, as if, now that he was captured, it was their turn to become "invisible beings."

"Do you have any complaints?" Robinson asked.

Magee appeared not to hear.

"I'm in charge of the investigation . . ." Robinson began to say.

Magee's eyes swiveled to the warrant badge clipped to the Special Branch chief's jacket. Robinson hastily covered it with his hand, not wanting to disclose his name.

Magee resumed his vigil of the wall.

A police mug shot of Patrick Magee taken after his capture in
Glasgow in June 1985. | Alamy Stock Photo

The other interrogators encountered the same trancelike silence. It
was a tactic enshrined in the IRA's Green Book, the training manual
derived from Gerry Adams's reorganization of the Provos into a cell-
based system in the 1970s. Strathclyde police initially did not realize
the full significance of their catch. They did not know the identities
of Gerard McDonnell, Ella O'Dwyer, or Martina Anderson, nor the
existence of the bombing plot. But the capture of Patrick Magee, now
identified as the main suspect for Brighton, was reason enough for
delight. And for extremely careful handling, everything by the book,
no rough stuff, nothing that could prejudice his eventual trial.

News of the capture zinged overnight across police forces and intelligence agencies. There were cheers and shouts in Scotland Yard. In
Sussex, Jack Reece probably made a prayer of thanks to Neptune before
notifying his boss, Chief Constable Roger Birch. They agreed to a low-
key public response, not saying anything that might hamper the prosecution. On the ferry back to Northern Ireland, Chief Inspector Ian
Phoenix celebrated at the bar and was rollicking drunk by the time he
got home.

But late that same night of Saturday, June 22, Detective Inspector Brian Watson made a discovery that chilled the mood at Stewart Street. Unzipping the money belt that McDonnell had worn, Watson found along with thousands of pounds in cash a list of dates and places, each with the letter *H* or *B*. It appeared to be a target list. One had a tick and extra detail: "London, 1st floor, 112, front, The Rubens Hotel, Buckingham Palace Road. BT plus 48." Another piece of paper had a sketch of what appeared to be a booby-trapped bomb, with the letters *M.S.* and *M.T.S.* presumed to signify "microswitch" and "mercury tilt switch." Realization dawned that this had been a full-fledged Active Service Unit on a bombing campaign. Ian Robinson had the documents immediately faxed to the Met.

As London woke to another drizzly Sunday, police vehicles quietly sealed off Buckingham Palace Road. Uniformed officers evacuated guests and staff from the Rubens Hotel and advised the palace to move the Queen's horses from the Royal Mews. Derek Pickford, the Met's duty "bomb doctor," his police driver, and two handlers with two dogs entered the deserted hotel. For three hours, they searched and sniffed room 112, removed a bath panel, peered into the cavity, searched and sniffed everything again. Nothing.

Pickford's driver, known as Chips, inspected the bedside cabinet screwed to the wall. He gripped it. "The screws are loose."

"Leave it!" said Pickford.

He ordered the others to leave in a tone that had the handlers racing their dogs out through the lobby and down the road. Pickford set up a portable X-ray and examined the base of the cabinet. There it was: an expertly concealed bomb.

Peter Gurney, the bomb burglar and Pickford's expo colleague, arrived. The two men studied the device's ghostly image. It indeed had a microswitch and mercury tilt switch, matching the sketch sent from Glasgow. If moved a fraction of an inch, it would explode.

Instead of defusing, they decided to disable the bomb with a disrupter, the device that fired an extremely powerful water jet to destroy the bomb without setting off the explosives. Gurney had used one four years earlier to disable the Oxford Street department store device just after a booby-trapped device had killed Ken Howorth. He had vowed to nail those responsible and celebrated when Thomas Quigley and Paul Kavanagh were convicted. Now Gurney was confronting the deadly skills of Patrick Magee, whose handiwork he had seen at Brighton, at Greenwich in 1979, and probably also in Belfast in the early 1970s during Magee's "blowy stuff" era with G Company. Gurney and Pickford positioned the disrupter, dropped the firing cable out the window, and ran it about seventy yards up the road to a sheltered doorway, where they huddled with their drivers. Farther down Buckingham Palace Road, people watched in silence from behind police tape. The cable was connected to a device that generated an electric current to fire the disrupter.

Pickford grinned at Gurney. "Go on, you do it."

Gurney shook his head. Chips had found the bomb and deserved the honor.

"Whoa," said Chips. "Not me."

"Look," said Gurney, "how often does a police constable have the chance to blow up a London hotel and not get blamed for it?"

Chips considered a moment. "Ah well, when you put it like that." He pressed the button.

There was a sound like a shotgun blast, but the Rubens did not blow up. The disrupter worked perfectly, blasting only the internal circuity of the bomb. The four men returned to 112. The bedside cabinet was wrecked and there were some marks on the wall; otherwise, the room was intact. Scattered across the carpet were fragments of the last bomb planted by Patrick Magee.

· · ·

RELIEF WAS SHORT-LIVED. The list had fifteen other targets. Were bombs planted there, too? The five suspects in Stewart Street said nothing.

On Monday, June 24, the Metropolitan Police commissioner, Sir Kenneth Newman, chaired a tense meeting at Scotland Yard with commanders from the Anti-Terrorist Branch, the Special Branch, eight provincial police forces, and the Home Office. Six years earlier, Newman had headed the RUC and successfully lobbied Thatcher, despite the slaughter at Mullaghmore and Narrow Water, to give his force primacy over the army in Northern Ireland. The decision now was whether to tell the public there might be bombs ticking across England. Some commanders wanted public warnings and massive searches, others favored discretion to avoid panic. A delicate compromise resulted in warnings and searches at hotels and resorts but no mass evacuations. The uncertainty was agonizing.

Then Gerard McDonnell's money belt yielded police another gift: Donal Craig. His neatly folded resignation letter led detectives to Craig's house on Teignmouth Road, in northwest London. The IRA's troubled, disillusioned fixer proved to be a cooperative, voluble contrast to his sphinxlike comrades. Flown to Glasgow, Craig led detectives to 17 James Gray Street, where he had once spent a night. When officers entered the top-floor flat, they found clothes, documents, and bric-a-brac belonging to the IRA unit—but no bombs. Yet a bomb detection device gave results almost off the charts. Officers assumed the machine was faulty and left.

The entire arsenal was in fact hidden in a cellar. The landlady's son, John Boyle, had discovered and moved everything after their former tenants were arrested, apparently in a panic, fearing police would think he was part of the plot. The next day, Detective Constable William Dorrian and a partner went back to James Gray Street for another nosy. Dorrian, chomping a lit cigar, noticed the cellar door was scuffed and ajar. When he pushed it open, a heavy black trash bag fell on him. It was part of a mound of bags, each with tightly wrapped parcels and electrical equipment.

"Stevie, get out of here," said Dorrian.

While his partner alerted headquarters, Dorrian, with his nerves jangling, hauled out twelve bags and a holdall and laid them in the yard. They contained detonators, batteries, alarm clocks, micro-switches, three rifles, a handgun, and twenty-five bundles of explosives with enough power to obliterate everything within a hundred yards. Two senior officers arrived, expressing skepticism about Stevie's dramatic report, only to pale when they saw the lethal stockpile. Their first words: "Oh shit." The bomb squad arrived and sealed off the area. Dorrian took this as a cue to march his partner to a pub around the corner to settle their nerves. They each downed a beer and a whiskey, then returned to the scene. "I gave up smoking after that," Dorrian said later.

With the bombs now accounted for, other pieces of the jigsaw fell into place. The RUC and Gardaí helped to identify Anderson, Mc-Donnell, and O'Dwyer. The group's Scottish fixer, Shaun McShane, and other suspected accomplices were arrested. In London, an estate agent led Detective Constable Paul Gibbon and other officers to the Hackney Road flat rented to the man who called himself Alan Cooper. Gibbon felt personally invested in the Brighton investigation; he had interviewed the chambermaid who serviced Magee's room at the Grand and confronted Paul Kavanagh in prison. Now, at the flat, they found Magee's pistol and bomb-making equipment and something else: a partially completed newspaper crossword with a distinctive *E*. It resembled the *E* on the Roy Walsh registration card.

"A eureka moment," Gibbon said. "Like scoring the winning try for England at Twickenham."

. . .

MEANWHILE, IN BELFAST, Chief Inspector Ian Phoenix experienced an aggravating postscript to his triumphant homecoming. Instead of being garlanded for E4A's role in catching the Brighton bomber, he tangled with RUC bureaucracy. The accounts department refused to reimburse Phoenix for his team's ferry tickets to Scotland, which he had paid for himself, saying he had not obtained pre-trip approval. The accountants were adamant, insisting in an increasingly fraught phone call that he had not followed procedure. Phoenix stared at the phone in disbelief. Anyone who has fought a losing battle against red tape might recognize the sentiment in the roar that followed: "You can fucking stick it up your ass, then." He never got the money back.

. . .

ON SATURDAY, JUNE 29, a week after their capture, Magee and the other four members of his unit were handcuffed to Met and Sussex officers and driven under heavy security to Glasgow Airport, motorcycle outriders leading the way. Fearing IRA reprisals, no major airline would fly the suspects, so police hired an aging charter plane.

No one spoke as the propellers droned south. The prisoners knew any word or gesture would be noted. One escort was a Gaelic-speaking sergeant, in case they communicated in Irish. At RAF Northolt, they were transferred to prison vans and driven to Paddington Green, the police fortress in West London.

There, at last, Magee was charged with five counts of "murder contrary to common law" in relation to Brighton. Other charges would follow.

A few miles away, Margaret Tebbit was making her first public appearance since the bomb. Three soldiers carried her into the Royal Box at Wimbledon's center court to watch a tennis match with her husband.

Jack Reece and his deputy, Bernie Wells, waited for Magee in an interrogation room. For eight months, the Sussex CID chief had sought his elusive fish, imposing order on a sprawling investigation, never doubting—in public at least—of one day reeling in the catch. The task now was to squeeze every drop of evidence into a watertight case. Reece did not expect Magee to confess, but hoped to extract some insight, a stray word that might prove useful. He had questioned Magee's parents and siblings in Kent in preparation—a psychological version of "wetting worms"—to try to catch Magee unawares and trigger a response.

Magee was frog-marched in and seated. He fixed his gaze at a spot on the desk. Reece introduced himself and went through a long list of questions. Magee ignored him. Then Reece played his trump card. He had visited the Magee family home in Kent, he said. Magee could visualize the scene—officers tramping through the house, opening drawers, firing questions, upsetting his elderly parents. Magee's youngest sister was a trainee nurse who wanted to save lives, said Reece, unlike her brother.

No response, not even a glance up.

"He didn't say a dickie bird, from the minute they wheeled him in. He never looked at us. He wouldn't have been able to tell you what I looked like," Wells recalled.

The Chancer remained as blank as one of Reece's dead, dangling sharks.

. . .

FIVE WEEKS LATER, under cover of night, a rubber dinghy sailed from a yacht off the east coast of Ireland. It delivered heavy wooden boxes to Clogga Strand, a remote stretch of County Wicklow. On the boxes were stenciled the words LIBYAN ARMED FORCES. It was the first of five planned weapons shipments to the IRA from Colonel Gaddafi. Impressed by the Brighton bomb, and embroiled in his own feud with Margaret Thatcher, the Libyan leader promised three hundred tons of guns and explosives—enough to unleash a Provo whirlwind and satisfy his own desire to punish the British. The IRA imported 150 tons in four shipments, but the fifth and biggest consignment was intercepted and Gaddafi, like Whitey Bulger, ended up frustrated. The failed shipment exposed his revolution-exporting secrets to Western intelligence agencies, and the IRA lacked the expertise and manpower to fully utilize what they did import. The ten tons of Semtex explosives would dramatically boost Provo bombs in years to come, but overall it was a disappointing return for Gaddafi. He bowed out of Ireland's revolution and sought other, bloodier ways to punish his enemies.

. . .

ON JUNE 23, 1986, one year after his arrest, Patrick Magee sat alone in the dock of court number two at the Central Criminal Court (the Old Bailey) in London. The oak-paneled chamber was silent. Everybody was looking at him: the packed public gallery, the journalists, the clerks in front of their great ledgers, the lawyers in their black gowns, the judge, Sir Leslie Boreham, in a red gown and horsehair wig yellowed with age. Magee, in jeans and a leather jacket, was supposed to stand. He refused. Two prison officers hauled him to his feet.

He gazed ahead, expressionless. He gave no hint that he felt drained and yearned for this to end, being on display like a specimen in a jar, a microscope on his every blink and twitch. For Magee, to show emotion was to betray weakness, to let them know they had him. He would give them nothing. His face was a mask.

He had already been found guilty of planting the Brighton bomb. A jury of six men and six women had delivered its verdict two weeks earlier, following a six-week trial. Magee was back in court now for sentencing. A staircase from the dock led to holding cells beneath the court. Trappings of English justice filled the Old Bailey, in the seats decorated with the words *Domine, Dirige Nos* ("Lord, direct us"), in the marbled halls, the busts and statues of monarchs, the allegorical paintings, the copper-roof dome topped by a statue holding a sword and the scales of justice. It was outside this court that the real Roy Walsh's IRA unit had detonated a car bomb in 1973, injuring two hundred people. A glass shard remained embedded in a wall above the main stairs as a reminder. Walsh had been caught and sentenced here just like Thomas Clarke, the Fenian bomber whose name Walsh used as an alias. Now it was Magee's turn.

He could not be executed. Because Thatcher had failed to convince

Parliament to restore hanging, now the man who had tried to kill her would live. So it was a question of how many years behind bars. Justice Boreham peered at the defendant through large black-rimmed glasses. He had a reputation as a heavy sentencer. His sonorous voice filled the chamber. "You intended to wipe out a large part of the government and you very nearly did," he said. "I am not concerned with your motives or what drives you. I am satisfied you enjoy terrorism. You are a man of exceptional cruelty and inhumanity."

Boreham paused, his damnation hanging in the air.

The journalists scribbled furiously.

Magee braced for the inevitable. For twelve months he had visualized this moment. There was not much else to do in the top-security D wing of Brixton prison, where he and his comrades were held as remand prisoners. Martina Anderson and Ella O'Dwyer had been in cells directly above the men. They would shout encouragement to each other. At night, Anderson sang rebel ballads and other songs upon request.

Magee's prosecution documents had included a welcome surprise—official confirmation of the police surveillance during his aborted mission to Lancashire in 1983, proof for the IRA that Magee had not panicked, but in fact eluded a trap. Magee considered this restoration of an unfairly tarnished reputation. "It was one of the most liberating days of my life. At the core, all I had was my name," he recalled.

Eileen had brought divorce papers, but felt duty bound to stand by him now that he was in jail. "Should we tear this up?" she asked. In a moment of weakness he would regret, Magee had said yes, shackling his long-suffering wife to his own fate.

The press plumbed Magee's past, interviewed childhood acquaintances, chased Eileen for quotes, speculated about training in Libya.

The others also received lurid media treatment, especially Sherry, who in tabloid imagining became a "lone wolf" sniper credited with twenty-one kills. Each day of the trial, which began on May 6, a prison van took different routes to court, while a police helicopter hovered overhead and police marksmen lined rooftops. Lest a loose comment prejudice proceedings, Margaret Thatcher reportedly forbade police briefings to the press before or during the trial. Robin Butler, the Downing Street mandarin who had been with Thatcher when the bomb exploded, watched from the public gallery. The accused were composed and well-groomed, he recalled. "They looked so good. The women were beautifully got out, as if butter wouldn't melt in their mouths."

Magee faced seven charges, including five of murder, for Brighton. He was also charged with the other four defendants with conspiracy to bomb in relation to the so-called seaside blitz. All pleaded not guilty. Magee's lawyer was Richard Ferguson, a skilled barrister and former Ulster Unionist MP. Despite the political gulf between them, Magee respected Ferguson and assented to his strategy. Magee stayed mute, not testifying, while Ferguson accused police of framing his client. In polished tones, he accused detectives of using the bomb timer found in rubble to nominate room 629 as the seat of the explosion and then planted Magee's fingerprints on the Roy Walsh registration card, with Scotland Yard's handwriting expert conveniently chiming in about the distinctive *E*.

"Were you party to a conspiracy wrongly to frame Mr. Magee?" Ferguson asked Jack Reece.

The Sussex CID chief glowered from the witness box. "That is a preposterous suggestion."

"Will you deal with it?" Ferguson prodded.

"Absolutely not at all," said Reece. "We wanted to bring the offender—not just anyone, the offender—to book."

Ferguson also confronted David Tadd. In addition to the right palm mark that originally identified Magee, Tadd had found a second print. Comparing the registration card's marks with fresh prints taken after Magee's arrest, Tadd's team identified the top of the little finger on his left hand, consistent with pushing the card back to the receptionist with the fingertip. Ferguson suggested Tadd had planted the prints.

"I most certainly did not," replied Tadd.

The jury did not buy the police conspiracy. On June 10, after twenty-four days of trial proceedings and five hours of deliberations, it found Magee guilty of all seven charges in relation to Brighton. The next day it also convicted him and the others accused of the seaside plot. Magee had expected it. The IRA had warned him when he joined in 1972 that a coffin or a cell awaited. In his case, it would be the austere otherworldliness of a Special Security Unit (SSU), a self-contained prison within a prison that inmates likened to a submarine. All that remained was the sentencing.

Wedged between prison officers, Magee gazed ahead as Judge Boreham's denunciation reached its climax, telling Magee he had murdered people in their beds and plotted cowardly, cynical, hideous terrorist crimes. "You plan them meticulously and with affection. Members of the public must be given the maximum protection that I can provide."

Boreham sentenced him to eight life terms, one for each charge, with a recommendation he serve at least thirty-five years before consideration for parole. In Britain, only spies had received longer sentences. Magee seized on the number. He *was* thirty-five. Based on his grandfathers' longevity, he might, if released in 2021 at the age of seventy, have four years of freedom before he died. Sherry, McDonnell, Anderson, and O'Dwyer were also sentenced to life.

As guards escorted Magee down to the cells, he raised a clenched fist. For the only time in the trial his voice rang out across the courtroom. The words were formulaic, but the tone was raw, defiant. "*Tiocfaidh ár lá,*" he shouted.

Our day will come.

He descended a few more steps and vanished from view.

. . .

THE ANTI-TERRORIST BRANCH celebrated the traditional way, with toasts in the office—Irish whiskey was reserved for such occasions—and drinks at the Feathers pub up the road from Scotland Yard. The Met Special Branch had its own celebration and hosted Hamish Innes, the Strathclyde surveillance officer, in honor of their collaboration in Glasgow. Some officers were invited to meet the Queen at Buckingham Palace and Margaret Thatcher at 10 Downing Street. Then it was back to work. There were other terrorists to hunt. The Brighton and seaside blitz investigations would soon become history, just like the murder relics in the Met's Black Museum.

For David Tadd, there was one final assignment in Brighton. One morning, he entered his team's fingerprint room and tapped Steve Turner on the shoulder. He told him to get his jacket. Jack Reece had invited them to lunch.

The Sussex detectives had had their own party at the police social club in Brighton. A sedate affair with wives and VIPs sipping sherry, after which the wives and VIPs went home and the proper piss-up began. It had been a farewell of sorts for Big Jack. He had delayed retirement to lead this final case. It rankled that they never identified the other man with Magee in room 629, nor did they catch the IRA planners in Dublin. But they put the Chancer and his Glasgow unit behind bars for life. Reece received the Queen's Police Medal for distinguished service. He looked forward to locking his CID badge in a drawer, hunting rabbits for Daphne to cook into a stew, and hunting sharks off the Azores. Before sailing off, Reece wanted to thank Tadd. Without the fingerprint evidence, Magee would not have been identified—nor, of course, convicted. It had been an unusual partnership, the big, bluff regional detective fronting the investigation, the smaller, younger Met man behind the scenes with his chemicals and epidiascopes. Physical opposites, they shared an old-school passion for villain catching. Tadd reckoned Turner, the "willing horse" who had identified the palm print, also deserved a feed in a fancy restaurant, so brought him to Brighton.

Reece and a police driver collected them from the train station. They headed out of town into the countryside. Hedgerows flashed past as they reminisced about the investigation's highs and lows. Down a lane, a pheasant appeared as if from nowhere and ran across their path. There was a thump. "Stop! Stop!" shouted Reece. He leaped out, grabbed the dead bird, opened the trunk, and threw it in. "That'll be okay for my Sunday lunch," he said, grinning.

Tadd exchanged wide-eyed looks with Turner. "I don't know if we've just witnessed an abduction or a murder."

They motored on. Tadd sensed he was going to miss Jack Reece.

. . .

ON THE MORNING of Thursday, August 28, 1986, a small convoy of discreetly armor-plated cars left Downing Street. It snaked south through London, then aimed for the sea. The Grand was reopening, and Margaret Thatcher and Norman Tebbit wanted to be there. It was almost two years since they had made the same journey for the October 1984 conference. The man who had tried to kill them was in a prison in the middle of England wearing oversized denim jeans and a prison-striped shirt, sixty-six days into his thirty years. His targets were returning to Brighton to show that the bomb had achieved nothing.

They reached the seafront just after midday. An aroma of fish and chips filled the air. Sunshine beamed on families promenading in gaudy summer colors and kiss-me-quick hats. Bars served trays of cold lager.

The presence of hundreds of police officers among the crowd and on rooftops, however, punctured the holiday aura. A block from the Grand, an exclusion zone termed a "sterile area" was in force. The security operation had begun before dawn with sniffer dogs waking hotel guests and officers checking drains.

The Grand gleamed in creamy splendor, fully rebuilt and

refurbished—though with no room 629. The £11 million budget had bought a new roof, a reinforced concrete frame, 3.3 miles of ornate plaster corniche, 75,000 square feet of carpet, 1,400 pictures and framed mirrors, and so many chandeliers that somebody forgot to count them all. Victorian-looking chimney stacks once again soared over the roof. They were fake now, fiberglass replicas.

Thatcher and Tebbit smiled and waved, the scene a radiant contrast to two years earlier. Instead of dust and screams, there were balloons and cheers. Instead of fire alarms, a Royal Marine brass band performed "Nimrod" from Elgar's *Enigma Variations*. A Concorde did a flyby.

Thatcher handed back the hotel's Union Jack flag, which had been lent to her for safekeeping after the bomb. "It will fly once again over the Grand Hotel, showing that, happen what may, the British spirit will once again triumph," she declared. Tebbit, sleek in a navy-blue suit, told the assembled press it was time to look ahead. "Even those who lost their lives would have wanted us to do what we are doing, surviving and going forward."

It was as if the bomb had dissolved into complete insignificance. A murderous act, duly punished, that left Britain unbowed and unchanged. But things had changed, and Britain was not quite the same, even if nobody wished to admit it. This reality was easy to overlook because the most conspicuous aspect of the bomb was what it *nearly* did. It almost killed Thatcher. The attack became one of the great what-ifs. Had Thatcher been in the Napoleon Suite bathroom, or had the avalanche of rubble swerved another way, she could have died. For want of two minutes, or a few feet, history could have turned, and with it the fate of Northern Ireland, Thatcherism, and the Cold War.

In November 1985, a year after the bomb, Thatcher signed the Anglo-Irish Agreement with Ireland's prime minister, Garret FitzGerald. The landmark treaty gave the Irish government an advisory role in Northern Ireland in return for which Dublin accepted there could be no change to the region's constitutional status without support from a majority of its people. It took guts to sign it; unionists called Thatcher a traitor and staged huge, clamorous protests.

The treaty did not end the Troubles, but it did transform British-Irish relations and laid a foundation for a future peace settlement. Thatcher's survival also enabled her to entrench her domestic revolution, a radical reorienting toward deregulation and individualism that reshaped Britain and unleashed what came to be called the Anglo-American New Right. It was also after Brighton that she chivvied Reagan and Gorbachev toward a détente that would recast global relations. If Thatcher had died at the Grand, it would have been a different world. It is doubtful a successor would have matched her ambition.

And yet, despite missing its principal target, the bomb did unsettle British politics, sending ripples beyond its shores, and in the process skewing history. It was as if grit from the explosion clogged a sense of what was normal, of how things should be.

The most visible global change came in the form of security. The exclusion zone on the promenade when Thatcher returned to Brighton attested to a dawning era of stifling checks and controls. No longer could the public mingle freely with senior elected representatives. "Instead of spontaneity, we do security," lamented one politician. "We play politics from behind bullet-proof screens and body scanners. . . . The first view a schoolchild will get on a visit to our parliament is of a police officer in body armor cradling a 9mm Heckler & Koch submachine gun." And it was not just Britain. Foreign governments and police forces studied and copied the new British protocols. There were enough discontented groups with access to explosives and precision timers to potentially turn any gathering of leaders into another Brighton.

The bomb also scrambled the relationship at the heart of Thatcherism, and thereby shaped its evolution. There was no telltale evidence the day Thatcher and Norman Tebbit returned to Brighton. As they stood shoulder to shoulder, gazing at the Concorde as it roared over the seafront, their political double act looked timeless. *Spitting Image* still portrayed Tebbit as the prime minister's loyal enforcer, and political pundits still spoke of him as her heir. But like the Grand's replica chimney stacks, appearances deceived.

Thatcher seemed to feel responsible for the suffering of her injured lieutenant and his paralyzed wife—she had been the target, but they had paid the price—producing an uncomfortable mix of sympathy and guilt. Plus, Tebbit, in chronic pain, had become querulous. "What did change after Brighton, and it was very understandable, was Norman's character. The physical injuries on his wife made him bitter . . . and harder to deal with," one aide recalled. "She found it harder to work with him." They had blazing rows. "If you think you can do your job better than I can, then do it!" Tebbit had once shouted, hurling papers on the floor. Colleagues whispered, "Norman is not the same Norman." Thatcher had moved him to a new job, Conservative Party chairman, but feared he was after her job. Tebbit, for his part, felt undermined, and suspected that critical stories about him in the press emanated from Downing Street.

None of this was apparent when they toured the restored Grand, trailed by TV crews. In the lobby ceiling where the Tebbits had been trapped, there were now freshly painted moldings and decorative carvings. Tebbit did not speak of pain or grief or fate. The old conference darling, a performer still, grinned and gave a jokey sound bite, one sure to make all the papers. "I do remember that room service was rather slow on that night. I had to wait three and a half hours before anyone came."

No one, not even Thatcher, knew that Tebbit was guarding a secret. He had come to realize two incompatible things. First, that he had the ability and possibly the support to become leader. But second, that his health—and even more so that of Margaret, *his* Margaret— made it impossible. So he had decided to quit frontline politics to focus on caring for her. And so, quietly, without fanfare, the prospect of Norman Tebbit becoming leader of the Conservative Party, and prime minister of Great Britain and Northern Ireland, was becoming alternate history.

Tour over, the convoy of armored government cars ferried Thatcher and Tebbit back to London, and police in Brighton dismantled the exclusion zone. The Union Jack flag once more flew over the Grand, and the Iron Lady was still prime minister, but her country and the ideology that bore her name were taking a path perceptibly altered by the bomb.

Overall, the British response to Brighton was marked by restraint, but such a traumatic incident could not be completely washed away. Indeed, in some vital moments it seemed to haunt the country—such as when Islamist terrorists inflicted their own "spectacular" on the US on September 11, 2001, and Britain followed the Americans into war, citing fears that the enemy possessed weapons of mass destruction, and needed to be lucky only once.

EPILOGUE

Margaret Thatcher won a third consecutive term in 1987, an extraordinary feat, and then succumbed to hubris. She introduced an unpopular tax, humiliated ministers, lost touch with her MPs, but carried on as if it were the same adoring party that had acclaimed her after the bomb. Colleagues forced her to resign in 1990.

In retirement, Thatcher lost caution and perspective. She poured vitriol on her successors and railed at European allies and their desire to integrate into the European Union, which ultimately took shape—despite her objections—in 1993. She became disillusioned about the Anglo-Irish Agreement, her own landmark achievement, fearing she had conceded too much. That it paved the way for the 1998 Good Friday Agreement, which ended the Troubles in Northern Ireland, brought no comfort.

Thatcher and Tebbit met for lunches to relive old times. Tebbit remained devoted to his own Margaret, cutting up her food, wheeling her around on rare public outings. She made the best of it. Her husband never disguised his contempt for Magee and expressed hope he would end up in a particularly hot corner of hell.

Thatcher died of a stroke in 2013, age eighty-seven. In her final years, though frail and sometimes muddled, she kept up public engagements. At a dinner for retired Metropolitan Police detectives, Paul Gibbon—the officer who had compared finding Magee's crossword to scoring at Twickenham—told her he had been part of the Brighton investigation. She placed her hands on his and said in a quiet voice, "We got them in the end, didn't we, my dear?"

That was not quite true. Magee's support team was never caught. And he was freed early, along with other convicted terrorists, in 1999. It was the price of IRA and loyalist paramilitary support for the Good Friday Agreement. This agreement was a collective leap of faith: republicans agreed to join unionists in governing Northern Ireland, which remained in the UK, while peacefully campaigning for a united Ireland.

Magee's comrades had mixed fortunes. Ella O'Dwyer tried in vain to forge an academic career. Martina Anderson married Paul Kavanagh—Ken Howorth's killer—and was elected to the European Parliament for Sinn Féin. Gerard "Blute" McDonnell returned to a low-key life in Belfast. Peter Sherry became a counselor at an addiction clinic. Donal Craig, the group's troubled fixer, died of cancer in 2009.

Gerry Adams transitioned to statesman—Prince Charles shook his hand—and stepped down as the Sinn Féin leader in 2018, an éminence grise revered by the movement. He continues to deny ever having been a member of the IRA.

Sinn Féin, meanwhile, has become a mainstream political force. In 2022 it became the biggest party in Northern Ireland. It is the main opposition party in the Dublin parliament and is expected to lead a future Irish government.

The police officers who hunted the IRA's England Department operators had varied fates. Peter Gurney survived more encounters with IRA bombs and wrote a memoir. Jack Reece became chairman of the National Federation of Sea Anglers and set a European record by landing a 1,069-pound six-gilled shark dubbed the "Monster of Monteiros." He died in 2015, age eighty-six. David Tadd finished his career as head of forensic investigation and operations for all of Scotland Yard, and still plays football. Ian Phoenix, the RUC's Captain Chaos, died in 1994 when a helicopter carrying intelligence officers crashed in fog in Scotland, killing all twenty-nine aboard.

David Tadd, who led the Scotland Yard team that identified
Patrick Magee's prints, returns to Brighton's Grand Hotel
in November 2021. | Rory Carroll, 2021

Patrick Magee's release in 1999, after serving fourteen years, less than half the judge's recommended sentence, was controversial. Tony Blair's Labour government called it "very hard to stomach." Augusto Pinochet, Chile's former dictator and a friend of Margaret Thatcher, chimed in: "My God! Him too?" Norman Tebbit rued a missed opportunity for revenge. "If I'd known when he was coming out I'd have gone there and shot him myself."

In prison, Magee had rediscovered books and obtained an Open University degree (first class honors), which led to a PhD dissertation on fictional literary depictions of republicans. He and Eileen eventually divorced. Magee's correspondence with an American writer, Barbara Byar, led to a prison wedding in 1997, and a son.

His post-prison life took several twists.

Walking down the Falls Road in Belfast one day, Magee encountered a crumpled-looking figure selling raffle tickets for republican prisoners.

"Pat!" the man called out.

It was Roy Walsh. The Old Bailey bomber had been released in 1994, after serving twenty-one years. He was a prematurely aged grandfather. "Pat," he repeated, "give me a pound."

It was a strange encounter, the two men recognizing but barely knowing each other. Walsh did not ask about the use of his name at Brighton, and Magee did not volunteer an explanation, in keeping with Provo operational etiquette. Magee handed over a pound. Walsh gave him a ticket and asked what name he should write on the stub. Magee smiled. "Care of Roy Walsh?"

To this day, Walsh says he does not know why Magee used his name. He jokingly refers to Magee as "Pat the Imposter."

A publisher turned Magee's thesis into a quasi-academic book, *Gangsters or Guerrillas? Representations of Irish Republicans in "Troubles Fiction."* But Magee struggled for employment. Notoriety trumped his doctorate—no university would touch him—so hopes of an academic career fizzled. He worked as a laborer on building sites.

In 2000, his life swerved again. Joanne Berry, the daughter of Anthony Berry, the MP killed in Brighton, asked to meet him. Spiritual and hippieish, she sought to find meaning in her father's death. Her empathy disarmed Magee, who for the first time perceived Anthony Berry as something other than a Tory. A realization struck him: *I had killed a fine human being.* Their dialogue evolved into a friendship and public discussions that continue two decades later. Berry and Magee speak at conflict resolution conferences around the world as a sort of reconciliation double-act. Harvey Thomas, the Tory conference organizer who survived the bomb, also befriended Magee. A devout Christian, Thomas forgave him.

Patrick Magee and Jo Berry, the daughter of Sir Anthony Berry, a Conservative MP killed in the Brighton bomb, at a reconciliation event in 2004. | © Guardian News & Media Ltd 2022

Magee expresses regret for the pain he inflicted, but still defends the Brighton bomb as a legitimate act of war. It is a moral murk—remorse without repentance. "When is the suffering worth it?" Jo Berry once asked him. Magee had no response at the time.

Magee is now in his seventies, separated from Byar, and walks with the aid of a cane. He sometimes visits the Sunflower pub on Kent

Street, near his old home in Unity Flats. It was here in 1972, when it was the Avenue Bar, that he received his first whispered orders as an IRA volunteer. These days it is a hub of students and artists. Magee takes the occasional beer, but he keeps to himself.

In 2021, he published a memoir, *Where Grieving Begins: Building Bridges after the Brighton Bomb*, with a foreword by Berry and an endorsement by Gerry Adams. It veiled the Brighton operation—Magee disclosed nothing about planning or execution—but the final section attempted to answer Berry's question, and to give some sort of accounting for his role in the Troubles.

"I am satisfied that we prevailed," he wrote. "But at terrible cost."

However one weighs the damage and grief, a great irony hangs over the IRA attempt to assassinate Thatcher. Because they failed to kill her, it gave her years to turn ever more hostile toward European integration, seeding in the Conservative Party a radical idea that would take time to bloom: quit the European Union. The UK voted to leave—"Brexit," the withdrawal was dubbed—in 2016. There are monumental consequences for Northern Ireland, which finds its borders, its inhabitants' allegiances, its very existence, all in question. There is perhaps no better illustration of the complexity of the Troubles: in the end it may be Margaret Thatcher's legacy, not IRA bombs, that delivers a united Ireland.

Acknowledgments

Writing a book like this starts lonely, like rowing a small boat across an ocean, but you don't get far without help.

My first thanks go to Steve Ramsey, author of *Something Has Gone Wrong: Dealing with the Brighton Bomb,* published in 2018, which vividly chronicles the experiences of survivors, emergency services, and police after the bomb detonated. I contacted Steve to ask for a phone number, with some trepidation. My book had limited overlap with his, but I was still treading on his turf. Steve floored me with his generosity and enthusiasm. He shared not only contacts but many of his own interview transcripts. When COVID lockdowns prevented me from traveling, Steve visited an archive called the Keep in Brighton and mined old newspapers and official records. He chased leads and scrutinized early drafts. When I finally made it to Brighton he gave me a tour, and we had a drink at the Grand.

In a story so full of politics, policing, and procedure, it is important to remember the human cost. I thank the friends and family members of those killed at Brighton who agreed to revisit a painful time and share their memories of love and loss.

Former IRA members parted veils on the cloistered world they once inhabited. Some defended the movement's actions during the Troubles, others condemned them. I thank them all. Those I can name include Anthony McIntyre, who is now an academic and writer; Shane Paul O'Doherty, also an author; Peter Sherry, the former "Armalite Kid"; Michael Hayes, the second-in-command of the England Department; Roy Walsh, whose name, and his own pseudonym, links generations of IRA operators. Patrick Magee was guarded but gracious.

I am indebted to journalists, scholars, and others who shared expertise and contacts: Ed Moloney, Tim Pat Coogan, Kevin Toolis, Tom Collins, Ian Cobain, Lena Ferguson, Brian Feeney, Aaron Edwards, Thomas Leahy, William Matchett, Tom McGurk, Henry McDonald, Robert Love, Tom Watson, Sean Boyne, Andy Oppenheimer, Gary O'Shea, Tom McCaughren, David Davin-Power, and Steven Farr. A special shout-out to Nick Davies, who excavated dusty notebooks from his investigations into the IRA's England campaign. The endnotes cite others whose articles, books, and documentaries I drew on.

Richard Nelsson, *The Guardian*'s information manager, deftly sifted through archives and uncovered gems. Thanks also to the staffs of the Linen Hall Library in Belfast, the National Library of Ireland in Dublin, the British Library in London, the Keep archive and Old Police Cells museum in Brighton, the Conflict Archive on the Internet (CAIN) at Ulster University, and Peter Heathwood, who maintains a private collection of television recordings.

Phil Mills, Jon Buss, and Adam Trimingham, alums of what used to be called the *Brighton Argus*, supplied evocative recollections about their town, the Tories, and the bomb. I benefited from the kaleidoscopic memory of Richard Baker, the Grand's former manager, and Pam Lelliott and Michael Forrester, of the Royal Sussex County

Hospital. Reminiscences from Jacqueline Shevlin, Derrick Francis, John Henty, Maria Pali, Nick Watkins, Lesley Ann Brett, among others, conjured life in 1980s Brighton.

I must also thank Iris Vloet, whose family hosted Patrick Magee in the Netherlands; the family of the IRA's London fixer Donal Craig; Ray Corcoran, a former Sinn Féin councillor in Ballymun; and Ken Maginnis, an Ulster Unionist MP who was in the IRA's crosshairs.

I am grateful to the retired police officers and soldiers who trusted me with their stories. Not all wished to be identified, but those I can name include Peter Gurney, the "bomb burglar," and his bomb-disposal colleagues Derek Pickford and Ian Jones; David Tadd, who patiently demystified the art of fingerprinting, and his Metropolitan police colleagues Paul Gibbon and Michael Colacicco, who shared his incomplete memoir. I hope he finishes it. Bob Fenton helpfully connected me with former colleagues at Scotland Yard, as did various branches of the National Association for Retired Police Officers.

From Sussex Police, I thank Roger Birch, Hilary Pownall, and Bernie Wells. The recollections of Dave Wilde, a first cousin and close friend of Jack Reece, breathed narrative life into Big Jack. Don Fraser and Steve Atkinson, Blackpool bobbies back in the day, plugged gaps in the story.

Ian Phoenix's son, Niven, and widow, Susan, shared memories of Ian and extracts from his private papers. Raymond White, a former assistant chief constable, generously connected me with Royal Ulster Constabulary colleagues. I also thank Jay Nethercott and John Shackles, who served in the Ulster Defence Regiment; Gerard Lovett, of the Garda Siochana Retired Members Association; plus all the other UDR, RUC, and Garda members who spoke to me. An entire book could—and should—be written about the RUC's Echo 4 Alpha unit. Ian Robinson, Hamish Innes, Brian Watson, William Dorrian, and Kenny Morrison, all formerly of the Strathclyde Police, helped to reconstruct events in Glasgow.

Talking to Norman Tebbit, Robin Butler, Charles Powell, and Harvey Thomas, all talented raconteurs, felt like having a ringside seat to the private world of Margaret Thatcher and those around her.

There would be no book without my agent, Will Lippincott, who is simply brilliant, a cocktail of energy, enthusiasm, and wisdom who has twice shepherded me to publication. I lucked out in working with Mark Tavani, a dream to work with, a consummate, gifted editor who improves everything he touches, along with Aranya Jain and the rest of the team at Putnam. Boundless thanks, too, to Joel Simons of Mudlark, who saw the potential for UK readers.

Finally, a mushy thanks to my parents, Joe and Kathy, and sisters, Mandy and Karina, for instilling in me a passion for story, and reading the manuscript; to my beautiful wife, Ligimat, light of my life, for her unstinting support; and to our daughter, Alma, who more than once reminded me it was time to finish the book already and come out and play. I dedicate it to them.

A Note on Sources

The book is based chiefly on original research encompassing dozens of interviews and reporting trips around Ireland, Northern Ireland, and Great Britain. However, I was able to chart the narrative framework from the vast trove of Troubles literature.

The opening chapter relied on Timothy Knatchbull's *From a Clear Blue Sky: Surviving the Mountbatten Bomb*. Later chapters drew on Ed Moloney's *A Secret History of the IRA* and *Voices from the Grave*, J. Bowyer Bell's *The Secret Army*, Toby Harnden's *Bandit Country*, Patrick Bishop and Eamonn Mallie's *The Provisional IRA*, Richard English's *Armed Struggle: The History of the IRA*, Kevin Toolis's *Rebel Hearts*, Sean O'Callaghan's *The Informer*, and Gary McGladdery's *The Provisional IRA in England*. This list could go on and on, but here I will add only Liam Clarke's *Broadening the Battlefield: H-Blocks and the Rise of Sinn Fein*, and Chris Ryder's *A Special Kind of Courage: 321 EOD Squadron*, and name the rest in the endnotes.

Several TV documentaries proved valuable: ITV's *The Brighton Bomber* (1986), Channel 4's *The Brighton Bomb* (2003), and three from the BBC: *To Kill the Cabinet* (1986), and Peter Taylor's twin documentaries in 2004.

Patrick Magee's memoir, *Where Grieving Begins*, was a rich source about his early life, less so about his activities in the IRA. One of his first commanders partly remedied that gap in the memoir *Insider: Gerry Bradley's Life in the IRA*, cowritten with Brian Feeney.

Gerry Adams declined to speak to me, so I drew on his numerous autobiographical writings and portraits by others, including Malachi O'Doherty's excellent biography, and David Beresford's unsurpassed book on the hunger strikes, *Ten Men Dead*.

My portrait of Margaret Thatcher funneled her memoirs, Charles Moore's magisterial three-volume biography, Jonathan Aitken's *Margaret Thatcher: Power and Personality*, Brenda Maddox's *Maggie: The First Lady*, and letters, cabinet papers, engagement diaries, and other documents on her foundation's website, margaretthatcher.org.

For the bomb and aftermath I repeatedly thumbed Steve Ramsey's *Something Has Gone Wrong*. David Briffett's *Sussex Murders* and Kieran Hughes's *Terror Attack Brighton: Blowing up the Iron Lady* (2014), which developed from an undergraduate dissertation, were also instructive.

Several books provided context to the police hunt for the bombers: Peter Gurney's memoir, *Braver Men Walk Away*, Robert Fleming and Hugh Miller's *Scotland Yard: The True Life Story of the Metropolitan Police*, Ray Wilson and Ian Adams's *Metropolitan Special Branch: A History, 1883–2006*, and Thomas Leahy's *The Intelligence War Against the IRA*. The remarkable career and tragic end of Ian Phoenix is chronicled in *Phoenix: Policing the Shadows* by Jack Holland and Susan Phoenix.

Of all that I read, the passage that struck me most was not in a book or diary or official document. It was on a poster in the dilapidated, crumbling Dublin home of Michael Hayes, the former deputy head of the IRA's England Department and a planner of the Brighton operation. He chain-smoked roll-ups and looked older than his seventy-four years, but blazed defiance. He would do it all again, for Irish freedom, he said. Hayes pointed his cigarette at the poster on his living room wall. It was a jail cell poem, "The Rhythm of Time," by the hunger striker Bobby Sands. It starts as a lyrical exhortation to resist oppression, then concludes with a declaration of righteousness, a bold, implacable certainty that could justify almost anything.

> It lights the dark of this prison cell,
> It thunders forth its might,
> It is "the undauntable thought," my friend,
> That thought that says "I'm right!"

Source Notes

PROLOGUE | INVISIBLE BEINGS

1. **"hold on to your nuts"**: Taxi driver Dennis Palmer quoted in the BBC1 documentary *To Kill the Cabinet*, 1986.

2. **"Ah, dear Brighton"**: Quote attributed to Noël Coward, cited in the *Evening Argus*, October 6, 2016.

4. **security forces called it the "Paddy Factor"**: Peter Gurney, *Braver Men Walk Away: Memoirs of the World's Top Bomb-Disposal Expert*, HarperCollins, 1993.

5. **He felt like a submarine captain**: Author interview with Harvey Thomas, citing a conversation with Magee in 2000.

5. **Autumnal bouquets and French polish**: Author interview with Jacqueline Shevlin, daughter of photographer Peter O'Byrne, who took portraits at the Grand.

5. **After midday it transitioned from cream teas**: Author interview with Richard Baker, general manager of the Grand, 1984–2004.

5. **required more than three million bricks**: Grand Hotel fact sheet on its construction and history.

5. **He had grown up poor in Belfast**: Patrick Magee, *Where Grieving Begins: Building Bridges After the Brighton Bomb*, Pluto Press, 2021.

5. **"A few active, intrepid and intelligent men"**: Jeremiah O'Donovan Rossa was a Fenian leader exiled in the United States who urged his comrades to stage guerrilla attacks in Victorian England. In the December 4, 1875, edition of the newspaper *Irish World*, which was edited by his friend Patrick Ford, Rossa wrote:
   "We should oppose a general insurrection in Ireland as untimely and ill-advised. But we believe in action nevertheless. A few active, intrepid and intelligent men can do so much to annoy and hurt England. The Irish cause requires Skirmishers. It requires a little band of heroes who will initiate and keep up without intermission a guerrilla warfare—men who will fly over land and sea like invisible beings.
   "Language, skin-color, dress, general manners, are all in favor of the Irish. Then, tens of thousands of Irishmen, from long residence in the enemy's country, know England's cities well. Our Irish skirmishers would be well disguised. They would enter London unknown and unnoticed. When the

night for action came; the night that the wind was blowing strong—this little band would deploy, each man setting about his own allotted task, and no man, save the captain of the band alone, knowing what any other man was to do, and at the same instant strike with lightning the enemy of their land and race. . . . In two hours from the word of command London would be in flames, shooting up to the heavens in fifty different places."
Cited in K. R. M. Short, *The Dynamite War: Irish-American Bombers in Victorian Britain*, Gill and Macmillan, 1979.

6. **A young receptionist, Trudy Groves:** Gareth Parry, "Brighton Bomb Man Guilty," *The Guardian*, June 11, 1986.

6. **his target was ninety miles north:** "MT Engagement Diary," Margaret Thatcher Foundation. Her engagement diary for September 15, 1984, is blank, as was often the case when she was at Chequers: https://www.margaretthatcher.org/document/147318.The next day's diary confirms she was there for Sunday morning Mass and lunch, and returned to London that evening: https://www.margaret thatcher.org/document/147319.

7. **she fretted the speech:** Author interview with Robin Butler.

7. **its grandeur was slipping:** Author interview with Richard Baker.

8. **scouts gathered intelligence:** Kevin McKinely, IRA member, quoted in Toby Harnden, *Bandit Country: The IRA & South Armagh*, Hodder & Stoughton, 1999, 273.

8. **Bank raids, kidnap ransoms:** J. Bowyer Bell, *The Secret Army*, Poolbeg Press, 1997.

8. **dreamed of being an artist:** Magee, *Where Grieving Begins*.

8. **erotic portraits:** Author interview with Jacqueline Shevlin, daughter of the photographer.

8. **A gathering of mystics:** "Psychics and Mystics Natural Health Exhibition and Conference," advertisement in *Evening Argus*, September 14, 1984.

CHAPTER ONE | MOUNTBATTEN

11. **Louis Mountbatten rose:** Timothy Knatchbull, *From a Clear Blue Sky: Surviving the Mountbatten Bomb*, Penguin, 2010.

12. **had graced Europe's palaces:** Andrew Lownie, *The Mountbattens: Their Lives & Loves*, Simon & Schuster, 2019.

12. **On this August morning:** Knatchbull, *From a Clear Blue Sky*.

12. **"Nick'las, Nick'las":** Knatchbull, *From a Clear Blue Sky*.

13. **"No place has ever thrilled":** Knatchbull, *From a Clear Blue Sky*.

13. **For weeks the weather:** Knatchbull, *From a Clear Blue Sky*.

14. **playing the same song:** Knatchbull, *From a Clear Blue Sky*.

14. **the greasy ladder:** Knatchbull, *From a Clear Blue Sky*.

14. **"Astern!" Mountbatten called:** Knatchbull, *From a Clear Blue Sky*.

14. **"Eleven thirty-nine and forty seconds":** Knatchbull, *From a Clear Blue Sky*.

16. **"The judgement of God":** From Charles Trevelyan's 1848 book *The Irish Crisis*, accessed via University College Cork's Corpus of Electronic Texts (Celt), https://celt.ucc.ie/published/E840001-002 /text001.html.

16. **hustled two thousand unwanted tenants:** Joe McGowan, *Even the Heather Bled*, Aeoleus, 2020.

16. **Palmerston, oblivious, built:** McGowan, *Even the Heather Bled*.

16. **a village, Mullach Gearr:** Mullach Gearr memorial pamphlet, 2017.

16. **no markers to indicate a burial ground:** Mullachan Heritage Group commemoration souvenir brochure, 2006.

18. **IRA units trained and hid arms:** Mullachan Heritage Group commemoration souvenir brochure.

18. **mined with explosives:** Mullachan Heritage Group commemoration souvenir brochure.

18. **big fella tumbled:** Diarmaid Ferriter, *Between Two Hells: The Irish Civil War*, Profile Books, 2021.

20. "quiet and friendliness all round": Knatchbull, *From a Clear Blue Sky*.

20. shadowed by bodyguards: Knatchbull, *From a Clear Blue Sky*.

21. In a classified intelligence report called "Future Terrorist Trends": Brigadier James Glover, the senior British army officer involved with intelligence work in Northern Ireland, prepared the classified report in November 1978. Known as the Glover report, it was leaked to the IRA and in 1979 widely reported in the media, including *An Phoblacht/Republican News*.

21. No single family in recorded history: Comment in the *Chicago Tribune* after Lord Mountbatten's death, cited in Knatchbull, *From a Clear Blue Sky*.

21. "The Irish are my friends": Andrew Lownie, "Who Killed Mountbatten?" *Sunday Times*, April 25, 2021. https://www.thetimes.co.uk/article/who-killed-mountbatten-8p9fkxrlx?t=ie.

21. storm was blowing over London: Knatchbull, *From a Clear Blue Sky*.

22. four-page appendix: Lownie, *The Mountbattens: Their Lives & Loves*.

22. lights inexplicably went out: Knatchbull, *From a Clear Blue Sky*.

22. "Did you just slam a door?": Knatchbull, *From a Clear Blue Sky*.

22. "blown up Mounty": Knatchbull, *From a Clear Blue Sky*.

22. Detective Henry, watching: Jim Gray, "'Spectacular' Murder Was Nothing but Butchery," *Irish Independent*, August 20, 2009.

23. "go on autopilot": Peter Murtagh interview with author, August 2019.

23. Lady Brabourne, in agony: Knatchbull, *From a Clear Blue Sky*.

24. "a beautiful target": Author interview with an IRA supporter in Belfast, April 2021.

25. "wash the death off you": Knatchbull, *From a Clear Blue Sky*.

25. line of sight: Toby Harnden, *Bandit Country: The IRA & South Armagh*, Hodder & Stoughton, 1999.

25. "All I can remember is a flash": Private Tom Caughey, quoted in Harnden, *Bandit Country*.

26. "There was another flash and a rumble": Caughey, quoted in Harnden, *Bandit Country*.

26. Captain Tom Schwartz: Paul Potts, "Paras Tell of Miraculous Escapes . . . and Carry On," *Daily Telegraph*, August 31, 1979.

CHAPTER TWO | THE FRIENDLY SKIES OF SOUTH ARMAGH

27. visitor spilled coffee: Anthony Seldon, "Living Above the Shop: Margaret Thatcher at Downing Street," *History of Government* blog, January 18, 2012, https://history.blog.gov.uk/2012/01/18/living-above-the-shop-margaret-thatcher-at-downing-street/.

28. "pretty, English sort of face": Katherine Hadley, "My Face, My Figure, My Diet: Margaret Thatcher Reveals Her Special Beauty Tips," *The Sun*, March 16, 1979.

28. This bank holiday weekend: "MT Engagement Diary: Sunday 26 August 1979," Margaret Thatcher Foundation, https://www.margaretthatcher.org/document/112889.

29. code-named "Carmen Rollers": Brenda Maddox, *Maggie: The First Lady*, Hodder & Stoughton, 2003.

29. "My dear Mrs. Rogers": "MT to Blairs," 790828 MT Letters to Families (81–132), Margaret Thatcher Foundation.

29. humbling truth about: Charles Moore, *Margaret Thatcher: The Authorized Biography, Volume One: Not for Turning*, Allen Lane, 2013, 587.

30. "I was not lucky": Maddox, *Maggie*.

30. beyond the grave: Maddox, *Maggie*.

30. "Methodists means method": Maddox, *Maggie*.

30. "higher aspirations": Maddox, *Maggie*.

31. "going to be an MP": Maddox, *Maggie*.

31. **"This woman is headstrong, obstinate"**: International Chemical Industries personnel department assessment, in rejecting job application from the then Margaret Roberts in 1948. Cited in BBC report "Margaret Thatcher," April 8, 2013, https://www.bbc.com/news/uk-politics-10377842.

31. **atomic bombing**: Maddox, *Maggie*.

31. **"it has warmth"**: Maddox, *Maggie*.

32. **bacon burned to a crisp**: Maddox, *Maggie*.

32. **"Bed, woman!"**: Maddox, *Maggie*.

32. **"look like rabbits"**: Maddox, *Maggie*.

32. **formidable and cold**: Maddox, *Maggie*.

32. **"men were agreeable, playful"**: Shirley Williams quoted in Maddox, *Maggie*.

33. **Edward du Cann**: Quoted in Maddox, *Maggie*.

33. **mockingly referred to her by her middle name, Hilda**: Matthew Parris, a Conservative Party researcher and MP, interviewed in the ITV documentary *Maggie: The First Lady*, March 2003. "The nickname that we all used for her was Hilda and it was not meant kindly."

34. **"I knew that we were of like mind"**: Thatcher recalled her first impression of Ronald Reagan in a 1997 speech at the Heritage Foundation in Washington, DC. A fuller quote: "As soon as I met Governor Reagan, I knew that we were of like mind, and manifestly so did he. We shared a rather unusual philosophy and we shared something else rather unusual as well: We were in politics because we wanted to put our philosophy into practice." Donna Leinwand Leger, "Thatcher, Reagan Relationship Altered History, *USA Today*, April 8, 2013, https://www.usatoday.com/story/news/world/2013/04/08/thatcher-reagan-political-soulmates/2063671.

35. **"Thank God one doesn't know"**: Quoted in a memoir by Thatcher's speechwriter, Sir Ronald Millar, *A View from the Wings: West End, West Coast, Westminster*, Weidenfeld & Nicolson, 1993.

35. **"Some devils got him"**: Interview with the BBC, quoted in Moore, *Margaret Thatcher*, vol. 1.

35. **"It sounds callous to say it"**: Moore, *Margaret Thatcher*, vol. 1.

36. **"Airey's death diminishes us"**: Thatcher statement to House of Commons on April 2, 1979, Margaret Thatcher Foundation, https://www.margaretthatcher.org/document/103992.

36. **a light mist**: Weather report, *Irish News*, August 29, 1979.

37. **"sentimental, imperialist hearts"**: "The Execution of Soldier Mountbatten," *An Phoblacht/Republican News*, September 1, 1979.

37. **"one mean bastard"**: Peter Gurney, *Braver Men Walk Away: Memoirs of the World's Top Bomb-Disposal Expert*, HarperCollins, 1993.

37. **"Every night is gelignite"**: Chris Ryder, *A Special Kind of Courage: 321 EOD Squadron*, Methuen, 2005, chapter 10.

38. **"without a result"**: David McKittrick, Seamus Kelters, Brian Feeney, Chris Thornton, and David McVea, *Lost Lives: The Stories of the Men, Women and Children Who Died as a Result of the Northern Ireland Troubles*, 2nd rev. ed., Mainstream, 2004, quoted by Fintan O'Toole, "All the Main Actors in the Troubles Tell Partial, Distorted and Deceitful Story," *Irish Times*, December 5, 2020.

38. **"hardboard millionaire"**: Ryder, *A Special Kind of Courage*.

38. **£300 government compensation**: Ryder, *A Special Kind of Courage*.

38. **Noel McConkey**: Quoted in Paul Potts, "Thatcher Sees IRA's Victims," *Daily Telegraph*, August 30, 1979.

39. **"jolly loyal to us"**: Moore, *Margaret Thatcher*, vol. 1.

39. **"No, no, I shouldn't"**: Moore, *Margaret Thatcher*, vol. 1.

40. **"If we do not defeat"**: Quoted in "Thatcher in and out on Whirlwind Tour of North," *Irish News*, August 30, 1979.

40. **"dress was £33.95"**: Quoted in "Thatcher in and out on Whirlwind Tour of North."

40. **"for God's sake help us"**: *Daily Mail*, August 30, 1979, cited in Margaret Thatcher Foundation.

40. **"will you clear H-Block?"**: "Harriet Kelly Challenges Maggie Thatcher," video, Gael Force Art, uploaded April 9, 2013, https://www.facebook.com/watch/?v=164070757085786.

41. **"If the Irish want to kill each other"**: Moore, *Margaret Thatcher,* vol. 1.

41. **"Whence does this mysterious power"**: Winston Churchill, speech to the House of Commons, December 15, 1921. https://api.parliament.uk/historic-hansard/commons/1921/dec/15/irish-free-state.

41. **"For God's sake bring me a large Scotch"**: Reginald Maudling, quoted in Kevin Meagher, *What a Bloody Awful Country: Northern Ireland's Century of Division*, Biteback Publishing, 2021.

42. **buffet lunch**: Desmond Hamill, *Pig in the Middle: The Army in Northern Ireland, 1969–84,* Methuen, 1985.

42. **"Come along! Let's get on with this"**: Hamill, *Pig in the Middle.*

42. **spring-loaded: his salute**: John Ezard, "David Thorne," obituary, *The Guardian*, April 25, 2000, https://www.theguardian.com/news/2000/apr/25/guardianobituaries.johnezard.

42. **He questioned the RUC's capacity**: Hamill, *Pig in the Middle.*

42. **"Madame Prime Minister"**: Hamill, *Pig in the Middle.*

42. **Other officers pressed**: Hamill, *Pig in the Middle.*

43. **"friendly skies of South Armagh"**: Pamphlet produced by Flight Lieutenant Brin Sharp, included in "790829 RAF Flier Heli Flight to South Armagh THCR 1-10-14 f9.pdf," Margaret Thatcher Foundation.

43. **Rats, a corgi/Jack Russell mix**: Toby Harnden, *Bandit Country: The IRA & South Armagh*, Hodder & Stoughton, 1999.

43. **nicknamed "the wee man"**: Duncan Campbell, "Sir Kenneth Newman Obituary," *The Guardian*, February 26, 2017, https://www.theguardian.com/uk-news/2017/feb/26/sir-kenneth-newman-obituary.

44. **removed her army jacket**: Hamill, *Pig in the Middle.*

44. **not interrupted once**: Hamill, *Pig in the Middle.*

CHAPTER THREE | THE CHANCER

46. **living in Shannon**: Patrick Magee, *Where Grieving Begins: Building Bridges After the Brighton Bomb*, Pluto Press, 2021.

47. **humiliated in Girdwood**: Magee, *Where Grieving Begins.*

47. **churn of emotions**: Magee, *Where Grieving Begins.*

47. **having nightmares**: Magee, *Where Grieving Begins.*

48. **"To me it was daft"**: Magee, *Where Grieving Begins.*

49. **"low esteem"**: Magee, *Where Grieving Begins.*

49. **"Just the sort of stunt that might convince you"**: Magee, *Where Grieving Begins.*

49. **"Never panic; hold your nerve"**: Magee, *Where Grieving Begins.*

49. **pacifist and a communist**: Magee, *Where Grieving Begins.*

49. **harvesting bohemian experience**: Magee, *Where Grieving Begins.*

50. **roughed him up**: Magee, *Where Grieving Begins.*

50. **Women and children evacuated**: Magee, *Where Grieving Begins.*

50. **destructive searches**: Gerry Bradley with Brian Feeney, *Insider: Gerry Bradley's Life in the IRA*, O'Brien Press, 2009.

50. **"marveled at their courage"**: Bradley, *Insider.*

51. **"IRA *were* the community"**: Magee, *Where Grieving Begins.*

51. **"What the hell can I do here?"**: Patrick Magee interview with the author, March 2021.

51. **Black boots pinned**: Magee, *Where Grieving Begins.*

51. **"The veil was lifted"**: Magee, *Where Grieving Begins.*

51. **young working-class males:** Paul Gill and John Horgan, "Who Were the Volunteers? The Shifting Sociological and Operational Profile of 1,240 Provisional Irish Republican Army Members," *Terrorism and Political Violence* 25, no. 3 (June 2013): 435–56.

51. **psychiatric study:** H. A. Lyons and H. J. Harbinson, "A Comparison of Political and Non-Political Murderers in Northern Ireland, 1974–84," *Medicine, Science, and the Law* 26, no. 3 (July 1986): 193–8.

51. **informal IRA survey:** Ian Cobain, *Anatomy of a Killing: Life and Death on a Divided Island*, Granta Books, 2020.

52. **"the 'Ra,":** Magee, *Where Grieving Begins.*

52. **Training was brief:** Magee, *Where Grieving Begins.*

52. **foxes and wild goats:** Sean O'Callaghan, *The Informer: The Real Story of One Man's War Against Terrorism*, Bantam, 1998.

52. **estimated at ten thousand:** Cobain, *Anatomy of a Killing.*

53. **seldom made it to brigade:** Bradley, *Insider.*

53. **daring, ruthless, and reckless:** Bradley, *Insider.*

53. **"blatter, blatter, blatter":** Bradley, *Insider.*

54. **biscuit tins:** Bradley, *Insider.*

54. **"couldn't be bate":** Bradley, *Insider.*

54. **"box of matches":** Magee, *Where Grieving Begins.*

54. **sulfuric acid dissolving:** Shane Paul O'Doherty interview with author, July 2020.

54. **"nutty professors":** Shane Paul O'Doherty, *The Volunteer: A Former IRA Man's True Story*, Strategic, 2011.

55. **"own goals":** Peter Gurney interview with author, February 2021.

55. **attitude than skill:** Magee interview with Peter Taylor in *The Brighton Bomb: The Hunt for the Bomber*, BBC1, September 14, 2004.

55. **hospital consultant:** Bradley, *Insider.*

55. **"blowy stuff":** Bradley, *Insider.*

55. **"pool of gray dust":** Shane Paul O'Doherty quoted in the PBS documentary *Bomb Squad*, October 21, 1997, https://www.pbs.org/wgbh/nova/transcripts/2413bombsquad.html.

56. **Third Batt had planted eleven:** Bradley, *Insider.*

56. **squad of paratroopers:** Magee, *Where Grieving Begins.*

56. **"Hands off cocks":** Magee, *Where Grieving Begins.*

57. **"hankie factory":** "The Brighton Bomber," *World in Action*, documentary series, ITV, June 11, 1986.

57. **Patsy O'Hara:** Magee interview with the author, March 2021.

57. **Jack Higgins thriller:** Patrick Magee, *Gangsters or Guerrillas? Representations of Irish Republicans in "Troubles Fiction,"* Beyond the Pale, 2001.

57. **looked like a hippie:** Magee, *Where Grieving Begins.*

57. **"Does anybody here":** Patrick Magee quoted in Richard English, *Armed Struggle: The History of the IRA*, Oxford University Press, 2003.

58. **"close to the forest floor":** Magee, *Where Grieving Begins.*

58. **"capacity to focus":** Magee, *Where Grieving Begins.*

58. **"Nothing was clearer to me":** Magee, *Where Grieving Begins.*

59. **extracted confessions:** *Report of an Amnesty International Mission to Northern Ireland (November 28, 1977–December 6, 1977)*, Amnesty International, 1978, https://cain.ulster.ac.uk/issues/police/docs/amnesty78.htm.

59. **slaps, punches:** Ian Cobain, "Inside Castlereagh: 'We Got Confessions by Torture,'" *The Guardian*, October 11, 2010.

59. **waterboarding:** *Inside the Torture Chamber*, documentary, BBC Radio Ulster, October 2012.

59. "slap and tickle": Cobain, *Anatomy of a Killing*.

59. thirty-two thousand soldiers: Chris Ryder, *The RUC: A Force Under Fire*, Mandarin, 1990.

59. long-delay timers: Ryder, *The RUC*.

59. "red light": Magee, *Where Grieving Begins*.

59. fire in the hearth: Magee, *Where Grieving Begins*.

60. "The timing mechanisms": Magee, *Where Grieving Begins*.

60. "bequeath that choice": Magee, *Where Grieving Begins*.

61. "You had to keep it tight": Magee interview with the author, March 2021.

61. assumed he had abandoned them: Magee interview with the author, March 2021.

61. picture of their newborn son: Magee interview with the author, March 2021.

61. shunted aside: Magee, *Where Grieving Begins*.

62. strange other self: Magee, *Where Grieving Begins*.

62. "My new existence": Magee, *Where Grieving Begins*.

62. wild impulse for action: Magee, *Where Grieving Begins*.

62. "I was of no use as a volunteer": Magee, *Where Grieving Begins*.

62. *Leave Ireland. Walk away*: Magee, *Where Grieving Begins*.

63. Meadows with poppies: Iris Vloet interview with author, September 2021.

63. polite, genial: Vloet interview with author, September 2021.

63. carpentry accident: Vloet interview with author, September 2021.

64. roared past: Paul van Gageldonk, *Ruger .357: De IRA in Limburg*, Media Groep Limburg, 2015.

64. "Stay down!": van Gageldonk, *Ruger .357*.

CHAPTER FOUR | HUNGER

65. *I'm about to die*: Patrick Magee, *Where Grieving Begins: Building Bridges After the Brighton Bomb*, Pluto Press, 2021.

65. notified Interpol: Paul van Gageldonk, *Ruger .357: De IRA in Limburg*, Media Groep Limburg, 2015.

65. tapping the phone: Iris Vloet interview with author, September 2021.

66. killed innocent civilians: Magee, *Where Grieving Begins*.

66. Brits chose violence: Magee, *Where Grieving Begins*.

66. "pray for a happy ending": van Gageldonk, *Ruger .357*.

66. "Befriended a Murderer": van Gageldonk, *Ruger .357*.

66. "Such a boy should be given a chance": van Gageldonk, *Ruger .357*.

68. forgo food over Christmas: Magee, *Where Grieving Begins*.

68. British detectives who attended the hearing: van Gageldonk, *Ruger .357*.

68. tears in his eyes: van Gageldonk, *Ruger .357*.

68. Its members hosted Magee: van Gageldonk, *Ruger .357*.

68. towering Amazonian: Magee, *Where Grieving Begins*.

69. "British pigs": Magee, *Where Grieving Begins*.

69. "gang of punk rockers": "Hiding Place," Tim Miles, *Daily Mail*, February 2, 1981, 13.

69. limousine festooned with US and British flags: "President Reagan at the Arrival Ceremony of Prime Minister Margaret Thatcher on February 26, 1981," Reagan Library video, YouTube, posted March 31, 2017, https://www.youtube.com/watch?v=qycXiuYE1PM.

69. "**The responsibility for freedom**": Ronald Reagan speech welcoming Thatcher to the White House, February 26, 1981. Records of the White House Television Office (WHTV) (Reagan Administration), 1/20/1981–1/20/1989. Viewed on YouTube: https://www.youtube.com/watch?v=qycXiuYE1PM.

69. "**We must have the courage to reassert**": White House Television Office.

70. "**This will even the score for H**": A confidential source related this conversation to the FBI in February 1981, according to FBI files released to *The Guardian* in 2014. Jon Swaine, "US Believed FBI Mole Passed Secrets to IRA in Thatcher Murder Plot, Files Reveal," *The Guardian*, December 8, 2014, https://www.theguardian.com/politics/2014/dec/08/us-fbi-mole-plot-kill-margaret-thatcher.

70. "**submit to hypnosis**": "MT's FBI File," Margaret Thatcher Foundation, https://www.margaretthatcher.org/archive/FBI.

71. **Years later, he would consistently deny:** Since running for elected office in the 1980s Adams has consistently denied ever being an IRA member, let alone a leader. He was never convicted of IRA membership or involvement in IRA violence. There is no evidence he ever personally fired a bullet or planted a bomb. Scholars and chroniclers of the Troubles—Ed Moloney, Tim Pat Coogan, J. Bowyer Bell, Richard English, Peter Taylor, Kevin Toolis, Eamonn Mallie, Patrick Bishop, Malachi O'Doherty, Patrick Radden Keefe, to name a few—have concluded Adams was a senior member of the IRA. Outspoken former IRA volunteers, such as Richard O'Rawe and Brendan Hughes, detailed Adams's leading role, an opinion shared by the Royal Ulster Constabulary and British army. This book agrees with that consensus. As a condition of secret talks with the British government in 1972, the IRA insisted that Adams be released from Long Kesh to join the delegation. In *A Secret History of the IRA*, Moloney cites evidence that Adams became a long-serving member of the IRA's seven-member Army Council, which directed strategy, but stepped back from any direct military role from the early 1980s to further his political ascent. Former IRA men and security force officials told this author that was accurate. Adams does not deny affinity with the IRA. "I have never disassociated myself from the IRA and I never will until the day I die," he said in 2019.

72. **father sexually abused:** Gerry Adams, "My Father Was a Child Sex Abuser," *The Guardian*, December 20, 2009, https://www.theguardian.com/politics/2009/dec/20/gerry-adams-sexual-abuse.

72. "**A meditative fellow**": Patrick Bishop and Eamonn Mallie, *The Provisional IRA*, William Heinemann, 1987.

72. "**Never showed his hand**": Bishop and Mallie, *The Provisional IRA*.

72. **Adams never smiled:** Malachi O'Doherty, *Gerry Adams: An Unauthorized Life*, Faber & Faber, 2017.

72. **under multiple names:** Gerry Adams, *Before the Dawn: An Autobiography*, Brandon, 2017.

72. **ordered the IRA to put away its guns and stand down:** O'Doherty, *Gerry Adams*.

72. "**Disperse or we will throw stones!**": Adams, *Before the Dawn*.

72. "**Adams, you bastard!**": Adams, *Before the Dawn*.

73. **informer had tipped off the Brits:** Ed Moloney, *A Secret History of the IRA*, Penguin Press, 2002.

73. **ragged sweater:** Moloney, *A Secret History of the IRA*.

73. **lecture on AK-47s:** O'Doherty, *Gerry Adams*.

73. **armchair generals:** Moloney, *A Secret History of the IRA*.

73. **float heretical notions:** Moloney, *A Secret History of the IRA*.

73. **Then he produced a rescue plan for the IRA:** According to Moloney's *A Secret History of the IRA*, Adams was instrumental in drafting the Green Book. Volunteers needed to read and digest it before being admitted, and thereafter would be described as having been "Green-Booked."

74. "**permanent leadership**": Moloney, *A Secret History of the IRA*.

74. **under their own rules:** Moloney, *A Secret History of the IRA*.

74. "**He hammered it home**": Moloney, *A Secret History of the IRA*.

75. "**Bobby, we are tactically**": Adams, *Before the Dawn*.

75. "**I am standing on the threshold of another trembling world**": Prison diary of Bobby Sands, https://www.bobbysandstrust.com.

75. **Leon Uris's *Trinity*:** Liam Clarke, *Broadening the Battlefield: H-Blocks and the Rise of Sinn Féin*, Irish Books & Media, 1987.

76. **blared republican songs:** David Beresford, *Ten Men Dead: The Story of the 1981 Irish Hunger Strike*, reprint ed., Atlantic Monthly Press, 1997.

76. **The Ford Escort wove:** Beresford, *Ten Men Dead*.

76. **"Bhi an bua againn":** Beresford, *Ten Men Dead*.

76. **"A crime is a crime is a crime":** Margaret Thatcher press conference in Saudi Arabia, April 21, 1981. Transcript at Margaret Thatcher Foundation, https://www.margaretthatcher.org/document /104501.

76. **freezing coldness:** Clarke, *Broadening the Battlefield*.

77. **"It is not my habit or custom":** Margaret Thatcher press conference in Saudi Arabia, April 21, 1981. Transcript at Margaret Thatcher Foundation, https://www.margaretthatcher.org/document/104501.

77. **protesters broke into Classiebawn:** Timothy Knatchbull, *From a Clear Blue Sky: Surviving the Mountbatten Bomb*, Penguin, 2010.

77. **"There Will Be Fire":** "There Will Be Fire," *An Phoblacht/Republican News*, April 25, 1981, 3.

77. **police discreetly padlocked:** Beresford, *Ten Men Dead*.

77. **won £500 in a sweepstake:** Chris Ryder, *The RUC: A Force Under Fire*, Mandarin, 1990.

78. **"starve a taig":** Richard English, *Armed Struggle: The History of the IRA*, Oxford University Press, 2003.

79. **"Mr. Sands was a convicted criminal":** Thatcher speech in House of Commons, May 5, 1981. Hansard transcript at Margaret Thatcher Foundation, https://www.margaretthatcher.org/document/104641.

79. **let envoys negotiate:** Cabinet documents cited in Owen Bowcott, "Thatcher Cabinet 'Wobbled' over IRA Hunger Strikers," *The Guardian*, December 30, 2011.

79. **admired their courage:** Charles Moore, *Margaret Thatcher: The Authorized Biography, Volume One: Not for Turning*, Allen Lane, 2013.

79. **"no visible emotion":** Bernadette McAliskey quoted in "The Honourable Member for Belfast West," *World in Action*, BBC documentary series, 1983.

80. **"absolute faith in Adams":** Richard O'Rawe quoted in O'Doherty, *Gerry Adams*.

80. **skin stretched across skull-like faces:** Adams, *Before the Dawn*.

80. **"Beidh an bua againn":** Adams, *Before the Dawn*.

81. **"I am the rebel head of an establishment government":** Brenda Maddox, *Maggie: The First Lady*, Hodder & Stoughton, 2003.

CHAPTER FIVE | THE ENGLAND DEPARTMENT

83. **Frankie Rafferty:** Patrick Magee, *Where Grieving Begins: Building Bridges After the Brighton Bomb*, Pluto Press, 2021.

84. **H-Block "comms":** Magee, *Where Grieving Begins*.

84. **Brigitte Bardot:** Magee, *Where Grieving Begins*.

84. **"every waking moment":** Magee, *Where Grieving Begins*.

84. **prolonged nightmare:** Magee, *Where Grieving Begins*.

85. **Clerkenwell prison:** Ray Wilson and Ian Adams, *Metropolitan Special Branch: A History, 1883–2006*, Biteback Publishing, 2015.

85. **"A few active, intrepid and intelligent men":** Jeremiah O'Donovan Rossa, cited in K. R. M. Short, *The Dynamite War: Irish-American Bombers in Victorian Britain*, Gill and Macmillan, 1979.

85. **William Lomasney:** Wilson and Adams, *Metropolitan Special Branch*, 17.

86. **"I believe we have struck":** Michael T. Foy, *Tom Clarke: The True Leader of the Easter Rising*, History Press Ireland, 2014.

86. **In early 1973, he assembled a team:** Ed Moloney, *Voices from the Grave: Two Men's War in Ireland*, Faber & Faber, 2010. Brendan Hughes, a close Adams lieutenant who later turned against him, said Adams conceived the Provisional IRA's first bombing attack in London and assembled a ten-strong team from a pool of Belfast volunteers.

Dolours Price, who was caught and convicted of being part of the bombing team, told newspaper interviewers that Adams planned the mission. Patrick Sawer, "'Republicanism Is Part of Our DNA', Says IRA bomber Dolours Price," *Sunday Telegraph*, September 23, 2012.

86. **Annie Walsh . . . never trusted Adams:** Brendan Hughes, quoted in Moloney, *Voices from the Grave.*

87. **James Earl Ray:** Hampton Sides, *Hellhound on His Trail,* Doubleday, 2010.

87. **Terminal 1, felt safe:** Roy Walsh interview with author, April 2021.

87. **appear relaxed:** Walsh interview with author, April 2021.

88. *Looney Tunes* **era:** Gareth Parry, "Why 'The Paddy Factor' Outwitted Police Security," *The Guardian,* October 14, 1984.

88. **fatally poisoned his dog:** Peter Gurney, *Braver Men Walk Away: Memoirs of the World's Top Bomb-Disposal Expert,* HarperCollins, 1993.

88. **chipped a balcony:** "Heath's Home in London Hit by Bomb 3 Hours Before Christmas Ceasefire," *New York Times,* December 23, 1974, https://www.nytimes.com/1974/12/23/archives/heaths-home -in-london-hit-by-bomb-3-hours-before-christmas.html.

88. **Ross McWhirter:** Peter Chippindale and Martin Walker, "Enemy of IRA Bombers Killed Outside Home," *The Guardian,* November 28, 1975, https://www.theguardian.com/news/1975/nov /28/mainsection.martinwalker.

89. **nom de guerre Gerry Fossett:** Ruan O'Donnell, *Special Category: The IRA in English Prisons,* Irish Academic Press, 2011.

89. **German Irishman named David Coyne:** O'Donnell, *Special Category.*

89. **"Secrecy assures confusion":** J. Bowyer Bell, *The Secret Army,* Poolbeg Press, 1997.

90. **"sky is red with flames":** Peter Kane, Roger Beam, and Garth Gibbs, "Gas Inferno," *Daily Mirror,* January 18, 1979, 1.

90. **"For goodness sake do":** "Gas Inferno," *Daily Mirror.*

90. **scaled a perimeter wall:** O'Donnell, *Special Category.*

90. **. . . earning a place in republican lore:** Peter O'Rourke, "Brixton Prison Escape, 1980," *An Phoblacht,* December 16. 2015, https://www.anphoblacht.com/contents/25569.

90. **Brassil's pub in Tralee:** Sean O'Callaghan, *The Informer: The Real Story of One Man's War Against Terrorism,* Bantam Press, 1998.

91. **Owen Coogan . . . Ownie:** Nick Davies, "How London Police Uncovered the IRA's Great Britain Brigade," *London Daily News,* June 23, 1987.

91. **Hayes was a romantic:** O'Callaghan, *The Informer.*

91. **Albert Flynn, careful, quiet:** O'Callaghan, *The Informer.*

91. **"flat caps":** O'Callaghan, *The Informer.*

91. **mussels from Cromane:** O'Callaghan, *The Informer.*

92. **Cathal Brugha:** Michael Farrell, "Brugha Aimed to Kill Cabinet," *Sunday Tribune,* October 14, 1984.

93. **Scottish oil terminal:** Christopher Andrew, *The Defence of the Realm: The Authorized History of MI5,* Allen Lane, 2009.

93. **the mislaying of Thatcher's engagement diary:** *An Phoblacht/Republican News,* May 16, 1981.

CHAPTER SIX | THE BOMB BURGLAR AND MR. T

97. **arrived early:** Peter Gurney, *Braver Men Walk Away: Memoirs of the World's Top Bomb-Disposal Expert,* HarperCollins, 1993.

97. **frightening, yes, but it was also** *interesting***:** Gurney, *Braver Men Walk Away,* 208.

97. **"bomb doctors":** Robert Fleming with Hugh Miller, *Scotland Yard: The True Life Story of the Metropolitan Police,* Michael Joseph, 1994.

98. **Gurney's great fear:** Gurney, *Braver Men Walk Away.*

98. **"bomb burglar":** Gurney, *Braver Men Walk Away.*

99.   **herding people away:** BBC TV News report, October 26, 1981.

99.   **eggs, bacon, steak:** Gurney, *Braver Men Walk Away*.

99.   **Grim Reaper:** Chris Ryder, *A Special Kind of Courage: 321 EOD Squadron*, Methuen, 2005.

100.   **"train a man to the nth degree":** George Styles autobiography quoted in Ryder, *A Special Kind of Courage*.

100.   **electromagnetic spectrum:** Toby Harnden, *Bandit Country: The IRA & South Armagh*, Hodder & Stoughton, 1999, 262.

100.   **"Tee-hee, Hee-hee":** A. R. Oppenheimer, *IRA: The Bombs and the Bullets: A History of Deadly Ingenuity*, 2008.

100.   **roped a captured bomber:** Ryder, *A Special Kind of Courage*.

100.   **"She has no face":** Gurney, *Braver Men Walk Away*.

100.   **"totally armless":** Gurney interview with author, February 2021.

101.   **TPUs:** Gurney interview with author, February 2021.

101.   **"If you take ten people":** Gurney interview with author, February 2021.

101.   **Ministry of Defence report:** Cited in "The Brighton Bomber," *World in Action*, documentary series, ITV, June 11, 1986.

102.   **1979, under floorboards:** Gurney, *Braver Men Walk Away*.

102.   **aviation fuel:** Gurney interview with author, February 2021.

102.   **an obsession that frayed his marriage:** Gurney interview with author, February 2021.

102.   **barrage balloons:** Gurney interview with author, February 2021.

102.   **"Queen Victoria's clitoris":** Gurney interview with author, February 2021.

103.   **grabbed his kit:** Gurney interview with author, February 2021.

103.   **forever remember as "the pit":** Gurney interview with author, February 2021.

103.   **filtered emotions:** Gurney interview with author, February 2021.

104.   ***Nail the bastards***: Gurney interview with author, February 2021.

104.   **on a cistern:** Gurney interview with author, February 2021.

105.   **Old Master paintings:** David Tadd interview with author, February 2021.

105.   **bath was a tin tub:** Tadd interview with author, February 2021.

105.   **ridge arrangement on every finger and palm of every human is unique:** "Fingerprint," *Britannica*, https://www.britannica.com/topic/fingerprint.

106.   **Lord Lucan:** "Fingerprint," *Britannica*.

106.   **sixteen points of similarity:** Robert Fleming with Hugh Miller, *Scotland Yard: The True Life Story of the Metropolitan Police*, Michael Joseph, 1994.

106.   **milk bottle, and a porcelain cup:** Paul van Gageldonk, *Ruger .357: De IRA in Limburg*, Media Groep Limburg, 2015.

107.   **dictated observations:** Tadd interview with author, February 2021.

107.   **"A mess":** Tadd interview with author, February 2021.

107.   **Santa's grotto:** Nick Davies, "How London Police Uncovered the IRA's Great Britain Brigade," *London Daily News*, June 23, 1987.

108.   **blue tunics . . . sprouted swallowtails:** Ray Wilson and Ian Adams, *Metropolitan Special Branch: A History, 1883–2006*, Biteback, 2015.

108.   **"light into these dark places":** Wilson and Adams, *Metropolitan Special Branch*.

108.   **"enemy by the throat":** Wilson and Adams, *Metropolitan Special Branch*.

109.   **black canvas bag:** Author interview with Michael Colaciccio, ex–Anti Terrorist Branch detective, March 2021.

109.   **crime scenes in waves:** Davies, "How London Police Uncovered the IRA's Great Britain Brigade."

109.   **stiff drink and slept:** Gurney, *Braver Men Walk Away*.

110.   **perpetually burning flame:** Fleming, *Scotland Yard*.

110. **desks, filing cabinets:** Colaciccio interview with author, March 2021.

110. **handpicked his fingerprint team:** Tadd interview with author, February 2021.

110. **"work stupidly long hours":** Tadd interview with author, February 2021.

111. **250,000 premises:** Ruan O'Donnell, *Special Category: The IRA in English Prisons*, Irish Academic Press, 2011.

111. **Cornish pasties:** David Tadd interview with author, November 2021.

CHAPTER SEVEN | FRIENDS

112. **nickname Bangers:** Patrick Bishop and Eamonn Mallie, *The Provisional IRA*, William Heinemann, 1987.

112. **Irish Special Branch detectives:** Niall Kiely, "Hard Liners Split Ard Fheis," *Irish Times*, November 2, 1981.

112. **he posed as a janitor:** "Venue History," Conference & Events Venue at the Mansion House, https://www.theconferenceandeventsvenue.ie/about-us/venue-history/.

113. **stuffy auditorium:** Kiely, "Hard Liners Split Ard Fheis."

114. **"Where the fuck":** Martin McGuinness quoted in Kevin Bean, *The New Politics of Sinn Féin*, Liverpool University Press, 2007, 63.

114. **"IRA Blasts Brits":** "IRA Blasts Brits," *An Phoblacht/Republican News*, October 22, 1981, 1.

115. **detailed graphic:** *An Phoblacht/Republican News*, October 17, 1981.

115. **Pringle's leg mocked:** *An Phoblacht/Republican News*, October 22, 1981.

115. **"Prestige Target":** "Prestige Target," *An Phoblacht/Republican News*, October 29, 1981.

115. **"expertise failed to defeat":** "Prestige Target."

115. **"armed propaganda":** Gerry Adams, *The Politics of Irish Freedom*, Brandon, 1986, 64.

116. **"give these bastards a Christmas":** Patrick Magee, *Where Grieving Begins: Building Bridges After the Brighton Bomb*, Pluto Press, 2021.

116. **Shortly after 6:00 p.m.:** Peter Murtagh, "Two Hit by Shots at SF Center," *Irish Times*, November 26, 1981, 1.

116. **foyer of Sinn Féin's:** "Two Hit by Shots at SF Center."

116. **Two bullets . . . did not feel anything:** Magee, *Where Grieving Begins*.

116. **"You were it":** Magee, *Where Grieving Begins*.

117. **"my constituency is":** Margaret Thatcher, Parliamentary Debates, sixth series, vol. 12, 238–39. Quoted in Richard English, *Armed Struggle: The History of the IRA*, Oxford University Press, 2003.

117. **bodyguard wore a raincoat:** Barry Stevens quoted in Ed Riley, "The Real-Life Bodyguard," *Daily Mail*, August 28, 2018, https://www.dailymail.co.uk/news/article-6105395/Margaret-Thatcher-protection-officer-recalls-years-working-former-PM.html.

117. **"dentist's appointment":** Brenda Maddox, *Maggie: The First Lady*, Hodder & Stoughton, 2003.

118. **busload of hockey fans:** Kevin Cullen and Shelley Murphy, *Whitey Bulger: America's Most Wanted Gangster and the Manhunt That Brought Him to Justice*, W. W. Norton, 2013, 247.

118. **audacious press conference:** Ed Moloney, *A Secret History of the IRA*, Penguin Press, 2002.

118. **caught the eye of a young Arab:** Brendan Anderson, *Joe Cahill: A Life in the IRA*, O'Brien Press, 2002.

118. **French sculptor:** Anderson, *Joe Cahill*.

118. **"everything would be possible":** Anderson, *Joe Cahill*.

118. **"awful hatred of England":** Anderson, *Joe Cahill*.

119. **old trailer by a beach:** Anderson, *Joe Cahill*.

119. **Joe Brown:** Dessie Mackin, Sinn Féin director of finance, quoted in Anderson, *Joe Cahill*.

119. **mascot was a leprechaun:** Cullen and Murphy, *Whitey Bulger*.

119. **hockey trick before:** Cullen and Murphy, *Whitey Bulger.*

120. **"bucket of blood":** Sam Savage, "History Shows Triple O's Has Quite the Past," *RedOrbit,* June 20, 2007, https://www.redorbit.com/news/business/975084/history_shows_triple_os_has_quite_the_past/.

120. **Nobody drank:** Cullen and Murphy, *Whitey Bulger.*

120. **"strange, complex amalgam":** Cullen and Murphy, *Whitey Bulger.*

121. **fished a videocassette:** Cullen and Murphy, *Whitey Bulger.*

121. **"The movie had pictures of little girls, dead":** Cullen and Murphy, *Whitey Bulger.*

121. **Patrick Nee:** Patrick Nee, Richard Farrell, and Michael Blythe, *A Criminal and an Irishman: The Inside Story of the Boston Mob,* Steerforth Press, 2006.

121. **floor of a Dodge van:** Nee et al., *A Criminal and an Irishman.*

122. **outsource car theft:** Cullen and Murphy, *Whitey Bulger,* 248.

122. **no longer wrote blank checks:** David Blundy and Andrew Lycett, *Qaddafi and the Libyan Revolution,* Weidenfeld & Nicolson, 1987, 159.

123. **aggravated his disdain:** Alison Pargeter, *Libya: The Rise and Fall of Qaddafi,* Yale University Press, 2012.

123. **With other Arab nationalist officers:** Ethan Chorin, *Exit the Colonel: The Hidden History of the Libyan Revolution,* Public Affairs, 2012.

123. **Padre, as he was known:** Steven Farr, *The Overseas Department: The Provisional IRA on Active Service in Europe,* self-published, 2012.

124. **shy young Englishwoman:** Nick Davies, "Exposing Father Patrick Ryan—Priest and Senior Terrorist," *London Daily News,* June 25, 1987, https://www.nickdavies.net/1987/06/25/exposing-father-patrick-ryan-priest-and-bomber/.

124. **"reservoirs as well":** Davies, "Exposing Father Patrick Ryan."

124. **"fine fella, best I ever met":** Patrick Ryan interviewed in *Spotlight on the Troubles: A Secret History,* documentary, BBC Northern Ireland, September 24, 2019.

124. **base in Le Havre:** Ryan interviewed in *Spotlight on the Troubles.*

124. **four hundred Memo-Park timers:** Ryan interviewed in *Spotlight on the Troubles.*

125. **"didn't do too badly":** Ryan interviewed in *Spotlight on the Troubles.*

CHAPTER EIGHT | REJOICE

126. **not chime at the same time:** Anthony Seldon, *10 Downing Street: The Illustrated History,* HarperCollins Illustrated, 1999.

126. **recalled Charles Powell:** Author interview with Charles Powell, May 2021.

127. **"Rawhide down":** Del Quentin Wilber, *Rawhide Down: The Near Assassination of Ronald Reagan,* Henry Holt, 2011.

127. **Larry Speakes:** Cited in Mary Kay Linge, "How Ronald Reagan's Nancy Let Her Astrologer Control the Presidency," *New York Post,* October 18, 2021, https://nypost.com/article/ronald-reagans-wife-nancy-astrologer-joan-quigley/.

127. **"unscheduled posy":** John Ezard and Dennis Barker, "President in a Low-Cost Remake," *The Guardian,* June 8, 1982, https://www.theguardian.com/world/1982/jun/08/usa.monarchy.

127. **"A" Squad:** Robert Fleming with Hugh Miller, *Scotland Yard: The True Life Story of the Metropolitan Police,* Michael Joseph, 1994.

128. **classified level two:** Fleming, *Scotland Yard.*

128. **Barry Stevens, recalled:** Fleming, *Scotland Yard,* 198.

129. **meeting that came to acquire mythical status:** Charles Moore, *Margaret Thatcher: The Authorized Biography, Volume One: Not for Turning,* Allen Lane, 2013, 587.

129. **floor by an electric heater:** Cynthia Crawford, "The Margaret Thatcher I Knew, by Her Personal Assistant," *The Guardian,* April 8, 2013, https://www.theguardian.com/politics/2013/apr/08/margaret-thatcher-personal-assistant-cynthia-crawford.

129. **humble enough to defer:** Moore, *Margaret Thatcher,* vol. 1, 587.

129. **Russians marveled:** Moore, *Margaret Thatcher*, vol. 1, 754, fn 237.

129. **"create the dangerous idea":** Moore, *Margaret Thatcher*, vol. 1.

130. **"only European leader I know with balls":** Moore, *Margaret Thatcher*, vol. 1.

130. **speech to MPs and lords:** Ronald Reagan, "Address to Members of the British Parliament," Ronald Reagan Presidential Library and Museum, June 8, 1982, https://www.reaganlibrary.gov/archives /speech/address-members-british-parliament.

130. **Many Britons were stunned:** Steven Rattner, "Britons Reassured by Reagan's Visit," *New York Times*, June 10, 1982, https://www.nytimes.com/1982/06/10/world/britons-reassured-by-reagan-s-visit.html.

130. **"rise and drink a toast":** "Toasts of the President and British Prime Minister Margaret Thatcher at a Luncheon Honoring the President in London," Ronald Reagan Presidential Library and Museum, June 8, 1982, https://www.reaganlibrary.gov/archives/speech/toasts-president-and-british-prime -minister-margaret-thatcher-luncheon-honoring.

130. **own money redecorating:** Seldon, *10 Downing Street*.

130. **Sir Thomas Knyvet:** Seldon, *10 Downing Street*.

131. **room overlooking Horse Guards Parade:** Seldon, *10 Downing Street*.

131. **"became my refuge":** Seldon, *10 Downing Street*.

131. **poached egg on Bovril:** Seldon, *10 Downing Street*.

131. **"simmering frozen peas":** Seldon, *10 Downing Street*.

131. **"entitled to be proud":** Margaret Thatcher, "Speech to Conservative Rally at Cheltenham," Margaret Thatcher Foundation, July 3, 1982, https://www.margaretthatcher.org/document/104989.

131. **"sincerity machine":** Author interview with Harvey Thomas, Conservative Party conference organizer, August 2020.

131. **"Behind the iron carapace":** Michael Dobbs, "Brighton Bombing: Thirty Years On, I Still Can't Be in the Same Room as Gerry Adams and Martin McGuinness," *Daily Telegraph*, October 12, 2014, https://www.telegraph.co.uk/news/politics/11155873/Brighton-bombing-Thirty-years-on-I-still -cant-be-in-the-same-room-as-Gerry-Adams-and-Martin-McGuinness.html.

132. **poem she had cut out and underlined:** Cynthia Crawford interviewed in *Thatcher: A Very British Revolution*, documentary, BBC, June 3, 2019.

132. **doctor's appointment:** "MT Engagement Diary: Tuesday, July 20, 1982," Margaret Thatcher Foundation, https://www.margaretthatcher.org/document/124897.

133. **Thatcher heard it:** Margaret Thatcher, *Margaret Thatcher: The Autobiography*, Harper Press, 1993, 469.

133. **Black smoke rose:** Steven Rattner, "IRA Bomb Attacks in London Kill 8," *New York Times*, July 21, 1982, https://www.nytimes.com/1982/07/21/world/ira-bomb-attacks-in-london-kill-8.html.

133. **Corporal Oliver Pitt:** Pitt's police statement quoted in Toby Harnden, *Bandit Country*, Hodder & Stoughton, 1999.

134. **conceived it in Dublin:** Michael Hayes interview with author, October 2021. In 1986, British press reports named Coogan as a suspect for the Brighton bomb, but he was never arrested or charged.

135. **Magee had surveilled:** Patrick Magee, *Where Grieving Begins: Building Bridges After the Brighton Bomb*, Pluto Press, 2021. Magee's memoir cites the surveillance of the Labour conference in Brighton without giving the date. In an interview with the author in March 2021, Magee said it was in the late 1970s. Asked if it was 1977, Magee appeared to assent, without explicitly saying yes. The author gave 1977 as the date in a *Guardian* article, "IRA Brighton Bomber 'Scouted Labour Conference Seven Years Earlier,'" March 15, 2021. Subsequently, another ex-IRA volunteer with insight into operations in England told the author the surveillance happened in 1979. Magee declined to elaborate. Since 1979 better fits the known timeline of Magee's activities in England, it is the date used in this book.

135. **pitched the proposal:** Hayes interview with author, October 2021.

136. **"spooked" by the furor:** Anthony McIntyre interview with author, September 2020.

136. **"'feasibility study'":** Hayes interview with author, October 2021.

136. **two scouts made a preliminary reconnaissance:** Patrick Bishop and Eamonn Mallie, *The Provisional IRA*, William Heinemann, 1987.

136. **code name: Lochinvar:** Hayes interview with author, October 2021.

CHAPTER NINE | BLACKPOOL

137. **Steve Atkinson, a rookie constable:** Steve Atkinson interview with author, March 2021.

137. **"It didn't make any sense":** Atkinson interview with author, March 2021.

138. **petty criminal called Raymond O'Connor:** "Detective Admits Informer Told Lies," *Irish Times*, September 20, 1986, https://www.irishtimes.com/newspaper/archive/1986/0920/Pg010.html#Ar01003.

138. **Maguire—who was later acquitted:** David Pallister, "Maguire Claims 'Set-Up' on Bomb Plot/ Irish Teacher Acquitted of Conspiracy with IRA's Patrick Magee," *The Guardian*, October 8, 1986.

138. **"given to the drink":** Alan Law, head of Lancashire Special Branch, quoted in "Detective Admits Informer Told Lies."

139. **secondary objective:** Michael Hayes interview with author, October 2021.

139. **Magee reckoned he was next:** Patrick Magee, *Where Grieving Begins: Building Bridges After the Brighton Bomb*, Pluto Press, 2021.

139. **"My life was too chaotic":** Magee, *Where Grieving Begins*.

140. **Murray a "classic sociopath":** Sean O'Callaghan, *The Informer: The Real Story of One Man's War Against Terrorism*, Bantam Press, 1998.

140. **Magee. "Highly intelligent":** O'Callaghan, *The Informer*.

140. **rendezvoused with Raymond O'Connor:** David Pallister, "Police 'Lost IRA Men in Chase,'" *The Guardian*, September 17, 1986.

140. **worked here as a waiter:** Magee, *Where Grieving Begins*.

140. **Hitler wanted an intact leisure town:** Mark Tran, "Hitler's Plans to Turn Blackpool into Nazi Resort Come to Light," *The Guardian*, February 23, 2009, https://www.theguardian.com/uk/2009/feb/23/hitler-blackpool-resort-plans.

140. **"Tories had much to answer":** Magee, *Where Grieving Begins*.

140. **O'Connor was the IRA team's fixer:** Pallister, "Police 'Lost IRA Men in Chase.'"

141. **redhead was "the minder":** Pallister, "Police 'Lost IRA Men in Chase.'"

141. **"bombing of Airey Neave?":** Pallister, "Police 'Lost IRA Men in Chase.'"

141. **April 16, the detectives sent their grainy:** David Pallister, "Maguire Claims 'Set-Up' on Bomb Plot/ Irish Teacher Acquitted of Conspiracy with IRA's Patrick Magee."

141. **had a manila folder on Magee:** Nick Davies, "The Foul-Ups and Loopholes Which Have Let IRA Bombers Go Free," *London Daily News*, June 24, 1987, https://www.nickdavies.net/1987/06/24/the-foul-ups-and-loopholes-which-have-let-ira-bombers-go-free/.

141. **On April 22, Magee and Murray:** Pallister, "Police 'Lost IRA Men in Chase.'"

142. **O'Connor was an agent provocateur:** Magee, *Where Grieving Begins*. Magee does not identify O'Connor by name.

142. **detectives hoped the suspects:** Ray Wilson and Ian Adams, *Metropolitan Special Branch: A History, 1883–2006*, Biteback, 2015.

143. **raced in pursuit:** Ian Henry, "Tip-Off 'Foiled IRA Bomb Plot in Britain,'" *Daily Telegraph*, September 17, 1986.

143. **"drew them away":** Patrick Magee interview with author, March 2021.

143. **windshield wipers going:** Magee interview with author, March 2021.

143. **fifteen minutes after:** Detective Chief Inspector Norman Finnerty, head of Lancashire CID, quoted in *Daily Telegraph* trial report, October 8, 1986.

143. **sold republican newspapers:** David Pallister, "Two Cleared of IRA Getaway: Magee's Helpers Did Not Know of Alleged Crime, Jury Accepts," *The Guardian*, October 16, 1986.

144. **jury later cleared Calvey and James:** Pallister, "Two Cleared of IRA Getaway."

144. **"my operational days were over":** Magee, *Where Grieving Begins*.

144. **"longest suicide note in history"**: Description by Labour MP Gerald Kaufman of his party's 1983 election manifesto, *The Guardian*, https://www.theguardian.com/politics/2017/feb/27/sir-gerald-kaufman-obituary.

145. **"prostrate before her"**: Charles Moore, *Margaret Thatcher: The Authorized Biography, Volume Two: Everything She Wants*, Allen Lane, 2015.

145. **"triumphalism horrified me"**: Peter Cropper quoted in Moore, *Margaret Thatcher*, vol. 2.

145. **"I have not long to go"**: Comment to John Coles, Thatcher's foreign affairs private secretary, quoted in Moore, *Margaret Thatcher*, vol. 2.

145. **"you people won the election"**: "History in the Making," *An Phoblacht/Republican News*, June 1983.

146. **Thatcher "to do something about Ireland"**: David Goodall, *The Making of the Anglo-Irish Agreement of 1985*, National University of Ireland, 2021, 5.

146. **to pitch Thatcher a radical idea**: Goodall, *The Making of the Anglo-Irish Agreement of 1985*.

146. **Five guards**: Ruan O'Donnell, *Special Category: The IRA in English Prisons*, vol. 2, Irish Academic Press, 2012.

146. *Andersonstown News*: O'Donnell, *Special Category*, vol. 2, 350.

CHAPTER TEN | SALCEY FOREST

148. **rake snagged on something**: Nick Davies, "How London Police Uncovered the IRA's Great Britain Brigade," *London Daily News*, June 23, 1987.

148. **bury weapons in the countryside**: Michael Hayes interview with author, October 2021.

149. **comprehensive collection of terrorist equipment**: Police cited in trial report of Kavanagh and Quigley, "Killers Trained to Hate," *Daily Mirror*, March 8, 1985.

149. **Gurney . . . aerial dogfight**: Peter Gurney interview with author, February 2021.

149. **detectives discovered that the car containing the Hyde Park bomb**: Davies, "How London Police Uncovered the IRA's Great Britain Brigade."

149. **"all about the chase"**: Davies, "How London Police Uncovered the IRA's Great Britain Brigade."

149. **"You had that little bit of power"**: Davies, "How London Police Uncovered the IRA's Great Britain Brigade."

149. **Regency furniture**: Nick Davies, "The Foul-Ups and Loopholes Which Have Let IRA Bombers Go Free," *London Daily News*, June 24, 1987, https://www.nickdavies.net/1987/06/24/the-foul-ups-and-loopholes-which-have-let-ira-bombers-go-free/.

150. **had tetchy relations with . . . the Special Branch**: Davies, "The Foul-Ups and Loopholes Which Have Let IRA Bombers Go Free."

150. **one frustrated spook told the journalist Nick Davies**: Davies, "The Foul-Ups and Loopholes Which Have Let IRA Bombers Go Free."

150. **"NKIL syndrome"**: Gareth Parry, "Why the 'Paddy Factor' Outwitted Police Security," *The Guardian*, October 14, 1984.

151. **"closest friend for twenty-five years, ma'am"**: Peter Gurney, *Braver Men Walk Away: Memoirs of the World's Top Bomb-Disposal Expert*, HarperCollins, 1993.

152. **"forensic Aladdin's cave"**: David Tadd interview with author, November 2021.

152. **only four scientists**: Davies, "The Foul-Ups and Loopholes Which Have Let IRA Bombers Go Free."

152. **"cradle to grave" protocols**: Tadd interview with author, November 2021.

152. **"didn't want to cock it up"**: Tadd interview with author, November 2021.

152. **spool of electrical cord**: Davies, "How London Police Uncovered the IRA's Great Britain Brigade."

152. **"light into these dark places"**: William Vernon Harcourt quoted in Ray Wilson and Ian Adams, *Metropolitan Special Branch: A History, 1883–2006*, Biteback, 2015.

153. **roster of potential candidates:** Hayes interview with author, October 2021.

153. **Downey . . . "blew" him in the press:** Davies, "The Foul-Ups and Loopholes Which Have Let IRA Bombers Go Free."

154. **Alighting from a taxi:** Ruan O'Donnell, *Special Category: The IRA in English Prisons*, vol. 2, Irish Academic Press, 2011.

154. **smuggled weapons in a trawler:** Davies, "How London Police Uncovered the IRA's Great Britain Brigade."

154. **Thatcher . . . outfits with Daphne Scrimgeour:** "MT Engagement Diary: Saturday, December 17, 1983," Margaret Thatcher Foundation, https://www.margaretthatcher.org/document/134670.

154. **playing for his beloved Nomads:** Tadd interview with author, November 2021.

154. **Gurney was driving home:** Gurney, *Braver Men Walk Away*.

154. **Officials notified Thatcher during a carol concert:** Margaret Thatcher, *Margaret Thatcher: The Autobiography*, Harper Press, 1993, 470–71.

155. **bags lay in the gutters:** Jon Nordheimer, "5 Killed in London as Bomb Explodes Outside Harrods," *New York Times*, December 18, 1983, https://www.nytimes.com/1983/12/18/world/5-killed-in -london-as-bomb-explodes-outside-harrods.html.

155. **The dusk was drenched in sweetness:** Gurney, *Braver Men Walk Away*.

155. **cloud of smoke boiling:** Nordheimer, "5 Killed in London as Bomb Explodes Outside Harrods."

155. **mother for a mannequin:** Gurney, *Braver Men Walk Away*.

155. **underpants adorned with a heart:** Gurney, *Braver Men Walk Away*.

155. *Who had she been, this girl?*: Gurney, *Braver Men Walk Away*.

155. **"car on top of a police sergeant":** Tadd interview with author, November 2021.

155. **Thatcher . . . saw the charred bodies:** Jonathan Aitken, *Margaret Thatcher: Power and Personality*, Bloomsbury, 2013, 410.

155. **"very evil people":** Thatcher quoted in Nordheimer, "5 Killed in London as Bomb Explodes Outside Harrods."

156. **"No damned Irishman":** Denis Thatcher quoted in Associated Press article, published in the *Montreal Gazette*, December 21, 1983.

156. **code-named Operation Abercorn:** Downing Street letter to Northern Ireland Office, December 20, 1983, National Archives, PREM 19/1547.

156. **medical team on standby:** Downing Street letter to Northern Ireland Office, December 20, 1983.

156. **One well-wisher, Mary Miller:** Miller quoted in Ric Clark, "Thatcher Pays Surprise Visit to Northern Ireland," UPI, December 23, 1983.

156. **"We're never, never":** Margaret Thatcher, "Remarks Visiting Northern Ireland," BBC Radio News Report 1800, Margaret Thatcher Foundation, December 23, 1983, https://www.margaretthatcher .org/document/105225.

156. **895 telexes, 3,060 phone messages:** Davies, "The Foul-Ups and Loopholes Which Have Let IRA Bombers Go Free."

157. **all they got was encouragement:** Davies, "The Foul-Ups and Loopholes Which Have Let IRA Bombers Go Free."

157. **"Years later, police briefed journalists":** In June 1987 the journalist Nick Davies, writing in the *London Daily News*, named John Connolly and Paul Kavanagh as prime suspects for the Harrods bombing. Davies cited Scotland Yard's Anti-Terrorist Branch. Article reprinted in https://www.nickdavies.net /1987/06/20/naming-the-prime-suspect-for-the-harrods-christmas-bombing/.

157. **bungled warning:** Kevin Toolis, *Rebel Hearts: Journeys Within the IRA's Soul*, St. Martin's Griffin, 1997, 279.

157. **"The Harrods operation":** IRA statement reprinted in *The Irish Times*, December 19, 1983.

158. **Gardaí . . . told Scotland Yard's Special Branch:** Wilson and Adams, *Metropolitan Special Branch*, 335.

158. **Eyes followed them, every step:** Davies, "The Foul-Ups and Loopholes Which Have Let IRA Bombers Go Free."

158. **not invisible, simply not memorable:** Former Special Branch surveillance specialist interview with author, 2020.

158. **He wore purple:** Davies, "The Foul-Ups and Loopholes Which Have Let IRA Bombers Go Free."

158. **At 2:15 p.m. he entered:** Davies, "The Foul-Ups and Loopholes Which Have Let IRA Bombers Go Free."

158. **It was 9:20 a.m.:** Davies, "The Foul-Ups and Loopholes Which Have Let IRA Bombers Go Free."

159. **did not recognize Kavanagh:** Wilson and Adams, *Metropolitan Special Branch*, 335.

159. **trekked into woodland:** Davies, "The Foul-Ups and Loopholes Which Have Let IRA Bombers Go Free."

159. **Belper, a milk tanker:** Davies, "The Foul-Ups and Loopholes Which Have Let IRA Bombers Go Free."

160. **"hadn't got the faintest idea":** Davies, "The Foul-Ups and Loopholes Which Have Let IRA Bombers Go Free."

160. **building a new kitchen:** Tadd interview with author, November 2021.

160. **Gurney, wearing boots:** Gurney interview with author, February 2021.

160. **laid on a white sheet:** Northamptonshire Police evidence exhibit photos from Salcey Forest, courtesy of Old Police Cells Museum, Brighton.

160. **timers had markings:** Gurney interview with author, February 2021.

160. **5L, 53E, 35E, 63E:** Gurney interview with author, February 2021.

160. **visit his native Belfast:** Davies, "The Foul-Ups and Loopholes Which Have Let IRA Bombers Go Free."

161. **RUC spotted and arrested him:** Davies, "The Foul-Ups and Loopholes Which Have Let IRA Bombers Go Free."

161. **Number 4 was missing:** Gurney interview with author, February 2021.

CHAPTER ELEVEN | TIGHTROPE

162. **"I was unsettled, a familiar feeling":** Gerry Adams, *A Farther Shore: Ireland's Long Road to Peace*, Random House, 2005, 23.

163. **"Gerry Adams will be next":** UVF informer Joe Bennett attributed this comment to UVF commander John Wilson in David Sharrock and Mark Devenport, *Man of War, Man of Peace? The Unauthorized Biography of Gerry Adams*, Macmillan, 1997, 220.

163. **included immolation in the bomb:** Brian Rowan, "UVF Sinn Féin Massacre Plot," *Belfast Telegraph*, July 4, 2008.

163. **magazine ran a "wanted" picture:** Sharrock and Devenport, *Man of War, Man of Peace?*

163. **purportedly from a policeman's father:** Sharrock and Devenport, *Man of War, Man of Peace?*, 220.

163. **90 percent chance he would be killed:** Sharrock and Devenport, *Man of War, Man of Peace?*, 220.

163. **"I have been involved in republican politics a long time":** Sharrock and Devenport, *Man of War, Man of Peace?*, 221.

163. **carrying a toothbrush:** Sharrock and Devenport, *Man of War, Man of Peace?*, 220.

163. **Magistrate Tom Travers. Mutual contempt:** Malachi O'Doherty, *Gerry Adams: An Unauthorized Life*, Faber & Faber, 2017, 178.

164. **loyalist snoop:** Colm Keena, *Gerry Adams: A Biography*, Mercier Press, 1990, 118.

164. **"In the enemy territory of the court building":** Adams, *A Farther Shore*.

164. **lingered in the big hall:** Sharrock and Devenport, *Man of War, Man of Peace?*

164. **They looked left and right:** Bob Murray quoted in *An Phoblacht/Republican News*, March 16, 1984.

164. **waiting gold-colored Cortina:** Murray quoted in *An Phoblacht/Republican News*.

164. **right on May Street:** Murray quoted in *An Phoblacht/Republican News*.

164. **occupants began to relax:** Gerry Adams quoted in Sharrock and Devenport, *Man of War, Man of Peace?*

164. **brown Rover 2000:** "No Evidence of Police Involvement in the Attempted Murder of Gerry Adams," Police Ombudsman for Northern Ireland, June 19, 2014, https://www.policeombudsman.org /Investigation-Reports/Historical-Reports/%E2%80%98No-evidence-of-police-involvement -in-the-attempte.

165. **"If we do not defeat":** Quoted in "Thatcher in and out on Whirlwind Tour of North," *Irish News,* August 30, 1979; see also chapter 2.

165. **heckler's warning about the H-Blocks:** "Harriet Kelly Challenges Maggie Thatcher," video, Gael Force Art, uploaded April 9, 2013, https://www.facebook.com/watch/?v=164070757085786; see also chapter 2.

165. **1982 memoir,** *Falls Memories:* Gerry Adams, *Falls Memories,* Brandon, 1982.

165. **biographer, Malachi O'Doherty:** O'Doherty, *Gerry Adams.*

165. **"sort of combat that suits him":** O'Doherty, *Gerry Adams.*

166. **"struggle for socialism in Britain":** Gerry Adams quoted in "The Honorable Member for Belfast West," *World in Action,* season 20, episode 11, Granada, December 19, 1983.

166. **"specific knowledge of military acts":** Adams quoted in "The Honorable Member for Belfast West."

166. **"Never showed his hand":** Patrick Bishop and Eamonn Mallie, *The Provisional IRA,* William Heinemann, 1987.

166. **regret for the civilian casualties:** Jon Nordheimer, "Harrods Reopens as London Mobilizes," *New York Times,* December 20, 1983, https://www.nytimes.com/1983/12/20/world/harrods-reopens-as-london -mobilizes.html.

167. **through a red light:** "No Evidence of Police Involvement in the Attempted Murder of Gerry Adams," 19.

167. **he had been chief of staff:** December 1977–February 1978. Ed Moloney, *A Secret History of the IRA,* Penguin Press, 2002.

167. **stood down from direct military roles:** Moloney, *A Secret History of the IRA.*

167. **remain on the seven-member Army Council:** Moloney, *A Secret History of the IRA.*

167. **shrunk to about 250:** Patrick Bishop and Eamonn Mallie, *The Provisional IRA,* William Heinemann, 1987, chap. 21.

168. **£2,500 a week to finance:** Bishop and Mallie, *The Provisional IRA,* chap. 21.

168. **£1 million alone for the 1983 election:** Bishop and Mallie, *The Provisional IRA,* chap. 21.

168. **Adams had recently visited to support . . . Sherry:** "Belfast and Dungannon By-Elections Campaigns in Top Gear."

168. **Armalite Kid:** Author interviews with Peter Sherry and ex–Ulster Defence Regiment personnel, 2021.

168. **bus shelters and fixing safety hazards:** Eamon Tracey, "Belfast and Dungannon By-Elections Campaigns in Top Gear," *An Phoblacht/Republican News,* March 16, 1984.

168. **eleven of the IRA's ninety-five kills:** Moloney, *A Secret History of the IRA.*

168. **shaken his fist when he saw the unit:** Liam Clarke, *Broadening the Battlefield: H-Blocks and the Rise of Sinn Féin,* Irish Books & Media, 1987, 227.

168. **Ivor Bell . . . suspected that Adams:** Moloney, *A Secret History of the IRA.*

168. **muster a 4–3 majority:** Moloney, *A Secret History of the IRA.*

168. **Shergar—had undermined Bell's authority:** Moloney, *A Secret History of the IRA.*

168. **.45 Colt and a Walther P38:** "No Evidence of Police Involvement in the Attempted Murder of Gerry Adams."

169. **"I felt the thumps and thuds":** Adams, *A Farther Shore,* 24.

169. *Jesus, Mary, and Joseph:* Adams, *A Farther Shore,* 24.

169. **Act of Contrition to Sean Keenan:** Keena, *Gerry Adams,* 117.

169. **Murray ran into the emergency:** Keena, *Gerry Adams,* 117.

170. **"a miraculous escape"**: Gerry Adams radio interview after the shooting. Adams, interviewed by Eamonn Mallie for Downtown Radio, a Belfast station, March 4, 1984.

170. **"reap what you sow"**: Ian Paisley quoted in Sharrock and Devenport, *Man of War, Man of Peace?*, 224.

170. **"her gentle heart pouring its pure blood"**: Tom Travers letter to the *Irish Times*, 1994. Author interview with Ann Travers, daughter of Tom Travers, in 2021.

171. **missed a fourth bullet**: Keena, *Gerry Adams*, 117, 118.

171. **copper jacket had fractured**: Keena, *Gerry Adams*, 118.

171. **Kevin McKenna, a gruff, monosyllabic**: Sean O'Callaghan, *The Informer: The Real Story of One Man's War Against Terrorism*, Bantam Press, 1998.

171. **"We knew she would be doing her speech"**: Michael Hayes interview with author, October 2021.

171. **"bring down the roof"**: Hayes interview with author, October 2021.

172. **worried killing Thatcher would leave them forever hunted**: Author interview with ex-IRA volunteer.

173. **alternatives to violence with a Belfast priest, Alec Reid**: Moloney, *A Secret History of the IRA*.

CHAPTER TWELVE | ROOM 629

174. **visit in 1979 to surveil the Labour Party Conference**: Patrick Magee, *Where Grieving Begins: Building Bridges After the Brighton Bomb*, Pluto Press, 2021.

174. **exuberant man named Dennis Palmer**: Dennis Palmer interviewed in *To Kill the Cabinet*, documentary, BBC1, 1986.

175. **Bookies were slashing odds**: "Hooray for New Prince," *Belfast News-Letter*, September 17, 1984.

175. **peeled off their jackets**: "Hooray for New Prince."

176. **"hold on to your nuts"**: Palmer interviewed in *To Kill the Cabinet*.

176. **sidelined him in Dublin**: Magee, *Where Grieving Begins;* see also chapter 9 regarding Blackpool.

176. **confined to logistical support**: Magee, *Where Grieving Begins.*

176. **supply chain, one of perhaps thirty people**: "There would maybe have been about thirty people involved in the Brighton bomb in 1984." Bradley quoted in Gerry Bradley with Brian Feeney, *Insider: Gerry Bradley's Life in the IRA*, O'Brien Press, 2009, 297.

176. **spoke of the operation in hushed tones**: Author interview with ex-IRA volunteer who served in the England Department.

176. **"A series of setbacks"**: Magee, *Where Grieving Begins.*

177. **home for Emperor Louis Napoleon III**: Essay by John Montgomery, "Down Memory Lane: The Grand Hotel, Brighton," undated, the Keep archives, Brighton.

177. **rogues' gallery of royalty**: Photographs of the Grand Hotel, the Keep archives, Brighton.

177. **no reservation but . . . had confirmed availability**: Patrick Magee interview with author, March 2021. Michael Hayes interview with author, October 2021.

177. **identified a short list of acceptable rooms**: Hayes interview with author, October 2021.

178. **"could have changed it but it suited"**: Magee interview with author, March 2021.

178. **Walsh**: "Walsh Family History," Ancestry.co.uk, https://www.ancestry.co.uk/name-origin?surname=walsh.

178. **million UK census records**: "Walsh Family History."

178. **"For some extraordinary reason"**: Hayes interview with author, October 2021.

179. **psychics and palm readers**: "Psychics & Mystics Exhibition and Conference, with Palmistry, at Hove Town Hall, 11am–7pm, 15–16 September," advert in the *Evening Argus*, September 15, 1984.

179. **Joe Cahill, itemizing the movement's every cent**: See chapter 7, "Friends."

179. **key with a metal fob**: Author interview with Richard Baker, general manager of the Grand, 1984–2004.

179. **pounded the steel hull of the *Valhalla***: Patrick Nee, Richard Farrell, and Michael Blythe, *A Criminal and an Irishman: The Inside Story of the Boston Mob*, Steerforth Press, 2006, 184.

179. **"How great is this?" he had murmured**: Kevin Cullen and Shelley Murphy, *Whitey Bulger: America's Most Wanted Gangster and the Manhunt That Brought Him to Justice*, W. W. Norton, 2013, 254.

179. **Cahill's heartfelt appeal at the Triple O**: See chapter 7, "Friends."

180. **"status symbol to have one of your guns on the *Valhalla*"**: Patrick Nee quoted in Cullen and Murphy, *Whitey Bulger*, 254.

180. **a historic act of charity for the old country**: Nee et al., *A Criminal and an Irishman*.

180. **decor had a dated look**: Baker interview with author.

180. **former manager later confided, was "tired"**: Baker interview with author.

180. **At 12:55 p.m., he appeared in the restaurant**: Sussex Police confidential timeline of "Roy Walsh" stay at the Grand Hotel, internal document shared after bomb, October 1984, courtesy of Old Police Cells Museum, Brighton.

180. **glass of milk and a cup of tea**: Sussex Police confidential timeline, October 1984.

180. **Magee refers to "we"**: Magee interview with author, March 2021.

181. **two female couriers, elegantly dressed**: Hayes interview with author, October 2021.

181. **did not stay overnight**: Only one bed slept in according to Sussex Police confidential timeline, October 1984.

181. **"To be certain of killing Thatcher"**: Magee, *Where Grieving Begins*.

181. **missing from the Salcey Forest cache**: See chapter 10, "Salcey Forest."

181. **bomb maker in Ireland had made the TPU's integrated circuits**: Hayes interview with author, October 2021.

181. **device had at least two timers**: Dr. Thomas Hayes of RARDE quoted in trial report, *Irish Times*, May 13, 1986.

181. **Patrick Ryan's shopping expeditions in Zurich**: See chapter 7, "Friends." An unrepentant Ryan admitted to the BBC in 2019 that he had supplied bomb parts for Brighton and other IRA attacks. "I regret that I wasn't even more effective." Julian O'Neill, "IRA Brighton Bomb: Patrick Ryan Admits Link to 1984 Attack," BBC News, September 24, 2019, https://www.bbc.com/news/uk-northern -ireland-49797327.

182. **method with the "blowy stuff"**: See chapter 3, "The Chancer"; Bradley with Feeney, *Insider*.

182. **to-do list, *always* draw diagrams**: Magee, *Where Grieving Begins*.

182. **Magee had shadowed Roy Mason**: Magee, *Where Grieving Begins*.

183. **"The enormity of it"**: Magee interview with author, March 2021.

183. **twenty arrests**: Philip Mills, "Gang of Soccer Fans Are Blamed for Fight," *Evening Argus*, September 17, 1984.

183. **Karl-Friedrich Merten**: "U-Boat Skipper Meets Victims," *Belfast News-Letter*, September 15, 1984, 7.

183. **a guest paid a photographer to take erotic portraits**: Author interview with Jacqueline Shevlin, daughter of O'Byrne, 2021.

184. **Paul Boswell, had a daily ritual**: Author interview with Richard Baker, general manager of the Grand Hotel, 1984–2004, in June 2021.

184. **"They're here," before taking the platter**: David Briffett, *Sussex Murders: County Murders and Mysteries*, Ensign, 1990, 141.

184. **To avoid "gelly headache"**: Gelignite odor caused headaches, see chapter 3, "The Chancer."

184. **tea and sandwiches**: Sussex Police confidential timeline, October 1984.

184. **"There was a voice"**: Pamela Plappert interview with Peter Taylor in *The Brighton Bomb: The Hunt for the Bomber*, BBC1, September 14, 2004.

184. **occupation of a runway at a US air base**: "Protestors Invade US Air Base," *Evening Argus*, September 17, 1984.

185. **In Derry, an IRA unit**: "IRA War News: Crossmaglen Culvert Bomb/Derry Telecom Attack," *An Phoblacht/Republican News*, September 20, 1984.

185. lead story in Brighton's local newspaper: Philip Mills, "Buried in Trap of Terror: Ordeal After Wall Collapsed," *Evening Argus*, September 17, 1984, 1.

185. Dutch prison reveries: See chapter 4, "Hunger"; Magee, *Where Grieving Begins*.

186. "target those we deemed most culpable": Patrick Magee interviewed on "The 'Brighton Bomber' Who Befriended the Daughter of the Man He Killed," Owen Jones Podcast, February 16, 2021, https://podcasts.apple.com/gb/podcast/25-brighton-bomber-who-befriended-daughter-man-he-killed/id1550331378?i=1000509193447.

186. wait another hour for the circuits: Briffett, *Sussex Murders*, 143.

186. Thatcher . . . supper in her flat: "MT Engagement Diary: Monday, September 17, 1984," Margaret Thatcher Foundation, https://www.margaretthatcher.org/document/147320.

186. "you don't dwell on it": Patrick Magee interview with Peter Taylor in *The Brighton Bomb: The Hunt for the Bomber*, documentary, BBC1, September 14, 2004.

186. bar charged per nip: Baker interview with author.

186. "We were still undercover": Magee interview with author, March 2021.

187. Only one bed had been slept in: Sussex Police confidential timeline, October 1984.

CHAPTER THIRTEEN | CLOCKWORK

188. Daimler shortly before 9:00 a.m.: "MT Engagement Diary: Tuesday, October 9, 1984," Margaret Thatcher Foundation, https://www.margaretthatcher.org/document/147342.

188. Yeomen of the Guard: "State Opening: Elements Unseen by the Public," UK Parliament, https://www.parliament.uk/about/living-heritage/evolutionofparliament/parliamentwork/offices-and-ceremonies/overview/state-opening/elements-unseen-by-the-public/.

188. symbolic search of the cellars: "The Ceremonial Search of the Cellars of the Palace of Westminster Is Conducted Ahead of the State Opening of Parliament," BBC Politics video, Twitter, December 19, 2019, https://twitter.com/bbcpolitics/status/1207612886530420736.

189. check sewers and service tunnels: Patrick Bishop and Eamonn Mallie, *The Provisional IRA*, William Heinemann, 1987, 337.

189. trimmed the interior, but stained easily: National Archives, cited in Owen Bowcott, "PMs' Cars: Thatcher Liked to Doze and Major Wanted More Leg Room," *The Guardian*, July 24, 2018, https://www.theguardian.com/politics/2018/jul/24/pms-cars-margaret-thatcher-liked-to-doze-and-john-major-wanted-more-leg-room.

189. bodyguards fretted about whiplash: Bob Kingston memo in National Archives, cited in Bowcott, "PMs' Cars."

189. vitamin B_{12} injections: Former aide Cynthia Crawford quoted in ITV documentary, cited in Steven Morris, "Whisky and B_{12} Shots Fortified Iron Lady," *The Guardian*, February 23, 2003, https://www.theguardian.com/politics/2003/feb/24/health.conservatives.

189. John Hester, opened proceedings: Conservative Party Conference program, October 9–12, 1984.

190. "Hilda," an old snickering tilt: See chapter 2, "The Friendly Skies of South Armagh"; Matthew Parris, a Conservative Party researcher and MP, interview in *Maggie: The First Lady*, documentary, ITV, March 2003. "The nickname that we all used for her was Hilda and it was not meant kindly."

190. speech . . . had to encapsulate its spirit: Margaret Thatcher, *Margaret Thatcher: The Autobiography*, HarperPress, 1993, 458. "You need to get the feel of the conference to achieve the right tone."

190. "on the boil, like some terrible peasant stew": Simon Hoggart, "The Fall-Out the Bomb Left Behind," *The Observer*, October 14, 1984.

190. recalled John Whittingdale: Former member of the Conservative Research Department, quoted in Brenda Maddox, *Maggie: The First Lady*, Hodder & Stoughton, 2003.

191. reflected in songs like "Gold" by Spandau Ballet: Michael Hann, "Spandau Ballet: The Sound of Thatcherism," *The Guardian*, March 25, 2009, https://www.theguardian.com/music/musicblog/2009/mar/25/spandau-ballet-thatcherism.

191. **new wave of shiny, aspirational pop music:** British music critic Stuart Maconie quoted in "The Thatcher Era's Effect on British Music," NPR Music, April 12, 2013, https://www.npr.org/2013/04/12/176952013/the-thatcher-eras-effect-on-british-music.

191. **Norman Tebbit—"on your bike":** Norman Tebbit, *Upwardly Mobile: An Autobiography*, Weidenfeld & Nicolson, 1988.

191. **Penny Rimbaud, of the punk band Crass:** Quoted in Dorian Lynskey, "Margaret Thatcher: The Villain of Political Pop," *The Guardian*, April 8, 2013, https://www.theguardian.com/music/musicblog/2013/apr/08/margaret-thatcher-pop-rock-music.

191. **worried about ideological zealotry:** Hoggart, "The Fall-Out the Bomb Left Behind."

191. **Jack Foster, an *Evening Argus* columnist:** Jack Foster, *Evening Argus*, October 5, 1984.

192. **draft speech . . . "enemy within":** "The Speech That Never Was—Thatcher Papers for 1984 Open to the Public," University of Cambridge, https://www.cam.ac.uk/research/news/the-speech-that-never-was-thatcher-papers-for-1984-open-to-the-public.

192. **roadworks near Pyecombe:** "All Quiet as Maggie Sweeps into Town," *Evening Argus*, October 9, 1984.

192. **instinctive distrust of the Irish:** David Goodall, *The Making of the Anglo-Irish Agreement of 1985*, National University of Ireland, 2021.

193. **drawn from an antique tombola:** *The Brighton Bomb*, part 1, documentary, BBC1, September 14, 2004.

194. **secure telegram to the UK's fifty-two chief constables:** Telegram supplied by Nick Davies, former journalist with the *London Daily News* and *The Guardian*, https://www.nickdavies.net/.

195. **Roger Birch . . . designed his strategy for the week:** Roger Birch interview with author, February 2021.

195. **color code for passes, red:** Conservative Party Conference program, October 9–12, 1984.

195. **"They didn't shut it down or anything":** Transcript of interview with officer, name withheld, supplied by Steve Ramsey, author of *Something Has Gone Wrong: Dealing with the Brighton Bomb*, Biteback, 2018.

195. **Met's close protection unit, were inside the Grand:** Report by Chief Constable Roger Birch to Sussex Police Authority, January 21, 1985.

196. **Loews Anatole hotel were awoken at 7:00 a.m.:** Jon Connell, "How They Protect the President," *Sunday Times*, October 14, 1984.

196. **Ministry of Defence's prophetic 1979 assessment:** See chapter 6, "The Bomb Burglar and Mr. T"; Ministry of Defence report cited in "The Brighton Bomber," *World in Action*, documentary series, ITV, June 11, 1986.

196. **"Such a system is very accurate":** British army report cited in *"The Brighton Bomber," World in Action*, documentary series, ITV, June 11, 1986.

196. **MI5 would later assert:** Christopher Andrew, *The Defence of the Realm: The Authorized History of MI5*, Allen Lane, 2009, 706, fn 135, "Recollections of Sir Stephen Lander." "For several years, the security service had been reporting intelligence that PIRA intended to bomb one of the annual Tory conferences—although the fact that no attempt was made until 1984 may have damaged the credibility of these warnings."

197. **daring to relax, just a little:** Harvey Thomas interview with author, August 2020.

197. **grandees grumbled at radical innovations:** Harvey Thomas with Judith Gunn, *In the Face of Fear*, Marshall, Morgan & Scott, 1985.

197. **still looked pink and portly:** Adam Trimingham's conference diary, *Evening Argus*, October 9, 1984.

198. **"You look gorgeous," gushed the mayor:** Adam Trimingham's conference diary, *Evening Argus*, October 10, 1984.

198. **threw a stink bomb:** "Stink Bomb Thrown in Monday Club Protest," *Evening Argus*, October 11, 1984.

198. **Thomas had snaffled one for himself:** Thomas interview with Peter Taylor, *The Brighton Bomb*, part 1, documentary, BBC1, September 14, 2004.

199. **Ivor Humphrey, a fifty-seven-year-old sales executive:** "No Sign of Dole Pity," *Evening Argus*, October 11, 1984.

199.   **mugger had stabbed Michael Keith Smith:** "Knife Thug Stabs Tory," *Evening Argus,* October 11, 1984.

199.   **fumed an organizer:** Kevin Williams quoted in "Maggie Slips Past Demo," *Evening Argus*, October 11, 1984.

199.   **semi-house-trained polecat:** Description of Tebbit by Labour leader Michael Foot in the House of Commons, March 2, 1978.

200.   **Tebbit the darling of the 101st conference:** Frank Johnson, *Times* columnist: "Mr. Tebbit became Darling at a simple ceremony involving his receiving a longer standing ovation than Mr. Heseltine the previous day," October 12, 1984, quoted in Tebbit, *Upwardly Mobile.*

200.   **speculation that he was Thatcher's heir:** See end of chapter 9, "Blackpool."

200.   **books, which he devoured:** Norman Tebbit interview with author, August 2020.

201.   **connived to bloat and featherbed:** Tebbit, *Upwardly Mobile.*

201.   **"Heard a chap on the radio":** Macmillan reportedly made the remark to friends at his gentlemen's club, Pratt's. In Chris Moncrieff, "When Labour MPs Wore Miners' Helmets," *The Guardian*, May 10, 2001, https://www.theguardian.com/politics/2001/may/10/redbox.houseofcommons.

201.   **"a rather warm glow inside you":** Tebbit interviewed in "The Brighton Bomb," *Secret History* documentary series, Channel 4, May 15, 2003.

201.   **felt duty bound to better it:** Robin Butler, cabinet private secretary, interview with author, April 2021.

201.   **love "sort of crept on us":** Margaret Tebbit interview on *Desert Island Discs*, BBC Radio 4, July 5, 1996.

201.   **Postnatal depression consumed her:** Tebbit, *Upwardly Mobile.*

202.   **grandparents and acquired a country retreat:** Tebbit, *Upwardly Mobile.*

202.   **Lest the press depict it as a snub:** Tebbit, *Upwardly Mobile*, 225.

202.   **had earlier hosted cockroaches:** Maria Pali, Top Rank cleaner, interview with author, July 2021.

203.   **Tebbits . . . chat to John Cole:** Tebbit, *Upwardly Mobile.*

203.   **climbing into bed around 2:30 a.m.:** Sarah Berry interview with Peter Taylor, *The Brighton Bomb*, part 1, documentary, BBC1, September 14, 2004.

204.   **Roberta, a vivacious personality:** Valerie Elliott, "Mrs. Roberta Wakeham, Lively and Devoted Supporter," *Daily Telegraph*, October 13, 1984.

204.   **Gordon and Jeanne Shattock:** Mark Elsdon-Dew, "The Lives That Were Shattered One Year Ago This Week," *Sunday Express*, October 6, 1985.

204.   **220 residents, 32 visitors, 11 staff:** Report by Chief Constable Roger Birch to Sussex Police Authority, January 21, 1985.

204.   **Magee . . . remote part of Cork:** Patrick Magee interview with author, March 2021.

205.   **bar napkin, he had sketched the Grand's facade:** Patrick Magee, *Where Grieving Begins: Building Bridges After the Brighton Bomb*, Pluto Press, 2021, 119.

205.   **Army Council had considered putting all volunteers:** IRA source to Ed Moloney, related to author in September 2021.

205.   **Thatcher . . . just approved final amendments:** Margaret Thatcher, *Margaret Thatcher: The Autobiography*, HarperPress, 1993.

206.   **Butler nodded. Of course she would:** Butler interview with author, April 2021.

CHAPTER FOURTEEN | A WHITE LIGHT

207.   **a few fishermen standing in the surf:** Author interview with Anthony Brooks, who was fishing for bass near the Grand when the bomb exploded, via Facebook, July 2021.

207.   **manager from the Pink Coconut nightclub:** Author interview with Lesley Brett, Pink Coconut's sales promotions manager, August 2021.

207.   **A police transit van, a rattling old Bedford:** From transcript of Steve Ramsey interview with police constable Paul Parton for Ramsey's *Something Has Gone Wrong: Dealing with the Brighton Bomb*, Biteback, 2018.

207. Bradford, in tuxedos and gowns: "To Kill the Cabinet," forty-page supplement, *Evening Argus*, December 3, 1984.

208. taxi back to the hotel of Richard Whitely: Richard Whitely interview with Peter Taylor, *The Brighton Bomb, part 1*, documentary, BBC1, September 14, 2004.

208. dazzling and blurring the surveillance camera: Tim Miles, "A White Flash—Then a Fireball," *Daily Mail*, October 15, 1984, 2.

208. Donald and Muriel Maclean: Michael McCarthy, "The Black Night When Terror Ripped a Happy World Apart," London *Times*, June 12, 1986.

208. Jeanne Shattock, age fifty-five: The opinion of Dr. Ian West, a pathologist who examined Shattock's body, quoted in "Horror of the Blast Injuries," *Daily Mirror*, and other press reports during trial of Patrick Magee, May 8, 1986.

208. She was decapitated: "Victim Inches from the Bomb," *Belfast Telegraph*, October 15, 1984.

208. Gordon Shattock glimpsed the flash: "Horror of the Blast Injuries," *Daily Mirror*.

208. Harvey Thomas . . . dreaming about asteroids: From transcript of Steve Ramsey interview with Thomas for Ramsey's *Something Has Gone Wrong*.

209. "I started to fall into a pit": Gordon Shattock testimony during Patrick Magee trial; David Williams, "IRA Plotted a Blitz on Seaside Britain," *Daily Mail*, May 8, 1986.

209. "It's a bomb," he shouted: Norman Tebbit interview with author, August 2020.

209. "I think you ought to come away from the window": Robin Butler interview with author, April 2021.

210. "I've never seen so much glass in my life": Jonathan Aitken, *Margaret Thatcher: Power and Personality*, Bloomsbury, 2013, 411.

210. "I think that was an assassination attempt, don't you?": Aitken, *Margaret Thatcher*.

212. attorney general would probably have designated Willie Whitelaw: Ronald Butt, "If the Bomb Had Found Its Target," London *Times*, October 18, 1984.

212. "Thank God you're all right": Michael Alison quoted in Aitken, *Margaret Thatcher*, 411, fn 18 and 19.

213. "Someone's broken a fire alarm to get Maggie out of bed": Fred Bishop, recalling an unnamed colleague's comment in *The Brighton Bomb: The Hunt for the Bomber*, BBC1, September 14, 2004.

213. discommoded the higher-ups: From transcript of Steve Ramsey interview with Bishop for *Something Has Gone Wrong*.

213. "Here, it's suddenly got misty": From transcript of Steve Ramsey interview with Bishop for *Something Has Gone Wrong*.

213. "The dust was so thick it looked like Sleeping Beauty": Pauline Banks, head telephonist, quoted in Angelique Chrisafis, "Regret but No Remorse, as Brighton Bomber Returns to Resort 20 Years On," *The Guardian*, October 12, 2004, https://www.theguardian.com/uk/2004/oct/12/northernireland .terrorism.

213. "you could hear crashes of masonry and metal": Brett interview with author.

213. "Um, it just went bang": Fred Bishop recalling policeman's comment in Ramsey, *Something Has Gone Wrong*.

214. "Everyone said, 'Well, if you're going in'": Fred Bishop quoted in "The Brighton Bomb," *Extreme Rescues* documentary series, ITV, October 16, 2007.

215. "Good morning, I'm delighted to see you": Thatcher quoted by Patrick Bishop et al., *Sunday Times*, October 14, 1984, 18.

215. "But you didn't say it back to her, obviously": From transcript of Steve Ramsey interview with Bishop for *Something Has Gone Wrong*.

215. making Thatcher cough: Aitken, *Margaret Thatcher*, 411.

215. nurses who had been at a dinner: From transcript of Steve Ramsey interview with Constable Simon Parr for *Something Has Gone Wrong*.

215. "'We're cold, we're cold'": From transcript of Steve Ramsey interview with Ivor Gaber for *Something Has Gone Wrong*.

216. **rumor spread that Thatcher was dead:** Aitken, *Margaret Thatcher*, 411.

216. **"It still never occurred to me that anyone would have died":** Margaret Thatcher, *Margaret Thatcher: The Autobiography*, HarperPress, 1993.

217. **Norman called for his wife:** Norman Tebbit, *Upwardly Mobile: An Autobiography*, Weidenfeld & Nicolson, 1988.

217. **photographer captured the moment:** The photographer was John Downing.

217. **"The IRA, those bastards":** Thatcher's driver, Denis Oliver, quoting Denis in *The Brighton Bomb*, pt. 1.

218. **"like a battleship":** Superintendent Dennis Williams cited in Jonathan Buss, *Paths of Political and Personal Conflict Resolution After the Brighton Bomb 1984*, Bachelor of Arts history thesis, University Campus Suffolk, May 9, 2016. Buss was a crime correspondent of the *Evening Argus* in 1984.

218. **US ambassador, Charles Price, was shoeless:** Thatcher, *Margaret Thatcher*.

218. **"You people, come in here out of the way":** "To Kill the Cabinet," 15.

218. **With a glint in her eye, she told a police officer:** "To Kill the Cabinet," 15.

218. **"Gentlemen, I have sat here listening to this discussion":** Recollection of Sir Andrew Bowden, Conservative MP, quoted in "The Day the Grand Was Bombed," *Evening Argus*, October 12, 2014, https://www.theargus.co.uk/news/11529122.the-day-the-grand-was-bombed/.

218. **climb out again to ask Cole if he needed another take:** BBC producer Ivor Gaber, interview with Ramsey, *Something Has Gone Wrong*.

219. **"Maggie's safe!":** Aitken, *Margaret Thatcher*.

219. **"Get out!" one government figure shouted:** Ramsey, *Something Has Gone Wrong*.

220. **"I'm having your guts for garters":** Fred Bishop, quoted in Ramsey transcripts, *Something Has Gone Wrong*.

220. **building surveyor arrived:** Fireman Peter Rodgers and police officer Alan Burt, quoted in Ramsey transcripts, *Something Has Gone Wrong*.

220. **"Where's Eric?" sobbed Jennifer:** Stephen White and Graham Barnes, "Haunted by Horror—The Tories Who Cannot Forget Brighton," *Daily Mirror*, October 7, 1988.

220. **"Hilp! Hilp!":** Harvey Thomas interview with author, August 2020.

221. **"If we'd realized what you weighed":** *The Brighton Bomb*, pt. 1.

221. **Chris Reid:** *The Brighton Bomb*, pt. 1.

221. **A pause . . . "Lady Berry":** *The Brighton Bomb*, pt. 1.

222. **three hands poking out:** "To Kill the Cabinet," 23.

222. **could hear his guts sloshing:** Tebbit, *Upwardly Mobile*.

222. **Norman shushed her. "Wait until":** Tebbit, *Upwardly Mobile*.

222. **"So this is death," he thought:** Tebbit, *Upwardly Mobile*.

222. **An unseen hand gripped his:** "To Kill the Cabinet," 23. Leading fireman Steve Tomlin was the first to reach the Tebbits.

223. *He knows the truth,* **thought Margaret:** Fred Bishop citing conversation with Margaret Tebbit years after the rescue in Ramsey, *Something Has Gone Wrong*. "She said I knew you knew, as soon as you put that collar round my neck."

223. **cracks a joke. Absolutely incredible:** Bishop citing conversation with Margaret Tebbit in Ramsey, *Something Has Gone Wrong*.

223. **"Margaret's fine," lied Bishop:** Bishop citing conversation with Margaret Tebbit in Ramsey, *Something Has Gone Wrong*.

224. **Colleagues thought him mad:** Fireman Paul Robb cited in Ramsey, *Something Has Gone Wrong*.

224. **"That was bloody marvelous":** Norman Tebbit quoted by Patrick Bishop et al., *Sunday Times*, October 14, 1984, 18.

225. **Patrick Magee remained awake:** Patrick Magee, *Where Grieving Begins: Building Bridges After the Brighton Bomb*, Pluto Press, 2021.

225. **Relief washed over Magee:** Magee, *Where Grieving Begins*.

226. **automated wake-up calls:** Pauline Banks, head telephonist, quoted in Chrisafis, "Regret but No Remorse, as Brighton Bomber Returns to Resort 20 Years On."

226. **Pauline Banks, the head telephonist:** Banks quoted in Chrisafis, "Regret but No Remorse, as Brighton Bomber Returns to Resort 20 Years On."

226. **Carlos Perez-Avila, a senior doctor, marveled:** Ramsey, *Something Has Gone Wrong*, 52–54.

226. **"I'm not known for my tolerance":** Michael Forrer, hospital administrator, interview with author, February 2021.

226. **Donald Maclean found himself being X-rayed:** Maclean interview in "The Brighton Bomber," *World in Action*, documentary series, ITV, June 11, 1986.

227. **hospital treated thirty-three:** Report by Chief Constable Roger Birch to Sussex Police Authority, January 21, 1985, appendix A.

227. **Calls from around the world, among them kings and presidents:** Forrer interview with author, February 2021.

227. **The organization, marveled Ivor Gaber:** Ramsey, *Something Has Gone Wrong*.

228. **Anthony McIntyre:** Anthony McIntyre interview with author, April 2021.

228. **"We all stood about like lemons at the back":** Roger Birch quoted in Buss, *Paths of Political and Personal Conflict Resolution After the Brighton Bomb 1984*, 19.

229. **kneeled and prayed in silence:** Aitken, *Margaret Thatcher*. "Crawfie and I knelt by the side of our beds and prayed for some time in silence."

229. **a telegram addressed to "Harvey Thomas":** Ramsey, *Something Has Gone Wrong*.

230. **"Dad's dead, Dad's dead":** Jo Berry interview in "Facing the Enemy," *Everyman*, documentary series, BBC2, December 13, 2001.

230. **Patrick Magee watched from a pub:** Magee, *Where Grieving Begins*.

231. **"What struck me forcefully":** Magee, *Where Grieving Begins*.

231. **"always be looking over my shoulder":** Magee, *Where Grieving Begins*.

CHAPTER FIFTEEN | WETTING WORMS

235. **Reece was making another ascent:** In a 2014 interview for Brighton's Old Police Cells museum, Reece said he trailed the pathologist Ian West around the ruins: "Ian had to be present every time a body was found and . . . I followed Ian about like a little lapdog, really."

235. **Jeanne Shattock's remains had been discovered nearby:** Shattock's body was found at 7:40 p.m., as in Kieran Hughes, *Terror Attack Brighton: Blowing Up the Iron Lady*, Pen & Sword, 2014, 59.

235. **Fred Bishop and his team had wanted to remove her:** Anti-Terrorist Branch detective Sergeant Michael Colacicco in Steve Ramsey, *Something Has Gone Wrong: Dealing with the Brighton Bomb*, Biteback, 2018.

236. **driven at high speed to Chequers:** "I was driven back to Chequers fasters than I had ever been driven before." Margaret Thatcher, *Margaret Thatcher: The Autobiography*, HarperPress, 1993, 461.

236. **Pinky Reece for his choleric temper:** Steve Ramsey interview transcript for Mike Rees, Sussex Police traffic officer, for *Something Has Gone Wrong*.

236. **"Always spoke his mind":** Steve Ramsey interview transcript for Bernie Wells for *Something Has Gone Wrong*.

236. **Reece's father, a Yorkshire coal miner:** "Jack Reece," obituary, London *Times*, December 9, 2015, https://www.thetimes.co.uk/article/jack-reece-c3bzfd350jj.

236. **"I clocked him a good 'un":** Dave Wilde, cousin and close friend of Jack Reece, interview with author, January 2021.

237. **They never had children, heartache:** Wilde interview with author, January 2021.

237. **spend hours hunched over manuals:** Wilde interview with author, January 2021.

237. **"Jack Reece was an amazing man, really":** Steve Ramsey interview transcript for Jon Buss for *Something Has Gone Wrong*.

238. **toss a coin in the sea as an offering to Neptune:** Wilde interview with author, January 2021.

238. **He had heard of "monster" sharks off the Azores:** Wilde interview with author, January 2021.

238. **Reece savored speed:** Wilde interview with author, January 2021.

238. **Reece had noticed potted shrubs:** Reece interview for Brighton's Old Police Cells museum, 2014.

239. **first time the Anti-Terrorist Branch had deployed:** Michael Colacicco, former ATB detective sergeant, interview with author, March 2021.

239. **"God, you know, what on earth are we going to do?'":** Ramsey, *Something Has Gone Wrong*.

239. **knocker boys—antique dealers:** Sussex Detective Constable Paul Gibbon in Steve Ramsey interview transcript for *Something Has Gone Wrong*.

239. **Rather than commute home, he took to sleeping in his office:** Wilde interview with author, January 2021.

239. **Ronald Reagan offered US help:** "Brighton Bomb: Reagan Letter to Thatcher (Message of Sympathy)," Reagan Archive, October 12, 1984, reproduced by Margaret Thatcher Foundation, March 28, 2000, https://www.margaretthatcher.org/document/109351.

239. **"Track down these pitiless Provos":** "The Sun Speaks Its Mind: Exterminate Them," editorial, *The Sun*, October 13, 1984, 6.

240. *Sunday Express* **foamed with xenophobic rage:** John Junor in the *Sunday Express*, October 14, 1984.

240. **Met's Special Branch accused Sussex Police:** Commander David Bickness critique cited in Ray Wilson and Ian Adams, *Metropolitan Special Branch: A History, 1883–2006*, Biteback, 2015, 337.

240. **MI5 chiefs said the bomb showed why:** Christopher Andrew, *The Defence of the Realm: The Authorized History of MI5*, Allen Lane, 2009.

240. **RUC accused its English colleagues:** Gareth Parry, "Why the 'Paddy Factor' Outwitted Police Security," *The Guardian*, October 13, 1984. "If it hasn't happened in London, well, it just hasn't happened," said an RUC officer.

240. **"Jon, I very much enjoyed reading my obituary":** Jon Buss recalling Roger Birch comment in Ramsey, *Something Has Gone Wrong*.

240. **"You feel pretty lonely":** Roger Birch interview with author, February 2021.

240. **"My job was to protect Jack Reece":** Birch interview with author, February 2021.

240. **"They're a blooming nuisance":** Roger Birch interviewed for Ramsey, *Something Has Gone Wrong*.

241. **"I expected our Special Branch to be filling us with names":** Steve Ramsey interview transcript for Bernie Wells for *Something Has Gone Wrong*.

241. **"Somewhere in that lot is the identity of the bomber:"** Unnamed officer quoted in *Evening Argus* Brighton bomb forty-page supplement, December 3, 1984, 33.

242. **Dennis Williams . . . phoned headquarters:** Sussex Chief Superintendent Williams interview in 2014 for Brighton's Old Police Cells museum.

242. **"How many more bloody dustbins do you want":** Recollection of Bernie Wells in Ramsey interview for *Something Has Gone Wrong*.

242. **The eventual answer:** Peter Gurney, *Braver Men Walk Away: Memoirs of the World's Top Bomb-Disposal Expert*, HarperCollins, 1993.

242. **labor left detectives bashed:** Michael Colacicco, Anti-Terrorist Branch detective sergeant, interview with author, March 2021.

242. **blowing a whistle if masonry wobbled:** *Evening Argus* Brighton bomb supplement, 1984, 34.

242. **masks were often unavailable:** Michael Colacicco in Ramsey, *Something Has Gone Wrong*. "They came back and issued us with some masks, which were crap. Up to that we'd used just filter, a piece of gauze with a steel plate over the front, these had things you screwed in at the side, but you couldn't work with them because, the amount of heavy work, they'd fill up with sweat on the inside and you'd drown."

243. **Jonathan Woods, was to die of mesothelioma:** Adrian Imms, "Police Kept Ignorant of Dangers at Bomb Blast Scene," *The Argus*, October 17, 2016, https://www.theargus.co.uk/news/14151628 .detective-who-investigated-grand-hotel-bombing-dies-from-inhaling-asbestos-family-pursuing -claim-against-police/.

243. **"We're not trained to abseil":** Imms, "Police Kept Ignorant of Dangers at Bomb Blast Scene."

243. **"We burned them out quite quickly":** Imms, "Police Kept Ignorant of Dangers at Bomb Blast Scene."

243. **contact lenses were identified and reunited:** "The Hunt for the Bomber," *The Brighton Bomb*, documentary, BBC1, September 14, 2004.

243. **"You can put tremendous weights on some floors":** Gurney, *Braver Men Walk Away*, 172.

243. **fear about a follow-up IRA attack:** Sussex police chiefs feared the IRA might mortar the John Street station.

244. **Some on Reece's team wondered if this was feasible:** "At the outset, it seemed an enormous task." Detective Chief Inspector Graham Hill in Ramsey, *Something Has Gone Wrong*.

244. **a team of two hundred detectives:** Home Office minister Leon Brittan told the House of Commons on October 22, 1984, that 228 officer were sifting through debris and more than 200 were pursuing those responsible for the bomb, https://api.parliament.uk/historic-hansard/commons/1984/oct/22/bomb-incident-brighton.

245. **some of Reece's detectives had trained on it:** Detective Inspector John Byford interviewed by Steve Ramsey for *Something Has Gone Wrong*.

245. **"It was a bit like an ant colony":** Sussex Detective Dave Gaylor, interview transcript, Ramsey, *Something Has Gone Wrong*.

245. **"Every inquiry is an action":** Byford interviewed by Ramsey for *Something Has Gone Wrong*.

245. **steel filing cabinets containing:** Colacicco in Ramsey, *Something Has Gone Wrong*.

245. **Paul Boswell, had been summoned:** Bernie Wells credited Boswell, "a little chap," with helping to extract the cards.

245. **"It was very eerie," Snelling said:** "Brighton Bomb: *Patrol* Special Report," *Patrol*, Sussex police magazine, June 1986, 5.

246. **Hilary Pownall's job to make two copies:** Hilary Pownall interview with author, January 2021.

246. **thwarted promotion had withered her ambition:** Pownall interview with author, January 2021.

246. **Jack Reece returned to the Grand:** *Evening Argus* photograph of Reece in Thatcher's suite, October 15, 1984, 3.

246. **Snelling pulled the hotel registration cards:** *Patrol*, 7.

247. **London detectives phoned back to say:** *Patrol*, 7.

247. **Thatcher was in Downing Street:** "MT Engagement Diary," https://www.margaretthatcher.org/document/147348; and Associated Press photograph, https://www.clickorlando.com/gallery/business/2020/01/23/britains-eu-journey-when-thatcher-turned-all-euroskeptic/.

247. **the handover of Hong Kong:** UK Embassy in Beijing's telegram to Foreign Office, 2596, https://www.margaretthatcher.org/document/230087.

248. **Mikhail Gorbachev . . . suddenly accepted:** Former Europe minister Malcolm Rifkind in BBC documentary, cited in Callum Hoare, "Margaret Thatcher: Secret 'No One Knows' About Former PM Revealed by Personal Assistant," *Express*, July 3, 2019, https://www.express.co.uk/news/uk/1148447/margaret-thatcher-secret-revealed-cynthia-crawford-bbc-documentary-spt.

248. **She was briefed on the investigation:** Bernie Wells in Steve Ramsey transcript, *Something Has Gone Wrong*. "Margaret Thatcher was briefed continually about how the investigation was going."

248. **"She had a huge respect for the law":** Lord Powell interview with author, May 2021.

248. **signaling indifference to danger:** Charles Moore, "After the Brighton Bomb," *The Spectator*, October 20, 1984, www.spectator.co.uk/article/after-the-brighton-bomb/.

248. **"We must go *very* slow on these talks":** Charles Moore, *Margaret Thatcher: The Authorized Biography, Volume Two: Everything She Wants*, Allen Lane, 2015, 315.

248. **"The IRA will probably get me in the end":** David Goodall, *The Making of the Anglo-Irish Agreement of 1985*, National University of Ireland, 2021, 52.

249. **"the day I was meant not to see":** Margaret Thatcher, "TV Interview for Channel 4 *A plus 4* (Brighton Bomb)," transcript, Margaret Thatcher Foundation, October 15, 1984, https://www.margaretthatcher.org/document/105764.

249. **Margaret Tebbit's paralysis might have been her own fate:** Denis Thatcher cited in Jonathan Aitken, *Margaret Thatcher: Power and Personality*, Bloomsbury, 2013.

249. **keep a torch beside her bed:** Robin Butler, cabinet private secretary, interview with author, April 2021.

249. **kept the bedroom door open to avoid being trapped:** Moore, *Margaret Thatcher*, vol. 2, 315.

249. **"marked on her soul," said Cynthia Crawford:** Crawford interviewed in "The Brighton Bomb," *Secret History*, documentary series, Channel 4, May 15, 2003.

249. **Indira Gandhi, further rattled Thatcher:** Aitken, *Margaret Thatcher*.

249. **She "doubted now if she would die in her bed":** The British cabinet secretary, Sir Robert Armstrong, told this to the Irish ambassador in London, Noel Dorr, as cited in John Bowman, "Thatcher Said After Brighton Bombing She 'Doubted She Would Die in Her Bed,'" *Irish Times*, December 27, 2014, https://www.irishtimes.com/news/politics/thatcher-said-after-brighton-bombing-she-doubted-she-would-die-in-her-bed-1.2042550.

249. **"It was a quote you wouldn't forget":** Powell interview with author, May 2021.

249. **IRA was following in the footsteps of Danny Morrison:** Author interviews with four ex-IRA members who believe Morrison authored the statement.

249. **anonymous GHQ spokesman:** "The Myth That the British Government Is Impregnable Has Been Blown," *An Phoblacht/Republican News*, October 18, 1984, 3.

250. **swerved through the gunfire and escaped:** For detailed insider description of the operation from the SAS perspective see Andy McNab, *Immediate Action: The Inside Story of the Toughest—and Most Highly Secretive—Strike Force in the World*, Dell, 1995.

250. **Peter Sherry . . . in a council election seven months earlier:** See chapter 11, "Tightrope."

250. **Three men with English accents:** Peter Sherry interview with author, April 2021.

250. **"Remember, we have only to be lucky":** Sherry interview with author, April 2021.

250. **Muammar Gaddafi disapproved:** Author interview with IRA source who was close to leadership, 2021.

250. **With his own reasons to loathe Thatcher:** The UK expelled Libyan diplomats after shots from Libya's London embassy killed WPC Yvonne Fletcher in April 1984.

250. **a D. R. Walsh, who was known to the Special Branch:** Police source to Nick Davies, author and journalist, 1985.

251. **under the name Roy Walsh:** Nick Davies, "The Foul-Ups and Loopholes Which Have Let IRA Bombers Go Free," *London Daily News*, June 24, 1987, https://www.nickdavies.net/1987/06/24/the-foul-ups-and-loopholes-which-have-let-ira-bombers-go-free/.

251. **"We really felt we'd got the man":** Steve Ramsey interview transcript for Bernie Wells for *Something Has Gone Wrong*.

251. **checked the Passport Office and the Driver:** "The Brighton Bomb; *Patrol* Special Report," *Patrol*, 7.

251. **wade through 750,000 reissues:** *Patrol*, 7.

251. **Plappert, the housekeeper:** Pamela Plappert interview with Peter Taylor in "The Hunt for the Bomber," *The Brighton Bomb*, BBC1, September 14, 2004.

251. **"behind the bath," said Paul Gibbon:** Sussex Detective Constable Paul Gibbon in Steve Ramsey interview transcript for *Something Has Gone Wrong*.

252. **Tadd had been expecting it:** David Tadd interview with author, November 2021.

252. **Metropolitan Police forensic science laboratory:** Background on Lambeth lab at "Metropolitan Police Service—Central Forensic Crime Laboratories," Critical Airflow, https://www.criticalairflow.com/projects/metropolitan-police/.

252. **a solution of ninhydrin:** Tadd interview with author, November 2021.

253. **Tadd packed away the bottles and tray:** Tadd interview with author, November 2021.

253. **chart in Byford's office:** Detective Inspector John Byford interviewed by Steve Ramsey for *Something Has Gone Wrong*.

253. **False leads multiplied: a group of Irishmen in the Metropole:** See David Briffett, *Sussex Murders: County Murders and Mysteries*, Ensign, 1990, 141.

254. **"We interviewed one woman":** "Hotel Lovers Face Quiz," *Evening Argus*, October 29, 1984.

254. **one asked journalist David Davin-Power:** David Power interview with author, February 2021.

254. **spanning Belgium to Botswana:** Sussex Police list of Interpol bureaus that undertook inquiries.

254. **2,700 messages, 6,000 statements:** *Patrol*, 7.

254. **Another record was the price tag: £1 million:** "Jack Reece," obituary, *London Times*, December 9, 2015, https://www.thetimes.co.uk/article/jack-reece-c3bzfd350jj.

255. **Detective Constable Ian Macleod spotted an ice cream cone–shaped:** Macleod quoted in Magee et al. trial reports, May/June 1986; and Gareth Parry and David Pallister, "Timer Clue to Brighton Bombing," *The Guardian*, May 10, 1986.

255. **RARDE to piece together the bomb's probable design:** Dr. Thomas Hayes quoted in "Murder Trial Told of Effects of Hotel Bomb Blast," *Irish Times*, May 13, 1986.

255. **"guys nearly drowning":** Ramsey interview transcript for *Something Has Gone Wrong*.

255. **ties and cuff links with a bin motif:** Ramsey interview transcript for *Something Has Gone Wrong*.

255. **November 6, Reece appeared:** "*Crimewatch* UK November 1984," Crimebox video, YouTube, uploaded October 3, 2021, https://www.youtube.com/watch?v=RT826JIMzu4.

256. **Roy Walsh not to phone:** *Patrol*, 7, quoted Reece telling other detectives: "I am the first police officer to come to *Crimewatch* requesting a person to come forward but hoping that he doesn't."

CHAPTER SIXTEEN | HYPOTHENAR EVIDENCE

257. **"From the look on his face":** Donald Maclean interview in "The Brighton Bomber," *World in Action*, documentary series, ITV, June 11, 1986.

257. **Jennifer Taylor wandered:** Mark Elsdon-Dew, "The Lives That Were Shattered One Year Ago This Week," *Sunday Express*, October 6, 1985.

258. **Gordon Shattock convalesced:** Elsdon-Dew, "The Lives That Were Shattered One Year Ago This Week."

258. **Sarah Berry sensed a darkness:** Jo Berry, daughter of Anthony and stepdaughter of Sarah, quoted in Adam Smith, "Remembering the IRA Bomb at the Grand Hotel in Brighton," *The Argus*, October 12, 2020, https://www.theargus.co.uk/news/18787152.look-back-ira-bomb-grand-hotel-brighton/.

258. **"In almost any murder you try and get close":** Jack Reece interview for Brighton's Old Police Cells museum, 2014.

258. **"That in my view is a cowardly act":** Jack Reece interview with Peter Taylor in "The Hunt for the Bomber," *The Brighton Bomb*, documentary series, BBC1, September 14, 2004.

258. **Reece had to give updates to Roger Birch:** Roger Birch interview with author, February 2021.

258. **cartoon in the satirical magazine *Private Eye*:** Appeared in the November 2, 1984, issue.

258. **"Get some light into these dark places":** William Vernon Harcourt quoted in Ray Wilson and Ian Adams, *Metropolitan Special Branch: A History, 1883–2006*, Biteback, 2015; see also chapter 6, "The Bomb Burglar and Mr. T."

259. **the IRA had used "clean skins":** Ex-IRA member told the author the England Department did in fact often use operatives with no criminal record.

259. **twenty thousand IRA suspects on file:** *New Hibernia*, July/August 1986.

259. **Patrick Magee was not on it:** This is the recollection of David Tadd. Magee believes he was on the short list. Author interview with Tadd, February 2021.

260. **spent days filling in blank registration cards:** Author interview with Tadd, February 2021.

260. **prints of approximately two hundred other IRA bombers:** Author interview with Tadd, February 2021.

261. **Japan came on rice paper:** WPC Hilary Pownall, member of hotel inquiry team, interview with author, January 2021.

261. **US forces sent verbatim transcripts:** Police interview in Steve Ramsey, *Something Has Gone Wrong: Dealing with the Brighton Bomb*, Biteback, 2018.

261. **The taxi driver, Dennis Palmer:** Palmer interviewed in *To Kill the Cabinet*, documentary, BBC1, 1986.

261. **"We plotted up that restaurant":** Ramsey, *Something Has Gone Wrong*.

261. **Walsh was a void:** Graham Hill interview by Steve Ramsey for *Something Has Gone Wrong*.

261. **Sussex Police briefing paper:** Copy supplied courtesy of the Old Police Cells museum, Brighton.

262. **"We weren't sort of, really making progress":** Hill interview by Ramsey for *Something Has Gone Wrong*.

262. **Gibbon churned with tension:** Detective Constable Paul Gibbon interview with author, February 2021.

263. **"My emotions, I want to get up":** Paul Gibbon interview by Steve Ramsey for *Something Has Gone Wrong*.

263. **first Walsh knew about the plot:** Roy Walsh interview with author, April 2021.

263. **"The screws were all whispering":** Walsh interview with author, April 2021.

263. **"'Fuck about with me, I'll get you done'":** Walsh interview with author, April 2021.

264. **He called it "The Haunty":** Kevin Cullen and Shelley Murphy, *Whitey Bulger: America's Most Wanted Gangster and the Manhunt That Brought Him to Justice*, W. W. Norton, 2013, 270.

264. **Sean O'Callaghan had tipped off Irish authorities:** Sean O'Callaghan, *The Informer: The Real Story of One Man's War Against Terrorism*, Bantam Press, 1998.

264. **US Coast Guard and Customs agents:** Cullen and Murphy, *Whitey Bulger*, 264.

264. **He suspected the crew's mechanic, John McIntyre:** Dick Lehr and Gerard O'Neill, *Whitey: The Life of America's Most Notorious Mob Boss*, Ebury Press, 2015, 257.

264. **Flemmi used pliers to extract the teeth:** Cullen and Murphy, *Whitey Bulger*, 267.

265. **lunch of beef and Dover sole:** Jo Thomas, "Thatcher and Russian Discuss Arms," *New York Times*, section A, 3, December 17, 1984, https://www.nytimes.com/1984/12/17/world/thatcher-and-russian-discuss-arms.html.

265. **her considered walking out:** Jonathan Aitken, *Margaret Thatcher: Power and Personality*, Bloomsbury, 2013, 480–85. "For a moment I wondered if we should leave," Gorbachev told Aitken in an interview for the book.

265. **"hair dryer treatment":** Aitken, *Margaret Thatcher*, 484.

265. **rebutting his host with confidence and humor:** Memo by translator Tony Bishop, "Mikhail Sergeevich Gorbachev: A Personal Assessment of the Man During His Visit to the United Kingdom, 15–21 December 1984," January 3, 1985, https://cb786b42ab2de72f5694-c7a3803ab0f7212d059698df03ade453.ssl.cf1.rackcdn.com/850103%20Bishop%20%281394-52%29.pdf.

265. **She flew to Camp David to tell Ronald Reagan:** National Security Archive memorandum of Thatcher-Reagan meeting at Camp David, December 22, 1984, https://nsarchive.gwu.edu/document/22548-document-01-thatcher-reagan-memcon-december-10.

265. **US president listened, rapt:** In a 1990 interview, Reagan credited MT with foresight. "She told me that Gorbachev was different from any of the other Kremlin leaders. She believed that there was a chance for a great opening. Of course, she was proven exactly right."

265. **history spun on a thread:** In an interview for *Thatcher: The Downing Street Years*, BBC, 1993, US secretary of state James Baker said MT's assessment of Gorbachev had a "profound influence" on US plans for its strategy and summitry.

266. **Tebbit had gratefully accepted:** Norman Tebbit, *Upwardly Mobile: An Autobiography*, Weidenfeld and Nicolson, 1988.

266. **housekeeper removed his supper tray:** Tebbit, *Upwardly Mobile*.

266. **He gave a breezy hospital bed interview:** "Tebbit Tells of 'Feeling Ragged,'" *The Guardian*, October 17, 1984, 6.

266. **"most likely to succeed, should he so wish":** Michael Jones, "A Time for Tory Zeal," *Sunday Times*, October 14, 1984, 16.

266. **Fred Bishop and two other firemen:** Bishop interviewed by Steve Ramsey for *Something Has Gone Wrong*.

266. **"get him coming back up again'":** Bishop interviewed by Ramsey for *Something Has Gone Wrong*.

267. **"I thought of our house, dark, lonely and silent":** Tebbit, *Upwardly Mobile*.

267. **"don't like to be reminded of your guilt":** Charles Moore on MT relationship with Norman Tebbit, in Steve Ramsey interview with Moore for *Something Has Gone Wrong*.

267. **Tebbit dragged blankets:** Tebbit, *Upwardly Mobile.*

267. **December 20 . . . Crimewatch:** "*Crimewatch* UK December 1984," redcard74 video, YouTube, uploaded August 9, 2018, https://www.youtube.com/watch?v=tFufAt4_f0U&t=189s.

269. **Crimewatch hotlines lit up, but none led anywhere:** The updated bulletin on December 20 said a viewer in the West Country had received a fraudulent check written with the distinctive E.

269. **Steve Turner stared at the screen of the epidiascope:** David Tadd interview with author, February 2021.

269. **"A willing horse," in David Tadd's words:** Tadd interview with author, February 2021.

270. **at the London Coliseum watching Rigoletto:** "MT Engagement Diary: Thursday, January 17, 1985," Margaret Thatcher Foundation, https://www.margaretthatcher.org/document/213651.

270. **names on the IRA files meant little to most of the team:** Tadd interview with author, February 2021.

271. **Egan was a strict disciplinarian:** Tadd interview with author, February 2021.

271. **He had feared the palm print, mark C:** Tadd interview with author, February 2021.

272. **"I need this now," he murmured:** Tadd interview with author, February 2021.

272. **"It was the first time I had got so excited":** Tadd interview with author, February 2021.

CHAPTER SEVENTEEN | DUBLIN

273. **surveillance officers who had been shadowing her:** BBC1 documentary *To Kill the Cabinet*, 1986, cited surveillance of Eileen Magee. Author interview with former Special Branch surveillance officer confirmed accuracy, March 2021.

274. **"An easy follow," one Special Branch detective recalled:** Author interview with former senior Garda Special Branch officer, February 2021.

275. **Irish courts routinely rejected British extradition requests:** Alpha Connelly, "Ireland and the Political Offense: Exception to Extradition," *Journal of Law and Society* 12, no. 2 (Summer 1985): 153–82, https://www.jstor.org/stable/1409965.

276. **circumvent this by allowing Irish courts:** Connelly, "Ireland and the Political Offense."

276. **nobbled Gerard Tuite in 1982:** See chapter 9, "Blackpool."

276. **attempt to extradite Evelyn Glenholmes:** Nick Davies, "The Bungle That Halted the Extradition of 36 Terrorists," *The Observer*, November 18, 1984, https://www.nickdavies.net/1984/11/18/the-bungle -that-halted-the-extradition-of-36-terrorists/.

276. **collapsed in acrimony:** Davies, "The Bungle That Halted the Extradition of 36 Terrorists."

276. **homesickness that had collared Thomas Quigley:** See chapter 10, "Salcey Forest."

276. **imposed a truce on the competing agencies:** *Daily Telegraph*, June 12, 1986. "A top level conference took place at which it was decided against publicizing the fact that Magee was the wanted man. Instead anti-terrorist chiefs played a waiting game, gambling that Magee would once again chance his luck on the mainland."

276. **home secretary, Leon Brittan:** "Brighton Bombing (Hoddinott Report)," House of Commons debate transcript, January 22, 1985, https://www.theyworkforyou.com/debates/?id=1985-01-22a.866.0.

277. **Reece took a calculated risk:** Steve Ramsey interviews with Bernie Wells, Paul Gibbon, and John Byford for Steve Ramsey, *Something Has Gone Wrong: Dealing with the Brighton Bomb*, Biteback, 2018.

277. **"In true detective style":** Ramsey interview with Paul Gibbon for *Something Has Gone Wrong.*

278. **"It was the best kept secret of my police career":** Ramsey interview with Paul Gibbon for *Something Has Gone Wrong.*

278. **wine and dine senior Met officers:** David Williams, "'They Trust Me and I Trust Them': How Police Contacts Took Daily Mail's Peter Burden, Who Has Died Aged 77, to the Top," *Press Gazette*, October 19, 2019, https://pressgazette.co.uk/they-trust-me-and-i-trust-them-how-police-contacts-took-daily -mails-peter-burden-who-has-died-aged-77-to-the-top/.

278. **"If you break this now":** Roger Birch recollection of Reece-Burden phone call in interview with Steve Ramsey for *Something Has Gone Wrong.*

278. **"You don't make a noise"**: Dave Wilde, cousin and close friend of Jack Reece, interview with author, January 2021.

278. **Patrick Magee wondered if he was getting paranoid**: Patrick Magee interview with author, April 2021.

279. **suspicious vehicles up the IRA chain**: Patrick Magee, *Where Grieving Begins: Building Bridges After the Brighton Bomb*, Pluto Press, 2021, 121.

279. *I would always be looking over my shoulder*: See chapter 14, "A White Light."

279. **snatch squad, just like the Dutch police years earlier**: See chapter 4, "Hunger."

279. **There was no way to know**: Magee interview with author, April 2021. "You had to allow that they knew, but I wouldn't have known for definite. . . . You didn't know."

279. **Jack McCabe accidentally blew himself up**: Brendan Anderson, *Joe Cahill: A Life in the IRA*, O'Brien Press, 2002.

280. **community vigilante group**: Donal Fallon, "Dealers Out! The Concerned Parents Against Drugs," *Dublin InQuirer*, March 6, 2019, https://www.dublininquirer.com/2019/03/06/dealers-out-the -concerned-parents-against-drugs.

280. **Ray Corcoran, a former Sinn Féin councillor**: Ray Corcoran interview with author, April 2021.

280. **"smell a cop a mile away"**: Detective Inspector Gerry O'Carroll interview with author, February 2021.

280. **"There were numerous shortcuts"**: Magee, *Where Grieving Begins*, 122.

280. **saw just one path: continued IRA operations**: Magee, *Where Grieving Begins*, 122.

280. **"We had upped the ante"**: Magee, *Where Grieving Begins*, 122.

281. **detached, arrogant, even an indulgence**: Sean O'Callaghan, *The Informer: The Real Story of One Man's War Against Terrorism*, Bantam Press, 1998.

281. **create and hold a "liberated zone"**: Magee, *Where Grieving Begins*, 122.

281. **made his move against Gerry Adams**: Ed Moloney, *A Secret History of the IRA*, Penguin Press, 2002.

281. **"After Brighton, as a direct consequence"**: Magee, *Where Grieving Begins*, 122.

282. **He could stay in Dublin, help with logistics**: Michael Hayes interview with author, October 2021.

282. **Harvey Thomas took a flight to Boston**: Harvey Thomas interview with author, August 2020.

282. **"What funny seatmates!"**: Thomas recollection of the conversation. Interview with author, August 2020.

282. **Basque separatist group ETA bombed**: James M. Markham, "Terrorists in Spain Strike at Tourism," *New York Times*, July 5, 1979, https://www.nytimes.com/1979/07/05/archives/terrorists-in-spain -strike-at-tourism-basque-separatist-group.html.

283. **team would switch to assassination**: Hayes interview with author, October 2021.

283. **"The complexity of the campaign required"**: Magee, *Where Grieving Begins*, 123. Magee mentions only the bombing campaign, not the VIP assassination plan.

283. **She skipped bail and moved to the republic**: Shane Paul O'Doherty, former IRA bomber, interview with author, September 2020.

284. **"You don't just walk into a bomb team"**: O'Doherty interview with author, September 2020.

284. **doctored by the same expert hand**: Toby Harnden, *Bandit Country: The IRA & South Armagh*, Hodder & Stoughton, 1999, 320.

284. **fifth member was assigned as a fixer**: "How IRA's Death Plan Was Blown," *Liverpool Echo*, June 23, 1986.

284. **"England was a big field of haystacks"**: Magee, *Where Grieving Begins*, 122.

285. **IRA's estimate of eleven cars surveilling the area**: Author interview with retired Garda Special Branch detective, February 2021.

285. **British did not tell the Irish government**: Author interview with minister from Garret Fitzgerald's government, February 2021.

285. **A retired sergeant told Tim Pat Coogan**: Tim Pat Coogan interview with author, January 2021.

285. **Magee bade farewell to Eileen and Padraig**: Magee, *Where Grieving Begins*.

286. **board a vessel**: Hayes interview with author, October 2021.

286. **Anne did most of the talking:** Gordon Petrie and David Steele, "The Forging of the Glasgow Link," *Glasgow Herald*, June 12, 1986, 7.

286. **"description was too imprecise to be released":** Jack Reece, quoted in *To Kill the Cabinet*, documentary, BBC1, 1986.

286. **The waiting and not knowing:** DCI John Byford interviewed by Steve Ramsey for *Something Has Gone Wrong*.

CHAPTER EIGHTEEN | LONDON

287. **crowds had streamed down the Mall:** For full BBC1 broadcast of Trooping of the Colour, June 15, 1985, see DavyFlute video on YouTube, uploaded June 3, 2020, https://www.youtube.com/watch?v=Czm2_MOV6k4.

287. **Trooping of the Colour:** For history and background of Trooping of the Colour ceremony, see Caroline Hallemann, "What Is Trooping the Colour, Anyway?" *Town & Country*, May 15, 2022, https://www.townandcountrymag.com/society/tradition/a10016954/trooping-the-color-facts/.

288. **on May 10, his face and name had been added:** Kevin Toolis, "Brighton—A Two Way Trail of Bungling and Incompetence," *Fortnight*, July 7, 1986.

289. **chain of explosions starting in mid-July:** Gareth Parry and David Pallister, "An Outrageous Plan to Create Havoc, Bloodshed/IRA Brighton Bomb Trial Continues," *The Guardian*, May 8, 1986.

289. **Royal Mews, a rear entrance to the palace:** "Visit the Royal Mews, Buckingham Palace," Royal Collection Trust, https://www.rct.uk/visit/the-royal-mews-buckingham-palace.

289. **palace was protected by Scotland Yard's Royal Palaces Division:** Robert Fleming with Hugh Miller, *Scotland Yard: The True Life Story of the Metropolitan Police*, Michael Joseph, 1994, 276.

289. **A six-story Edwardian edifice:** For structural details about the hotel, now renamed the Rubens at the Palace, see its website, https://rubenshotel.com/about.

289. **"Few hotels can claim to be neighbors of the Queen":** Police discovered the brochure, with Magee's fingerprints on it, at his unit's hideout at 17 James Gray Road, Glasgow.

289. **pianist tinkled a soft tune:** *To Kill the Cabinet*, documentary, BBC1, 1986, retrieved on YouTube, February 12, 2022, https://www.youtube.com/watch?v=gmta9UIz5Dk.

289. **phoned half an hour earlier to book a room:** *To Kill the Cabinet*.

289. **he had a female companion:** Unidentified newspaper clipping from 1986 trial. "The receptionist said she could remember nothing about the woman and all she could recall of the man was that he paid in advance for the double room without question." "Woman Booked In with Bomber," *Irish News*, May 8, 1986.

290. **paid £70 up front:** Parry and Pallister, "An Outrageous Plan to Create Havoc, Bloodshed."

290. **Margaret Thatcher was at Chequers:** Downing Street engagement diary. https://www.margaretthatcher.org/document/213919.

290. **David Tadd was at his home:** David Tadd interview with author, February 2021.

290. **Jack Reece liked to spend Saturday evenings at home:** Dave Wilde, cousin and friend of Reece, interview with author, January 2021.

290. **bright yellow *Masters of the Universe* lunch box:** "The Hunt for the Bomber," The Brighton Bomb, documentary series, BBC1, September 14, 2004.

290. **Three pounds and nine ounces:** Gordon Petrie and David Steele, "How a Courting Couple Trapped Bombers," *Glasgow Herald*, June 12, 1986, 6.

290. **stolen from Irish Industrial Explosives:** Testimony of Alan Fereday, principal scientific officer at the Royal Armament Research and Development Establishment, reported in David Pallister, "'Explosives Enough to Make 24 Bombs'/Old Bailey Trial of Alleged IRA Terrorists," *The Guardian*, May 21, 1986.

290. **wrapped in plastic wrap more than seventy times:** Alan Burt, Metropolitan Police dog unit, interviewed by Steve Ramsey in *Something Has Gone Wrong: Dealing with the Brighton Bomb*, Biteback, 2018.

290. **A long-delay timer:** Fereday testimony in Pallister, "'Explosives Enough to Make 24 Bombs.'"

290. **Memo-Park timer and travel alarm clock:** Author interview, January 2021, with Derek Pickford, the Metropolitan explosives officer (Expo) who disarmed the Rubens device.

290. **A nine-volt battery powered the device:** Pickford interview with author, January 2021.

290. **two booby traps, a microswitch on the lid and a mercury tilting device:** Pickford interview with author, January 2021.

290. **hiding spot was beside a disused chimney:** Pickford interview with author, January 2021.

290. **device could bring down one floor:** Pickford interview with author, January 2021.

291. **headed to Finsbury Park:** *To Kill the Cabinet.*

291. **smuggling personnel and material:** RUC Special Branch detective interview with author, February 2021.

291. **easy for operators to blend in:** Former Strathclyde detective inspector Brian Watson interview with author, January 2021.

291. **Local Special Branch detectives tended to focus:** Ian Robinson, former Strathclyde police detective chief superintendent, interview with author, January 2021.

291. **sort of Celtic Ho Chi Minh Trail:** Sean O'Callaghan, *The Informer: The Real Story of One Man's War Against Terrorism*, Bantam Press, 1998.

291. **connected Magee and O'Dwyer to Frances Boyle:** See chapter 17, "Dublin," for Magee and O'Dwyer meeting Frances Boyle. In his 1986 trial McShane pleaded guilty to assisting the IRA unit and was sentenced to eight years, reduced on appeal to six years; see "UDA Murder Plot Accused Anton Duffy Met IRA 'Helper,'" BBC News, June 1, 2015, https://www.bbc.com/news/uk-scotland-glasgow-west -32965672.

292. **families with children who tromped:** At various times, six children lived on the same floor as the unit, according to Gordon Petrie and David Steele, "The Forging of the Glasgow Link," *Glasgow Herald*, June 12, 1986, 7.

292. **put extra bolts on their door:** David Pallister, "Man Cleared of Sheltering IRA Bomb Team/Old Bailey Trial of John Boyle," *The Guardian*, June 21, 1986.

292. **told to puff by the window:** Pallister, "Man Cleared of Sheltering IRA Bomb Team."

292. **handguns, automatic rifles, more than 130 pounds of gelignite:** Evidence from June 1986 trial plus author interview with former Strathclyde detective constable William Dorrian, who discovered the cache, April 2021.

292. **John Boyle, noted high electricity usage:** Boyle was found not guilty of helping the IRA team at his trial in 1986. Pallister, "Man Cleared of Sheltering IRA Bomb Team."

292. **Shaun McShane, the team's Glasgow gofer:** Petrie and Steele, "The Forging of the Glasgow Link," 7.

292. **"They're making fucking bombs up there":** McShane's wife kept a diary, which police recovered. Petrie and Steele, "The Forging of the Glasgow Link," 7.

292. **The IRA team sorted timetables:** Author interview with Dorrian, who itemized evidence at the IRA unit's properties and discovered the arms cache.

293. **a bombing calendar:** "Diary of Destruction," London *Times*, June 12, 1986. Other trial reports give slightly different dates for the bomb calendar, for instance the *Daily Mail* reported that the first bomb was planned for June 29, 1985. David Williams, "IRA Plotted a Blitz on Seaside Britain," *Daily Mail*, May 8, 1986.

293. **revive the old graffiti:** See chapter 2, "The Friendly Skies of South Armagh," and Thatcher's first visit to Belfast.

293. **appeared to shadow the Queen:** Tabloids extrapolated this partial calendar/royal itinerary overlap as a plan to assassinate royals, as in George Hollingbery and John Kay, "Four Blasts to Wipe Out the Royal Family," *The Sun*, June 12, 1986.

293. **Paul Kavanagh ... sent her greetings:** Tom Brady, "IRA's Deadliest Terror Team," *Irish Press*, June 12, 1986.

294. **Magee ... received two cards:** Petrie and Steele, "How a Courting Couple Trapped Bombers," 6.

294. **under the name Alan Woods:** *To Kill the Cabinet.*

294. **bought an Alfasud car with just two doors:** "How IRA's Death Plan Was Blown," *Liverpool Echo*, June 23, 1986.

294. **Blute and Anderson had got a close view of his disintegration:** Craig drove them to Wembley stadium for apparent reconnaissance during the FA Cup final on May 18, 1985.

294. **Whitehaven when he drove the wrong way:** "How IRA's Death Plan Was Blown"; Stewart Tendler, "Woman Ready to Shoot Policeman at Traffic Check, Court Is Told," London *Times*, June 24, 1986.

295. **Only later would his manic depression be diagnosed:** Enda Craig interview with author, September 2021.

295. **England Department wanted Craig shot:** Mick Hayes, deputy head of England Department, interview with author, October 2021.

295. **Craig handed Magee a resignation letter:** "How IRA's Death Plan Was Blown"; Tendler, "Woman Ready to Shoot Policeman at Traffic Check."

295. **53 Hackney Road in London's East End. Using the name Alan Cooper:** *To Kill the Cabinet.*

295. **hid a loaded handgun, a soldering iron:** Detective Constable Paul Gibbon interview with author, February 2021.

295. **Magee did a newspaper crossword:** Gibbon interview with author, February 2021.

295. **waiting for surveillance photographs to develop:** Drawn from a segment of Ian Phoenix's private, handwritten, unpublished work diary, detailing Operation Drain, June 1985.

296. **portacabin . . . base in Lisnasharragh:** E4A offices, work practices, and operations supplied by former mid-ranking E4A member "Michael" in interview with author, March 2021.

296. **tending beehives, glazing windows:** Susan Phoenix, Ian Phoenix's widow, interview with author, December 2021.

296. **possibly the worst-dressed plainclothes officer:** Phoenix interview with author, December 2021.

296. **"what the fuck are you doing about it?":** Phoenix interview with author, December 2021.

297. **grown up playing cowboys and Indians:** Jack Holland and Susan Phoenix, *Phoenix: Policing the Shadows: The Secret War Against Terrorism in Northern Ireland*, Hodder & Stoughton, 1996.

297. **considered himself Irish:** Holland and Phoenix, *Phoenix.*

297. **trained at an SAS-style boot camp:** William Matchett, ex-E4A member and author of *Secret Victory: The Intelligence War That Beat the IRA*, Matchett, 2016.

297. **ordinary looking—not too short or tall:** "Michael" interview with author, March 2021.

297. **"You had to be happy to pee into a plastic bucket":** "Michael" interview with author, March 2021.

297. **nickname was Captain Chaos:** Holland and Phoenix, *Phoenix.*

297. **combative streak extended even to the English language:** Phoenix interview with author, December 2021.

298. **Operation Drain:** Details drawn from Ian Phoenix's private diary.

298. **soft-spoken, with a slight build:** Author interview with ex-RUC and UDR officer "Jonathan," who knew Sherry as a boy and an adult, February 2021.

298. **masked their fear by calling him "Little Peter":** Author interview with ex-UDR major "Norman," April 2021.

298. **Adams canvassed for Sherry in March 1984:** See chapter 11, "Tightrope."

298. **surviving the SAS ambush:** See chapter 15, "Wetting Worms."

298. **Ken Maginnis, the unionist MP:** Ken Maginnis (now Baron Maginnis of Drumglass) interview with author, January 2021.

299. **"It made life more difficult":** Peter Sherry interview with author, April 2021.

299. **"The logic was that things were too hot":** Sherry interview with author, April 2021.

299. **"We were told to lay off":** "Norman" interview with author, April 2021.

299. **a crude magnetic tracking device:** "Michael" interview with author, March 2021.

299. **"Okay, that's him coming off the motorway":** "Michael" interview with author, March 2021.

300. **not a known republican safe house:** "Michael" interview with author, March 2021.

300. **not even boot men could safely keep watch:** "Michael" interview with author, March 2021.

300. **everyone knew their names:** Ian Phoenix's diary says the operatives were so popular that other drinkers invited them to other pubs. They declined.

300. **later revealed to be a £5,000 payment:** Phoenix diary.

300. **crewman contacted his handler:** Phoenix diary.

301. **meant catching that evening's 6:30 p.m. ferry:** Phoenix diary.

301. **raced to the Port of Larne:** Author interview with Susan Phoenix, widow of Ian Phoenix, December 2021.

301. **Captain Chaos paid the fares himself:** Susan Phoenix interview with author, December 2021.

CHAPTER NINETEEN | GLASGOW

302. **Special Branch monitored passenger ferries:** RUC Special Branch detective interview with author, February 2021.

302. **cash, a fake passport:** Gareth Parry, "IRA Team Is Found Guilty of Terror Blitz/Five Convicted at Old Bailey of British Coastal Bombing Campaign," *The Guardian*, June 12, 1986.

302. **message written in tiny letters on cigarette paper:** Parry, "IRA Team Is Found Guilty of Terror Blitz."

302. **made his way through railway sidings:** *To Kill the Cabinet*, documentary, BBC1, 1986.

303. **disembarked at the ferry port of Stranraer:** From Ian Phoenix's handwritten work diary, detailing Operation Drain, June 1985.

303. **meeting with two detective constables:** Phoenix diary of Operation Drain.

303. **as if auditioning for *Miami Vice*:** Jack Holland and Susan Phoenix, *Phoenix: Policing the Shadows: The Secret War Against Terrorism in Northern Ireland*, Hodder & Stoughton, 1996.

303. **"The two plebs had no foresight":** Phoenix diary of Operation Drain.

303. **visitors said the undercover officers:** Author interview with E4A member "Michael," March 2021.

303. **watchers in the neighboring carriage:** Author interview with Hamish Innes, a detective sergeant and surveillance specialist with Strathclyde Special Branch who tailed Sherry from Ayr, January 2021.

303. **saw him buy another ticket:** Author interview with Brian Watson, a detective inspector with Strathclyde Special Branch who observed Sherry at Glasgow Central Station, January 2021.

303. *You can always tell a Met man, but not much*: See chapter 10, "Salcey Forest."

304. **studied photographs of fugitive Provos:** Met Special Branch surveillance officer Brian McDowell quoted in Steve Ramsey, *Something Has Gone Wrong: Dealing with the Brighton Bomb*, Biteback, 2018.

304. **mustache and stubble:** Author interview with Strathclyde detective inspector Brian Watson, who arrested Magee that night, January 2021.

304. **troubled teen from Norwich:** See chapter 3, "The Chancer."

304. **"Just the sort of stunt":** Patrick Magee, *Where Grieving Begins: Building Bridges After the Brighton Bomb*, Pluto Press, 2021.

304. **an Inter-City 125, so-called because:** "Intercity 125: Workers Say Farewell to British Rail Icon," BBC News, May 17, 2021, https://www.bbc.com/news/uk-england-south-yorkshire-57069437.

304. **Carlisle, a border city, was built by watchers:** "Carlisle," Hadrian's Wall Country, https://hadrianswallcountry.co.uk/visit/carlisle.

304. **Peter Sherry checking out of his hotel:** McDowell quoted in Ramsey, *Something Has Gone Wrong*.

305. **entering a nearby pub, where he sipped a few drinks:** In an interview with the author, Peter Sherry disputed the police version that he waited in a pub and said he waited in a café or a store with a café. He also said he did not carry any medallions with secret messages.

305. **canoodling couple occupied a nearby bench:** McDowell quoted in Ramsey, *Something Has Gone Wrong*.

305. **emerged from the throng and greeted Sherry:** *To Kill the Cabinet*.

305. **"I think it's Magee":** McDowell quoted in Ramsey, *Something Has Gone Wrong*.

305. **A veteran Met undercover operative:** McDowell quoted in Ramsey, *Something Has Gone Wrong*.

306. **"I started looking for the finger"**: McDowell quoted in Ramsey, *Something Has Gone Wrong*.

306. **He remained oblivious**: Patrick Magee interview with author, March 2021.

306. **on a police circular of wanted fugitives**: See end of chapter 17, "Dublin."

306. **attempt to grab the bastards now**: Author interviews with RUC E4A members, 2021.

307. **Let the targets run, Phoenix implored**: Author interviews with RUC E4A members, 2021; Niven Phoenix interview with author, January 2021.

307. **"had to be prepared for the hindsight experts"**: Author interview with retired senior RUC officer, June 2021.

307. **"I have confidence in this team"**: McDowell quoted in Ramsey, *Something Has Gone Wrong*.

307. **London-based officers**: Ian Robinson, detective chief superintendent and head of Strathclyde Police Special Branch in 1985, interview with author, February 2022.

308. **took seats close to the IRA men**: "The Hunt for the Bomber," *The Brighton Bomb*, documentary series, BBC1, September 14, 2004.

308. **painting his back garden gate**: Ian Robinson, former head of Strathclyde Police Special Branch, interview with author, January 2021 and February 2022.

308. **Sometime before 4:00 p.m.**: Ian Robinson believes the phone call must have been earlier in the day, otherwise he would not have had time to organize surveillance at Glasgow Central Station and rustle up guns and men for the raid at Langside Road by 7:40 p.m. This would mean Magee and Sherry caught an earlier train. Other protagonists give slightly conflicting accounts of the timeline. Police records that could clarify it remain sealed. The author has selected the timeline that matches multiple accounts in the aftermath of the arrests and the trial.

308. **Robinson's wife came out to the garden**: Robinson interview with author, January 2021 and February 2022.

308. *Jesus Christ,* **he thought**: Robinson interview with author, January 2021 and February 2022.

309. **Robinson was good at catching them**: Strathclyde Special Branch had arrested dozens of loyalist suspects under the Prevention of Terrorism Act.

309. **"Call in the surveillance team"**: Robinson interview with author, January 2021.

309. **Strathclyde's radios used a different frequency**: Robinson interview with author, January 2021.

310. **canopy of Central Station**: For background on the Glasgow Central Station, see Alicia Queiro, "Station Secrets: Behind the Scenes at Glasgow Central," BBC News, November 7, 2014, https://www.bbc.com/news/uk-scotland-glasgow-west-29961895.

310. **It was packed**: Detective Inspector Brian Watson, who was at the station, interview with author, January 2021.

310. **suspects vanished into the human froth**: Hames Innes, who tailed Sherry and Magee from the train station, interview with author, January 2021.

310. **making their way toward the east exit**: Watson, who observed Sherry at Glasgow Central Station, interview with author, January 2021.

310. **Detective Sergeant Hamish Innes was suddenly glad**: Innes interview with author, January 2021.

311. **woman rapped on the window**: Innes interview with author, January 2021.

311. **double-decker bus, number 57**: Gordon Petrie and David Steele, "How a Courting Couple Trapped Bombers," *Glasgow Herald*, June 12, 1986, 6.

311. **targets had gone upstairs, then downstairs**: Watson interview with author, January 2021.

311. **left their ride and followed on foot**: Innes interview with author, January 2021.

311. **"It was a tense moment"**: Innes interview with author, January 2021.

312. **"Heading back to the park"**: Innes interview with author, January 2021.

312. **Queen's Park Cafe**: Innes interview with author, January 2021.

312. **briefly stepped into a grocery shop**: Innes interview with author, January 2021.

312. **wooden and glass door**: Footage of the building exterior and inside of the apartment was recorded soon after the arrests and shown on *To Kill the Cabinet*.

312. **dimly lit hallway**: *To Kill the Cabinet*.

312. **decor pink, beige, and cream:** *To Kill the Cabinet*.

313. **The two men had almost certainly met before:** Sherry hinted at this in an interview with the author, but did not disclose details.

313. **noise in the courtyard turned out to be some drunks:** Petrie and Steele, "How a Courting Couple Trapped Bombers," 6.

313. **expecting a visitor later, the landlord:** Magee interview with author, March 2021.

313. **McDonnell, who had experience shooting:** See chapter 17, "Dublin."

313. **second handgun hid in Anderson's gray handbag:** Innes interview with author, January 2021.

314. **Hamish Innes and his Met colleague:** Innes interview with author, January 2021.

314. **Robinson's counterpart in London:** Robinson interview with author, February 2022.

314. **Maintaining surveillance overnight:** Robinson interview with author, February 2022.

314. **Robinson didn't like it. Too volatile:** Robinson interview with author, February 2022.

314. **"I decided to do it the way we were used to":** Robinson interview with author, February 2022.

315. **police in Britain had been mostly unarmed:** See chapter 6, "The Bomb Burglar and Mr. T."

315. **"There is a serious situation":** Robinson interview with author, February 2022.

315. **prisoners were herded out of cells:** Robinson interview with author, February 2022.

316. **"They have to be arrested":** Robinson interview with author, February 2022.

316. **it could all go violently wrong:** Robinson interview with author, February 2022.

316. **observed the external layout at Langside Road:** Watson interview with author, January 2021.

316. **Watson divided the officers into squads:** Watson interview with author, January 2021.

317. **Dorneywood, an estate near Chequers:** According to MT's engagement diary, at 7:45 p.m., she sat down to dinner with Denis, several ministers and peers, Chief Constable Brian Hayes, and their spouses; see https://www.margaretthatcher.org/document/213926.

317. **"You, come with me":** Innes interview with author, January 2021.

317. **afforded him a view of the stairwell:** Watson interview with author, January 2021.

317. **dinner of potatoes, sprouts, and steak:** Petrie and Steele, "How a Courting Couple Trapped Bombers," 6.

317. **The landlord, he thought:** Magee interview with author, March 2021.

318. **Maybe they were investigating a burglary:** Magee interview with author, March 2021.

318. **"Can I help you?" he asked:** Watson interview with author, January 2021.

318. **shocked them into muteness:** Sherry interview with author, April 2021.

319. **Chancer let his imagination take flight:** Magee, *Where Grieving Begins*, 124.

CHAPTER TWENTY | RECKONINGS

320. **"Do you have any complaints?":** Ian Robinson, former Strathclyde police detective chief superintendent, interview with author, January 2021.

320. **hastily covered it with his hand:** Robinson interview with author, January 2021.

321. **Gerry Adams's reorganization of the Provos:** See chapter 4, "Hunger."

321. **everything by the book:** Two officers were assigned to each suspect and every interaction, every question, and response, or nonresponse, was logged. Magee acknowledged there was no physical abuse, unlike interrogations by the RUC and army in Northern Ireland; Patrick Magee, *Where Grieving Begins: Building Bridges After the Brighton Bomb*, Pluto Press, 2021.

321. **cheers and shouts in Scotland Yard:** Detective Constable Paul Gibbon in interview transcript for Steve Ramsey, *Something Has Gone Wrong: Dealing with the Brighton Bomb*, Biteback, 2018.

321. **made a prayer of thanks to Neptune:** See chapter 15, "Wetting Worms."

321. **rollicking drunk by the time he got home:** Niven Phoenix interview with author, January 2021.

322. **Brian Watson made a discovery:** Brian Watson interview with author, January 2021.

322. **Robinson had the documents immediately faxed:** Robinson interview with author, January 2021.

322. **evacuated guests and staff from the Rubens:** Derek Pickford, former Met bomb disposal officer, interview with author, January 2021.

322. **"The screws are loose":** Pickford interview with author, January 2021.

322. **"Leave it!":** Pickford interview with author, January 2021.

322. **Gurney, the bomb burglar:** See chapter 6, "The Bomb Burglar and Mr. T."

323. **booby-trapped device had killed Ken Howorth:** See chapter 6, "The Bomb Burglar and Mr. T."

323. **Thomas Quigley and Paul Kavanagh were convicted:** See chapter 18, "London."

323. **handiwork he had seen at Brighton:** See chapter 15, "Wetting Worms," and Gurney inspecting the ruins of the Grand.

323. **at Greenwich in 1979:** See chapter 5, "The England Department." Magee is believed to have been part of the teams that blew up a gas depot that ignited seven million cubic feet of natural gas in East London.

323. **during Magee's "blowy stuff" era:** See chapter 3, "The Chancer," which details Magee's time as an engineering officer, or bomb maker, in North Belfast.

323. **"Go on, you do it":** Dialogue taken from Peter Gurney, *Braver Men Walk Away: Memoirs of the World's Top Bomb-Disposal Expert*, HarperCollins, 1993, 175.

323. **bedside cabinet was wrecked:** Pickford interview with author, January 2021.

324. **Sir Kenneth Newman, chaired a tense meeting:** Nick Davies, "Seven Charged over IRA Plot to Bomb Seaside Towns," *The Observer*, June 30, 1985, https://www.nickdavies.net/1985/06/30/seven-charged -over-ira-plot-to-bomb-seaside-towns/?catid=147.

324. **Six years earlier, Newman had headed the RUC:** See chapter 2, "The Friendly Skies of South Armagh."

324. **Craig led detectives to 17 James Gray Street:** See chapter 18, "London."

324. **results almost off the charts:** Robinson interview with author, January 2021.

324. **had discovered and moved everything:** Boyle was found not guilty of helping the IRA team at his trial in 1986. David Pallister, "Man Cleared of Sheltering IRA Bomb Team/Old Bailey Trial of John Boyle," *The Guardian*, June 21, 1986.

324. **Detective Constable William Dorrian:** William Dorrian interview with author, April 2021.

325. **enough power to obliterate everything within a hundred yards:** Robinson interview with author, January 2021, citing bomb squad opinion.

325. **"Oh shit":** Dorrian interview with author, April 2021.

325. **march his partner to a pub around the corner to settle their nerves:** Dorrian interview with author, April 2021.

325. **Alan Cooper:** See chapter 18, "London."

325. **Gibbon . . . had interviewed the chambermaid:** See chapter 16, "Hypothenar Evidence."

325. **"Like scoring the winning try":** Gibbon in interview transcript for Ramsey, *Something Has Gone Wrong*.

326. **increasingly fraught phone call:** Phoenix interview with author, January 2021.

326. **"You can fucking stick it up your ass":** Phoenix interview with author, January 2021.

326. **no major airline would fly the suspects:** Detective Constable Paul Gibbon, who was part of the escort, interview with author, February 2021.

326. **No one spoke as the propellers droned south:** Gibbon interview with author, February 2021.

326. **One escort was a Gaelic-speaking sergeant:** Gibbon interview with author, February 2021.

326. **Royal Box at Wimbledon's center court:** "A Royal Salute to Bomb Victim," *Sunday Mirror*, June 30, 1985.

326. **He had questioned Magee's parents:** Magee says Reece was "bullying, nasty" to his family even though they knew nothing of his IRA activities. Magee, *Where Grieving Begins*, 127.

327. **"He didn't say a dickie bird":** Bernie Wells interview with Steve Ramsey for *Something Has Gone Wrong*.

328. **in jeans and a leather jacket:** *Six O'Clock News* bulletin, BBC1, June 23, 1986.

328. **yearned for this to end, being on display:** Magee, *Where Grieving Begins*, 129. "It was an extraordinarily stressful time . . . the pressure came from having to handle the daily presence in court, where I felt under constant scrutiny."

328. **to show emotion was to betray weakness:** Magee, *Where Grieving Begins*, 129.

328. **the busts and statues of monarchs:** For background on the Old Bailey, see "History of the Old Bailey Courthouse," Proceedings of the Old Bailey, https://www.oldbaileyonline.org/static/The-old -bailey.jsp.

328. **outside this court that the real Roy Walsh's IRA:** See chapter 5, "The England Department."

328. **just like Thomas Clarke:** See chapter 5, "The England Department."

328. **Thatcher had failed to convince Parliament:** See chapter 9, "Blackpool."

329. **reputation as a heavy sentencer:** "Sir Leslie Boreham: Though Sympathetic to Women, a Hard Sentencing Judge," obituary, *The Guardian*, May 12, 2004, https://www.theguardian.com/news /2004/may/12/guardianobituaries.

329. **"I am not concerned with your motives or what drives you":** Tyler Marshall, "IRA Man Gets Life Term in Bombing at Thatcher Hotel," *Los Angeles Times*, June 24, 1986, https://www.latimes.com /archives/la-xpm-1986-06-24-mn-20958-story.html.

329. **Martina Anderson and Ella O'Dwyer had been in cells:** Magee, *Where Grieving Begins*, 128.

329. **Anderson sang rebel ballads:** Magee, *Where Grieving Begins*, 128.

329. **his aborted mission to Lancashire in 1983:** See chapter 9, "Blackpool."

329. **Magee had not panicked:** Magee, *Where Grieving Begins*, 129.

329. **"At the core, all I had was my name":** Magee, *Where Grieving Begins*, 129.

329. **"Should we tear this up?":** Magee, *Where Grieving Begins*, 129.

329. **speculated about training in Libya:** Multiple outlets reported this, citing anonymous security sources. Magee denies having visited Libya. There is no evidence he did.

329. **became a "lone wolf" sniper:** Neil Walis and Chris Boffey, "The Man They Call the Butcher," *The Star*, June 12, 1986; Brian Crowther and Bob Graham, "Ghost Squad Nail Hitman," *Daily Mirror*, June 12, 1986.

330. **Thatcher reportedly forbade police briefings:** Liam Clarke, "Police Blunders Galore," *New Hibernia*, July/August 1986.

330. **watched from the public gallery:** Robin Butler interview with author, April 2021.

330. **"The women were beautifully got out":** Butler interview with author, April 2021.

330. **Magee respected Ferguson:** Magee, *Where Grieving Begins*, 130.

330. **"Were you party to a conspiracy":** David Pallister, "Brighton Bomb Police Deny They Framed Suspect/ Old Bailey Trial of Alleged Terrorist Patrick Magee," *The Guardian*, May 14, 1986.

330. **"a preposterous suggestion":** Pallister, "Brighton Bomb Police Deny They Framed Suspect."

331. **Ferguson suggested Tadd had planted the prints:** Gareth Parry, "Fingerprint Clue 'Led to Brighton Hotel Bomber'/Trial of Alleged IRA Terrorists," *The Guardian*, May 23, 1986.

331. **found Magee guilty of all seven charges:** Gareth Parry, 'Brighton Bomb Man Guilty/Patrick Magee Convicted of IRA Attack," *The Guardian*, June 11, 1986.

331. **Magee had expected it:** Patrick Magee interview with author, March 2021.

331. **IRA had warned him . . . a coffin or a cell:** Magee interview with author, March 2021.

331. **likened to a submarine:** Magee, *Where Grieving Begins*, 138. Magee cites one such inmate, armed robber John McVicker.

331. **"You plan them meticulously":** David Briffett, *Sussex Murders: County Murders and Mysteries*, Ensign, 1990, 159.

331. **only spies had received longer sentences:** *Six O'Clock News* bulletin, BBC1, June 23, 1986.

331. **Based on his grandfathers' longevity:** Magee, *Where Grieving Begins*, 133.

332. **hosted Hamish Innes:** Hamish Innes interview with author, January 2021.

332. **murder relics in the Met's Black Museum:** See chapter 6, "The Bomb Burglar and Mr. T."

332. **wives and VIPs sipping sherry:** Jonathan Buss, the *Evening Argus* crime correspondent, attended the party. He told Steve Ramsey, for *Something Has Gone Wrong*: "Everyone sips sherry, and then the VIPs and their wives go home, and all hell lets loose, it was one of those parties."

332. **hunting sharks off the Azores:** "As for the future, I shall be doing a lot of fishing starting in the Azores at the end of August." Reece was quoted in "Top Job in CID Changes Hands," *Patrol* magazine, August 1986.

332. **Tadd reckoned Turner, the "willing horse":** See chapter 16, "Hypothenar Evidence."

333. **pheasant . . . ran across their path:** David Tadd interview with author, February 2021.

333. **"Stop! Stop!" shouted Reece:** Tadd interview with author, February 2021.

333. **"witnessed an abduction or a murder":** Tadd interview with author, February 2021.

333. **denim jeans and a prison-striped shirt:** Magee, *Where Grieving Begins*.

333. **reached the seafront just after midday:** "Speech Reopening Brighton Grand Hotel," Margaret Thatcher Foundation, August 28, 1986, https://www.margaretthatcher.org/document/106277.

333. **fish and chips filled the air:** Jonathan Buss, the former *Evening Argus* crime correspondent, included a vivid account of the visit in his Bachelor of Arts history thesis, *Paths of Political and Personal Conflict Resolution After the Brighton Bomb, 1984*, University Campus Suffolk, 2016.

333. **families promenading in gaudy summer colors:** Buss, *Paths of Political and Personal Conflict Resolution After the Brighton Bomb, 1984*.

333. **A block from the Grand, an exclusion zone:** Buss, *Paths of Political and Personal Conflict Resolution After the Brighton Bomb, 1984*.

333. **before dawn with sniffer dogs:** A. J. McIlroy, "Thatcher Returns to Grand Hotel," *Daily Telegraph*, August 29, 1986.

334. **3.3 miles of ornate plaster corniche:** Jill Faulds, the Grand's reopening press release, Communications Strategy Ltd., August 28, 1986.

334. **Victorian-looking chimney stacks:** Joan Gray, "The Grand Hotel Is Restored to Glory," *Financial Times*, June 30, 1986.

334. **performed "Nimrod":** Buss, *Paths of Political and Personal Conflict Resolution After the Brighton Bomb, 1984*.

334. **Thatcher handed back the hotel's Union Jack:** McIlroy, "Thatcher Returns to Grand Hotel."

334. **"Even those who lost their lives":** John Passmore, "'Flag of Courage Flies on Grand'/Premier's Pride at Triumph over the Terrorists," *Daily Mail*, June 28, 1986.

335. **foundation for a future peace settlement:** Also see David Goodall's own verdict on the impact of the 1985 agreement: "It remained in force long enough to change the political chemistry in the north and oblige all the political parties—even in the end Sinn Féin—reluctantly and privately to realize that it would not go away unless and until they could jointly agree on a mutually acceptable alternative." David Goodall, *The Making of the Anglo-Irish Agreement of 1985*, National University of Ireland, 2021, 168.

335. **"Instead of spontaneity, we do security":** Conservative peer and author Michael Dobbs, "Thirty Years I Still Can't Be in the Same Room as Gerry Adams and Martin McGuinness," *Daily Telegraph*, October 12, 2014, https://www.telegraph.co.uk/news/politics/11155873/Brighton-bombing-Thirty-years-on-I-still-cant-be-in-the-same-room-as-Gerry-Adams-and-Martin-McGuinness.html.

335. **Foreign governments and police forces:** Birch interview with Ramsey for *Something Has Gone Wrong*. Birch said Sussex police officers toured the world, including Asia and the US, with a presentation on conference security in light of the Brighton bomb.

335. *Spitting Image* **still portrayed Tebbit:** See chapter 13, "Clockwork."

336. **Thatcher seemed to feel responsible for the suffering:** Charles Moore, *Margaret Thatcher: The Authorized Biography, Volume Two: Everything She Wants*, Allan Lane, 2015, 432. Tebbit told Moore that his presence near Thatcher provoked in her "not a guilty conscience, but a feeling that somehow she was responsible. She had been the target but others had paid the price. Every time I walked into the room she remembered how narrowly she'd escaped death. Because she was a good woman there was an element of feeling bad about this." Moore then notes: "Thus did her sympathy for her injured minister make her feel that his presence was almost unwelcome."

336. **"What did change after Brighton"**: Lord Charles Powell interview with author, May 2021. A fuller quote: "What did change after Brighton, and it was very understandable, was Norman's character. The physical injuries on his wife made him bitter. And understandably bitter and harder to deal with. I think he was less tolerant of some of her more outrageous ways of talking sometimes and she found it harder to work with him. She was determined to keep him as part of her government for as long as it was possible to do so. So the relationship changed in that sense, it became harder to manage."

336. **"If you think you can do your job better than I can"**: Jonathan Aitken, *Margaret Thatcher: Power and Personality*, Bloomsbury, 2013, 501. The source is Norman Lamont, then Tebbit's junior minister.

336. **"Norman is not the same Norman"**: Moore, *Margaret Thatcher*, vol. 2. Moore cites the Conservative Party treasurer, Alistair McAlpine, as the key whisperer against Tebbit.

336. **Tebbit, for his part, felt undermined**: Norman Tebbit, *Upwardly Mobile: An Autobiography*, Weidenfeld and Nicolson, 1988.

336. **realize two incompatible things**: Moore, *Margaret Thatcher*, vol. 2, 433. Moore cites Tebbit's private secretary: "In Andrew Lansley's view, the effect of the Brighton bomb on Tebbit was extremely painful psychologically. He realized two incompatible things at the same time—that he had the ability and possibly the party backing to become leader, but that his own health, and even more that of his wife, made it impossible. This 'added a bitter edge. He had a sense of lost ambition afterward, without having fully had that ambition before.'"

336. **decided to quit frontline politics**: Norman Tebbit interview with author, January 2021.

337. **perceptibly altered by the bomb**: The Brighton bomb emboldened the IRA to stage more audacious attacks in England in the 1990s, arguably with some success. US congressman Bruce Morrison told a BBC documentary about the 1996 bombing: "Canary Wharf got republicans to the table . . . the actions (of the British) said: 'Yes, you can bomb your way to the conference table.'" "Docklands Bomb: IRA Bombed Its Way to Talks Table," *Belfast Telegraph*, February 6, 2016, https://www.belfasttelegraph.co.uk/news/northern-ireland/docklands-bomb-ira-bombed-its-way-to-talks-table-with-canary-wharf-claims-former-us-congressman-bruce-morrison-34428103.html. Also: Thomas Leahy, a lecturer in British and Irish Politics and Contemporary History at Cardiff University, and author of *The Intelligence War Against the IRA*, Cambridge University Press, 2020, cites an RUC officer who believes the IRA's England attacks led to negotiations.

EPILOGUE

338. **lost touch with her MPs**: Jonathan Aitken, *Margaret Thatcher: Power and Personality*, Bloomsbury, 2013, 350. "His departure was a more grievous blow to the stability of the government than the prime minister realized." Thatcher missed Norman Tebbit's counsel, which had helped connect her to grassroots sentiment.

338. **Thatcher lost caution and perspective**: Charles Powell, her former private secretary, said she never had a happy day after retirement. BBC, 2013.

339. **She placed her hands on his**: Gibbon first related this to Steve Ramsey in *Something Has Gone Wrong: Dealing with the Brighton Bomb*, Biteback, 2018, and repeated the anecdote in an interview with this author in February 2021.

339. **tried in vain to forge an academic career**: Patrick Magee interview with author, March 2021.

339. **elected to the European Parliament for Sinn Féin**: In 2021, Sinn Féin purged Martina Anderson of her positions, blaming her for Sinn Féin election losses to the SDLP in Derry. Anderson's family accused the party of humiliating her. Brian Hutton, "Sinn Féin Using Martina Anderson as 'Sacrificial Lamb,' Says Family," *Irish Times*, May 11, 2021, https://www.irishtimes.com/news/politics/sinn-f%C3%A9in-using-martina-anderson-as-sacrificial-lamb-says-family-1.4562167.

339. **counselor at an addiction clinic**: Peter Sherry runs a team of six addiction counselors. In interviews with the author in April and June 2021, he spoke guardedly of his role in the IRA and his ill-fated mission to Britain in June 1985. He supports the peace process and is proud of his role in the Troubles.

339. **died of cancer in 2009**: Enda Craig, Donal's brother, told the author that despite their disputes in 1985, Gerry McDonnell had looked after Craig while in prison.

339. **Adams transitioned to statesman**: Deftly chronicled by Ed Moloney in *A Secret History of the IRA*, Penguin Press, 2002.

340. **He died in 2015, age eighty-six**: Reece told interviewers that Magee's early release made a laughingstock of justice. "Jack Reece: Police Officer Who Caught Patrick Magee, the Man Who

Bombed the Grand Hotel in Brighton," obituary, *The Independent*, November 29, 2015, https://www
.independent.co.uk/news/people/jack-reece-police-officer-who-caught-patrick-magee-the-man-who
-bombed-the-grand-hotel-in-brighton-a6753381.html.

340. **helicopter carrying intelligence officers crashed:** Richard Norton-Taylor, "Chinook Crash Reports
'Clears Pilots of Blame,'" *The Guardian*, July 10, 2011, https://www.theguardian.com/uk/2011/jul
/10/chinook-crash-report.

340. **Labour government called it "very hard to stomach":** John Mullin, "Freedom for the Brighton
Bomber," *The Guardian*, June 23, 1999, https://www.theguardian.com/uk/1999/jun/23/northern
ireland.johnmullin.

341. **"My God! Him too?":** Pinochet interview with the *Sunday Telegraph*, July 18, 1999, cited in Patrick
Magee, *Where Grieving Begins: Building Bridges After the Brighton Bomb*, Pluto Press, 2021.

341. **"If I'd known when he was coming out":** Michael White, the *Guardian*'s political editor, recalled
Tebbit saying this in a conversation with him—not an interview—at Westminster. There is no
suggestion Tebbit then or later actually planned to attack Magee. Author interview with White,
August 2022.

341. **"Pat!" the man called out:** Roy Walsh interview with author, April 2021.

341. **Walsh did not ask about the use of his name:** Walsh interview with author, April 2021.

341. **"Care of Roy Walsh?":** Walsh interview with author, April 2021.

341. *Gangsters or Guerrillas*: Beyond the Pale Publications, 2001.

341. **Joanne Berry, the daughter of Anthony Berry:** See brief mention in chapter 14.

342. *I had killed a fine human being*: Magee, *Where Grieving Begins*.

342. **dialogue evolved into a friendship:** A 2001 BBC2 documentary, "Facing the Enemy" (part of
Everyman, a documentary series), showed their early meetings. Many subsequent encounters were
filmed and are available on YouTube.

342. **Harvey Thomas, the Tory conference organizer:** See chapters 13, 14, 17.

343. **"I am satisfied that we prevailed":** Magee, *Where Grieving Begins*.